SPINOZA'S
CRITIQUE OF RELIGION

SPINOZA'S CRITIQUE OF RELIGION

by

LEO STRAUSS

Professor of Political Science
The University of Chicago

SCHOCKEN BOOKS · NEW YORK

Translated by E. M. Sinclair

The main body of this book was published as
Die Religionskritik Spinozas als Grundlage seiner Bibelwissenschaft Untersuchungen zu Spinozas Theologisch-Politischem Traktat
Akademie-Verlag, Berlin, 1930

Library of Congress Catalog Card No. 65-10948
PRINTED IN THE UNITED STATES OF AMERICA

To the memory of

FRANZ ROSENZWEIG

CONTENTS

CONTENTS

PREFACE TO THE
ENGLISH TRANSLATION

PREFACE TO THE ENGLISH TRANSLATION

THIS STUDY on Spinoza's *Theologico-political Treatise* was written during the years 1925-28 in Germany. The author was a young Jew born and raised in Germany who found himself in the grip of the theologico-political predicament.

At that time Germany was a liberal democracy. The regime was known as the Weimar Republic. In the light of the most authoritative political document of recent Germany—Bismarck's *Thoughts and Recollections*—the option for Weimar reveals itself as an option against Bismarck. In the eyes of Bismarck Weimar stood for a leaning to the West, if not for the inner dependence of the Germans on the French and above all on the English, and a corresponding aversion to everything Russian. But Weimar was above all the residence of Goethe, the contemporary of the collapse of the Holy Roman Empire of the German Nation, and of the victory of the French Revolution and Napoleon—Goethe whose sympathetic understanding was open to both antagonists and who identified himself in his thought with neither. By linking itself to Weimar the German liberal democracy proclaimed its moderate, non-radical character: its resolve to keep a balance between dedication to the principles of 1789 and dedication to the highest German tradition.

The Weimar Republic was weak. It had a single moment of strength, if not of greatness: its strong reaction to the murder of the Jewish Minister of Foreign Affairs, Walther Rathenau, in 1922. On the whole it presented the sorry spectacle of justice without a sword or of justice unable to use the sword. The election of Field-Marshal von Hindenburg to the presidency of the German Reich in 1925 showed everyone who had eyes to see that the Weimar Republic had only a short time to live: the old Germany was stronger—stronger in will—than the new Germany. What was still lacking then for the destruction of the Weimar Republic was the opportune moment; that moment was to come within a few years. The weakness of the Weimar Republic made certain its speedy destruction. It did not make certain the victory of National Socialism. The victory of National Socialism became necessary in Germany for the same reason that the victory of Communism had become necessary in Russia: the man with the strongest will or single-mindedness, the greatest ruthlessness, daring, and power over his following, and the best judgment about the strength of the various forces in the immediately relevant political field was the leader of the revolution.[1]

Half-Marxists trace the weakness of the Weimar Republic to the power of monopoly capitalism and the economic crisis of 1929, but there were other liberal democracies which were and remained strong although they had to contend with the same difficulties. It is more reasonable to refer to the fact that the Weimar Republic had come into being through the defeat of Germany in World War I, although this answer merely leads to the further question of why Germany had not succeeded in becoming a liberal democracy under more auspicious circumstances (for instance, in 1848), i.e. why liberal democracy had always been weak in Germany. It is true that the Bismarckian regime as managed by William II had already become discredited prior to World War I and still more so through that war and its outcome; correspondingly, liberal democracy had become ever more attractive; but at the crucial moment the victorious liberal democracies discredited liberal democracy in the eyes of Germany by the betrayal of their principles through the Treaty of Versailles.

It is safer to try to understand the low in the light of the high than the high in the light of the low. In doing the latter one necessarily distorts the high, whereas in doing the former one does not deprive the low of the freedom to reveal itself fully as what it is. By its name the Weimar Republic refers one back to the greatest epoch of German thought and letters, to the epoch extending from the last third of the eighteenth century to the first third of the nineteenth. No one can say that classical Germany spoke clearly and distinctly in favor of liberal democracy. This is true despite the fact that classical Germany had been initiated by Rousseau. In the first place Rousseau was the first modern critic of the fundamental modern project (man's conquest of nature for the sake of the relief of man's estate) who thereby laid the foundation for the distinction, so fateful for German thought, between civilization and culture. Above all, the radicalization and deepening of Rousseau's thought by classical German philosophy culminated in Hegel's *Philosophy of Right*, the legitimation of that kind of constitutional monarchy which is based on the recognition of the rights of man, and in which government is in the hands of highly educated civil servants appointed by an hereditary king. It has been said, not without reason, that Hegel's rule over Germany came to an end only on the day Hitler came to power. But Rousseau prepared not only the French Revolution and classical German philosophy, but also that extreme reaction to the French Revolution which is German romanticism. To speak politically and crudely, "the romantic school in Germany . . . was nothing other than the resurrection of medieval poetry as it had manifested itself . . . in art and in life."[2] The longing for the middle ages began in Germany at the very moment when the actual middle ages—the Holy Roman Empire ruled by a German—ended, in what was then thought to be the moment of Germany's deepest humiliation. In Germany, and only there, did the end of the middle ages coincide with the beginning of the longing for the middle ages. Compared with the medieval Reich which had lasted for almost a millennium until 1806, Bismarck's Reich (to say nothing of Hegel's Prussia) revealed itself as a little Germany not only in size. All profound German longings—for those for the middle ages were not the only ones nor even the most profound—all these longings for the origins or, negatively expressed, all German dissatisfaction with modernity pointed toward a third Reich, for Germany was to be the core even of Nietzsche's Europe ruling the planet.[3]

The weakness of liberal democracy in Germany explains why the situation of the indigenous Jews was more precarious in Germany than in any other Western country. Liberal democracy had originally defined itself in theologico-political treatises as the opposite, not of the more or less enlightened despotism of the seventeenth and eighteenth centuries, but of "the kingdom of darkness," i.e. of medieval society. According to liberal democracy, the bond of society is universal human morality, whereas religion (positive religion) is a private affair. In the middle ages religion— i.e. Catholic Christianity—was the bond of society. The action most characteristic of the middle ages is the Crusades; it may be said to have culminated not accidentally in the murder of whole Jewish communities. The German Jews owed their emancipation to the French Revolution or its effects. They were given full political rights for the first time by the Weimar Republic. The Weimar Republic was succeeded by the only German regime—the only regime ever anywhere—which had no other clear principle than murderous hatred of the Jews, for "Aryan" had no clear meaning other than "non-Jewish." One must keep in mind the fact that Hitler did not come from Prussia, nor even from Bismarck's Reich.

At a time when German Jews were politically in a more precarious situa- tion than Jews in any other Western country, they originated "the science of Judaism," the historical-critical study by Jews of the Jewish heritage. The emancipation of Jews in Germany coincided with the greatest epoch of German thought and poetry, the epoch in which Germany was the foremost country in thought and poetry. One cannot help comparing the period of German Jewry with the period of Spanish Jewry. The greatest achievements of Jews during the Spanish period were rendered possible partly by the fact that Jews became receptive to the influx of Greek thought, which was understood to be Greek only accidentally. During the German period, however, the Jews opened themselves to the influx of German thought, the thought of the particular nation in the midst of which they lived—a thought which was understood to be German essentially: political dependence was also spiritual dependence. This was the core of the predicament of German Jewry.

Three quotations may serve to illustrate the precarious situation of the Jews in Germany. Goethe, the greatest among the cosmopolitan Germans, a "decided non-Christian," summarizes the results of a conversation about a new society to be founded, between his Wilhelm Meister and "the gay Friedrich," without providing his summary with quotation marks, as follows: "To this religion [the Christian] we hold, but in a particular manner; we instruct our children from their youth in the great advantages which [that religion] has brought to us; but of its author, of its course, we speak to them only at the end. Then only does the author become dear and cherished, and all reports regarding him become sacred. Drawing a conclusion which one may perhaps call pedantic, but of which one must at any rate admit that it follows from the premise, we do not tolerate any Jew among us; for how could we grant him a share in the highest culture, the origin and tradition of which he denies?"[4] Two generations later Nietzsche could say: "I have not yet met a German who was favorably disposed toward the Jews."[5] One might try to trace Nietzsche's judgment to the narrowness of his circle of acquaintances: no one would expect to find people favorably disposed toward Jews among the German Lutheran pastors among whom Nietzsche grew up, to say nothing of Jakob Burckhardt in Basel. Nietzsche has chosen his words carefully; he surely excluded himself when making the judgment, as appears, in addition, from the context. But his remark is not trivial. While his circle of acquaintances was limited, perhaps unusually limited, he was of unusual perspicacity. Besides, being favorably disposed toward this or that man or woman of Jewish origin does not mean being favorably disposed toward Jews. Two generations later, in 1953, Heidegger could speak of "the inner truth and greatness of National Socialism."[6]

In the course of the nineteenth century many Western men had come to conceive of much, if not all, sufferings as consisting of problems which as such were soluble as a matter of course. In this manner, too, they had come to speak of the Jewish problem. The German-Jewish problem was never solved. It was annihilated by the annihilation of the German Jews. Prior to Hitler's rise to power most German Jews believed that their problem had been solved in principle by liberalism: German Jews were Germans of the Jewish faith, i.e. they were no less German than the Germans of the Christian faith or of no faith. They assumed that the German state (to say nothing of German society or culture) was or ought to be neutral to the difference between Christians and Jews or between non-Jews and Jews. This assumption was not accepted by the strongest part of Germany and hence by Germany. In the words of Herzl: "Who belongs and who does not belong, is decided by the majority; it is a question of power." At any rate it could seem that in the absence of a superior recognized equally by both parties the natural judge on the German-ness of German Jews was the non-Jewish Germans. As a consequence, a small minority of German Jews, but a considerable minority of German-Jewish youth studying at the universities, had turned to Zionism. Zionism was almost never wholly divorced from traditional Jewish hopes. On the other hand, Zionism never intended to bring about a restoration like the one achieved in the days of Ezra and Nehemiah: the return to the land of Israel was not seen as culminating in the building of the third temple and restoration of the sacrificial service.

The peculiarity of Zionism as a modern movement comes out most clearly in the strictly political Zionism presented first by Leon Pinsker in his *Autoemancipation* and then by Theodor Herzl in his *The Jewish State*. Pinsker and Herzl started from the failure of the liberal solution, but continued to see the problem to be solved as it had begun to be seen by liberalism, i.e. as a merely human problem. They radicalized this purely human understanding. The terrible fate of the Jews was in no sense to be understood any longer as connected with divine punishment for the sins of our fathers or with the providential mission of the chosen people and hence to be borne with the meek fortitude of martyrs. It was to be understood in merely human terms, as constituting a purely political problem which as such cannot be solved by appealing to the justice or generosity of other nations, to say nothing of a league of all nations. Accordingly, political Zionism was concerned primarily with cleansing the Jews of their millennial degradation, with the recovery of Jewish dignity, honor or pride. The failure of the liberal solution meant that Jews could not regain their honor by assimilating as individuals to the nations among which they lived or by becoming citizens like all other citizens of the liberal states: the liberal solution brought at best legal equality, but not social equality; as a demand of reason it had no effect on the feelings of non-Jews. To quote Herzl again: "We are a nation—the enemy makes us a nation whether we like it or not." In the last analysis this is nothing to be deplored, for "the enemy is necessary for the highest effort of the personality." Only through securing the honor of the Jewish nation could the individual Jew's honor be secured. The true solution of the Jewish problem requires that the Jews become "like all the nations" (1 Samuel 8), that the Jewish nation assimilate itself to the nations of the world or that it establish a modern, liberal, secular (but not necessarily democratic) state. Political Zionism, then, strictly understood was the movement of an elite on behalf of a community constituted by common descent and common degradation, for the restoration of their honor through the acquisition of statehood and therefore of a country—of any country: the land which the strictly political Zionism promised to the Jews was not necessarily the land of Israel.

This project implied a profound modification of traditional Jewish hopes, a modification arrived at through a break with these hopes. For the motto of his pamphlet Pinsker chose these words of Hillel: "If I am not for myself, who will be for me? And if not now, when?" He omitted the sentence which forms the center of Hillel's statement: "And if I am only for myself, what am I?" He saw the Jewish people as a herd without a shepherd to protect and gather it; he did not long for a shepherd, but for the transformation of the herd into a nation that could take care of itself. He regarded the Jewish situation as a natural sickness that could be cured only by natural means. What the change effected by strictly political Zionism means, one sees most clearly when, returning to the origin, one ponders this sentence of Spinoza: "If the foundations of their religion did not effeminate the minds of the Jews, I would absolutely believe that they will at some time, given the occasion (for human things are mutable), establish their state again."

Strictly political Zionism became effective only through becoming an ingredient, not to say the backbone, of Zionism at large, i.e. by making its peace with traditional Jewish thought. Through this alliance or fusion it brought about the establishment of the state of Israel and therewith that cleansing which it had primarily intended; it thus procured a blessing for all Jews everywhere regardless of whether they admit it or not.[7] It did not, however, solve the Jewish problem. It could not solve the Jewish problem because of the narrowness of its original conception, however noble. This narrowness was pointed out most effectively by cultural Zionism: strictly political Zionism, concerned only with the present emergency and resolve, lacks historical perspective: the community of descent, of the blood, must also be a community of the mind, of the national mind; the Jewish state will be an empty shell without a Jewish culture which has its roots in the

Jewish heritage. One could not have taken this step unless one had previously interpreted the Jewish heritage itself as a culture, i.e. as a product of the national mind, of the national genius.[8] Yet the foundation, the authoritative layer, of the Jewish heritage presents itself, not as a product of the human mind, but as a divine gift, as divine revelation. Did one not completely distort the meaning of the heritage to which one claimed to be loyal by interpreting it as a culture like any other high culture? Cultural Zionism believed it had found a safe middle ground between politics (power politics) and divine revelation, between the sub-cultural and the supra-cultural, but it lacked the sternness of these two extremes. When cultural Zionism understands itself, it turns into religious Zionism. But when religious Zionism understands itself, it is in the first place Jewish faith and only secondarily Zionism. It must regard as blasphemous the notion of a human solution to the Jewish problem. It may go so far as to regard the establishment of the state of Israel as the most important event in Jewish history since the completion of the Talmud, but it cannot regard it as the arrival of the Messianic age, of the redemption of Israel and of all men. The establishment of the state of Israel is the most profound modification of the Galut which has occurred, but it is not the end of the Galut: in the religious sense, and perhaps not only in the religious sense, the state of Israel is a part of the Galut. Finite, relative problems can be solved; infinite, absolute problems cannot be solved. In other words, human beings will never create a society which is free of contradictions. From every point of view it looks as if the Jewish people were the chosen people in the sense, at least, that the Jewish problem is the most manifest symbol of the human problem as a social or political problem.

To realize that the Jewish problem is insoluble means ever to bear in mind the truth proclaimed by Zionism regarding the limitations of liberalism. Liberalism stands or falls by the distinction between state and society, or by the recognition of a private sphere, protected by the law but impervious to the law, with the understanding that, above all, religion as particular religion belongs to the private sphere. Just as certainly as the liberal state will not "discriminate" against its Jewish citizens, so is it constitutionally unable and even unwilling to prevent "discrimination" against Jews by individuals or groups. To recognize a private sphere in the sense indicated means to permit private "discrimination," to protect it and thus in fact to foster it. The liberal state cannot provide a solution to the Jewish problem, for such a solution would require a legal prohibition against every kind of "discrimination," i.e. the abolition of the private sphere, the denial of the difference between state and society, the destruction of the liberal state. Such a destruction would not by any means solve the Jewish problem, as is shown in our days by the anti-Jewish policy of the USSR. It is foolish to say that that policy contradicts the principles of Communism, for it contradicts the principles of Communism to separate the principles of Communism from the Communist movement. The USSR owes its survival to Stalin's decision not to wait for the revolution of the Western proletariat, i.e. for what others would do for the USSR, but to build up socialism in a single country where his word was the law, by the use of any means however bestial, and these means could include, as a matter of course, certain means successfully used previously, not to say invented, by Hitler: the large-scale murder of party members and anti-Jewish measures. This is not to say that Communism has become what National Socialism always was, the prisoner of an anti-Jewish ideology, but it makes use of anti-Jewish measures in an unprincipled manner when and where they seem to be expedient. It is merely to confirm our contention that the uneasy "solution of the Jewish problem" offered by the liberal state is superior to the Communist "solution."

There is a Jewish problem that is humanly soluble,[9] the problem of the Western Jewish individual who or whose parents severed his connection with the Jewish community in the expectation that he would thus become a normal member of a purely liberal or of a universal human society, and who is naturally perplexed when he finds no such society. The solution to his problem is return to the Jewish community, the community established by the Jewish faith and the Jewish way of life—*teshubah* (ordinarily rendered by "repentance") in the most comprehensive sense. Some of our contemporaries believe such a return to be altogether impossible because they believe that the Jewish faith has been overthrown once and for all, not by blind rebellion, but by evident refutation. While admitting that their deepest problem would be solved by that return, they assert that intellectual probity forbids them to sacrifice intellect in order to satisfy even the most vital need. Yet they can hardly deny that a vital need legitimately induces a man to probe whether what seems to be an impossibility is not in fact only a very great difficulty.

The founder of cultural Zionism could still deny that the Jewish people have a providential mission on the ground that Darwin had destroyed the most solid basis of teleology.[10] At the time and in the country in which the present study was written, it was granted by all except the most backward that the Jewish faith had not been refuted by science or by history. The storms stirred up by Darwin and to a lesser degree by Wellhausen had been weathered; one could grant to science and history everything they seem to teach regarding the age of the world, the origin of man, the impossibility of miracles, the impossibility of the immortality of the soul and of the resurrection of the body, the Jahvist, the Elohist, the third Isaiah, and so on, without abandoning one iota of the substance of the Jewish faith. Some haggling regarding particular items, issuing sometimes in grudging concessions, was still going on in outlying districts, but the battle for the capital had been decided by the wholesale surrender to science and history of the whole sphere in which science and history claim to be or to become competent, and by the simultaneous depreciation of that whole sphere as religiously irrelevant. It had become religiously relevant, it was affirmed, only through a self-misunderstanding of religion, a self-misunderstanding which was inevitable in earlier times and which on the whole was even harmless in earlier times. That self-misunderstanding consisted in understanding revelation as a body of teachings and rules that includes such teachings and rules as could never become known as true and binding to the unassisted human mind, such as the human mind would reject as sub-rational were they not proven to be supra-rational by the certainty that they are the word of God; men who were not ear-witnesses of God's declaring these teachings and rules could have that certainty only through a reliable tradition that also vouches for the reliable transmission of the very words of God, and through miracles. The self-misunderstanding is removed when the content of revelation is seen to be rational, which does not necessarily mean that everything hitherto thought to be revealed is rational. The need for external credentials of revelation (tradition and miracles) disappears as its internal credentials come to abound. The truth of traditional Judaism is the religion of reason, or the religion of reason is secularized Judaism. But the same claim could be made for Christianity, and however close secularized Judaism and secularized Christianity might come to each other, they are not identical, and as purely rational they ought to be identical. Above all, if the truth of Judaism is the religion of reason, then what was formerly believed to be revelation by the transcendent God must now be understood as the work of the human imagination in which human reason was effective to some extent; what has now become a clear and distinct idea was originally a confused idea.[11] What except demonstrations of the existence of God by theoretical reason or postulations of His existence by practical reason, which were becoming ever more incredible, could prevent one from taking the last step, i.e. to assert that God Himself is a product of the human mind, at best "an idea of reason"?

These and similar denials or interpretations suddenly lost all their force by the simple observation that they contradict not merely inherited opinions but present experience. At first hearing one may be reminded of what Leibniz had said when overcoming Bayle's doubt regarding revelation: "toutes ces difficultés invincibles, ces combats prétendus de la raison contre la foi s'évanouissent.

> Hi motus animorum atque haec discrimina tanta
> Pulveris exigui jactu compressa quiescunt."[12]

God's revealing Himself to man, His addressing man, is not merely known through traditions going back to the remote past and therefore now "merely believed," but is genuinely known through present experience which every human being can have if he does not refuse himself to it. This experience is not a kind of self-experience, of the actualization of a human potentiality, of the human mind coming into its own, into what it desires or is naturally inclined to, but of something undesired, coming from the outside, going against man's grain. It is the only awareness of something absolute which cannot be relativized in any way as everything else, rational or non-rational, can; it is the experience of God as the Thou, the father and king of all men; it is the experience of an unequivocal command addressed to me here and now as distinguished from general laws or ideas which are always disputable and permitting of exceptions. Only by surrendering to God's experienced call which calls for one's loving Him with all one's heart, with all one's soul and with all one's might can one come to see the other human being as one's brother and love him as oneself. The absolute experience will not lead back to Judaism —for instance, to the details of what the Christians call the ceremonial law—if it does not recognize itself in the Bible and clarify itself through the Bible, and if it is not linked up with considerations of how traditional Judaism understands itself and with meditations about the mysterious fate of the Jewish people. The return to Judaism also requires today the overcoming of what one may call the perennial obstacle to the Jewish faith: traditional philosophy, which is of Greek, pagan origin. For the respectable, impressive or specious alternatives to the acceptance of revelation, to the surrender to God's will, have always presented themselves and still present themselves as based on what man knows by himself, by his reason. Reason has reached its perfection in Hegel's system; the essential limitations of Hegel's system show the essential limitations of reason and therewith the radical inadequacy of all rational objections to revelation. With the final collapse of rationalism the perennial battle between reason and revelation, between unbelief and belief has been decided in principle, even on the plane of human thought, in favor of revelation. Reason knows only of subjects and objects, but surely the living and loving God is infinitely more than a subject and can never be an object, something at which one can look in detachment or indifference. Philosophy as hitherto known, the old thinking, so far from starting from the experience of God, abstracted from such experience or excluded it; hence, if it was theistic, it was compelled to have recourse to demonstrations of the existence of God as a thinking or a thinking and willing being. The new thinking as unqualified empiricism speaks of God, man and the world as actually experienced, as realities irreducible to one another, whereas all traditional philosophy was reductionist. For if it did not assert that the world and man are eternal, i.e. deny the creator-God, it sought for the reality preceding world and man as it precedes world and man and as it succeeds world and man, i.e. for what cannot be experienced by man, by the whole man, but can only be inferred or thought by him. Unqualified empiricism does not recognize any such Without or Beyond as a reality, but only as unreal forms, essences, or concepts which can never be more than objects, i.e. objects of mere thought.[13]

The new thinking had been originated above all by Franz Rosenzweig, who is thought to be the greatest Jewish thinker whom German Jewry has brought forth. It was counteracted by another form of the new thinking, the form originated by Heidegger.[14] It was obvious that Heidegger's new thinking led far away from any charity as well as from any humanity. On the other hand, it could not be denied that he had a deeper understanding than Rosenzweig of what was implied in the insight or demand that the traditional philosophy, which rested on Greek foundations, must be superseded by a new thinking. He would never have said as Rosenzweig did that "we know in the most precise manner, we know with the intuitional knowledge of experience, what God taken by Himself, what man taken by himself, what the world taken by itself 'is.' " Nor did Heidegger assume, as Rosenzweig did, that we possess without further ado an adequate understanding of Greek philosophy, of the basic stratum of that old think-ing which has to be overcome: with the questioning of traditional philos-ophy the traditional understanding of the tradition becomes questionable. For this reason alone he could not have said as Rosenzweig did that most Platonic dialogues are "boring."[15] This difference between Rosenzweig and Heidegger, about which much more could be said, was not un-connected with their difference regarding revelation. At that time Heidegger expressed his thought about revelation by silence or deed rather than by speech. Rosenzweig's friend Martin Buber quotes a much later utterance of Heidegger which gives one, I believe, an inkling of Heidegger's argument—especially if it is taken in conjunction with well-known utter-ances of Nietzsche whom Heidegger evidently follows in this matter.

"The 'prophets' of these religions [sc. Judaism and Christianity]," says Heidegger according to Buber, "do not begin by foretelling the word of the Holy. They announce immediately the God upon whom the certainty of salvation in a supernatural blessedness reckons."[16] Buber comments on this statement as follows: "Incidentally, I have never in our time encountered on a high philosophical plane such a far-reaching mis-understanding of the prophets of Israel. The prophets of Israel have never announced a God upon whom their hearers' striving for security reckoned. They have always aimed to shatter all security and to proclaim in the opened abyss of the final insecurity the unwished for God who demands that His human creatures become real, they become human, and confounds all who imagine that they can take refuge in the certainty that the temple of God is in their midst." Heidegger does not speak of the prophets' "hearers," but he clearly means that the prophets themselves were con-cerned with security.[17] This assertion is not refuted by the well-known facts which Buber points out—by the fact, in a word, that for the prophets there is no refuge and fortress except God: the security afforded by the temple of God is nothing, but the security afforded by God is everything. As Buber says seventeen pages earlier in the same publication, "He who loves God only as a moral ideal, can easily arrive at despairing of the guidance of a world the appearance of which contradicts, hour after hour, all principles of his moral ideality."[18] Surely the Bible teaches that in spite of all appear-ances to the contrary the world is guided by God or, to use the traditional term, that there is particular providence, that man is protected by God if he does not put his trust in flesh and blood but in God alone, that he is not completely exposed or forsaken, that he is not alone, that he has been created by a being which is—to use Buber's expression—a Thou. Buber's protest would be justified if the Biblical prophets were only, as Well-hausen may seem to have hoped, prophets of insecurity, not to say of an evil end,[19] and not also predictors of the Messianic future, of the ultimate victory of truth and justice, of the final salvation and security, although not necessarily of the final salvation and security of all men. In other words, the Biblical experience is not simply undesired or against man's grain: grace perfects nature, it does not destroy nature. Not every man but every noble man is concerned with justice or righteousness and therefore with any possible extra-human, supra-human support of justice, or with the security of justice. The insecurity of man and everything human is not an absolutely terrifying abyss if the highest of which a man knows is absolutely secure. Plato's Athenian Stranger does not indeed experience that support, that refuge and fortress as the Biblical prophets experienced it, but he does the second best: he tries to demonstrate its existence. But for Heidegger there is no security, no happy ending, no divine shepherd, hope is replaced by thinking, the longing for eternity or belief in anything eternal is understood as stemming from "the spirit of revenge," from the desire to escape from all passing-away into something that never passes away.[20]

The controversy can easily degenerate into a race in which he wins who offers the smallest security and the greatest terror. It would not be difficult to guess who would be the winner. But just as an assertion does not become true because it is shown to be comforting, so it does not become true because it is shown to be terrifying. The serious question concerns man's certainty or knowledge of the divine promises or covenants. They are known through what God Himself says in the Scriptures. According to Buber, whose belief in revelation is admittedly "not mixed up with any 'orthodoxy,' " what we read in the Bible is in all cases what the Biblical authors say, (even when God is said to have said something, as for example and above all in the case of the Ten Commandments) and what the Biblical authors say is never more than a human expression of God's speechless call or a human response to that call or a man-made "image," a human interpretation, an experienced human interpretation to be sure, of what God "said." Such "images" constitute not only Judaism and Christianity but all religions. All such "images" are "distorting and yet correct, perishable like an image in a dream and yet verified in eternity."[21] The experience of God is surely not specifically Jewish. Besides, can one say that one experiences God as the creator of heaven and earth, i.e. that one knows from the experience of God, taken by itself, that He is the creator of heaven and earth, or that men who are not prophets experience God as a thinking, willing and speaking being? Is the absolute experience necessarily the experience of a Thou?[22] Every assertion about the absolute experience which says more than that what is experienced is the Presence or the Call, is not the experiencer, is not flesh and blood, is the wholly other, is death or nothingness, is an "image" or interpretation; that any one interpretation is the simply true interpretation is not known but "merely believed." One cannot establish that any particular interpretation of the absolute experience is the most adequate interpretation on the ground that it alone agrees with all other experiences, for instance with the experienced mystery of the Jewish fate, for the Jewish fate is a mystery only on the basis of a particular interpretation of the absolute experience, or rather the Jewish fate is the outcome of one particular interpretation of the absolute experience. The very emphasis on the absolute experience as experience compels one to demand that it be made as clear as possible what the experience by itself conveys, that it not be tampered with, that it be carefully distinguished from every interpretation of the experience, for the interpretations may be suspected of being attempts to render bearable and harmless the experienced which admittedly comes from without down upon man and is undesired; or of being attempts to cover over man's radical unprotectedness, loneliness and exposedness.[23]

Yet—Buber could well have retorted—does not precisely this objection mean that the atheistic suspicion is as much a possibility, an interpretation and hence is as much "merely believed" as the theistic one? And is not being based on belief, which is the pride of religion, a calamity for philosophy? Can the new thinking consistently reject or (what is the same thing) pass by revelation? Through judging others, Nietzsche himself had established the criterion by which his doctrine is to be judged. In attacking the "optimistic" as well as the "pessimistic" atheism of his age, he made clear that the denial of the Biblical God demands the denial of Biblical morality however secularized, which, far from being self-evident or rational, has no other support than the Biblical God; mercy, compassion, egalitarianism, brotherly love or altruism must give way to cruelty and its kin.[24] But Nietzsche did not leave things at "the blond beast." He proclaimed "the over-man," and the over-man transcends man as hitherto known at his highest. What distinguishes Nietzsche in his view from all earlier philosophers is the fact that he possesses "the historical sense,"[25] i.e. the awareness that the human soul has no unchangeable essence or limits but is essentially historical. The most profound change which the human soul has hitherto undergone, the most important enlargement and deepening which it has hitherto experienced is due, according to Nietzsche, to the Bible. ". . . these Greeks have much on their conscience—falsification was their particular craft, the whole European psychology suffers from the Greek *superficialities*; and without that little bit of Judaism, etc. etc." Hence the over-man is "the Roman Caesar with Christ's soul."[26] Not only was Biblical morality as veracity or intellectual probity at work in the destruction of Biblical theology and Biblical morality; not only is it at work in the questioning of that very probity, of "*our* virtue, which alone has remained to us";[27] Biblical morality will remain at work in the morality of the over-man. The over-man is inseparable from "the philosophy of the future." The philosophy of the future is distinguished from traditional philosophy, which pretended to be purely theoretical, by the fact that it is consciously the outcome of a will: the fundamental awareness is not purely theoretical but theoretical and practical, inseparable from an act of the will or a decision. The fundamental awareness characteristic of the new thinking is a secularized version of the Biblical faith as interpreted by Christian theology.[28] What is true of Nietzsche is no less true of the author of *Sein und Zeit*. Heidegger wishes to expel from philosophy the last relics of Christian theology like the notions of "eternal truths" and "the idealized absolute subject." But the understanding of man which he opposes to the Greek understanding of man as the rational animal is, as he emphasizes, primarily the Biblical understanding of man as created in the image of God. Accordingly, he interprets human life in the light of "being towards death," "anguish," "conscience," and "guilt"; in this most important respect he is much more Christian than Nietzsche.[29] The efforts of the new thinking to escape from the evidence of the Biblical understanding of man, i.e. from Biblical morality, have failed. And, as we have learned from Nietzsche, Biblical morality demands the Biblical God.

Considerations of this kind seemed to decide the issue in favor of Rosenzweig's understanding of the new thinking, or in favor of the unqualified return to Biblical revelation. As a matter of fact, Rosenzweig's return was not unqualified. The Judaism to which he returned was not identical with the Judaism of the age prior to Moses Mendelssohn. The old thinking had brought about, since the days of Mendelssohn, to say nothing of the middle ages, some more or less important modifications of native Jewish thought. While opposing the old thinking, the new thinking was nevertheless its heir. Whereas the classic work of what is called Jewish medieval philosophy, the *Guide of the Perplexed*, is primarily not a philosophic book but a Jewish book. Rosenzweig's *Star of Redemption* is primarily not a Jewish book but "a system of philosophy." The new thinking is "experiencing philosophy." As such it is passionately concerned with the difference between what is experienced, or at least capable of being experienced, by the present day believer and what is merely known by tradition; that difference was of no concern to traditional Judaism. As experiencing philosophy it starts in each case from the experienced, and not from the non-experienced "presuppositions" of experience. For instance, we experience things "here" or "there," in given "places"; we do not experience the homogeneous infinite "space" which may be the condition of the possibility of "places." I experience a tree; in doing so, I am not necessarily aware of my "Ego" which is the condition of possibility of my experiencing anything. Accordingly, when speaking of the Jewish experience, one must start from what is primary or authoritative for the Jewish consciousness and not from what is the primary condition of possibility of the Jewish experience: one must start from God's Law, the Torah, and not from the Jewish nation. But in this decisive case Rosenzweig proceeds in the opposite manner; he proceeds, as he puts it, "sociologically." He notes that the Jewish dogmaticists of the middle ages, especially Maimonides, proceeded in the first manner: traditional Jewish dogmatics understood the Jewish nation in the light of the Torah; it was silent about the "presupposition" of the Law, *viz.* the Jewish nation and its chosenness. One begins to wonder whether our medieval philosophy, and the old thinking of Aristotle of which it made use, was not more "empirical," more in harmony with the "given," than an unqualified empiricism which came into being through opposition to modern constructionist philosophy as well as to modern scientific empiricism: if the Jewish nation did not originate the Torah but is manifestly constituted by the Torah, it is necessarily preceded by the Torah which was created prior to the world and for the sake of which the world was created. The dogma of Israel's chosenness becomes for Rosenzweig "the truly central thought of Judaism" because, as he makes clear, he approaches Judaism from the point of view of Christianity, because he looks for a Jewish analogue to the Christian doctrine of the Christ.[30] It is not necessary to emphasize that the same change would have been effected if the starting point had been mere secularist nationalism.

Rosenzweig never believed that his return to the Biblical faith could be a return to the form in which that faith had expressed or understood itself in the past. What the author of a Biblical saying or a Biblical story or the compilers of the canon meant is one thing; how the text affects the present day believer and hence what the latter truly understands, i.e. appropriates and believes, is another. The former is the concern of history as history which, if it regards itself as self-sufficient, is one of the decayed forms of the old thinking; the latter, if it is practiced with full consciousness, calls for the new thinking. Since the new thinking is the right kind of thinking, it would seem that the understanding of the Bible of which it is capable is in principle superior to all other forms. At any rate, Rosenzweig agrees with religious liberalism as to the necessity of making a selection from among the traditional beliefs and rules. Yet his principle of selection differs radically from the liberal principle. The liberals made a distinction between the essential and the unessential, i.e. they made a distinction which claimed to be objective. Rosenzweig's principle is not a principle strictly speaking but "a force": the whole "reality of Jewish life," even those parts of it which never acquired formal authority (like "mere" stories and "mere" customs) must be approached as the "matter" out of which only a part can be transformed into "force"; only experience can tell which part will be so transformed; the selection cannot but be "wholly individual."[31] The sacred law, as it were the public temple, which was a reality, thus becomes a potential, a quarry or a store-house out of which each individual takes the materials for building up his private shelter. The community of the holy people is henceforth guaranteed by the common descent of its members and the common origin of the materials which they transform by selecting them. This conscious and radical historicization of the Torah—the necessary consequence of the assumed primacy of the Jewish people under the conditions of modern "individualism"[32]—is in Rosenzweig's view perfectly compatible with the fact that the Jewish people is the a-historical people.

Rosenzweig could not believe everything that his orthodox Jewish contemporaries in Germany believed. His system of philosophy supplies the reasons why he thought that in spite of their piety they were mistaken. He has discussed by themselves two points regarding which he disagreed with them and which are of utmost importance. First, he opposed their inclination to understand the Law in terms of prohibition, denial, refusal and rejection rather than in terms of command, liberation, granting and transformation, and proposed the opposite inclination. It is not immediately clear, however, whether the orthodox austerity or sternness does not rest on a deeper understanding of the power of evil in man than Rosenzweig's view, which is at first glance more attractive, and which resembles one of "the favorite topics" of Mittler in Goethe's *Elective Affinities*.[33] Second, Rosenzweig was unable simply to believe all Biblical miracles. All Biblical miracles were indeed susceptible of becoming credible to him. For instance, when the story of Balaam's speaking she-ass was read from the Torah, it was not a fairy-tale for him, whereas on all other occasions he might doubt this miracle.[34] The orthodox Jew would reproach himself for his doubts as for failings on his part, for he would not determine what he is obliged to believe by his individual and temporary capacity or incapacity to believe; he would argue, with Maimonides' *Treatise on the Resurrection of the Dead*, that if God has created the world out of nothing and hence is omnipotent, there is no reason whatever for denying at any time any miracle vouched for by the word of God.

Considerations like those sketched in the preceding paragraphs made one wonder whether an unqualified return to Jewish orthodoxy was not both possible and necessary—was not at the same time the solution to the problem of the Jew lost in the non-Jewish modern world and the only course compatible with sheer consistency or intellectual probity. Vague difficulties remained like small faraway clouds on a beautiful summer sky. They soon took the shape of Spinoza—the greatest man of Jewish origin who had openly denied the truth of Judaism and had ceased to belong to the Jewish people without becoming a Christian. It was not the "God-intoxicated" philosopher but the hard-headed, not to say hard-hearted, pupil of Machiavelli and philologic-historical critic of the Bible. Orthodoxy could be returned to only if Spinoza was wrong in every respect.

That Spinoza was wrong in the decisive respect had been asserted about a decade earlier by the most authoritative German Jew who symbolized more than anyone else the union of Jewish faith and German culture: Hermann Cohen, the founder of the Neo-Kantian school of Marburg. Cohen was a Jew of rare dedication, the faithful guide, defender and warner of German Jewry, and at the same time, to say the least, the one who by far surpassed in spiritual power all the other German professors of philosophy of his generation. It became necessary to examine Cohen's attack on Spinoza. That attack had been occasioned by a particularly striking act of celebration of Spinoza on the part of German Jews.

There were two reasons why contemporary Jews were inclined to celebrate Spinoza. The first is Spinoza's assumed merit about mankind and only secondarily about the Jews; the second is his assumed merit about the Jewish people and only secondarily about mankind. Both reasons had induced contemporary Jews not only informally to rescind the excommunication which the Jewish community in Amsterdam had pronounced against Spinoza, but even, as Cohen put it, to canonize him.

The great revolt against traditional thought or the emergence of modern philosophy or natural science was completed prior to Spinoza. One may go further and say that, far from being a revolutionary thinker, Spinoza is only the heir of the modern revolt and the medieval tradition as well. At first glance he might well appear to be much more medieval than Descartes, to say nothing of Bacon and Hobbes. The modern project as understood by Bacon, Descartes and Hobbes demands that man should become the master and owner of nature; or that philosophy or science should cease to be essentially theoretical. Spinoza, however, attempts to restore the traditional conception of contemplation: one cannot think of conquering nature if nature is the same as God. Yet Spinoza restored the dignity of speculation on the basis of modern philosophy or science, of a new understanding of "nature." He thus was the first great thinker who attempted a synthesis of pre-modern (classical-medieval) and of modern philosophy. His speculation resembles Neo-Platonism; he understands all things as proceeding from, not made or created by, a single being or origin; the One is the sole ground of the Many. Yet he no longer regards this process as a descent or decay but as an ascent or unfolding: the end is higher than the origin. According to his last word on the subject, the highest form of knowledge, which he calls intuitive knowledge, is knowledge not of the one substance or God, but of individual things or events: God is fully God not qua substance or even in His eternal attributes but in His non-eternal modes understood *sub specie aeternitatis*. The knowledge of God as presented in the First Part of the *Ethics* is only universal or abstract; only the knowledge of individual things or rather events qua caused by God is concrete.[35] Spinoza thus appears to originate the kind of philosophic system which views the fundamental *processus* as a progress: God in Himself is not the *ens perfectissimum*. In this most important respect he prepares German idealism. Furthermore, just as he returned to the classical conception of *theoria*, he returned in his political philosophy to classical republicanism. The title of the crowning chapter of the *Theologico-political Treatise* is taken as literally as possible from Tacitus. But just as his theoretical philosophy is more than a restatement of classical doctrines and in fact a synthesis of classical and modern speculation, his political philosophy is more than a restatement of classical republicanism. The republic which he favors is a liberal democracy. He was the first philosopher who was both a democrat and a liberal. He was the philosopher who founded liberal democracy, a specifically modern regime. Directly and through his influence on Rousseau, who gave the decisive impulse to Kant, Spinoza became responsible for that version of modern republicanism which takes its bearings by the dignity of every man rather than by the narrowly conceived interest of every man. Spinoza's political teaching starts from a natural right of every human being as the source of all possible duties. Hence it is free from that sternness and austerity which classical political philosophy shares with ancient law—a sternness which Aristotle expressed classically by saying that what the law does not command it forbids. Hence Spinoza is free from the classical aversion to commercialism; he rejects the traditional demand for sumptuary laws. Generally speaking, his polity gives the passions much greater freedom and correspondingly counts much less on the power of reason than the polity of the classics. Whereas for the classics the life of passion is a life against nature, for Spinoza everything that is is natural. For Spinoza there are no natural ends and hence in particular there is no end natural to man. He is therefore compelled to give a novel account of man's end (the life devoted to contemplation): man's end is not natural, but rational, the result of man's figuring it out, of man's "forming an idea of man, as of a model of human nature." He thus decisively prepares the modern notion of the "ideal" as a work of the human mind or as a human project, as distinguished from an end imposed on man by nature. The formal reception of Spinoza took place in 1785 when F. H. Jacobi published his book *On the Doctrine of Spinoza, in Letters to Herr Moses Mendelssohn*. Jacobi made public the fact

that in Lessing's view there was no philosophy but the philosophy of
Spinoza. The philosophy of Kant's great successors was consciously a
synthesis of Spinoza's and Kant's philosophies. Spinoza's characteristic
contribution to this synthesis was a novel conception of God. He thus
showed the way toward a new religion or religiousness which was to
inspire a wholly new kind of society, a new kind of Church. He became the
sole father of that new Church which was to be universal in fact and not
merely in claim, like other Churches, because its foundation was no
longer any positive revelation. It was a Church whose rulers were not
priests or pastors but philosophers and artists and whose flock were the
circles of culture and property. It was of the utmost importance to that
Church that its father was not a Christian but a Jew who had informally
embraced a Christianity without dogmas and sacraments. The millennial antagonism between Judaism and Christianity was about to disappear.
The new Church would transform Jews and Christians into human
beings—into human beings of a certain kind: cultured human beings,
human beings who because they possessed Science and Art did not need
religion in addition. The new society, constituted by the aspiration
common to all its members toward the True, the Good, and the Beautiful,
emancipated the Jews in Germany. Spinoza became the symbol of that
emancipation which was to be more than emancipation but secular
redemption. In Spinoza, a thinker and a saint who was both a Jew and a
Christian and hence neither, all cultured families of the earth, it was
hoped, will be blessed. In a word, the non-Jewish world, having been
molded to a considerable extent by Spinoza, had become receptive to
Jews who were willing to assimilate themselves to it.

The celebration of Spinoza had become equally necessary on purely
Jewish grounds. As we have seen, the emphasis had shifted from the Torah
to the Jewish nation, and the Jewish nation could not be considered the
source of the Torah if it was not understood as an organism with a soul of
its own; that soul had expressed itself originally and classically in the
Bible, although not in all parts of the Bible equally. From the days of the
Bible, there always had been the conflict between prophet and priest,
between the inspired and the uninspired, between profound subterraneous
Judaism and official Judaism. Official Judaism was legalistic and hence
rationalistic. Its rationalism had received most powerful support from the
philosophic rationalism of alien origin that had found its perfect expression
in the Platonic conception of God as an artificer who makes the universe
by looking up to the unchangeable, lifeless ideas. In accordance with this,
official Judaism asserted that God has created the world and governs it
sub ratione boni. Precisely because he believed in the profoundly understood
divinity of the Bible, Spinoza revolted against this official assertion, in
the name of the absolutely free or sovereign God of the Bible—of the God
who will be what He will be, who will be gracious to whom He will be
gracious and will show mercy to whom He will show mercy. Moved by the
same spirit, he embraced with enthusiasm Paul's doctrine of predestination.
The Biblical God has created man in His image: male and female did He
create them. The male and the female, form and matter, cogitation and

extension are then equally attributes of God; Spinoza rejects both Greek idealism and Christian spiritualism. The Biblical God forms light and creates darkness, makes peace and creates evil; Spinoza's God is simply beyond good and evil. God's might is His right, and therefore the power of every being is as such its right; Spinoza lifts Machiavellianism to theological heights. Good and evil differ only from a merely human point of view; theologically the distinction is meaningless. The evil passions are evil only with a view to human utility; in themselves they show forth the might and the right of God no less than other things which we admire and by the contemplation of which we are delighted. In the state of nature, i.e. independently of human convention, there is nothing just and unjust, no duty and no guilt, and the state of nature does not simply vanish when civil society is established: pangs of conscience are nothing but feelings of displeasure that arise when a plan has gone wrong. Hence there are no vestiges of divine justice to be found except where just men reign. All human acts are modes of the one God, who possesses infinitely many attributes each of which is infinite and only two of which are known to us; who is therefore a mysterious God, whose mysterious love reveals itself in eternally and necessarily bringing forth love and hatred, nobility and baseness, saintliness and depravity; and who is infinitely lovable not in spite of but because of His infinite power which is beyond good and evil.

Compared with the fantastic flights of the Spinoza enthusiasts in the two camps, of the moralists and the immoralists, Cohen's understanding of Spinoza is sobriety itself. All the more impressive is his severe indictment of Spinoza.[36] He shows first that in his *Theologico-political Treatise* Spinoza speaks from a Christian point of view and accordingly accepts the entire Christian critique of Judaism, but goes much beyond even that Christian critique in his own critique. Spinoza accepts against his better knowledge the assertion of Jesus that Judaism commands the hatred of the enemy. He opposes spiritual and universalistic Christianity to carnal and particularistic Judaism: the core of Judaism is the Mosaic law as a particularistic not to say tribal law that serves no other end than the earthly or political felicity of the Jewish nation; the Torah does not teach morality, i.e. universal morality; the Mosaic religion is merely national; Moses' God is a tribal and in addition a corporeal God. By denying that the God of Israel is the God of all mankind Spinoza has blasphemed the God of Israel. He reduces Jewish religion to a doctrine of the Jewish state. For him, the Torah is of merely human origin. Cohen shows next that the Christianity in the light of which Spinoza condemns Judaism is not historical or actual Christianity but an idealized Christianity, and hence while idealizing Christianity, he denigrates Judaism. He shows then that Spinoza admits the universalistic character of the Old Testament prophecy, thus contradicting himself grossly. This contradiction clearly proves his lack of good faith.[37] Nor is this all. While taking the side of spiritual and transpolitical Christianity against carnal and political Judaism, Spinoza contradicts this whole argument by taking the side of the State not only against all churches but against all religion as well. "He put religion altogether [i.e. not merely Judaism] outside the sphere of truth." Starting

like all other sophists from the equation of right and might, he conceives of
the State entirely in terms of power politics, i.e. as divorced from religion
and morality, and he puts the State thus conceived above religion. This
does not mean that he deifies the State. On the contrary, he is concerned
above everything else with what he calls philosophy which he assumes to
be wholly inaccessible directly or indirectly to the large majority of men.
He has no compunction whatever about affirming the radical and un-
modifiable inequality of men without ever wondering "how can nature,
how can God answer for this difference among men?" Hence his sympathy
for democracy is suspect. He is compelled to erect an eternal barrier
between popular education and science or philosophy, and therewith
between the State and Reason. There is no place in his thought for the
enlightenment of the people. He has no heart for the people, no compassion. He cannot admit a Messianic future of mankind when all men will
be united in genuine knowledge of God. This is the reason why he is
altogether blind to Biblical prophecy and hence to the core of Judaism.[38]

On the basis of all these facts Cohen reached the conclusion that far
from deserving celebration, Spinoza fully deserved the excommunication.
Far from rescinding the excommunication, Cohen confirmed it acting as a
judge in the highest court of appeal. The grounds of his verdict were not
the same as the grounds of the lower court. He was not concerned with
Spinoza's transgression of the ceremonial law and his denial of the Mosaic
authorship of the Pentateuch. He condemned Spinoza because of his
infidelity in the simple human sense, of his complete lack of loyalty to his
own people, of his acting like an enemy of the Jews and thus giving aid and
comfort to the many enemies of the Jews, of his behaving like a base traitor.
Spinoza remains up to the present day the accuser *par excellence* of Judaism
before an anti-Jewish world; the disposition of his mind and heart toward
Jews and Judaism was "unnatural," he committed a "humanly incomprehensible act of treason," he was possessed by "an evil demon."[39]

Our case against Spinoza is in some respects even stronger than Cohen
thought. One may doubt whether Spinoza's action is humanly incomprehensible or demoniac but one must grant that it is amazingly unscrupulous.
Cohen is justly perplexed by the fact that "the center of the whole
[theologico-political] treatise" is the disparagement of Moses and the
idealization of Jesus, although the purpose of the work is to secure the
freedom of philosophizing. He explains this anomaly by Spinoza's belief
that the suppression of philosophy goes back to the Mosaic law. Cohen
does not assert that Moses championed the freedom of philosophy but he
raises the pertinent question whether Jesus championed it.[40] Why then
does Spinoza treat Judaism and Christianity differently? Why does he take
the side of Christianity in the conflict between Judaism and Christianity,
in a conflict of no concern to him as a philosopher? Cohen believes that
Spinoza had a genuine reverence for Jesus' teachings. According to
Spinoza's own statements he preferred spiritual Christianity to carnal
Judaism.[41] But is Spinoza a spiritualist? Cohen says that spirit or mind, if
applied to God, is no less a metaphor than hand, voice or mouth. He thus
merely repeats what Spinoza himself asserts; Spinoza may be said to have

denied that God has a spirit or mind. The question returns: why does
Spinoza treat Christianity differently from Judaism? Cohen comes closest
to the truth in saying that Spinoza's motive was fear,[42] surely a "humanly
comprehensible" motive. Or, to start again from the beginning, Spinoza,
attempting to achieve the liberation of philosophy in a book addressed to
Christians, cannot but appeal to the Christian prejudices which include
anti-Jewish prejudices; he fights Christian prejudices by appealing to
Christian prejudices; appealing to the Christian prejudice against Judaism,
he exhorts the Christians to free essentially spiritual Christianity from
all carnal Jewish relics (e.g. the belief in the resurrection of the body).
Generally speaking, he makes the Old Testament against his better knowledge the scapegoat for everything he finds objectionable in actual
Christianity. In spite of all this he asserts that the prophets were as universalistic as Jesus and the apostles or, more precisely, that both Testaments
teach with equal clarity everywhere the universal divine law or the
universal religion of justice and charity. Why this strange reversal, this
flagrant contradiction? At this point Cohen fails to follow Spinoza's
thought. The purpose of the *Treatise* is to show the way toward a liberal
society which is based on the recognition of the authority of the Bible,
i.e. of the Old Testament taken by itself and of the two Testaments taken
together. The argument culminates in the 14th chapter, in which he
enumerates seven dogmas which are the indispensable fundamentals of
faith, of Biblical faith, the seven "roots," as the Jewish medieval thinkers
would say. They are essential to "the catholic or universal faith," to the
religion which will be the established religion in the well-ordered republic;
belief in these seven dogmas is the only belief necessary and sufficient for
salvation. They derive equally from the Old Testament taken by itself and
from the New Testament taken by itself.[43] They do not contain anything
specifically Christian nor anything specifically Jewish. They are equally
acceptable to Jews and to Christians. The liberal society with a view to
which Spinoza has composed the *Treatise* is then a society of which Jews
and Christians can be equally members, of which Jews and Christians can
be equal members. For such a society he wished to provide. The establishment of such a society required in his opinion the abrogation of the
Mosaic law in so far as it is a particularistic and political law, and especially
of the ceremonial laws: since Moses' religion is a political law, to adhere
to his religion as he proclaimed it is incompatible with being the citizen
of any other state, whereas Jesus was not a legislator but only a teacher.[44]
It is for this reason that Spinoza is so anxious to prove that Moses' law
lost its obligatory power, and that the Jews ceased to be the chosen people
with the loss of the Jewish state: the Jews cannot be at the same time the
members of two nations and subject to two comprehensive legal codes.
Spinoza stresses the abrogation of the ceremonial law, however, not only
because that abrogation is in his opinion a necessary condition of civic
equality of the Jews but also as desirable for its own sake: the ceremonial
law is infinitely burdensome, nay, a curse.[45] In providing for the liberal
state, Spinoza provides for a Judaism that is liberal in the extreme. The
"assimilationist" "solution to the Jewish problem" which Spinoza may

be said to have suggested was more important from his point of view than the "Zionist" one which he likewise suggested. The latter as he understood it could seem to require the preservation of the ceremonial law even with the abandonment of the spirit which has animated it hitherto.[46] The former suggestion and the general purpose of the *Theologico-political Treatise* are obviously connected: freedom of philosophy requires, or seems to require, a liberal state, and a liberal state is a state which is not as such either Christian or Jewish. Even Cohen sensed for a moment that Spinoza was not entirely free from sympathy with his people.[47] Spinoza may have hated Judaism; he did not hate the Jewish people. However bad a Jew he may have been in all other respects, he thought of the liberation of the Jews in the only way in which he could think of it, given his philosophy. But precisely if this is so, we must stress all the more the fact that the manner in which he sets forth his proposal—to say nothing of the proposal itself—is Machiavellian: the humanitarian end seems to justify every means; he plays a most dangerous game;[48] his procedure is as much beyond good and evil as his God.

All this does not mean however that Cohen's critique of Spinoza's *Theologico-political Treatise* is altogether convincing. His political thought claims to be inspired by Biblical prophecy and hence is Messianic. In opposition to Spinoza it starts from the radical difference between nature and morality, the Is and the Ought, egoism and pure will. The state is essentially moral, and morality cannot be actual except in and through the state. The difficulty presented by the fact that morality is universal and the state is always particular is overcome by the consideration that the state is part of a universal moral order, as is shown by the existence of international law and by the intrinsic possibility which is at the same time a moral necessity, of a universal league of states. The radical difference between nature and morality does not amount to a contradiction between nature and morality: nature does not render impossible the fulfillment of the moral demands. The morally demanded infinite progress of morality, and in particular the "eternal progress" toward "eternal peace," nay, every single step of morality requires for its "ultimate security" the infinite duration *a parte post* of the human race and hence of nature; this infinite duration or eternity is secured by the idea of God "who signifies the harmony of the knowledge of nature and of moral knowledge," who is not a person, nor living, nor existing, nor a spirit or mind but an idea, "our" idea, i.e. our *hypothesis* in what Cohen regards as the Platonic meaning of the term. This is the Cohenian equivalent of Creation and Providence. Without "the idea of God" as Cohen understands it morality as he understands it becomes baseless. That idea is the basis of his trust in infinite progress or of his belief in history, of his "optimism," of his certainty of the ultimate victory of the good: "there is no evil." But eternal progress also requires eternal tension between the actual state and the state as it ought to be:[49] immorality is coeval with morality. Here Cohen seems to join Spinoza whose political thought is based on the truth allegedly proven by experience that there will be vices as long as there will be human beings, and who takes it therefore for granted that the state is necessarily repressive or coercive. Cohen too cannot well deny that the state must use coercion but, opposing the Kantian distinction between morality and legality, he denies that coercion is the principle of law: coercion means nothing other than law and therefore need not be mentioned. He is as uneasy about coercion as he is about power: the state is law, for the state is essentially rational, and coercion begins where reason ends. All this follows from the premise that morality is self-legislation and that it can be actual only in and through the state. A further consequence is that Cohen must understand punishment not in terms of the protection of society or other considerations which may be thought to regard the criminal not as "an end in himself" and only as a means, but in terms of the self-betterment of the criminal alone.[50] Cohen obscures the fact that while the self-betterment is necessarily a free act of the criminal, his forcible seclusion for the purpose of that self-betterment in which he may or may not engage, is not. In other words, all men are under a moral obligation to better themselves, but the specific difference of the condemned criminal is that he is put behind bars. For it goes without saying that Cohen denies the justice of capital punishment. However justly Spinoza may deserve condemnation for his Machiavelli-inspired hard-heartedness, it is to be feared that Cohen has not remained innocent of the opposite extreme. Since he attacks Spinoza in the name of Judaism, it may suffice here to quote a Jewish saying: "but for the fear of the government, men would swallow each other alive."[51]

One may doubt whether Cohen's political teaching is unqualifiedly superior to Spinoza's from the moral point of view. Cohen "rejects war." On the other hand he does not reject revolution although, as he emphasizes, Kant had "coordinated wars to revolutions." Revolutions are political but not legal acts and hence the state is not simply law; they "suspend" positive law but are justified by natural law. They do not necessarily occur without the killing of human beings; Cohen, the sworn enemy of capital punishment, reflects only on the death of "the revolutionary martyrs" who voluntarily sacrifice their lives, but not on the death of their victims. Kant had questioned the legitimacy of revolution on the ground that its maxim does not stand the test of publicity which in his view every honest maxim stands: the preparation of every revolution is necessarily conspiratorial or secret. To counter this argument Cohen observes that the moral basis of revolutions is the original contract which, "being only an idea, is always only an interior, hence secret presupposition." The same reasoning would lead to the further conclusion that the original contract, nay, Cohen's theology must never be publicly mentioned, let alone be taught. It is altogether fitting that Cohen, who was no friend of "the irrational" or of "mysticism," should be driven in his defense of the revolutionary principle to become friendly to the "irrational" and to "mysticism."[52] To say nothing of other things, he would never have been driven to this surrender of reason if he had taken seriously the law of reason or the natural law which may be said to indicate the right mean between hard-heartedness and soft-heartedness.

While admitting "the deep injustice" of Cohen's judgment on Spinoza,

Rosenzweig asserts that Cohen has honestly complied in his critique of the *Theologico-political Treatise* with the duty of scholarly objectivity.[53] This assertion must be qualified. Since Cohen accuses Spinoza of having been unfair in his treatment of the universalism of the prophets, one must consider in fairness to Spinoza whether the Jewish tradition with which Spinoza was directly confronted had preserved intact that universalism. Cohen failed to make this investigation. Once one makes it, one observes that Spinoza recognized the universalism of the prophets in some respects more clearly than did some of the greatest traditional Jewish authorities. In his critique of Spinoza Cohen is silent about the fact, which he mentions elsewhere, that prophetic universalism had become obscured in later times for easily understandable reasons.[54] Cohen is particularly indignant about Spinoza's using a remark of Maimonides in order to prove that according to Judaism non-Jews cannot be saved unless they believe in the Mosaic revelation,[55] i.e. unless, as one is tempted to say, they are Christians or Muslims. More precisely, Spinoza quotes a passage from Maimonides' Code in which it is said that a Gentile is pious and has a share in the world to come if he performs the seven commandments given to Noah qua commanded by God in the Torah, but that if he performs them because of a decision of reason, he does not belong to the pious Gentiles or to the wise ones. Cohen accuses Spinoza of having used a false reading of a single passage of the Code—of a passage which expresses only Maimonides' private opinion and which in addition is contradicted by two other passages of the Code—in order to deny the universalism of post-biblical Judaism. He (or the authority to which he defers) notes that according to the most authoritative commentator on the Code, Joseph Caro, the qualification stated by Maimonides (*viz.* that piety requires recognition of the Mosaic revelation) is his private opinion, but Cohen fails to add that Caro adds that the opinion is correct. Caro would not have said this if Maimonides' opinion contradicts the consensus of Judaism. Cohen (or his authority) also notes that, according to the most authentic text of the Code, the Gentile who performs the seven Noahidic commandments because of a decision of reason does not indeed belong to the pious Gentiles but to the wise ones.[56] But Cohen does not show that Spinoza knew that reading to be the most authentic reading. The reading used by Spinoza is still the common reading which it would not be if it were in shocking contrast to the consensus of Judaism as Cohen asserts and hence would have shocked every Jewish reader.[57] In addition, the allegedly best reading does not necessarily improve the fate of the wise Gentiles unless one proves first that the fate of the wise Gentiles is as good as that of the pious Gentiles. Cohen finally asserts that the passage in question contradicts two other passages of the Code which in his opinion do not demand that the pious Gentile believe in the revealed character of the Torah. It suffices to say that the two passages are silent on what precisely constitutes the piety of the Gentiles and are therefore irrelevant to the issue.[58] Cohen also refers to a different treatment of the subject in Maimonides' commentary on the Mishna; but this merely leads to the further question whether that commentary, composed much earlier than the Code, is equal in authority to it. But, to return to the main issue, i.e. whether the ordinary reading, used by Spinoza, of the passage under consideration makes sense as a Maimonidean utterance: can Maimonides have taught, as Spinoza asserts he did, that Gentiles who perform the seven Noahidic commandments because reason decides so are not wise men? The answer is simple: Maimonides must have taught it because he denied that there are any rational commandments. Cohen might have objected to this argument on the ground that if Maimonides' denial of the rationality of any commandments or laws were his last word, he could not well have attempted to show that all or almost all commandments of the Torah have "reasons."[59] The reply is obvious: according to Maimonides all or almost all commandments of the Torah serve the purpose of eradicating idolatry, an irrational practice, and are in this sense "rational"; they are rational in the sense in which, not a healthy body but a medicine is "healthy."[60] One could say that Maimonides' denial of the rationality of any law is implied in the incriminated passage itself regardless of which of the two readings one prefers; for the term which Cohen renders by "reason" (da'at) does not necessarily mean reason in particular but may mean thought or opinion in general:[61] it makes sense both to assert and to deny that opinion justifies the seven Noahidic commandments.

These and similar considerations do not affect the main issue, namely, the fact that Cohen may well be right in asserting that Spinoza acted ignobly in basing his denial of the universalism of traditional, post-prophetic Judaism on a single Maimonidean utterance. In the words of Rosenzweig, beneath the deep injustice of Cohen's judgment lies its still much deeper justification. What Rosenzweig meant may be stated as follows. Cohen was a more profound thinker than Spinoza because unlike Spinoza he did not take for granted the philosophic detachment or freedom from the tradition of his own people; that detachment is "unnatural," not primary, but the outcome of a liberation from the primary attachment, of an alienation, a break, a betrayal. The primary is fidelity, and the sympathy and love which go with fidelity. Genuine fidelity to a tradition is not the same as literalist traditionalism and is in fact incompatible with it. It consists in preserving not simply the tradition but the continuity of the tradition. As fidelity to a living and hence changing tradition, it requires that one distinguish between the living and the dead, the flame and the ashes, the gold and the dross: the loveless Spinoza sees only the ashes, not the flame, only the letter, not the spirit. He is not excusable on the ground that Jewish thought may have declined in the centuries preceding him from its greatest height; for he "on whose extraction, whose gifts, whose learning the Jews had put the greatest hope" was under an obligation to understand contemporary Judaism, and still more Maimonides, to say nothing of Scripture itself, in the light of the highest or, if necessary, better than they understood themselves. Within a living tradition, the new is not the opposite of the old but its deepening: one does not understand the old in its depth unless one understands it in the light of such deepening; the new does not emerge through the rejection or annihilation of the old but through its metamorphosis or reshaping. "And it is a question whether such reshaping is not the best form of annihilation."[62] This is indeed the question: whether the loyal and loving reshaping or reinterpretation of the inherited, or the pitiless burning of the hitherto worshiped is the best form of annihilation of the antiquated, i.e. of the untrue or bad. On the answer to this question the ultimate judgment on Spinoza as well as on Cohen will depend: is the right interpretation "idealizing" interpretation, i.e. the interpretation of a teaching in the light of its highest possibility regardless of whether or not that highest possibility was known to the originator, or is it historical interpretation proper, which understands a teaching as meant by its originator? Is the conservativism which is generally speaking the wise maxim of practice also the sacred law of theory?

It would not be reasonable to demand from Cohen that he should give the benefit of idealizing interpretation to Spinoza who had become an ingredient of the modern tradition on which Cohen's philosophy as a philosophy of culture is based. For the kind of interpretation which Spinoza calls for is not idealizing, since his own doctrine is not idealistic. As was shown before, Cohen's political philosophy did not pay sufficient attention to the harsh political verities which Spinoza has stated so forcefully. Accordingly, he does not pay sufficient attention to the harsh necessity to which Spinoza bowed by writing in the manner in which he wrote. He did not understand Spinoza's style, which was indeed entirely different from his own. Cohen sometimes writes like a commentator on a commentary on an already highly technical text and hence like a man whose thought is derivative and traditional in the extreme, and yet he surprises time and again with strikingly expressed original and weighty thoughts. Be this as it may, he goes so far as to deny that in Spinoza's time the freest minds were compelled to withhold and to deny the truth; "Think only of Jean Bodin who in his Heptaplomeres not only directed the strongest attacks against Christianity but also celebrated Judaism most highly. It must appear strange that this writing, which was known to Leibniz and Thomasius, which was at that time widely distributed, should have remained unknown to Spinoza." He forgets here to say what he says elsewhere: "Leibniz had seen the manuscript of the Heptaplomeres and had advised against its being printed."[63] It was not printed before the nineteenth century. Once one takes into consideration the consequences of persecution, Spinoza's conduct in the *Theologico-political Treatise* ceases to be that "psychological riddle" which Cohen saw in it. He wondered whether that conduct could not be traced to the fact that the Spanish Jews' feelings of anxiety caused by the terrors of the Inquisition had eventually turned into hatred for that for the sake of which they had been so cruelly persecuted. A different explanation was suggested by Nietzsche in his verses addressed to Spinoza. After having paid homage to Spinoza's *amor dei* and to his being "blissful through intelligence," he goes on to say that beneath the love of the "One in all" there was eating a secret desire for revenge: *am Judengott frass Judenhass*. Nietzsche understood Spinoza in his own image. He traced his own revolt against the Christian God to his Christian conscience. The premise of this explanation

is Hegelian dialectics: every form of the mind perishes through its antithesis which it necessarily produces. Spinoza's break with the Torah is the
consequence of the *Sithrei Torah* in the double sense of the expression, the
secrets of the Torah and the contradictions of the Torah. Spinoza was not
swayed by Hegelian dialectics but by the Aristotelian principle of contradiction.

Cohen read Spinoza on the one hand not literally enough and on the
other hand much too literally; he understood him too literally because he
did not read him literally enough. Hence he did not find his way among
the contradictions in which the *Theologico-political Treatise* abounds. As
he exclaims on one occasion, "no reason of reasonable men can understand,
let alone overcome, these difficulties." A single example must here suffice.
He wonders whether Spinoza does not contradict himself by admitting
that the Mosaic law is a divine law although he understands by a divine
law a law that aims only at the highest good, i.e. true knowledge of God
and love of God, or intellectual love of God; and he denies that the Mosaic
law aims at that highest good. The contradiction disappears once one
considers the fact, which Cohen observes, that according to Spinoza a
law may also be called divine with a view to its origin: the Mosaic law is
human as regards its end, since it aims only at political felicity, but it is
divine qua divinely revealed. Cohen quotes Spinoza's explanation: the
Mosaic law "may be called the law of God or divine law since we believe
that it is sanctioned by the prophetic light." He remarks: "But why do we
believe this? This question is not answered by the anonymous author."
But does not the community consisting of the anonymous author who
speaks as a Christian and his Christian readers believe it as a matter of
course, so that the question as to "why we believe it" does not have to
arise? Spinoza had originally said that the divine law aims only at the
highest good; immediately before saying that the Mosaic law can be called
divine with a view to its origin as distinguished from its aim, he says according to Cohen that the divine law "consists chiefly in the highest good":
hence, Cohen infers, Spinoza admits now a secondary content of the
divine law without stating immediately what that secondary content is,
namely, the sensual means which sensual men need. But Spinoza did not
say that the divine law consists in the highest good; he says that it consists
in the prescriptions regarding the means required for achieving the highest
good: the divine law consists chiefly of the prescriptions regarding the
proximate means and secondarily of the prescriptions regarding the
remote means; since "sensual man" is incapable of intellectual love of God,
his needs fall wholly outside of the divine law as here considered by
Spinoza. It must be added that according to Spinoza even the divine law
in the strictest sense is of human origin; every law is prescribed by human
beings to themselves or to other human beings. Cohen throws some light
on Spinoza's teaching regarding the divine law by making this remark on
Spinoza's assertion that "the highest reward of the divine law is the law
itself": "here he has literally taken over a sentence of the Mishna from the
well-known Sayings of the Fathers, only adding the word 'highest.'"
Cohen underestimates the importance of Spinoza's addition: Spinoza's

egoistic morality demands for the fulfillment of the commandments rewards other than the commandments or perhaps additional commandments; it does not leave room for martyrdom.[64]

Rosenzweig finds Cohen guilty of injustice to Spinoza not because of defective objectivity but rather because of defective "subjectivity," i.e. of "insufficient reflection about the conditions and foundations of his own person. He ought to have made his attack with a clearer consciousness of the fact that, not indeed he himself, but the times which had born and raised him, Cohen himself, would not have been possible without Spinoza." The distinction between Cohen himself and his time, which is due to idealizing or apologetic interpretation, is immaterial here, for if Cohen's thought had nothing to do with the thought of his time, he would not have met Spinoza by reflecting about the presuppositions of "his own person." Cohen accuses Spinoza of blindness to Biblical prophetism, but this phenomenon as Cohen understood it was brought to light by what he calls "the historical understanding of the Bible," and this understanding is not possible without higher criticism of the Bible, i.e. without a public effort which was originated with the necessary comprehensiveness by Spinoza. Cohen blames Spinoza for disregarding the difference between mythical and historical elements of the Bible, a distinction which, as Cohen states, was alien to our traditional exegesis; and as regards the doctrinal elements of the Bible, he blames him for not distinguishing between the less and the more mature Biblical statements; he blames him for the immaturity or incompetence of his Biblical criticism, not at all for his Biblical criticism itself: for Cohen, Biblical criticism is a matter of course. Similarly, he states that Spinoza opposed rabbinical Judaism, especially its great concern with the ceremonial law, and that his sharp opposition had a certain salutary effect on the liberation of opinion; he notes without any disapproval that "modern Judaism" has freed itself from part of the ceremonial law; he fails to admit that modern Judaism is a synthesis between rabbinical Judaism and Spinoza. As for Spinoza's denial of the possibility of miracles, Cohen gives an extremely brief summary of the chapter which Spinoza devotes to the subject of miracles without saying a word in defense of miracles.[65] In brief, Cohen does not discuss at all the issue between Spinoza and Jewish orthodoxy, i.e. the only issue with which Spinoza could have been concerned, since there was no modern or liberal Judaism in his time. One may say that in his critique of Spinoza Cohen commits the typical mistake of the conservative, which consists in concealing the fact that the continuous and changing tradition which he cherishes so greatly would never have come into being through conservatism, or without discontinuities, revolutions, and sacrileges committed at the beginning of the cherished tradition and at least silently repeated in its course.

This much is certain: Cohen's critique of Spinoza does not come to grips with the fact that Spinoza's critique is directed against the whole body of authoritative teachings and rules known in Spinoza's time as Judaism and still maintained in Cohen's time by Jewish orthodoxy. Cohen took it for granted that Spinoza had refuted orthodoxy as such. Owing to the collapse of "the old thinking" it became then necessary to examine the

Theologico-political Treatise with a view to the question of whether Spinoza
had in fact refuted orthodoxy. Cohen's critique remained helpful for this
purpose almost only in so far as it had destroyed the prejudice in favor of
Spinoza, or the canonization of Spinoza by German or Jewish romanticism, to say nothing of the canonization by liberalism. Cohen's critique had
the additional merit that it was directed chiefly against the *Theologico-
political Treatise*. The seeming neglect of the *Ethics* proved to be sound, and
thus to be obligatory for the re-examination of Spinoza's critique of
orthodoxy, for the following reason. The *Ethics* starts from explicit premises
by the granting of which one has already implicitly granted the absurdity
of orthodoxy and even of Judaism as understood by Cohen or Rosenzweig;
at first glance these premises seem to be arbitrary and hence to beg the
whole question. They are not evident in themselves but they are thought
to become evident through their alleged result: they and only they are held
to make possible the clear and distinct account of everything; in the light
of the clear and distinct account, the Biblical account appears to be
confused. The *Ethics* thus begs the decisive question, the question as to
whether the clear and distinct account is as such true and not merely a
plausible hypothesis. In the *Theologico-political Treatise*, however, Spinoza
starts from premises that are granted to him by the believers in revelation;
he attempts to refute them on the bases of Scripture, of theologoumena
formulated by traditional authorities, and of what one may call common
sense. For in the *Treatise* Spinoza addresses men who are still believers
and whom he intends to liberate from their "prejudices" so that they can
begin to philosophize; the *Treatise* is Spinoza's introduction to philosophy.

The results of this examination of Spinoza's critique may be summarized
as follows. If orthodoxy claims to know that the Bible is divinely revealed,
that every word of the Bible is divinely inspired, that Moses was the writer
of the Pentateuch, that the miracles recorded in the Bible have happened
and similar things, Spinoza has refuted orthodoxy. But the case is entirely
different if orthodoxy limits itself to asserting that it believes the afore-
mentioned things, i.e. that they cannot claim to possess the binding
power peculiar to the known. For all assertions of orthodoxy rest on the
irrefutable premise that the omnipotent God whose will is unfathomable,
whose ways are not our ways, who has decided to dwell in the thick
darkness, may exist. Given this premise, miracles and revelations in
general, and hence all Biblical miracles and revelations in particular, are
possible. Spinoza has not succeeded in showing that this premise is contradicted by anything we know. For what we are said to know, for example,
regarding the age of the solar system, has been established on the basis of
the assumption that the solar system has come into being naturally;
miraculously it could have come into being in the way described by the
Bible. It is only naturally or humanly impossible that the "first" Isaiah
should have known the name of the founder of the Persian empire; it was
not impossible for the omnipotent God to reveal to him that name. The
orthodox premise cannot be refuted by experience or by recourse to the
principle of contradiction. An indirect proof of this is the fact that Spinoza
and his like owed such success as they had in their fight against orthodoxy

to laughter and mockery. By means of mockery they attempted to laugh orthodoxy out of its position from which it could not be dislodged by any proofs supplied by Scripture or by reason. One is tempted to say that mockery does not succeed the refutation of the orthodox tenets but is itself the refutation. The genuine refutation of orthodoxy would require the proof that the world and human life are perfectly intelligible without the assumption of a mysterious God; it would require at least the success of the philosophic system: man has to show himself theoretically and practically as the master of the world and the master of his life; the merely given world must be replaced by the world created by man theoretically and practically. Spinoza's *Ethics* attempts to be the system but it does not succeed; the clear and distinct account of everything that it presents remains fundamentally hypothetical. As a consequence, its cognitive status is not different from that of the orthodox account. Certain it is that Spinoza cannot legitimately deny the possibility of revelation. But to grant that revelation is possible means to grant that the philosophic account and the philosophic way of life are not necessarily, not evidently, the true account and the right way of life: philosophy, the quest for evident and necessary knowledge, rests itself on an unevident decision, on an act of the will, just as faith does. Hence the antagonism between Spinoza and Judaism, between unbelief and belief, is ultimately not theoretical but moral.

For the understanding of that moral antagonism the Jewish designation of the unbeliever as Epicurean seemed to be helpful, especially since from every point of view Epicureanism may be said to be the classic form of the critique of religion and the basic stratum of the tradition of the critique of religion. Epicureanism is hedonism, and traditional Judaism always suspects that all theoretical and practical revolts against the Torah are inspired by the desire to throw off the yoke of the stern and exacting duties so that one can indulge in a life of pleasure. Epicureanism can lead only to a mercenary morality whereas traditional Jewish morality is not mercenary: "The reward for [the fulfillment of] the commandment is the commandment." Epicureanism is so radically mercenary that it conceives of its theoretical doctrines as the means for liberating the mind from the terrors of religious fear, of the fear of death, and of natural necessity. Characteristically, modern unbelief is indeed no longer Epicurean. It is no longer cautious or retiring, not to say cowardly, but bold and active. Whereas Epicureanism fights the religious "delusion" because of its terrible character, modern unbelief fights it because it is a delusion: regardless of whether religion is terrible or comforting, qua delusion it makes men oblivious of the real goods, of the enjoyment of the real goods, and thus seduces them into being cheated of the real, "this-worldly" goods by their spiritual or temporal rulers who "live" from that delusion. Liberated from the religious delusion, awakened to sober awareness of his real situation, taught by bad experiences that he is threatened by a stingy, hostile nature, man recognizes as his sole salvation and duty, not so much "to cultivate his garden" as in the first place to plant a garden by making himself the master and owner of nature. But this whole enterprise requires, above all, political action, revolution, a life and death struggle: the

Epicurean who wishes to live securely and retiredly must transform himself into an "idealist" who has learned to fight and to die for honor and truth. But in proportion as the systematic effort to liberate man completely from all non-human bonds seems to succeed, the doubt increases whether the goal is not fantastic—whether man has not become smaller and more miserable in proportion as the systematic civilization progresses. Eventually the belief that by pushing ever farther back the "natural limits" man will advance to ever greater freedom, that he can subjugate nature and prescribe to it his laws, begins to wither. In this stage the religious "delusion" is rejected not because it is terrible but because it is comforting: religion is not a tool which man has forged for dark reasons in order to torment himself, to make life unnecessarily difficult, but a way out chosen for obvious reasons in order to escape from the terror, the exposedness and the hopelessness of life which cannot be eradicated by any progress of civilization. A new kind of fortitude which forbids itself every flight from the horror of life into comforting delusion, which accepts the eloquent descriptions of "the misery of man without God" as an additional proof of the goodness of its cause, reveals itself eventually as the ultimate and purest ground for the rebellion against revelation. This new fortitude, being the willingness to look man's forsakenness in its face, being the courage to welcome the most terrible truth, is "probity," "intellectual probity." This final atheism with a good conscience, or with a bad conscience, is distinguished by its conscientiousness from the atheism at which the past shuddered. Compared not only with Epicureanism but with the unbelief of the age of Spinoza, it reveals itself as a descendant of Biblical morality. This atheism, the heir and the judge of the belief in revelation, of the secular struggle between belief and unbelief, and finally of the short-lived but by no means therefore inconsequential romantic longing for the lost belief, confronting orthodoxy in complex sophistication formed out of gratitude, rebellion, longing and indifference, and in simple probity, is according to its claim as capable of an original understanding of the human roots of the belief in God, as no earlier, no less complex-simple philosophy ever was. The last word and the ultimate justification of Spinoza's critique is the atheism from intellectual probity which overcomes orthodoxy radically by understanding it radically, i.e. without the polemical bitterness of the Enlightenment and the equivocal reverence of romanticism. Yet this claim however eloquently raised can not deceive one about the fact that its basis is an act of will, of belief, and, being based on belief, is fatal to any philosophy.

The victory of orthodoxy through the self-destruction of rational philosophy was not an unmitigated blessing, for it was a victory not of Jewish orthodoxy but of any orthodoxy, and Jewish orthodoxy based its claim to superiority to other religions from the beginning on its superior rationality (Deut. 4:6). Apart from this, the hierarchy of moralities and wills to which the final atheism referred could not but be claimed to be intrinsically true, theoretically true: "the will to power" of the strong or of the weak may be the ground of every other doctrine; it is not the ground of the doctrine of the will to power: the will to power was said to be a fact.

Other observations and experiences confirmed the suspicion that it would be unwise to say farewell to reason. I began therefore to wonder whether the self-destruction of reason was not the inevitable outcome of modern rationalism as distinguished from pre-modern rationalism, especially Jewish-medieval rationalism and its classical (Aristotelian and Platonic) foundation. The present study was based on the premise, sanctioned by powerful prejudice, that a return to pre-modern philosophy is impossible. The change of orientation which found its first expression, not entirely by accident, in the article published at the end of this volume, compelled me to engage in a number of studies in the course of which I became ever more attentive to the manner in which heterodox thinkers of earlier ages wrote their books. As a consequence of this, I now read the *Theologico-political Treatise* differently than I read it when I was young. I understood Spinoza too literally because I did not read him literally enough.

L. S.

The University of Chicago
August, 1962

THE TRADITION OF THE CRITIQUE OF RELIGION

INTRODUCTION[1]

IN OUR TIME scholars generally study the Bible in the manner in which they study any other book. As is generally admitted, Spinoza more than any other man laid the foundation for this kind of Biblical study. In the seventh chapter of his *Theologico-political Tractate*, he determines the fundamental themes and goals of the new discipline; in the subsequent chapters he arrives at fundamental results which remained accepted in the later development of the discipline. One may describe this kind of study of the Bible as historical. The philosophic question to which the modern study of the Bible gives rise is primarily the methodological question, the question of the methods of historical studies or of "the sciences of culture," as distinguished from natural science. Spinoza's achievement in this respect is far less significant than the achievement of, say, Erasmus of Rotterdam; this is the consequence of his limiting view that the method of Biblical study is fundamentally the same as that of natural science. To leave it at this judgment, however, would mean to be blind to the peculiar character of Spinoza's work. To found the historical study of the Bible is obviously an achievement of a higher order than to found the disciplines of investigating, say, Egyptian or Babylonian culture. Once it is assumed that the Bible is a literary document like any other, it must be studied and interpreted like any other literary document; it becomes the object of the sciences of culture like all their other objects; the foundation of Biblical science is no longer a problem. Hence the justification of that assumption, i.e. the critique of the opposed presupposition, that of revealed religion, is the true foundation of Biblical science in the modern sense. It is for this reason and only for this reason that Spinoza's work is of fundamental importance. The context to which it belongs is the critique of Revelation as attempted by the radical Enlightenment. That critique in its turn is only one particular form, one particular stage of the critique of religion which was originated in Greek antiquity and continued and renewed in the age in which belief in Revelation predominated. In order to gain some access to Spinoza's critique of revealed religion and to gain some standard for judging it, we begin with a survey of the tradition of the critique of religion in general.

CHAPTER I

THE TRADITION OF THE CRITIQUE OF RELIGION[2]

IN THE extreme case—and the extreme case is the common one —radical criticism of religion is by intent scientific criticism. It is rendered no less scientific by the general situation that opposition to religion points at the pernicious nature of religion, or the positive harm it does, rather than at the error of its doctrines. Nor is the claim to being scientific rendered questionable by the fact that opposition to religion passes beyond theoretical rejection and into practical revolt. For both the rejection of religion as harmful and the practical revolt against it can be justified by the critic on scientific grounds.

But, we must ask, is not the very idea of scientific criticism of religion inherently absurd? Are not religion and science by their inherent intent so basically different that they cannot come into conflict with one another? The concept of science that underlies this view of the relation of science and religion (science as positive, man-conceived science) is not applicable, one must concede, to the metaphysics underlying the traditional criticism of religion. Inherent in the idea of this metaphysics, as the knowledge essentially of God, is the possibility of criticism of the false notions of God; also inherent is the idea of a scientific criticism of religion. Must the difference between positive science, which offers no possibility of criticism of religion, and metaphysics, which in principle permits criticism of religion, be defined as it has been defined by Kant in his transcendental dialectics, namely by the statement that this difference has its basis in theoretical consciousness? Is the difference between metaphysics and positive science not rather the fact that metaphysics by origin is *more* than pure theory? Is it not perhaps this extra something that throws a bridge between religion and science over the gulf dividing them, a bridge that makes scientific criticism of religion possible? These early critics of religion speak with a naiveté, which never ceases to startle us, of the happiness which they owe to their science, and which they confidently expect to receive from their science—the liberation from religion. By this happiness they do not mean the joy of disinterested investigation aiming, it is true, at results, but not at these or those particular results. Their interest aims at particular results. Their particular happiness requires that they should arrive at particular "truths." Their scientific inquiry serves a particular purpose. And is this purpose not prior to the pursuit of science? Does it not define the limits of their questioning? Does it not foreshadow their answers? Certainly these metaphysicians by their systems prove that the interest which directs their science is the only justifiable human interest, the sole interest in harmony with nature and with truth. But is the reality and the effectiveness of this interest due to its scientific foundation? Is it not much more plausible and convincing that this interest guides their science, and by so doing directs the scientific justification adduced for the interest? We need not take for granted that this question is settled on one side or the other. But we must assume the possibility here adumbrated that the criticism of religion undertaken, in intent scientific and objective, nevertheless has its origin in an original interest springing from the heart, in an original motive. This possibility becomes reality, if ever, in the philosophy of Epicurus. Epicurus' criticism of religion is one source, and the most important one, of seventeenth century criticism of religion.

Epicurus is conscious of his motive. It is expressly the root first of his criticism of religion and then of his science. Were we not in awe of active and effectual gods, science, according to Epicurus' expressed opinion, would be in essential part superfluous. For Epicurus, the basic aim of knowledge is to achieve a condition of *eudaimonia*, by means of reasoning. This *eudaimonia* does not consist in the scientific investigation itself; science is no more than the indispensable means of attaining the condition.[3] The concrete meaning attached to *eudaimonia* defines the task of science as the elimination of all fear of the gods.

We shall first retrace the exposition of his objective as given by Epicurus himself. The only standard is pleasure. Any and every pleasure is as such a good, and any and every pain is as such an evil. Nevertheless, we do not welcome every pleasure, nor do we avoid every pain. For it is better to endure much toil in order to gain greater pleasure, and it is more profitable to refrain from certain pleasures so as to avoid paying the price of still greater pain. Therefore, taking into account the fact that pleasures and pains are often inextricably coupled, what is required for the sake of the highest possible return in pleasure is a prudent weighing in the balance, a comparative assessment which sets against the probability of pleasure, as given at any specific moment, the probability of pain.[4] What is to be understood as the greatest pleasure is not, however, the highest possible surplus of any pleasure over the pain mingled with it, but the purest pleasure, free of any pain. The elimination of every pain—this is "the limit for the magnitude of pleasure." The greatest pleasure is thus unambiguously defined as the purest pleasure. What above all imperils purity of pleasure is the recall of past pain and the premonition of future pain. Pleasure must be safeguarded not only against the admixture of present pain, but also against the intrusion of past and future pain. The security of pleasure is for Epicurus only the more general form of the achievement of pure pleasure. But it is manifest that, if certainty is divorced from its association with purity of pleasure, and one can disregard the particular premise that the greatest pleasure is the purest, then pleasure may also be understood and desired as secure. This observation is necessary for understanding the Epicurean tradition in criticism of religion. Epicurus' critique of religion is founded on the achievement of security divorced from the achievement of purity.

The most certain pleasures are those of the past; "they are safe behind impregnable fortifications." Memory holds them for us as ever-present, and thus builds round us a world in which present pains are felt no more. Of past sorrows Epicurus takes no heed. He recalls his past only in so far as it is pleasurable. It is the decisive characteristic of the Epicurean that he is incapable of suffering from his past. Present pleasures are not yet entirely secure, they are still exposed to the grasp of fate. Future pleasure is altogether uncertain. Therefore interest in pleasure, understood as interest in certain pleasure, is focused sharply on past pleasures, on living in memory of pleasures past. It is not the youth but the old man, if his cup of happiness has brimmed, whom Epicurus accounts happy. Just as pleasure, which consists not in present joys, but in the memory of those past, is stronger than the greatest present pain, so also the expectation of future pain is in its turn stronger than the greatest present pleasure. Here, however, the countervailing force of expectation, memory, on which one might well

have expected to be able to count, must fall short. For it is not a
case of expecting some future pain unknown and uncharacter-
ized. We hold that we are threatened by eternal and limitless
pain. It follows that Epicurus cannot but direct the whole of his
energy to the elimination of this anxiety by which all pleasure is
brought to nothing: The fear of the gods and fear of death.[5]

The opposite of man's perfect state, *eudaimonia*, is the condition
of confusion due to fear. Liberation from fear is achieved by denial
of the fearful quality of what is taken to be fearful. It is science
which provides proof that there is no cause for fear, that there is
nothing to fear. That is the very intent and meaning of science:
were we not harassed by apprehensions regarding Olympus and
death, there would be no need for a science of physics (*Sententiae
Selectae* 10–13).

That science will achieve this, that the unveiling of truth will
bring us tranquillity of mind and not still greater anxiety, is
taken for granted by Epicurus. The justice of this hope, of this
belief that outward events are keyed to human peace of mind,
which is thought to be needlessly disturbed by fear of celestial
things and by fear of death, is the pre-condition for the success of
his undertaking. What cannot be traced back to this motive is his
conviction of the truth of certain theorems which favor the
effectiveness of this motive.

What throws a bridge between these heterogeneous elements,
the motive and the theorems? Does the definition of the purpose of
science rest on results of science? But how are these results
reached by science? There is justification for the misgiving that
the interest which science serves and which doubtless is active
prior to its being justified by results, on its part influences these
results and distorts them. This suspicion becomes stronger, the
less Epicurus' science proves to be consistent. Furthermore, if
his theorems—in correspondence with the whole structure of his
science—are to be understood as *his* theorems only, in the light
of their function as furthering the object of his science, it then
becomes obligatory to interpret his science in the light cast upon
it by his motive. For him the theorems are only means. His lack
of scruple in the choice of means may lead to the oft-repeated
charge that his theory is "superficial," but the unity and consistency of his intent are beyond all doubt.

It is to be conceded that the word "means" overstates the case,

for it is in no sense to be said that Epicurus consciously recon-
structs the world as a figment in harmony with his impelling
interest. Rather is it that his dominant will to self-liberation from
fear predisposes him to seek out and prefer facts which work for
equanimity and consolation. It is not only the specific scientific
findings which are modified by this tendency, but the specific
scientific approach as a whole.

Since the connection between Epicurus' motive and the science
corresponding with that motive is so important for understanding
the criticism of religion in the seventeenth century, the features
of this connection must be treated in some detail. If science is to
do away with fear and confusion of mind, there must first of all
be unambiguous criteria which permit the final settling of at least
those questions which touch on principles. It is for this reason
that dialectic is rejected, and only a few rules, and those unconditionally valid, are admitted to be "canonic." This underlies
the insistence on maximum simplicity, palpability and clarity.[6]
The truths unveiled by reason using these epistemological
principles must at all times be ready to hand in the form of
propositions, to quell perturbation in the moment of its arising.
This explains the terse formulation of the basic propositions—
those most frequently needed—into apophthegms, designed to be
learned by heart.[7] Let it be borne in mind that it is not truth
qua truth which brings calm, but the particular truth that there
is no ground for fear. The world itself must be of such a nature that
we need not fear finding ourselves confronted with surprising,
dangerous occurrences. A soothing regularity and necessity must
prevail. This necessity must not tyrannize over us, it must leave us
our freedom. Hence the notorious resort to the theory of the
arbitrary movements of atoms, so that human tranquillity may
persist, even in the face of the otherwise inexorable necessity of
atomic events.[8]

If all the theories of Epicurus, in the sense of being Epicurus'
own theories, are to be understood essentially as a means of liberating men from fear, the question arises whether the means are at
least necessary means. According to the express opinion of
Epicurus himself, they are necessary. However, he himself
indicates another possibility. "It were better to follow the tale of
the gods than to be enslaved to the doom of which the physicists
speak: for that tale leaves the hope that the gods may be swayed

by being honored, but this is of inexorable necessity" (Diogenes Laertius x, 134). Taking this proposition in all seriousness, the possibility opens that fear could be eliminated through faith in effective gods, provided that these gods themselves are kind. We interpolate this observation only to bring out that Epicurus' predominant motive is independent, not only of his concrete theorems, but also of hostility towards religion. It also brings out that Epicurus' motive is inseparable from his hostility towards any position which assumes that fear of the divine must ever operate to prevent peace of mind. Such a position looms large in Epicurus' mind—the thought that belief in willing and acting gods is the mightiest impairment of human peace of mind (ibid., x, 81). Against this, according to Epicurus, there is no recourse except by adherence to the theology and physics of his teaching. The whole of Epicurus' scientific endeavor assumes—more than any other—the fear of the gods as an ever-menacing danger.[9]

The history of criticism of religion has every reason to devote particular attention to the only thinker who saw in criticism of religion his highest task, the fulfillment of his intent. This is no divagation under stress of circumstance. His own basic intention drives him undeviatingly along the straight and narrow path to this goal. In this sense, Epicurus' teachings merit the epithet "classical." It is in this light that Lucretius sees his master and teacher, when he sings his praise

> Primum Graius homo mortalis tollere contra
> est oculos ausus primusque obsistere contra.

For this reason we must pay careful attention to his motive. Epicurus' concern is for tranquillity of mind and life unbeset by fear. He sets his face resolutely against all that confuses and disturbs. The drive behind his philosophy is of such nature that it must have affected not only the adherents of a particular school of philosophy, i.e. those who choose a certain particular means. Rather is it the case that in Epicureanism a universal human motive for rebellion against religion finds its expression—the most universal human motive, which changes little, if at all, amid all the modifications and developments in the evolution of human consciousness.[10]

Epicurus' analysis of religion must be kept sharply distinct from the motive underlying that criticism. It is to be assumed from the outset that the motive will cause Epicurus to adopt analyses from other sources, and, on the other hand, that his own analysis will be called on to serve critical analysis born of different motives. It is, however, to be expected that the analysis of religion characteristic of original Epicureanism will stand within the framework of his system; in other words, within the general means available to him for his basic purpose.

When Epicurus anticipates that liberation from fear of the gods will come from physics, the search for causes, in particular causes of celestial events, he is implicitly stating that ignorance of causes is in fact the condition *sine qua non* for fear of the gods. If one puts the further question, what is the sufficient cause of this fact, the sources available to us fail to provide us with the answer given by Epicurus. Taking into account the relationships which exist in other connections between Epicurus and Democritus, and further taking into account the context in which Lucretius gives the answer returned by Democritus, we can without hesitation assume that the answer of Epicurus was the same. Celestial events (lightning, thunder, eclipses of sun and moon, etc.) evoked in ancient times the belief that it was the gods who were responsible, and, because of this, men became frightened (Diels 55 A 75). Sextus, who handed down this theory of Democritus, interprets it in this way: 'it was because of unanticipated untoward events that men came to the concept of gods.' This is the sense in which we must interpret Democritus; the unforeseeable and exceptional event, against whose effects on the mind there was no means of reassurance by knowledge of causes, were to be attributed to the gods.

The full import of this thought becomes plain from the connection in which it stands to the science of Democritus and Epicurus. The context is clear in the interpretation of the statement: "Nothing comes into existence from nothing: for if this were the case, anything might come into being from anything, fatherless and unneedful of semen" (Diogenes Laertius x, 38), which in Lucretius (Book I, lines 180–190) reads:

> quod si de nilo fierent, *subito* exorerentur
> *incerto* spatio atque *alienis* partibus anni; . . .
> nec porro augendis rebus *spatio* foret usus,
> seminis ad coitum si e nilo crescere possent;

nam fierent juvenes *subito* ex infantibu' parvis
e terraque exorta *repente* arbusta *salirent,*
quorum nil fieri manifestumst, omnia quando
paulatim crescunt, ut par est semine *certo*
crescentesque genus servant;

These verses are to prove the following proposition (line 150):

nullam rem e nilo gigni *divinitus* unquam.

It is from the proof of the thesis "nihil ex nihilo" that physics takes its very first step, so that on the basis of this proposition it may cut away every available ground for the perplexing and frightening belief in gods who create and rule. It is in this Epicurean context that we find the confrontation of the "mythical" and the "scientific" categories; on the one hand, the indeterminate and the sudden, the jump, the discontinuous (for the explanation of which recourse must be had by *foeda religio* to the doings of the gods), and on the other hand, the definite, the gradual, growth, the continuous, from which, as the genuine and only real progress of events, the merely apparent irregularity can be comprehended "without divine aid," by the assumption of minute, no longer visible changes. This shows the direct connection between the epicurean intention and the choice of a system of physics such as that of Democritus.

Accordingly, we may assume Democritus' and Epicurus' answer to the question of the origin of men's fear of the gods: men in the earliest times, and also all other men in so far as they are not in possession of knowledge of the actual (or possible) causes, lay the blame for all striking facts, for events which occur contrary to all expectation, on the gods. And so they fall into fear. Belief in gods is prior to fear of gods. This fear stems from the belief that certain events must be taken as originating with the gods.

Nevertheless, what has been said here does not reach the full intent of Democritus' thought. Cleanthes the Stoic, who draws on Democritus for his own account of the origin of our knowledge of the gods, represents the matter thus: men, alarmed by lightning, storm, snow, hail, earthquakes, comets and similar happenings, assumed that there was some celestial or divine power (Cicero, *De natura deorum* ii, 5, 14). In the light of this representation,

Democritus holds the view that belief in the gods stems from fear. It is not the mere perception of striking natural phenomena as such or an inference drawn from these, but fear of such occurrences, the experience of feeling imperiled by them, that leads to the belief in gods, to fear of the gods. We may take Democritus as the originator of the theory on which, as on a foundation, the theories of Hobbes, Spinoza, Hume, Holbach, Feuerbach, Bruno Bauer, Marx[11] take their stand to characterize and define a great tradition which extends into the present. The school of Epicurus is the first torch-bearer of this tradition.

Does belief in gods as a whole, or only belief in the frightening character of the gods, stem from fear? The question how fear should have taken objective form in belief in gods could scarcely be raised by Democritus and Epicurus, since neither of them denied the existence of gods. So little has come down to us concerning Democritus' conception of gods that it is impossible to state his view with certainty. The basic concept of Epicurus' theology is that the gods, eternal and blissful, cannot care for the world or for mankind, and that their due is veneration and not fear. In this case, it is only the delusory belief in dire and terrible gods that stems from human fears, and not the true belief in gods itself. There is no ground for the element of fear and awe in this justified belief. Extraordinary and unheard of perils awaken so great a fear in men that they attribute the dire quality to the gods. The terrifying character of the gods is born of human anxiety and disquiet of exceptional nature, reflects this terror and heightens it (Lucretius v, 1181–1227).

Epicureanism, spurred by the wish to contend against fear, traces the illusion of gods to fear. By intent, Epicureanism must fight also against the fear which precedes fear of the gods and is not yet referred to the gods, fear of real dangers. But it can nevertheless scarcely fail to find this fear relatively justified. What force is it that brings about the heightening of common fears, which have some justification in reality, into fear of the gods? Is there no field of experience particularly apt to call forth fear of the gods, as intensified fear and as fear of the unreal? It is dreams that provide that experience. They, according to Epicurean teaching, like other similar phenomena, are a by-product and residue of sensory perception. Let us call the basic lines of this theory to mind.

All knowledge of truth can be traced back to sensory perception. This, like all real processes, is a bodily process. Sight, for instance—and *mutatis mutandis* the other modes of sensory perception—is the product of minute particles of matter, which in accord with their function are called images, and which are released from the surface of the body, fly through the air with extraordinary velocity, and—though themselves not visible— strike the eye. Images collide and merge, and in this way arise images of unreal objects. In sleep, the senses cannot receive the images of objects actually present. Thus, when we are asleep, the images of objects previously present, even of persons now dead, affect us as though they were continuing to live after death. All these images of unreal objects alarm us on waking, and especially in sleep, and thus provide a major part of religious concepts.

If we summarize the conceptions of religion prevailing in Epicurean thinking, which are demonstrably present in the work of Lucretius, and which were handed down in various ways to the seventeenth century, we find a characteristic conviction that there is a fundamental cleavage between science and religion: to the effect that fear of the gods can arise and persist only on condition that knowledge of real causes is lacking. Fear of the gods arises from the powerful effect which cosmic events have on us. Especially important are the exceptional and striking events—those which alarm and imperil. Experience of mortal danger, which leads to despair and to contempt of human resources—this is the mood which is most favorable to the birth of religion. The real perils are reinforced in this effect by imaginary ones experienced in dreams. It is science that frees us from the onus of religion, itself born of terror and dream.

The Epicurean critique of religion continued effective during the period dominated by revealed religion. This was possible because the distinction asserted in revealed religion between superstitious and genuine fear of God was denied or overlooked. Revealed religion itself came to be contested as mere superstition. Criticism changed its character not only because the object of criticism had changed with the transition from paganism to revealed religon but also because the critics' attitude ceased to be pagan under the influence of revealed religion. Nevertheless, Epicurean criticism of religion remains essentially unchanged, even given the changed premises of the age. To this extent, Epicurean criticism is not characteristic of the climate of opinion prevailing at the time during the epoch dominated by belief in revealed religion. Fear of God as taught by the Bible took the place once occupied by fear of the gods, and brought forth a new type of criticism. It was now not only the Epicurean concern which induced men to undertake criticism of religion; every concern indifferent to revelation, or at least to conformity with revelation, led to heresy, denial or doubt. Whereas Epicurus had led the battle against religion by means of theory, but not for the sake of theory, now it was also and in particular the representatives of pure theory (to the extent that their theories taught a different doctrine than did religion), who found themselves obliged to wage a more or less concealed war against religion. For it was no longer possible, or not yet possible, simply to disregard religion or to live as if religion did not exist. Even those whose original position towards religion was one of indifference or disbelief found themselves obliged to come to grips with religion at every step. A tradition which has remained active for about five hundred years within Western Christianity traces this type of criticism back to Averroës.[12] As this type will be treated in more detail when we come to the analysis of Spinoza's criticism of Maimonides, we limit ourselves here to recounting the points which are needful for marking the frontiers between Averroist and Epicurean criticism of religion.

Since *eudaimonia* is found in contemplation or theory, and theory is accessible only to the few who are wise, special precautions are needed for the guidance of the ignorant many, for the sake of social law and order. This assumes that civil government, which regulates and supervises only external human actions, is not in itself sufficient for orderly corporate life within society.[13] Religion is a regulator of order in social life. It bears on the life of the populace. It is not a necessary and spontaneous product of the life of the many, but a code of law prescribed for the many by higher intelligences (prophets). Religion is not by nature but by institution. Here we have a sharp contrast between the Epicurean and the Averroist conception of religion. The prevailing order of society in Averroës' time, based as it was on revealed religion, itself originating in the action of outstanding individuals, may here have been of influence. We shall understand the historical

connection between the Averroist and the Epicurean traditions
only when the modes of prophetic leadership of the many have
been more closely described. According to Averroism, the gift
which enables the prophet, as distinct from the philosopher, to
perform his function is imagination, the capacity which operates
most purely in our dreams. Prophecy, born of the joint activity
of imagination and intelligence, makes its appeal to the imagination of the many. Prophecy appeals to the striving of the many
after material satisfactions in order to move the many to externally
virtuous behavior (the many being considered incapable of true
virtue). It promises rewards and punishments. It teaches that the
wrath of God falls on those who do not obey Him, and that He is
therefore to be feared and obeyed (Moses ben Maimon, *Moreh
Nebukhim* III, 28: Salomon Munk, *Le Guide des Égarés*: accom-
pagné d'une traduction française et des notes, Paris, 1856, III,
214). Religion is thus an excellent means also for princes to
restrain their peoples and to exact obedience. This conception of
religion, which found crude expression in the catch-phrase of the
three impostors, is originally supported by the interest in theory
as the perfection of man. It is this very connection which is still
an element in Spinoza's thinking. During the Middle Ages the
unbelievers of this type often become undistinguishable from the
Epicureans. In Christian Europe knowledge of the true Averroës is
more and more replaced by the legend of Averroës. It is significant that to the legendary Averroës is ascribed the tenet that
pleasure is the highest good. After the rediscovery of Epicurean
philosophy by the humanists—a discovery which reaches its
climax in the work on Epicurus by Gassendi—the two traditions
are fused in the thought of the free-thinkers of the sixteenth and
seventeenth centuries.

When we meet in this period with the theory that religion is a
deception practiced by princes and priests, one can take it that
this is certainly to a great extent due to the persisting Averroist
tradition. And yet, at the time, this anti-religious theory was given
fresh impetus by a new motive. The passions for "worldly honor"
or "worldly glory" which animate political life and which
manifest themselves in terrible and vigorous deeds, and not
merely in endurance of sufferings, are the nexus out of which
Machiavelli and Giordano Bruno draw their rejection of the
Christian ideal, which allegedly fosters quietism.[14] This trans-

valuation gives new life to the Averroistic conception of prophecy as a product of the imagination. Giordano Bruno resolutely draws the full consequences from this characterization. He rejects prophecy root and stock as, in comparison with philosophy, a lower form of inspiration, a form to be despised.[15]

It is from the political motive that Machiavelli offers only a critique of Christianity, and not a rejection of religion in itself. He connects the rule of religion over a people with their political virtue, love of freedom, simplicity and purity of manners, and thus justifies it.[16] This assessment takes its origin not in political calculation but from profound sympathy with what is spontaneous, unsophisticated and genuine in the face of decadence and corruption. For the free-thinkers of the following age, this kind of critique is effective only through those elements which it shares with the Averroistic kind. This combination penetrates the "politiques" of the seventeenth century. Become an article of faith, it is taken up also in the Epicurean movement of the age. That movement is not guided by political fervor, but by Epicurean hostility toward religion. This movement makes use of the positive Machiavellian revaluation for polemical purposes. The campaign against fear becomes a campaign against the way in which kings and priests use this fear for the increase of their own power.[17]

Three tendencies and traditions of very different origin underlie seventeenth-century criticism of religion. They are traditionally designated by the names Epicurean, Averroist and Machiavellian. From an early time they were in such close association that it becomes difficult to characterize the general movement of criticism of religion in the seventeenth century by one name rather than another. We have preferred the name of Epicurus for the reason that of the three motives which brought forth that criticism— ataraxia, theory, virtù—the first is the least mediate, in the sense of not having been called forth under pressure from a particular historical situation. The meaning of the term is originally defined by the opposition to religion.

We are further justified in keeping Epicurus' motive separate from his theory by the manner in which Epicureanism has influenced the modern age. It is only with reserve that one can speak of a renewal or renaissance of Epicureanism. On the other hand, the effect of the Epicurean doctrines is not easily overestimated. It is, at the least, equal to that of the Stoa. But in most cases the linkage occurs only at particular points: for instance, with the new science via the atomic theory, which was, however, handed down rather than evolved by the Epicureans; and with modern political theory via the doctrine originated by the sophists. The very effective identification of Epicureanism with hedonism as such provides what are often deceptive agreements. But even the genuine, conscious and avowed adoption of the Epicurean motive takes place with far-reaching modifications. Particularly in the case of men most responsible for the rediscovery of Epicurus, Valla and Gassendi, it strikes one that it is a Christian interest which motivates them. Epicurus' theory that human virtues develop out of animal instincts is affirmed as in harmony with the Christian mistrust of purely *human* virtue, for the sake of humiliating human pride in its own virtues. Epicurean animalism and Christian pessimism converge in rejection of the Stoa. They enter into a union to which the most famous monument is La Rochefoucauld's *Maxims and Reflections*.[18] In the context of this association, which marks a basic departure from the original (anti-religious) motive, the Epicurean concern and the Epicurean concept are still effective in the modern physiology of mental life.

The radical analysis of religion carried on in the seventeenth century finds its appropriate place in this comprehensive field as a subsidiary enterprise. It can, however, prove acceptable only to the thinkers who, after the break with religion, find themselves faced with the task of explaining the phenomenon of "religion." For this, it is by no means needful that the motive for rejection of religion should be the same as that of the Epicureans: just as, conversely—since a great gulf yawns between the fear of the gods as known to the ancients and the fear of God as taught in the Bible—Christian and Epicurean interests could form an alliance and thus counter the trend against religion present in Epicureanism.

However, in the Age of Enlightenment the general concern, in which men of the most varied types concur, is such that recourse must be had to Epicureanism not only for an understanding of man or the understanding and analysis of religion, but also with reference to the motive underlying criticism of religion.

Even in their own time, the Epicureans of antiquity had to meet the charge that their attack on fear of the gods was at the same time an attack on the very foundations of social life. The elimination of fear of the gods means the elimination of piety, and therefore of justice. And already then, in its own time, Epicureanism had the answer that no power bore guilt for more fearful crimes than did religion itself (Cicero, *De Natura deorum* i, 2, 4; Lucretius i, 74–95). Lucretius cites the sacrifices of Iphigenia as a case in point. His successors in later centuries had no difficulty in remarking, instead of the mythical example, the atrocities being committed before their eyes in the name of religion. The ancient Epicurean motive, opposition to religion in the name of human peace of mind, took on, in the age of the Inquisition and of the wars of religion, a compelling topicality which Epicurus himself could never have foreseen. It must however be borne in mind that the original Epicurean motive was concern for peace of mind—and this concern is the prevailing one also in the case of Lucretius, whereas in later centuries criticism of religion aimed predominantly toward peace within society. But is it possible to combine individual peace of mind and peace within society under the formal heading "Life in tranquillity and absence of fear"? This heading is certainly no more formal than the traditional term "hedonism" which no one would discard as meaningless. In our context the formal heading is preferable, because it regains the distinction which makes criticism of religion possible: "not pleasure merely, but certainty of pleasure." This kind of hedonism we can call Epicureanism, and mean by the term not the teachings of a philosophic school as handed down to us, but the original inclination of the human heart—an inclination of the heart which found its classical expression in the philosophy of Epicurus.

There remains the question whether the interest in social peace is primary, as immediately and directly understandable as was the Epicurean interest in individual peace of mind. The Enlightenment attempted to secure peace within society and between societies against the perils arising from the cleavage of Europe on religious grounds. Must not its striving for social peace be understood in the light of this social situation? It is not the striving, but the situation from which that striving arises, that gives its character to the criticism of religion in the Age of Enlightenment. Two cases must be distinguished here. The interest in social peace need not necessarily be taken in the limited sense that peace is preferable to senseless conflict between the different religions, confessions and sects. This type of criticism, which is prompted by desire for peace, usually takes its stand on the theoretical criticism of the doctrines of the various currents within revealed religion, even of revealed religion itself. Yet social peace may be sought as a good so absolute that already the peace-endangering manifestations of essentially particular revealed religion—not "common to all men"—may count as a decisive argument against revealed religion. Only in the first case is the criticism accidental, in deciding against revealed religion from the fact of religious persecution. It is accidental to the extent that its cause, the particular social conditions of the century, must be taken as the distinctive reason. In the second case, the criticism of religion directed by interest in social peace is no less primary than was Epicurus' own.

These preliminary characterizations of the motive underlying criticism of religion in the Age of Enlightenment are now to be given more concrete character by analysis of the efforts made by some precursors of Spinoza in this field. Since in this investigation the analysis of criticism of religion is undertaken only for the purpose of making the founding of Biblical science understandable, we shall here consider as Spinoza's precursors only such men as found themselves, in the course of their criticism of religion, compelled to make observations of a most fundamental kind regarding the Bible: Uriel da Costa, Isaac de la Peyrère, and Thomas Hobbes. The two men first named have a specific background in common with Spinoza, by the fact that they were of Jewish origin and Marranos. It is relevant to inquire particularly into the question whether this background has any significant bearing on the criticism of religion originating in these two men, as has of late been asserted.

CHAPTER II

URIEL DA COSTA[19]

THE MARRANOS' CRITIQUE of Christianity would not be an enigma if their adherence to Christianity had no other basis than compulsion on the part of the Church and on the part of the Iberian monarchies, which were at that time in process of consolidation. But it is to be remembered in the first place that many Jews had gone over to Christianity from conviction,[20] and in the second place that descendants of Jews who had been compelled by force to adopt Christianity were certainly in many cases devout Christians. Da Costa's father was a good Catholic (Gebhardt, p. 105). Nevertheless, for these Marranos the ties with the traditions of their families were not entirely loosed. Such family ties kept awake in the converts a sense of separation from Christian society and the Christian church. This background, even for those Marranos who at first lived untroubled in mind within the Christian order, would tend—for whatsoever reason they came to harbor misgivings as to Christianity—to direct the converts back towards Judaism. This Judaism was itself no longer the concrete and unquestioning Judaism of earlier times. For the spiritual content of Judaism had—after several generations of un-Jewish living—inevitably faded from the minds of the Marranos. The connection with Judaism was still strong enough to inhibit unquestioning life within the Christian world. On the other hand, the connection was too tenuous to make life possible within the Jewish world.

It is beyond dispute that the situation of the Marranos favored doubt of Christianity quite as much as doubt of Judaism, that it disposed to alienation from all revealed religion. But one does not pierce to the heart of da Costa's critique of religion by reference to his Marranism. One does not thus understand the substantive reasons that underlie his relinquishing Christianity and returning to Judaism, and later impel him to relinquish Judaism in turn. It is only these reasons to which da Costa refers. He mentions his Marrano origin, and he describes his path from Christianity by way of Judaism to unbelief, without indicating any connection

between the two facts. In so doing he may have gone too far.
He may himself have failed to recognize a concomitant factor.
But that this element is not an essential condition of his critique
of religion is clearly proved by the fact that this critique does not
basically deviate from that to be found in other writers of his time
who were not of Marranist or even of Jewish origin. This fact
alone is sufficient to discourage us from seeing in Marranism a
"religio-psychological fact of unique nature,"[21] except in the
sense that one may attribute "uniqueness" to any accidental
personal situation.

Da Costa's critique of religion as it has come down to us in a
developed form has two parts: it is directed against the Jewish
tradition and against the doctrine of the immortality of the soul.
The critique of the Jewish tradition is basically identical with the
biographically earlier critique of Christianity, on the motives for
which da Costa reports in his autobiography, *Exemplar humanae
vitae.*

As the son of a devout Catholic father, da Costa grew up in
Catholic surroundings. For fear of eternal damnation he meticulously followed all the behests of the Church. As an adult, he
found it impossible that the forgiveness of sin should be granted
in the confessional, and furthermore, he found it impossible to
meet the demands made by the Church. Since he thus despaired
to find salvation and peace of mind on the way prescribed by the
Church, he began—impelled by the desire for a firm foothold—
to read the books of Moses and of the Prophets. He observed that
the New Testament in some points significantly contradicts those
books which are recognized as revelation by Christianity. More
precisely he observed that the deviations were of such a nature
that the doctrines of the Old Testament are more acceptable to
the judgment of reason than those of the New Testament. A
further indication of the truth of the Old Testament for him is the
fact that Jew and Christian alike believe in the Old Testament,
whereas it is the Christians alone who believe in the New Testament.[22]

It is thus by his own reflection and not through considerations
influenced by revelation that he comes to give his faith to Moses
rather than to the Catholic Church, and to recognize as revealed
the Law given to Moses. With the acceptance of revelation,
acceptance of the truth of the doctrine is also given—truth which

cannot be scrutinized and tested in the detail of the doctrine. At this point in the critique, reason and revelation are recognized as two different sources of knowledge. Reasonableness is a criterion of truth only in the sense that truth cannot run counter to reason. For if God were to prescribe through reason, which He Himself has implanted in man, the contrary of what He has prescribed in Holy Writ, God would contradict Himself (*ibid.*, p. 110). The positive criterion of truth is consensus. If this consensus speaks for Moses against Jesus it speaks equally against the teachings of the Jewish tradition, as recognized by the Pharisees only, and which has come down by word of mouth. This tradition is rejected because it deviates from Mosaic Law.[23] If this criterion is applied to the full, it becomes an argument against Mosaic Law itself. Universal recognition can be given only to a law which is innate and common to all men, inherent in humanity: the law of nature, which is determined and defined by *recta ratio* (*ibid.*, p. 118).

It is not in a single step that da Costa comes to this radical stand. When he for the time being halts halfway—i.e. at the written law of Moses—he does so because the criticism of revealed religion has a criterion independent of every "rational" criterion, a criterion founded in the revealed religion itself. In this criterion it is possible to recognize a tendency—one still potent but destined to die soon—which dominates da Costa's thought, and which can be historically placed, using the category "Renaissance." Inherent in the Renaissance striving after a rebirth of life from its origins is the conviction that the existing state of living is decay and fall from an original perfect condition. For Renaissance thought, this formula is valid: truth is to be found in the beginning, at the origin. This belief, which revealed religion nourished by its concept of final and complete revelation, given in the remote past, setting forth the true aim and the true rule of life—at least for the present state of the world—comes, within revealed religion, and in relation to revealed religion, to its fullest expression in the Reformation. All later teachings or laws are, as contrasted with the original revelation, no more than falsifying additions, fictions, untruth and the work of men. Priestly lust for power and greed for wealth have corrupted and befouled the pure doctrine. Because of these views, the worst aspersion that can be cast in the polemics of the age is the reproach of innovation. This mistrust

of the new, and as such, bad,[24] informs da Costa's critique, and
particularly his critique of the Jewish tradition. He is the advocate
for the pure observance of the Law, for the strictest division between
the divine and the human, between what is commanded and what
is added by individual judgment. He sets his face against what the
Jewish sages, "not without hope of their own advantage," had
invented.

At this stage in criticism, and only at this stage, da Costa finds
himself compelled to proffer criticism of the Bible. His Biblical
criticism sets out to rid divine revelation of all human additions
and adulterations. His criticism teaches nothing new on the
content of revelation, nothing which could not already be known
from the Torah, the revealed character of which is taken for
granted. In fact, it presupposes complete knowledge of the
content of revelation. It does no more than prevent the clear
content of revelation from being clouded by human additions.
All the canonical books are submitted to criticism except the
Torah itself. The Torah is true: therefore all the passages from
other canonical books, which run counter to the sayings of the
Torah on the same topics, in other words, which are all untruths,
have been added by men. The distrust of tradition becomes
distrust of the text itself, in its character of a heritage passed from
generation to generation. For the time being, distrust stops at the
text of the Torah (*ibid.*, pp. 81, 85, 95). The doctrine of immortality is false because it contradicts the Law. Thus the books in
which, according to the opinion of the critic, there is really
reference to immortality, as Samuel 1 and the Book of Daniel,
are excised as an invention of the Pharisees. All that is needed for
detection of the spurious is comparison with the doctrines of the
Torah. In fact, since revelation cannot run counter to the findings
of reason, the proof that a passage is unreasonable suffices for
recognition that the passage is spurious. So criticism of the dogma
calls for criticism of the text, and criticism concerned with truth
calls for philological criticism.

What is the relationship between criticism of the doctrine of the
immortality of the soul and criticism of the Jewish tradition? Does
da Costa reject the doctrine only because it is in conflict with the
teaching of Moses? It is thus that he himself presents the case, as
though he has arrived at denial of immortality solely as a result of
exclusive recognition of the Mosaic Law: "Post caeptum opus

[sc. study of the Bible] *accidit* etiam . . . ut . . . accederem sententiae illorum, quis legis veteris praemium et poenam definiunt temporalem, et de altera vita et immortalitate animorum minime cogitant"—but he continues immediately with: "eo praeter alia nixus fundamento, quod praedicta Lex Mosis omnino taceat super his, et nihil aliud proponat observantibus et transgressoribus, quam praemium, aut poenam temporalem" (*ibid.*, p. 108). Not only Holy Writ but reason itself speaks against the doctrine of immortality (*ibid.*, pp. 66 ff.). It seems actually to be the case that it is not on account of Scripture that da Costa denies immortality, but rather that—on grounds of his own spontaneous doubt, founded on reason, as to immortality—he recognizes the Mosaic law because of its silence on immortality as in harmony with reason. His own account also bears out this view: he reports that when he had come to doubt of the Catholic church and despaired of salvation, he came to question the doctrine of another life, and on the basis of this doubt he attained to peace of mind (*ibid.*, p. 106). He did not, at that time, need to deny immortality, but only eternal damnation, which he greatly feared (*ibid.*, p. 105). In any case, the problem of another life as such had greatly preoccupied him early, even before his return to Judaism, and the denial of immortality is in no sense a mere secondary result of his fidelity to the Law of Moses. It can further be shown that da Costa's critique of the doctrine of immortality is fully conditioned by the theory of the soul put forward by the Spaniard Michael Servetus.[25] Whether da Costa became acquainted with the anti-Trinitarian teachings of Servetus while he was still a Christian and whether this theory played its part in his break with the Church, cannot be determined from any documentary material at present available.[26] It is, however, probable that this theory did play such a part. If so the connection existing between Servetus' criticism of the dogma of the Trinity and his theory of the soul would confirm that da Costa's criticism of the immortality of the soul is of greater weight for him than his "Judaism."

Servetus came to his theory of the soul through his studies of physiology; he is the discoverer of the pulmonary circulation of the blood. The theory which da Costa takes over states that the soul, the vital spirit, springs from the union that takes place in the heart between the air breathed in through the lungs with the blood, the finest and most ethereal blood transmitted from the liver to the heart. The finer this *spiritus vitae* becomes, the more does it aspire upward toward the brain, in which it receives its ultimate refinement into the *spiritus animalis*. Thus in breath, blood, vital spirit and soul there is one and the same power at work.[27] Just as the souls of animals are, so the souls of men are propagated by procreation.[28] From this of necessity follows the assertion that the soul itself is mortal. The teaching of the Scriptures bears it out: for hell and the grave are one and the same. Numerous passages dwell on the brevity and vanity, above all the basic hopelessness of human life. Servetus limits this proposition by the statement that Christ's descent into hell had made the total absence of hope breathed forth from these passages untenable. Through redemption in Christ immortality would have been granted.[29] Da Costa disregards this limitation, and, by so doing, demonstrates that he follows an intent different from that of his Christian precursor.

An interest springing direct from the heart, and not mere reflections based on reason and Holy Writ, conditions his denial of life after death. When his opponent da Silva calls him "one who resurrects the disgraceful and long buried sects of Epicurus" he strikes home—whether he knew this at the time and intended it or not—not only to the theory put forward by da Costa, but also to his motive. Replying to da Silva's reproach, da Costa resolutely takes up the defence of Epicurus, of the Epicurus whom he himself does not know directly by acquaintance with his works, but only through his doctrines and through the judgment of certain men who are lovers of truth (*ibid.*, pp. 108 f., 174). Da Costa has his place, by inborn kinship of mind, in the Epicurean movement of his time, a trend against which the institutions of the Jewish and Christian religions no longer offered a sufficient defense.

Epicurean criticism of religion assumes that all men are by nature predisposed to fear of gods and fear of death. Its aim is to ensure that human peace of mind will not be thus beset. If this particular threat to peace of mind did not exist, the whole enterprise undertaken by Epicurus would on his own showing be superfluous. Da Costa himself labored under the besetting fear of eternal damnation. It is because of this fear that he faithfully and meticulously follows all the observances of the Catholic Church. When he finds himself unable to accept the way to salvation laid down by the Church, and therewith despairs of salvation, there can be no peace of mind for him except by casting doubt on the accepted doctrines (*ibid.*, pp. 105 ff.). It is the fear of eternal damnation which impels him to cast doubt on eternal damnation. This doubting frees him from the fear. The Epicurean motive is unmistakable. This motive runs counter not only to the notion of eternal evil, but also to the notion of eternal beatitude. Da Costa rejects eternal beatitude as "a wager against long odds." The Epicurean aspiration toward assured happiness stands in the way of so great a risk. By denying the immortality of the soul he frees himself from what "in truth had distressed him and beset him more than aught else in this life," that is, from the notion that "there is for man either eternal bliss or eternal woe, and according to his actions this bliss or this woe will be his future lot" (*ibid.*, p. 101).

The Epicurean motive undergoes no essential change by modification in its field of application and in particular by limitation of that field. It has already been pointed out that interest in peace and tranquillity in life does not of necessity demand criticism of religion. Epicurus himself prefers the tales of gods to the teachings of the natural philosophers on inexorable fate. If God is venerated as pure mercy and loving-kindness in such a way as expressly to deny the conception of God as judge and avenger,[30] or to divest it of any concrete significance in life as lived under the eye of God, the Epicurean interest is not only compatible with religious concepts, but must recognize the religious concepts as those fulfilling the Epicurean requirement to the highest degree, for they best further peace of mind and liberation from fear, and must therefore be recognized as uniquely consolatory and therefore true. It is then sufficient to contest "false religion" which insults God by "presenting Him as the most cruel executioner and terrible torturer to the eyes of men," to contest *this* religion as the source of the most besetting "terrors and fears" (*ibid.*, pp. 120 f.).

What is true of belief in God is also true of the belief in the immortality of the soul. When Frederick the Great, in his "Imitation du troisième livre de Lucrèce sur les vaines terreurs de la mort et les frayeurs d'une autre vie," took up the Epicurean arguments against the doctrine of immortality, Moses Mendelssohn in his review could write: "Can one in our times, for instance, really still say that the belief in eternal life makes death a matter of fear for us, so that, in order to be freed from this fear, one must lay aside this prejudice? Or is it not the case that the most reasonable part has the most consolatory thoughts of the future, which make of death even an object of desire? Whoever would set out to-day to write on *les vaines terreurs de la mort* must rather assert that the soul is immortal."[31] Mendelssohn does not contest the legitimacy of the Epicurean interest. He aims only at determining which system of metaphysics—the materialist or the spiritualist —best serves that interest. This interest is common to all the efforts made in the Age of Enlightenment, whose spirit is not properly defined as eudaimonistic. For in the final instance, the heart of the matter is not that regard for happiness is the principle of the morality of that age, but rather that this regard conditions also the answers given by the science of the period, and the regard for the truth is narrowed to interest in truth which consoles. And it is as a consoling truth that an influential wing of the philosophy of the period felt the doctrine of immortality. If da Costa thus accepts Mosaic law and the Old Testament, because in neither of these is there mention or implication of immortality of the soul, and if other exponents[32] of the Enlightenment reject the Old Testament for that very reason, there persists within that opposition of assumptions a consensus at a deeper level: the same motive underlies both rejection and acceptance.

Da Costa's criticism of religion therefore does not find its sufficient explanation in the Epicurean motive alone. In the same way as Epicurus' own criticism of religion, it presupposes the conviction—which is not due to the motive—that this theorem is true: the soul of man dies with his body. On the other hand, the significance of the theorem, the interest which the theorem arouses and which compels assent, is not to be understood from the theorem as such. The theorem in itself does not conduce to peace of mind. And yet it is in this sense that it is embraced by Epicurus himself and by his follower da Costa. In the case of da Costa it is not exclusively on the count of its power to console. In spite of all the kinship with Epicurus' own interest, his interest is peculiarly different.

When Epicurus contests the dreadful illusion of belief in active gods, his opposition is directed originally and above all against the terrifying, and not against the illusory character of that belief. What he seeks is certain pleasure. This he finds in the memory of past pleasure, pleasure no longer present in experience. For pleasure present, pleasure in the moment of experience, is at hazard, basically uncertain. Admittedly, the memory of pleasures past is itself present pleasure. But the particular quality of remembered pleasure is that it is *always* present, unthreatened by any hazards to come. This pleasure dies only with death itself, and with death dies also all pain, and pain ceases to be any concern. For Epicurus the primary and principal good is inner tranquillity. Basically he is independent of the suffering which men and events may impose. Only the gods might jeopardize his inner tranquillity. But the gods are not active. Da Costa, on the other hand, is concerned with the real, in other words, the present good. He opposes belief in immortality not only because this belief "torments him and weighs him down," because it is cause for fear, but as much because this belief decoys us away from the only real and assured good and ill, the present good and ill, because this belief is a delusion (*ibid.*, pp. 73 f., 101). For this reason, liberation of the mind by the action of the mind is not enough. It becomes needful to ensure present good, exposed as it is to the onslaught of men and of events, by external measures. Above all it becomes necessary to ensure external peace, social peace. The fearful aspect of religion is now seen mainly in its devastating effect on social peace. Religion is to be fought against as the origin of the most heinous crimes. Emphasis shifts more and more away from the task of the individual living in seclusion to achieve self-liberation from fear of the gods and of death, by his recognition of true causes. Emphasis falls now on liberating human society from its worst enemies (the "priests") by political action. The battle against religion becomes a bitter and passionate attack on other men, who are arraigned as responsible for the unendurable condition of social hostility and are branded as enemies of humanity.

It is a battle not so much against illusory thinking as against *enemies*, which presupposes and favors all combative emotions. This war is waged with the full sense of its justice as war for truth and freedom against untruth and bondage. It appears to be demanded by honor. This same da Costa, who found no word too harsh for discrediting religious martyrdom, who poured ridicule on the men "who were fools and prodigals enough to

submit their soul to martyrdom and to death under the executioner's axe and cast away life itself which preceding generations
had valued highly," now praises in the highest terms the noble
death for peace and freedom (*ibid.*, pp. 115 ff., 99). The originally Epicurean intent in the conflict acquires not a little of the
intent which animates the opponents. The Epicurean interest
now takes on a charge of moral content which is not to be accounted for by that interest itself.

The engagement in this not originally intended but externally
imposed conflict influences the attitude of the contestant. But
does the situation of being forced into waging a war, the situation
of finding oneself persecuted, define the objective for which the
battle is being waged? Is social peace an unconditional good for
da Costa only when he finds himself at odds with all sides, persecuted from all sides? We should have to assume this to have been
the case, if his critique of the Mosaic Law took on its essential
meaning only as a result of the experience gained in conflict with
his Jewish opponents. It is in fact only *after* this experience that he
rejects the Mosaic Law as a product of the human mind. When
that law rends the natural bonds of affection between parents
and children, between friends and brothers, it runs counter to the
law of nature which binds humankind in mutual love, since it
commands a man to kill or betray a son, a brother or a friend
for the sake of religion. Whatever contradicts natural law must of
necessity be a human ordinance, a man-made law. Whereas
natural law favors harmony, man-made laws lead to hatred,
conflict and confusion.[33] But the experience mentioned is not
the sole reason of that change. An essential reason for his having
previously recognized Mosaic Law was his view that Mosaic Law
shows the way to enjoyment of present good, and does not delude
us, as does the teaching of the Catholic Church, into disregarding present good by holding out the hope of eternal well-being
(*ibid.*, pp. 73 f.) If, however, present good is valued as the only
good, then peace within society must be demanded without
qualification. What da Costa learns from his conflict with his
Jewish opponents is merely that the Mosaic Law does not fulfil
and cannot fulfil the function for the sake of which he had recognized it. But it is not from this conflict that he first gains the
standard which he applies to the Law of Moses.

Did he not originally show himself to be a zealous upholder of this law as the pure doctrine? That his zeal was genuine seems to be corroborated by the fact that he stands to the harsh literal meaning of "an eye for an eye" in opposing the more clement interpretation handed down in Jewish tradition (*ibid.*, p. 7). Yet the basis for his explanation of this "Thesis against the Tradition" is not only the relevant and unambiguous passages in Scripture, but also his own reflections on the laws of the nations, and the general intention of the Torah, to awaken fear in the heart of the transgressor. He holds that this intention is insufficiently met by fines as penalties and can be met only by corporal punishment. Thus even his critique of the Jewish tradition, even his zeal for pure doctrine, arises already from his interest in ensuring security in social life. Against this, one may say that da Costa also lent his support to literal interpretations of commandments contained in the Torah, interpretations which are not any more rational than the traditional interpretations. But if—as we can scarcely doubt—it was his horror of eternity, of the harassing and torturing concept that "for man there is eternal good and eternal ill," and not submission to the authority of the Torah that furnished the actual reason for da Costa's denial of immortality, we are also entitled to assume that this horror—or, more positively expressed, the value he attaches to present good and to present good only—led him away from Christianity to the more "this-worldly" Mosaic law. The recognition of Mosaic law can then be put forward in accord with the way of thought prevailing in the period, as a return to the pure doctrine. And this way of thought in its turn imposes conclusions which are not fully understandable from the primary motive.

CHAPTER III

ISAAC DE LA PEYRÈRE

LA PEYRÈRE presented his doctrine in two works which were published together in 1655: 1) *Prae-Adamitae, Sive Exercitatio super versibus duodecimo, decimotertio, et decimoquarto, capitis quinti Epistolae D. Pauli ad Romanos. Quibus inducuntur Primi Homines ante Adamum conditi.* 2) *Systema theologicum, ex Praeadamitarum hypothesi. Pars prima.*

The title and also the structure of the introductory work give rise to the opinion that the interpretation of the passage from the Epistle to the Romans designated in the title led La Peyrère to his theory that there were men living before the creation of Adam. And as this interpretation was justifiably taken as very strange indeed, and as the theory itself—with less justification—was rejected as "fanatical and bizarre," as a mere *idée fixe* born of La Peyrère's imagination, an over-venturesome opinion, a "queer notion," the idea lay ready to hand that La Peyrère had come to an abstruse theory by way of an abstruse interpretation.[34] But the very Preface to the *Systema theologicum* itself shows that the order should be reversed. The theory arose from the widening of the horizon in ethnology and from the difficulties in interpreting the first chapter of Genesis, and was subsequently corroborated —to La Peyrère's mind decisively corroborated—by the new interpretation of the Epistle to the Romans 5:12–14.[35] This theory itself, however, is "the first memorable attempt on the beginnings of the human race."[36]

It therefore seems apposite to quote the opinion of an anthropologist: ". . . le polygénisme, habituellement regardé comme un résultat de la libre pensée, a commencé par être biblique et dogmatique. La Peyrère avait attaqué le dogme adamique au nom du respect dû au texte d'un livre sacré. . . ."[37] Yet La Peyrère belongs among the first of those who openly declared their departure from unquestioning acceptance of the Bible. This fact favors the suggestion that the recourse to Scripture, which has caused so much ridicule to be poured on La Peyrère, is no more than an adventitious trimming to a naturalistic and rationalistic theory.[38] This interpretation at least serves for grasping his main thesis. It does not serve to explain the extensive theological disquisitions, which fill hundreds of pages. Closer consideration shows that the basis on which La Peyrère's criticism of religion and his Biblical science arise, and from which they branch out and deviate, is not the rationalistic, or the naturalistic position, but the Socinian. La Peyrère's theological system is to be interpreted as a development and extension of Socinianism. We must therefore first inquire into the trend of thought prevailing in Socinian criticism of religion, and then into the reasons why La Peyrère developed and extended this trend.

The significance of Socinianism within the field of criticism of religion becomes manifest in its criticism of Mosaic law. The Socinians contest the validity of this law mainly on two grounds: the first is the inhuman hardness of that law, and the second is its lack of any teaching on the immortality of the soul.[39] This charge demonstrates the same impulse toward the mitigation of the harshness of existence, toward tranquillity, as does da Costa's critique, among many others. It would, however, seem that the Socinians, with their retention of the belief in the immortality of the soul, deviate less from revealed religion. But this very belief of theirs is connected with a principle, which is not yet in action in the case of da Costa, and which belongs to a more advanced stage in the criticism of religion. The Socinian view of man is in diametrical opposition to the view which can be summed up in the formula "the new is bad in itself."

For the Socinian, the Christian religion is the way revealed by God toward eternal life (*Racovian Catechism, Qu.* I). True religion could not be other than revealed religion, since there is no natural religion.[40] All men do in fact have this in common, that they recognize and admit that justice must be preferred to injustice, and the honorable to the dishonorable. This arises from the interior word of God, which does not presuppose knowledge of God.[41] The moral attitude is a necessary condition for belief in the revelation of the New Testament.[42] No man holding this view and applying his reason to the historical reports as given in the New Testament can doubt the reality of the events there reported, and he must therefore put faith in the teaching of Christianity there recorded, nay forming part of the narrative.[43] From the morality which all men have in common, rational historical investigation leads to recognition of the Christian revelation. The essential content of the Christian revelation is the promise of immortality. This provides the complement required by nature to morality known from nature. This is the first morality to be established on a basis that ensures the fulfillment of its demands, and not on a standard of virtue too strict and harsh for human nature.[44] By its moral prescriptions and also by its promises, the Christian religion stands far above all other religions, and in particular far above Judaism. Mosaic Law teaches "an eye for an eye," but the Gospel lays upon men the duty of loving their enemies. Ceremonial law was imposed on the Jews because they were a stiff-necked and rebellious generation, and inclined to idolatry. The Gospel requires worship in spirit and in truth. Mosaic law promises worldly goods as reward for obeying the Law. In so doing, it is inferior even to the teachings of the pagan philosophers, who require that virtue shall be followed for its own sake, or for the sake of some other spiritual good. Immortality—the true reward for virtue—is unknown within the Mosaic law as it is within pagan philosophy. Whereas Moses, to whom only temporal good was promised, in actual fact knew nothing in his whole life but toil and trouble, and from whom entry into the Promised Land was withheld, Christ attained the far greater good promised to him—resurrection.[45] The historical fact of the Resurrection of Jesus is the decisive guarantee for the certainty of the Christian promise. The proof taken from the Resurrection is beyond all doubt: since the first Christians asserted that they had seen the Resurrection, and continued to maintain this assertion, even though in so doing they exposed themselves to the severest persecution, it necessarily follows that either Jesus did in fact rise from the dead, or that the early Christians were prepared to endure the most terrible modes of dying for the sake of bearing witness to an event which they knew to be untrue. The second possibility runs counter to all reason, the first is only above and beyond reason. The supra-rational fact of the Resurrection, this fact above and beyond all reason, is thus proved for reason.[46] Through the authority thus established, the authority of the Old Testament is also proved. But belief in the Old Testament is not necessary to salvation. Christians can even entirely dispense with it. Thus corruption of Old Testament texts need not be of serious import for religion.[47] It is by this argument that Socinus in principle throws the Old Testament open to philological and historical criticism. When La Peyrère sets out on this criticism, he unquestionably goes beyond the bounds of Socinian doctrine. But in so doing he only completes what the Socinians had begun in the way of undermining the authority of the Old Testament, for whom the ultimate reason is the conception of religion as exclusively concerned with the hope of immortality.

The Socinian denial that the Mosaic Law has any significance for salvation, and the resulting denial of the Old Testament as a whole, is not to be taken merely as meaning that the promise of eternal life is not contained in the Old Testament. Socinianism denies the assumption on the basis of which Paul defines the part that the Mosaic law played in the history of salvation. It was not first by the sin of Adam that man became subject to mortality. Man was created mortal, because he was formed out of earth. The outcome of Adam's sin is only that natural mortality took on the character of a punishment and thus became necessary.[48] Sin and the remission of sin have in no sense altered the natural condition of man. It was not sin that first made man mortal, and the remission of sin has not given him immortality.[49] What is needful, if man who was created mortal is to attain immortality, is a change of his nature, a second creation. This change is the fulfillment of the promise given by Jesus and vouched for by the resurrection of Jesus himself. Therefore the way that leads from human mortality to immortality is essentially independent of the process that leads from sin to the redemption from sin. The bond of union between the two lines is established for Socinus by the tenet that repentance and turning from sin are the condition for "both," i.e. for forgiving of sins and for eternal life. La Peyrère makes this connection more compelling by asserting, in line with Manichean thinking, that all men are fallen into sin because the matter out of which they are formed is itself perishable and liable to corruption. Thus sin and death stem from the same cause.[50] Sin, understood in this sense, cannot be equated with the sin of Adam. For the sin of Adam is remitted, but death—which was imposed on man by reason of Adam's transgression, which is inseparably connected with death—is not remitted.

The sin of Adam, the transgression of the prohibition imposed on him, is distinguished as *peccatum legale* from the *peccatum naturale* inborn in all men. The legal sin is imputed to man, the natural or innate sin is not. Natural sin is *followed* by natural death. Sin against the law is *avenged* by death according to the law.[51] Sin against the law has changed nothing of man's sinful nature. Sin against the Law has done no more than add a mystic sin. This mystic sin has been mystically washed away by the death of Christ as sacrifice for all men. But there remains what has been from the beginning and always shall be, even unto the end of the world, natural sin and the natural death which follows from it. Thus Christ by his death has again brought men into that state in which Adam lived before the Fall. Only when Christ returns at the end of time will natural sin and natural death be overcome and done away with.[52] What then is the significance of the whole "mystic" story from Adam's sin to the redeeming death of Christ? In La Peyrère's view, we misunderstand the history of salvation if the point of departure is taken to be the sin of Adam, and not the redeeming death of Christ. The sin of Adam was imputed to mankind only so that the death of Christ could be imputed to them. The mystic salvation by the death of Christ is but the preparation of mankind for its true salvation at the end of time, for the second creation through which man, first created from impure matter and subject to death and corruption, will find the gate of eternal life open to him. The ultimate purpose of the prohibition imposed on Adam is the raising of mankind to immortal life. The transgression of that law, the imputation of that transgression to all mankind, the abolition of the Law and of reward and punishment by the sacrificial death of Christ, is the parabolic, or mystic presentation of what will, in the fulness of time, be the election of man from his mortal state to immortality.[53] Of this economy of salvation it can not be said, as can be said of the economy of salvation as generally understood, that it is harsh and cruel.[54] La Peyrère can safely take up the doctrine of original sin rejected by Socinus, since La Peyrère considers original sin to be no more than the merely mystical imputation of merely mystical guilt for the purpose of merely mystical salvation, and in the final instance, for the purpose of the real salvation of mankind from mortality. His conception is no less "gentle" than Socinus' own. Impelled by the same motive, it formally does away with the lack of clarity in determining the relation between sin and death, immortality and redemption, which Socinus found himself unable to master and resolve.

La Peyrère did not evolve this extension of Socinus' theory because of difficulties inherent in that theory, but for two quite other reasons, which are themselves each of quite different character. The first of these to be treated here is admittedly already at work within the assumptions of Socinianism. Since the hope of immortality is the motive force of Socinianism, it is a very striking fact that Socinus, who himself asserted with so much decision that man is by nature created mortal, never came to adopt the solution which lay ready to hand, and which was so favorable to the interest nearest his heart—the proposition that man (the soul) was created immortal. There is a close connection between the denial of man's original immortality and the denial of man's original perfection, righteousness and knowledge of God. It is easy to attribute these denials to the opposition against the doctrine of original sin. But that raises the further question: to what must we attribute that opposition itself? Dilthey says: "In opposition to the theory of the original perfection of man, the Socinians, with sound feeling and incipient anthropological insight, assume man in his first emergence as it were still wrapped in swaddling clothes, totally without experience, knowing neither good nor evil and yet for all that, destined to be lord of the earth. They demonstrate not only the non-sense in the Oriental picture of man's life as originally of endless duration, but also the non-sense in the theory of a righteousness due to creation: moral perfection is not innate, it must always be acquired."[55] The dawning anthropological insight of which Dilthey speaks is originated or occasioned by the widening of the anthropological horizon, due to the discoveries of the fifteenth and sixteenth centuries. Socinus refers to these in support of his denial of natural religion as originating without revelation: "Religio res naturalis nequaquam (est), alioqui non invenirentur nationes omni prorsus religione carentes; quales *nostra aetate* quibusdam in locis inventae sunt, ac nominatim in regione Bresilia"; elsewhere he also writes: ". . . non singuli tantum alioqui homines, sed integri populi *hodie* inveniuntur, qui nullum, penitus sensum, aut suspicionem Divinitatis alicujus habent."[56] Through these discoveries it was not only the traditional conception of human nature, of what is common to all men, but also the traditional attitude toward the world of the Bible which was shaken. Men were discovered for whom the history of salvation could mean nothing, since they were not descended from Adam. The discovery of new peoples (but also traditions handed down from antiquity) led La Peyrère to the assumption that pre-Adamite men had existed, and that long before Adam, men from whom the greater part of all men living were descended, in fact, all the peoples except the Jews.

Thus it was not only the new conception of knowledge, expressing itself in the new mathematical physics, but also and in particular the findings of such strictly empirical sciences as geography and ethnology that might direct men's minds to a critique of religion. The *dissemination and extension of empirical knowledge* as such underlies the change in the attitude to the world of the Bible. The extension of the anthropological horizon is a fact which affects all minds, which is accessible to all, regardless of what each man may have had as his primary notion of man, or what his motive. For great as might be the divergences in relation to the primary conception of man, "what is common to all men" suffices for grasping with sufficient definiteness the facts that we are here considering. These facts, it must be admitted, like all facts, are capable of and in need of interpretation, for their definiteness is limited. On what primary notion of man does this extension of the anthropological horizon impinge in the case of Socinus and La Peyrère?

The assertion of man's original perfection means within the context against which Socinus and after him La Peyrère rebel that the original perfection is now lost and is to be regained only by the grace of God: redemption is not to be expected from man's own power. Socinus' assertion of the original imperfection of man signifies that perfection, and in particular moral perfection, can be acquired only by human effort and action. Man's moral effort is, according to Socinus, not left without direction: the directives are "innate" in him. His goodness or badness therefore depends entirely on what the originally imperfect man, "inexperienced in good or evil," does with this seed of goodness which is given him by nature. It depends entirely on the way in which his nature is trained and nurtured. The correlate of this proposition that man is by nature imperfect is the belief that man's own achievement, in the sense of how he cultivates his natural endowment, is decisive. Socinus, a whole-hearted believer in revelation, asserts this only in relation to the moral effort of the individual. In La

Peyrère's theory, however, we glimpse the comprehensive import of his critical approach to the assumption basic to the doctrine of original sin, to the assumption of man's original perfection. Adam was created perfect in the sense that he was endowed with all that belongs to man as man by nature. The seeds of the arts and sciences were implanted in him at his creation. That this seed should blossom and bear fruit demands labor, cultivation, a long time, gradual advance.[57] The specific cast of mind of the modern centuries, the belief in method, in culture—let us not forget that "culture" means "culture of nature"—implies directedness towards the future, belief that perfection is to be sought in the future, the denial of perfection as lost forever, as not to be recovered by human striving. This is the attitude that supports Socinus' attack on the dogma of original sin, and La Peyrère's re-interpretation of that criticism—a re-interpretation in which Socinus' criticism is both negated and conserved.

Socinus' theory should be an excellent theme for historical consideration, since in this theory naturalistic anthropology appears as an active factor prior to the emergence of naturalistic cosmology. As it is essential for a fully developed naturalism that anthropology be felt as part or adjunct of natural science, it is always difficult to distinguish which elements in naturalistic anthropology are based on original anthropological insight and which are primarily due to inferences from the naturalistic premises.[58] This difficulty does not arise then in the analysis of Socinianism, since its "line of argument . . . is negatively conditioned by the absence . . . of any conception of the ineluctable force and validity of the laws of nature."[59] We must here bear in mind that Socinianism cast no doubt on Biblical miracles or on freedom of will. In La Peyrère's work however there is already apparent the influence of the new natural science that has arisen after the time of Socinus. The broadening of the anthropological horizon was a pre-condition even of Socinus' theory. It is not this particular advance that is the decisive reason for La Peyrère's consistently naturalistic re-casting of Socinianism. La Peyrère's theological system is to be seen rather as an attempt to reconcile the history of salvation with the new natural science. He attained this end by a sharp distinction between the "natural" and the "mystical," and by assigning each to its own plane: these planes at no time intersect.[60] He thus does away with the root of possible conflict between science and revealed religion. This end is served especially by the sharp distinction between natural sin arising from natural reasons and leading to natural results, and legal sin, the consequence of which is the "mystic" imputation. It is extensively demonstrated that the natural wretchedness of human nature is grounded in natural causes: wars break out as a result of desire for gain or revenge or domination, disease arises from corruption of the air or of the human body itself. The truth of these assertions is vouched for by all the doctors and all the statesmen. But on the other hand, sins against the law have no natural ill effects at all. Thus Adam, in all the nine hundred and thirty years of his life, was never, as far as we know, at any time ill. Cain, the slayer of his brother, prospered. Unfaithful wives do not lose their good looks. Imputation of transgressions of others— as distinct from the natural results of one's own transgressions —exists only for jurists as a legal fiction and for theologians as a mystery. But it is certain that these mysteries and fictions have no effect whatsoever on nature.[61] The chain of natural effects and causes is not broken by "mystic" intervention. The connection linking the extension of empirical knowledge and the continuously widening acceptance of the concept of nature (nature as opposed to the supernatural) is at least plausible.

From this position La Peyrère advances to a denial of miracles, a denial scarcely veiled by the appearance of being no more than an interpretation. The objection advanced against the traditional conception of miracles as recounted in the Scriptures is that the specific is there too readily given the validity of the general.[62] For instance, Adam is not the progenitor of all mankind but only of the Jews. The darkness that covered the world during the crucifixion of Christ did not extend over the whole earth, but only over the whole land, i.e. Palestine. The miracle granted to Hezekiah bore only upon the sundial belonging to Ahas, and not upon the sun itself. The sun did not stand still over Gibeon, but the sunset lingered overlong in the sky. The day of the battle of Gibeon was the longest day there ever was—in Gibeon, but not on the whole earth; for instance, not in the Polar regions, where unbroken daylight endures for months.[63] Such interpretation is meaningful only on the presupposition that the Scripture is true. This interpretation is meant to uphold this presupposition in the face of rational objections,[64] or to make room for reason while not questioning that presupposition. That the presupposition of the literal truth of Scripture is not taken seriously by La Peyrère, that the rationalistic "explaining away" of miracles only conceals the denial of miracles altogether, is shown by his critique of the Bible. It is merely shown by that critique; that critique does not form the foundation for doubting the authority of the Scriptures. Criticism of what is conveyed by tradition precedes criticism of the medium that conveys it. La Peyrère disputed the authority of the Pentateuch only because and only when his opponents deduced, from the fact that these books speak of Adam as the first man, the conclusion that therefore the founding of all the arts and sciences is to be attributed to Adam or Adam's descendants, whereas the traditions handed down from the most ancient races prove that long before Adam there had been men who had achieved a scientific culture.[65]

La Peyrère's theory can be summed up in the single proposition, that there were men prior to Adam. For the defense of his proposition in the face of the authority of the Scriptures, La Peyrère makes use of both the ways open to him: he proves from the Scriptures themselves that there were men before Adam, and he casts doubt on the authority of the Scriptures. He proves from a passage in Paul's Epistle to the Romans that there were men prior to Adam, and he casts doubt on the authority of the Old Testament Scriptures. We see here an after-effect of the Socinian point of view on the relation between the Old and the New Testament. Because of Socinus' motive Mosaic Law is bereft of its religious import in the matter of salvation. La Peyrère's proof from the Scriptures of the theory of the pre-Adamites implies the express elimination of Mosaic Law from the history of salvation, so that the door to philological and historical critique of the Pentateuch (and thus also of all the other books composing the Old Testament) is opened wide.[66]

In the Epistle to the Romans 5:13, Paul speaks of a law prior to which sin existed in the world but was not imputed to man's responsibility. The generally accepted view is that the period prior to the Law extends from Adam to Moses. During this period, sin undoubtedly existed in the world, but was not imputed. The imputation of sin began only with the Mosaic law. La Peyrère takes the view that this interpretation is directly contrary to what the Apostle intended. For the dominion of death depends

on the dominion of sin as sin imputed: death is the wages of sin.
The dominion of imputed sin depends, on the dominion of law:
sin was not imputed before the law was given. But the dominion
of death begins with Adam. Thus, as in addition all the stories
recounted in Genesis bear out, it is with Adam that the dominion
of law begins. The law given unto Adam was the prohibition on
eating the fruit of the tree of knowledge. It was through transgression against this commandment that sin entered the world,
and with sin death. The function of this prohibition consists
entirely in evoking the result of its transgression: the mystic sin of
the sinning man Adam is the condition for the mystic expiation
contained in the death of the God-man Christ. That mystic
redemption is the mystic representation of the real redemption
at the end of time. It is therefore the commandment as given to
Adam, and that commandment alone which has universal
significance in the matter of redemption. It is the "law of laws,"
and to be distinguished carefully from the law of nature as well as
from all civil law, pagan or Jewish. Mosaic law by its nature can
not fulfil the function of the "law of laws." For Mosaic law was
given to the Jews alone. In no part of the Scripture is the transgression of the law of Moses imputed to any heathen. The validity
of this law for the Jewish people only is revealed by Scripture
itself. For instance, long prior to Moses behests had been given
(Gen. 26:4 f.), and therefore Mosaic Law was not the first body
of law. Mosaic law contains amid its tenets laws which are
common to all divine and human laws and which spring direct
from the natural law. Seen over against this primal law, the law of
Moses is only one particular law among others. It was the
particular law for the particular people of the Jews, and even
with them, only at a particular time, between other bodies of
law prior and subsequent. It contains particular ordinances on
sacrifice and priesthood, ordinances which had no validity before
Moses and which were abrogated by Christ.[67] Since the law
mentioned in Romans 5:13 is the prohibition imposed on Adam,
and also since, according to the words of the Apostle, there was a
time "prior to the law" in which sin was in the world but was not
imputed, we must assume that there were men before Adam.
This assumption, based on the passage quoted from Holy Writ,
does not run counter to Christian faith. Rather, it is apt to
harmonize the Scriptures among themselves and with the scientific

knowledge of the ancients and the moderns. In the accounts given in the first chapters of Genesis the presence of men other than the children of Adam is everywhere assumed. The time from the creation of Adam up to the time of the highly developed science of the Chaldeans and Egyptians is much too brief for the evolution of all this science, which itself used experience gained in much greater time-spans. Finally, the peoples discovered by Columbus in America cannot possibly be taken as descended from Adam.[68]

The Biblical proof of the theory of the pre-Adamites from Romans 5:13 (and from the accounts given in the first chapters of Genesis) is clearly insufficient to controvert the opposed theory upheld by the Churches and founded on the Scriptures. The authority of the Scriptures, and in particular of the Old Testament, must be overthrown. The path to this goal is discrimination between those elements of Scripture which are necessary to salvation and those which are not—a distinction which La Peyrère takes over from the Socinians. The part necessary to salvation is clear. It is only in those portions not necessary to salvation that obscurities are found.[69] It is thus that La Peyrère understands the case: ". . . quae ad salutem nostram unice spectant, paucis constant. Et in illis tantum curae, tantum diligentiae, et tantum lucis adhibuit Spiritus sanctus, quantum captui humano convenit. Pluribus mandata sunt quae de aliis tractant. Et de illis aperiam quod omnes sentiunt, quodque plerique mussant dicere. Tanta scilicet incuria, et caligine tanta scripta fuisse; ut nihil plerumque intricatius, nihil obscurius legi possit."[70] What then are the reasons for the obscurity of the major portion of the Bible? "The Lord said, that he would dwell in the thick darkness" (I Kings 8:12): hence the obscure and enigmatic words used by God in His revelations. (What may well underlie this "reasoning" is the traditional Averroist critique of prophetic knowledge.)[71] By being committed to writing, the obscurity has been made, according to God's will, still more obscure. As the third reason we have the fact that the source-writings have not come down to us. The following arguments establish the fact that the individual books of the Bible are copies, not originals:

(a) The books of Joshua, Kings, and Chronicles are copies: Joshua 10:13 quotes the "Book of Jasher"; in the books of Kings and Chronicles various passages quote the Book of Nathan and the Book of Gad, the Chronicles of the Kings of Israel and of the Kings of Judah and similar books as sources.

(b) The Pentateuch was not written by Moses: for 1) the death of Moses is recounted in the book; 2) in Deuteronomy we several times find "beyond Jordan" at points where Moses would have said "on this side of Jordan"; 3) In Num. 21:14 "the book of the wars of the Lord" is quoted as source; 4) in Deut. 3:14 we read "unto this day," which indicates that the passage was written long after the time of Moses: the writer's intention is to explain "the reason for that name [sc. that of the long since dead Jair] having come down from the time of Moses to the writer's own time"; 5) Deut. 3:11 gives as evidence for the victory gained by Israel over the King of Bashan the fact that the king's iron bed-stead is still to be seen in Rabbath: "Quorsum, inquam, opus erat, Judaeos alio mittere, ut lectum Gigantis viderent; qui Gigantem ipsum, coram, in terra sua viderant, vicerant, et campis Basan ipsis prostratum vulgo mensi erant?" 6) Deut. 2:12 mentions the expulsion of the Edomites from Seir by the Israelites; but as we know from Deut. 2:4 f., Psalm 108:10, and I Chron. 18:12 f., the subjection of Edom by Israel took place only in the reign of King David; this portion of Deuteronomy must therefore have been written after the time of David. That the Pentateuch as we know it is not the original text is to be inferred from the very numerous truncations, repetitions, omissions and other flaws of the text. For instance, the passage about Lamech (Gen. 4:23) is incomplete, since at no point is anything recounted of the boy whom Lamech boasts of slaying. The account of the circumcision of Moses' son is truncated (Exod. 4:24 f.). Genesis 20, the account of Abraham's journey to Abimelech, king of Gerar, is misplaced, for it seems improbable that Abimelech should have felt desire for old Sarah ("it had ceased to be with Sarah after the manner of women"). The same objection can be raised against the passage in Genesis 26. It is not credible that Abimelech—was it the same king of that name as in the case of Sarah?—should have lusted after Rebecca, who was already old at the time, "because she was fair to look upon." These and very numerous other similar obscurities in the text are to be accounted for only by the assumption that the Pentateuch was compiled from various sources.[72] This insight into the character of the text as a copy sets the task of distinguishing what shows through in the text as original from the copy. The best possibility of making this distinction is given in cases where the writer explicitly states from which sources he has compiled his book. In all this La Peyrère holds fast to the view that the original text is more in accord with reason than the copy, that the original stood in the same relation to the copy as the divine does to the human, and that therefore our human reason, as a particle of the divine reason, is as such capable of recognizing the original.[73]

La Peyrère sets up the following hypothesis on the original of the Pentateuch: Moses recounted the exodus of the Israelites out of Egypt, the legislation on Mount Sinai, and the forty years in the desert in his diaries. It may be surmised that long after the death of Moses, the "Book of the Wars of God" mentioned in Num. 21:14 was drawn from these diaries as a summary, and that finally what we know today as the Pentateuch developed partly from that compilation. In addition, Moses set down a history of the Jews from the creation of Adam to his own time. The older part of that history was known to Moses by accounts handed down by word of mouth or in writing. In that history, Moses treated in detail only what was of moment to the Jews, and dealt cursorily with the rest, including the most ancient history of the Jews. The compilers of the copies were more cursory still. This would explain why the story of the Creation in the first chapter of Genesis is so succinctly recounted.[74]

Thus in any case lucidity is not to be expected of the Scriptures for the reason that God "will dwell in darkness and mystery." This primary obscurity is further deepened by the spuriousness of very large portions of the Scriptures as we know them. If the Scriptures, even the original Scriptures, are obscure, we cannot hope from this source to reach an unambiguous version of the truth. It is thus particularly impossible that we should hope to use the Scriptures as the means of attaining perfect clarity on the history of early man.[75] What is clear and incapable of misinterpretation is those parts which related to our salvation, which are necessary for salvation, the promise that mortal man shall attain immortality. This promise is given in the New Testament. Obscure or spurious passages in the Old Testament are therefore, as Socinus pointed out, of no moment.

When Paul in the Epistle to the Romans 5:13, speaks of the time "until the Law," and thus makes a distinction between the

time before the Law and the time after the giving of the Law,
he distinguishes, according to La Peyrère, between the Pre-
Adamite age, during which death and sin were indeed in the
world, but did not "reign," did not "live," and the post-Adamite
age, in which sin and death hold reign. The human condition
before Adam was the state of nature. In that age, death was only
a privation. In the age between Adam and the coming of Christ,
death has become something positive, alive and ruling.[76] La
Peyrère introduces a pre-Adamite, who has seen the human
condition in both ages, and puts words into his mouth. The tone of
the speech shows that what we have here is a direct polemical
confrontation of the Christian ideal with the naturalistic ideal.
In the state of nature,[77] Right Reason ruled alone. God was known
to man only by the instinct which cannot be satisfied except by
the recognition of a single creative principle. Man knew only
the law of nature and the laws made by man, but no divine law:
Deus legislator mihi ignotus erat. Sin there was, and the sense of
shame for sin, for having sinned, as an action unworthy of man;
there was also punishment of sin administered by the ruling
power, but there was no sin against God. Therefore there was also
no "imputation" of sin, and no twofold death through the entry
of sin into the world. Men did indeed die, but they did not die
unto death. They died *naturaliter*, and did not die in addition
*spiritualiter.*The moral life in the first state of nature was that of
Socrates and Cato.[78] If one compares with this the passage in
which La Peyrère both concedes and denies the difficulty of his
theory of the mystic imputation of sin by deriding the Church's
doctrine of the imputation of sin,[79] which he does in such a way as
seemingly to indicate that his own theory is a parody of the
orthodox theory; if one bears in mind his naturalism in its
entirety, his denial of miracles, his critique of the Scriptures, one
gains the impression that his concern is not with *harmonizing*
his naturalism with the Gospel of salvation, but only with "some
adjustment with the forms of the Church's body of dogma."[80]
Indeed, at bottom, his concern is no more than the masking of his
unbelief by formulations soothingly couched in the terminology
used in orthodox dogmatics. It is not hard to hit on the reason for
La Peyrère's procedure: he was not born for martyrdom. When
the Inquisition began to view him with suspicion, he recanted not
only his Calvinism, which did not lie very deep, but also his

"Pre-Adamites," of whom he said that he loved them more
than his own eyes. In the Deprecatio which he sent in 1658 to
Pope Alexander VII, he speaks as a believing Catholic. His
contemporaries were justified in not taking his Protestantism any
more seriously than his Catholicism: "La Peyrère était le meilleur
homme du monde, le plus doux et qui tranquillement croyait fort
peu de chose." And other reports of him do not belie this.[81]
So it is highly questionable whether and to what extent his
"theological system" is to be taken seriously, whether any of it
was seriously intended except the naturalism which shines through
at various passages in the work. His naturalism, it must be
conceded, differs from naturalism unqualified, in that his is
conditioned and restricted by his hope of future salvation, of the
elevation of human nature into a nature transcending this, and of
mortal man into immortality. By this very hope, it betrays its
origin in Socinianism.

La Peyrère's hope of salvation is modified by the fact that it
includes the hope for the temporal salvation of the Jews. Apart
from the new natural sciences, the strong interest in the re-establishment of the Jewish State induces La Peyrère to recast Socinianism in the direction of his "theological system." We must in fact
regard it as possible that, because of his interest in the temporal
re-establishment of the Jews, he adopted the Christian hope of
salvation, as understood by the Socinians, and in a form acceptable to his own enlightened mind compatible with the more
developed naturalism of his own time.

Man, who was created mortal, can not attain immortality
except by a new, a second creation. It is not to all men that God
will grant immortality, but only to the elect. This divine election
is from all eternity, "before the foundations of the world were
laid." The symbol of this election is the mystic election by which
God singles out men and nations, so that, in the fullness of time, as
from a fountain, redemption will flow forth over the others chosen.
Thus it was that God first chose the Jews, and then when the
Jews rejected and crucified Christ who had been made flesh and
sent among them as a Jew, God rejected the Jews and took unto
Himself other peoples. In the fulness of time, when Christ will
come again in the spirit, God will crown with eternal life Jews
and Gentiles alike. At the end of this mystic election, in which
first the Jews were chosen and the heathen neglected, and

subsequently the heathen were chosen and the Jews neglected,
God's choice will become final and effective in a choice for all
eternity.[82] Christ, who will then return in spirit and in truth,
will bring to the Jews not only eternal salvation but also temporal
salvation. When Jesus came in the flesh the Jews were looking
forward to the coming of the Messiah, who would restore their
kingdom. But Jesus destroyed their kingdom. The Jews failed to
grasp the spiritual or mystical significance of this destruction, and
they could not possibly grasp it. They knew not what they did,
and therefore it was forgiven them. They could not believe in a
Jesus who had come as a man. But when He comes again, in the
spirit, he will re-establish their kingdom, and will convince them
that he is the Messiah of the Promise. Just as their forefathers had,
on impulse and unaware, given up their brother Joseph into
bondage in Egypt so that their own lives might be spared, so had
the Jews surrendered Jesus, who will, at the end of all the ages,
reveal Himself as the Christ of the Jews. He will, as the Messiah
of their expectation, re-establish their Kingdom. He will rise
again from the dead as their avenger and king, will gather together
his people now dispersed among all the nations, will vanquish
their enemies, go up in triumph on Mount Zion, and there set up
His banner of victory before God.

The re-establishment of the Jewish kingdom was intended as
the theme of the second part of La Peyrère's *Systema theologicum*.
This second part has never been published, and it is to be supposed that the manuscript has been destroyed. We therefore draw
on La Peyrère's earlier work, *Du rappel des Juifs* as complement.
This work had already appeared in 1643. It does not yet
contain the theory of the pre-Adamites. Taking as his point of
departure that Jesus as the Messiah came mainly for the sake of
the Jews, La Peyrère makes a plea to the Jews to turn from their
old faith to Christ. This seriously intended summons is based on
the view that Christianity is "la foy intellectuelle et universelle"
which gathers all mankind to one and the same Apostolic creed,
one and the same Lord's prayer, and one and the same Law as was
given in the two tables on Mount Sinai. In his view, the Jews will
be converted to Christianity only if and when they have been
convinced that the yoke imposed by Christianity is lighter than
that of the Law. If, however, the Christian, himself overloaded
with the confused lumber of dogmas and articles of faith, should

come before the Jews with the intent of converting them, the Jews would be fully justified in their answer that all this inheritance from the Church is a burden heavier far than that imposed on them by the Law of Moses. Furthermore, the load of dogma and articles of faith weighing on the Christians is not the true Apostolic faith, which, as taught by the Apostles, is brief and simple. Just as by the recall to evangelical simplicity the multiple complexities and controversies of the dogmatists are done away with, so also by the call to the Gospel commandment "Love ye one another" there will be an end to the fanaticism of the Church. These two arguments, which run through the whole movement of the Englightenment, are used by La Peyrère mainly on behalf of the Jews.[83] He states as the condition of the spiritual salvation of the Jews their recognition of Christ as the Redeemer, in other words, of the universal and rational religion. He requires the spiritual salvation of the Jews as the precondition for their temporal salvation. He shows that the election of the Jews as God's chosen people is by intent as much temporal as spiritual. The Scriptures tell of the victories of Israel, the strength of its men, the beauty of its women, the fertility of its land, the glory of its capital Jerusalem and so on. Spiritual rejection occurred simultaneously with the temporal rejection. Since that time, the Jews have been dispersed over all the world. They have lost their kings and rulers, and have lost the very name of the nation. For, as they do not form a society recognized in the eyes of the law, they also lack a legitimate sovereignty. Thus since that time, the Jews have stood defenseless and unprotected against the world. Lacking spirit and without honor, the Jews are exposed to the insults and injuries of all peoples. This rejection within the temporal order will be followed by a restoration within the temporal order, and under a temporal king. The Jews will flee to France, the land of temporal freedom, *terre de franchise*. There, they will convert to Christianity, and from France they will set forth for the re-conquest of the Holy Land.[84] In *Du rappel des Juifs* La Peyrère sets his hopes on the king of France (the lilies of the French royal arms recall to La Peyrère's mind the lilies of the Song of Solomon), in the "Deprecatio" he looks to Pope Alexander VII as the man manifestly chosen by God to carry out this work of salvation, the crowning glory of which will be the inclusion of the Jews within Christendom.[85]

Thus La Peyrère's hope for the temporal redemption of the Jews has a concrete political bearing, and in particular a bearing on the politics and policies of the Church. If one takes into account that the no less unbelieving Hobbes also sets conversion to Christianity as the precondition for entry into the Kingdom of God, and this for purely political considerations, because of the need to take into account the (at that time still unimpaired) force of Christian consciousness, it is justifiable to assume that La Peyrère wrote his whole "theological system," in so far as it refrains from overt or implied attacks on the accepted teaching of the Church, for the sake of the political rehabilitation of the Jews, on purely political considerations, on the assumption that all concessions to the orthodox doctrine are justified not only as personal prudence on his own behalf, but also and in particular in relation to the concrete political conditions prevailing within and outside the Church in regard to the political rehabilitation of the Jews, the re-establishment of the Jews within a State of their own. If one rejects this assumption, one must leave matters at saying that La Peyrère unites the hope of salvation as the Socinians understood it with the hope of earthly salvation as it was understood in the Jewish expectation of the Messiah.

In La Peyrère's own time the attempt was made to relate his marked interest in the temporal reconstitution of Jewry to his Marrano origin. Richard Simon wrote to him that Jona Salvador, an Italian Jew, with whom Simon had discussed La Peyrère, "ne peut pas s'imaginer qu'après toutes les louanges que vous avez données à la nation juive à la fin de vos Préadamites, vous ne soyez de la race de quelque Marane: et ce qui le confirme dans cette pensée, c'est qu'on lui a dit à l'Hôtel de Condé,[86] que vous êtes de Bordeaux où il croît qu'il y a plusieurs qui cachent leur religion in petto."[87] The reason given does not seem to have convinced Simon. He certainly states, in information given by him after La Peyrère's death, that La Peyrère came of a Huguenot family in Bordeaux, and without even mentioning Jona Salvador's supposition.[88] Yet it is certain that Simon was ill-informed on La Peyrère's earlier life. He was unaware that La Peyrère had completed his Du Rappel des Juifs in 1643 and published it. A contemporary epigram, which directs its shafts against his indifference to religion and change of religion, calls him "Ce bon Israélite."[89]

More significance is to be attached to direct evidence, to the appeal appended to the *Systema theologicum*; it is to this appeal that the Jona Salvador mentioned by Richard Simon refers. The appeal is inscribed to the "Synagogis Judaeorum universis, quotquot per totum Terrarum orbem sparsae." It begins thus: "Natio sancta et electa! filii Adam, qui fuit filius Dei: atque adeo et ipsi filii Dei. Salutem vestram vobis precatur, nescio quis: atque *utinam ex Vobis unus*. Magna sunt quae de vobis dixi in Tractatu hoc; ubi egi de Electione vestra. Multo majora sunt quae de vobis dicam in sequenti; ubi agam des Restauratione vestra. Quam futuram esse certo scio. Et, si quid Deus agit secretis cogiationibus apud nos, quam *brevi* futuram spero et confido. Eripiet Deus caligantem nubem illam, quae nostros et vestros, Christianorum et Judaeorum oculos hebetat. Videbitis Judaei secundum Prophetam vestrum, Jesum eundem nostrum quem Patres vestri transfixerunt, venientem vobis et nobis in nubibus . . . Vos sperabatis in eum qui restiturus erat regnum Israel. At Jesus in carne evertebat regnum Israel; ut in locum Israel substitueret gentilem. Mysterio, vobis et seculis ipsis incognito. Quocirca, neque credidistis in Jesum, neque potuistis credere in illum . . . Quin et Jesus idem ille a vobis crucifixus, se vobis de coelo exeret. Et qui regnum vestrum evertit, cum venit in carne: regnum ille idem vestrum vobis restituet, cum veniet in spiritu. Stabitis attoniti ad tantum miraculum. Sed nolite commoveri. Auctius et melius vobis erit, quam Patribus vestris: qui fratrem suum Josephum quem vendiderant, non noverant: a quo tamen et victum, et vitam accipiebant. Accedet ultro ad vos Jesus ille, qui Christus et Messias vester est; dicetque vobis, quae dicebat Joseph fratribus suis: Misit me Deus ante vos in viveficationem . . ."—And then the contemporary of Sabbatai Zwi continues: "Neque vero illud tantum; restituet vobis regnum vestrum Deus, per spiritum Jesu et Christi sui, Messiae vestri. Sed etiam exorietur (si non exortus est) vestris ex ossibus et fratribus, ultor et Rex vester: qui virtute Dei, et spiritu Christi fretus; gentes vobis inimicas conteret, vosque in manu forti et brachio extento, patriae vestrae et Terrae sanctae restituet: ut illam, In Aeternum, Confidenter, Et Soli, habitetis. Quod vobis authentice promissum fuit. Quod expressum notavi in hac parte mei Systematis. Quodque expressius demonstrandum mihi erit in sequenti. Gestiunt mihi praecordia, quoties recordor Regem illum vetrum: Pulchrum prae filiis hominum . . .

Salit mihi cor, et nescio quod insolitum gaudium pertentat tacitum meum pectus; quoties imago subit futuri illius reditus vestri: quo exciti omnes ex omnibus Terrarum omnium partibus, in quas dispersi estis, confluetis ad dulcem illam patriam vestram possidendam, pro qua tam diu est quod imo de pectore suspiria ducitis . . . Totus exulto, quoties reputo semitas omnes undique ferventes in reditu illo vestro . . . Sed ad coelos ipsos meditatione evehor; quoties in animum induco meum, reditum illum vestrum, et restaurationem illam vestram, Plenitudinem fore gentium . . . Quo tempore, inquam, laudabunt Dominum omnes gentes cum populo ejus . . ." The final words: "Hoc mihi certe cum Vobis commune est: quod vitam duco erraticam . . . At, si vivo vitam vestram; moriar morte vestra: et moriar morte Justorum; quae vestra est. Vos autem sospitet Deus. Vivite felices in spe vestra: quae fortitudo vestra est. Durate! et Vosmet rebus servate secundis."

We believe that the tone of this appeal makes certainty of Salvador's surmise. It is not likely that a Christian concerned with converting the Jews would write in this way. And La Peyrère, whose Christianity, according to the opinion of all those who knew him, is so much called in question, can scarcely figure in the role of one who converts Jews to Christianity. But on the other hand, what interest could he take in Judaism, this follower of Socinus, who rejects the Law of Moses as abrogated, who sees as the essential content of religion the hope of immortality and, for that very reason, can scarcely be inclined to give his preference to Judaism rather than to Christianity? If this man lived for several decades in the belief that the Kingdom of the Jews would once more be set up,[90] the fact seems to be intelligible only under the assumption that La Peyrère was of Marrano origin, and that his expectation of the coming of the Messiah springs from the affection felt by a man for the people of his own race, and not for a traditional faith.

For completeness it is still needful to indicate what connection exists between the theory of the Pre-Adamites and the theory that the Jews are the people chosen of God. In Genesis the creation of man is twice recounted, once in the first chapter and again in the second. The men of the "first creation" are the heathen, created by the Word of God. The descendants of the man of the second creation, of the man Adam, who was created not by the word of

God, but formed by the hand of God, are the Jews. It would seem that La Peyrère sees in the creation of Adam as recounted in the second chapter of Genesis, as compared with the creation described in the first chapter, a symbol or parable of the "second creation" at the end of all the ages.[91]

CHAPTER IV

THOMAS HOBBES

OUR ANALYSIS has so far identified three characteristics of the modern criticism of religion. 1) The authentic Epicurean concern with tranquillity of mind (the halcyon calm of the soul) receded, and interest in peace of within society took foremost place. 2) Thus religion is rejected, not primarily because it causes distress of mind, but essentially because the hopes which it awakens are illusory. 3) The reliance on man's achievement, on labor, on culture and progress, opposes the belief in the original perfection of man, and—thought through to its final consequences—opposes any interest in, or belief in, revelation. The connection between the first two characteristics and the third has not as yet been explicitly treated in this study, since da Costa's concern is limited to the first and second characteristics, and La Peyrère's is limited to the third. Hobbes, incomparably more radical-minded, established the lacking connection, and brought it into full light. His philosophy is the classic form in which the positivist mind comes to understand itself. His critique of religion, implied in that self-understanding, is the classic manifestation of the positivist attitude to religion. Hobbes was therefore able, in a way impossible to da Costa or to La Peyrère, to undertake an explicit analysis of religion. For analysis of religion, the explanation of religion in terms of human nature, is the complement and culmination of critique of religion. The more definite the break with religion, the more compelling is the obligation to supply such an analysis. If the critic finds himself in radical opposition to religion, he cannot rest content with merely refuting the teachings of religion, so that religion and critique of religion, still seem in principle to belong to the same plane of thought. He finds himself compelled to uncover the origin from which the whole complex of fallacious thinking characteristic of religion arises. Thus with Hobbes, critique of religion once more takes on the archetypal originality, the integral breadth and depth, which characterized that critique in the case of Epicurus and of Lucretius. He grasps afresh—and in a manner entirely different—that religion and science are by their nature opposed.

If science and religion are radically opposed, it seems to follow that science and critique of religion are identical. No such identification exists for Epicurus in the final instance. To his mind, science and critique of religion are so little related that he sees science only as a means for the critique of religion, and even as such, as he himself at least indicates, and as the later development of philosophy clearly bears out, in no sense an indispensable or irreplaceable means. In regard to the end which science is to be called upon to serve, Epicurus' view of man and of the human situation impels him to take science and religion as serving the same end—pleasure, maximum pleasure. Science and religion are thus related in this way: science does in fact lead to the unique goal of life, whereas religion is an inadequate means to that end. Characteristically enough, this view of the relation between science and religion does not figure prominently in Epicurus' work. For his hostility to religion does not spring primarily from the view that religion falls short as a means to happiness, but from the view that the failure of religion in this respect is so complete that in point of fact nothing so undermines human peace of mind as does religion. In any case, Epicurus does not see science and religion as two opposed *attitudes of mind*. The determining factor in Hobbes' thinking, on the other hand, is the scientific attitude as opposed to the attitude of the preachers and prophets. This does not mean that Hobbes simply rejects the more obvious view according to which science actually achieves what religion set out to perform but cannot achieve. The question must now be put: How are these two characteristics of religion—characteristics which manifestly belong to different ranges of thought—to be reconciled?

The external tripartite division of the *Elementa philosophiae* into doctrine of body, doctrine of man, and doctrine of the citizen is less adequate than the internal division into doctrine of natural bodies and doctrine of political bodies. This division splits *De Homine* into two parts.[92] The internal organization of the *Elementa* takes its bearings from the ontological distinction between nature and art,[93] and from the difference in the method applied—between proof (deduction) and experience (human experience, in particular the experience which each man has of himself).[94]

This articulation finds its deepest reason in the difference between the *purpose* of natural science (physics) and the *purpose* of politics. Physics is concerned with man's happiness, anthropology (philosophia moralis et civilis) with man's misery.[95] The greatest misfortune is death by violence; happiness consists in the limitless increase of power over men and over things. Fear of violent death, and the pursuit of domination over things—it is basically these two determinants of willing which Hobbes accepts as justified. Thus the distinction between the aim of natural science and the aim of anthropology (politics) is based on consideration of the fundamental duality of man's legitimate aims. The distinction between the two parts of knowledge is therefore so deeply rooted in Hobbes' conception of man that his formal forswearing of that distinction in favor of uni-dimensional "progress from the most general to the most particular," which Hobbes later preferred,[96] could do no more than externally modify the whole of his philosophy. To each of these two sciences (in the final instances to each of the two fundamental and legitimate directions of man's will) there corresponds a peculiar meaning of "illusion," or a peculiar slant in his critique of religion. Since the distinction between physics and anthropology itself points back to his conception of man, it is in his anthropology that we must seek the reason for the end or the spirit of both the anthropology and the physics.

A. The Spirit of Physics (Technology) and Religion

If one disregards all the trappings of traditional formulas and the anomalies in the presentation itself, one finds oneself face to face with the following order, characteristic of Hobbes, of the ends of human desires: pleasure, reputation, power, security. Pleasure (of the senses and of the flesh) finds its fulfillment in the present. It ends in satiety or even revulsion. The three higher grades of desire are constituted by expectation, anticipation. These have their foundation in the striving after pleasure. In desire, pleasure (the pleasure-giving object, the good) is looked forward to; in enjoyment the pleasure is present. Now whoever looks forward to any particular pleasure in the future must seek the means of attaining that pleasure: the sum total of these means at the disposal of any given man is called his power. Since in any conflict between two human beings for the same good, the excess power of one contestant over the other is decisive, that excess is power simply. Recognition of this excess or superiority by others is called honor. The striving after power and the striving after honor (reputation) take on independence over against the seeking after sensual pleasure which underlies both of them. They are also superior to the seeking after sensual pleasure, for they are limitless, because they permit of enduring pleasure that does not end in satiety and disgust, and because their origin lies in a greater vitality and a more potent *élan vital*. Happiness, enduring pleasure, the highest good, does not consist in a cessation of desire, in achievement of a final goal (there is no final goal: life is constant movement, constantly renewed desire), but in the maximum possible progress from one stage of power to a higher stage of power, to ever greater power, from honor to honor, to ever greater honor.[97] Assessed in regard to happiness, taken in the sense of enduring and ever-growing pleasure, what is at stake is not the enjoyment of the object desired at any one time, but simply and solely the attainment of the object as a means to power or to the recognition of one's power: the end becomes a means, the means becomes an end.

This reversal of the natural relationship is found only in the striving after reputation, but not in the striving after power as such. Concern with permanence, the long view, care for the future, which is the work of reason, justifies the continuing process of advancing from one desire to the next, from attainment of the one object desired to that of the next object of desire, with a view to the fact that man strives not only toward the unique pleasure of the moment, but toward ensuring his enjoyment in the future. The incessant striving after power is not—or not exclusively— founded in dissatisfaction with moderate power, in irrational craving, but in the fact that present power (one's present capacity to ensure lasting enjoyment for oneself) can be maintained only by the acquisition of more power.[98] Reason, the provident outlook on the future, thus justifies the striving after power, possessions, gain, wealth, since these provide the means to gratify the underlying desire for pleasures of the senses. Reason does not justify, but indeed refutes, all striving after reputation, honor, fame: in a word, and that word used in the sense applied by Hobbes, vanity. For vanity is occupied with ridiculous trifles, preoccupied by every word, every smile, every opinion, every indication of contempt. The good sought by human vanity is not good in the meaning of sensual goods, but of pleasures of the mind, which here conveys, at least as subsidiary connotation, illusionary good.[99]

The legitimate striving after pleasure is sublated into striving after power. What is condemned is the striving after reputation. Philosophy (or more accurately physics as distinct from anthropology) is to be understood as arising from the striving after power: *scientia propter potentiam*. Its aim is cultivation, the cultivation of nature.[100] What nature offers to man without supplementary activity on the part of man is sufficient for no more than a life of penury. So that life may become more comfortable, human exertion is required, and the regulation of unregulated nature. Cultivation does not bring to bear on nature an alien order, but follows the lines seen within nature. Cultivation does regularly what nature herself does sporadically and haphazardly. Cultivation is fundamentally method.

Science exists for the sake of power. In other words, science carries out the task of procuring means for the comfort and convenience of life. Science seeks after means and only after means. It searches out only the efficient causes.[101] The man who disposes of the causes which will bring forth a specific effect, can procure this effect for himself. Man, unlike other animals, is capable of observing causal relations. Because man has this capacity, he can take thought and action for the future, just as, on the other hand, it is care for the future that impels man to investigate causes.[102] Science, which has culture as its aim, consists in the cultivation of man's natural urge to seek causes, in the methodical search for causes.[103] The unmethodical search for causes produces religion.[104] Thus science and religion spring from the same root. Both presuppose thinking in terms of causes. This accord, which is in effect recognized also in the Epicurean analysis of religion, comes to clearer expression in Hobbes because for him the opposition between science and religion is primarily an opposition not of content but of method, the opposition of methodical and unmethodical thought. He does not contend against religion, but against unmethodical seeking after causes. The anti-religious implication is not primarily intended. His critique of religion is not the object, but only the subsidiary result of analyzing and defining science. This must be stressed because his analysis of religion is in many points in harmony with Epicurean analysis of religion.

Philosophy, the striving for knowledge of causes, is innate in every human being: each man reflects to some extent about some things. But since the right method is lacking, most men go astray. Seeking after causes is arbitrarily limited to the question of what causes our happiness and unhappiness. This preoccupation with happiness and unhappiness is heightened into anxiety—permanent anxiety—by the widening of the horizon brought about by seeking after causes. This anxiety diverts men from investigating the true causes. This diversion from the true to the merely apparent causes is already founded in the quest for the causes of happiness and unhappiness. This search does not aim at the causes of an event as such but it connects the circumstances accompanying a fortunate or unfortunate event with its being fortunate or unfortunate; it is not concerned with the real connection of the facts among themselves, but with their external connection with our happiness or unhappiness; it does not establish its findings in order to take the appropriate steps for the future, but seeks some being as responsible, so that he may be accused if misfortune occurs; it arises not from active foresight, but from inactive expectation. Now in most cases it is not even possible to find, among the matters perceived, an apparent cause for the good or evil fortune which befell. And thus man, living as they do in ever-present anxiety due to their lack of knowledge of the causal relations linking all things, assume as causes of good and evil fortune invisible powers, gods. The gods originate as offspring of human fear.[105]

Science is cultivation of our innate, natural reason. Knowledge immediately supplied by nature, perception, and memory is excluded from science, precisely because it is a gift of nature.[106] Also excluded as a matter of course is imagination, which is only a pale reflection of perception, and, in particular the dream. It is dream which provides the matter for the conception of the gods. It is from dream that there arises the positive complement to the negative, invisible powers. Just as men and other bodies appear in dream or in a mirror, souls are thought of as real, but tenuous, bodies. As such, they are called "spirits." The gods are spirits.[107] Hobbes here differs but little from Lucretius. The contrast between the contexts in which the doctrine appears in the two cases is all the more striking. For the sensualist, the critique of dreams is focal; for Hobbes it is a concomitant of his critique of sensory perception. Even if one can justifiably assert that Hobbes' critique of sensory perception is based on his critique of dreams, and that he extends his critique of dreams to include sensory perception itself (since sensory perception cannot be precisely distinguished from dream),[108] his aim—unlike that of the Epicureans, who contrast the fear-inspiring nature of dream with reality—remains fixed on the illusory dreamlike character as such.[109]

The purpose pursued by science is conquest over nature: science is essentially method. Thus the intent of criticism of religion is rejection of unmethodical seeking after causes, as leading to the assumption of illusionary causes. Religion is a divagation. It fails to recognize true causes. Therefore it cannot serve the happiness of mankind. What religion is incapable of doing, and nevertheless sets out to do, that is, to serve the happiness of mankind, is a task performed by science. Religion is an attempt made with ineffective means.

B. The Spirit of Commonwealth (Morality) and Religion

The striving after reputation and after power is to be preferred to striving after pleasures of the senses;[110] the striving after power is to be preferred to the striving after reputation.[111] The reason adduced is that man strives not only after satisfaction of the moment, but also to assure satisfaction in the future. From this arises the objection to complete preoccupation with pleasure of the moment, also to striving after reputation. This latter has, it is true, a certain record for the future, but it is divorced from our natural preoccupation with worldly goods, and is therefore set only on "pleasures of the mind," on empty show. If we go to the root of the matter, the distinction between striving after power and striving after reputation loses its importance. The sharper scrutiny both cancels and preserves the greater justification inhering in the striving after power. There is no highest good, no final goal for desire, for life itself is desiring. But there remains nevertheless, a *primary* good, a *conditio sine qua non* of all other goods: life, bare life itself. Correspondingly, there is a *primary* evil, death, "the fearful enemy of nature," and there is, in particular, death in pain by violence.[112] This is in itself the greatest evil.[113] There is no highest good, but only a worst evil. To this formulation the anthropology of Hobbes can be reduced.

Since only the evil is limited, not the good, it follows that the conduct of life, the goal set to life, is conditioned by evil. The conduct of life takes on the character of foreseeing the greatest evil and taking precaution against it. Expectation of future evil is called fear. Fear is not only alarm and flight, but also distrust, suspicion, caution, care lest one fear.[114] Now it is not death in itself that can be avoided, but only death by violence, which is the greatest of possible evils. For life itself can be of such misery that death comes to be ranked with the good. In the final instance what is of primary concern is ensuring the continuance of life in the sense of ensuring defense against other men. Concern with self-protection is the fundamental consideration, the one most fully in accord with the human situation. This is the origin of the distinction made between (moral) good and (moral) evil. The fear of death, the fear of death by violence, is the source of all right, the primary basis of natural right.[115]

For the mind prepared to follow the problem to its root, the striving after reputation and the striving after power cannot be justified. The one and the other seeks after inequality, power over others, or a position of superiority. But in the final instance, it is manifest that all men are equal. For each and all of them may cause any other man to suffer the utmost evil. The constitution of the human body is so frail, that even the weakest man may kill the strongest, and that easily. Therefore there is no reason why any man should trust in his own strength and believe himself naturally superior to other men. Such belief is based on empty vainglory and misjudgment of forces. What corresponds to the condition of men, what is rational and based on due assessment of the power of the individual, is the resolve and intention to grant to all others what one permits oneself to do. In other words, recognition of man's equality with man. It is this attitude that characterizes the modest man, and the opposite that characterizes the arrogant man.[116]

Radical thinking recognizes the superiority of the will to power over striving after reputation. From fear of death by violence, from love of security, men seek after peace, after an ordered society. To bring this out, Hobbes takes into account such other factors as are capable of bringing men to a state of peace and sociality. In so doing Hobbes establishes a basic dualism of all apparent good as sensual good and as mental good. Concomitantly,

it becomes apparent that striving after reputation by its very
nature isolates the individual. For if all men achieve fame and
reputation, no one achieves them. He who sets out to prevail in
this sense dare not, in the nature of things, be under obligation
to others and owe them gratitude for their assistance to him on his
road to prominence. As far as power is concerned, in the sense of
means of acquiring the means of enjoyment and of ensuring
the security of that enjoyment—in other words, power over things
—these means of enjoyment can be increased by mutual aid.
Nevertheless, the one in sole possession has the advantage over
those who share. Thus the striving after power over means of
enjoyment of things develops by its very nature into striving after
power over other men.[117] Striving after power leads, just as does
the striving after reputation—by manifesting itself as striving to
secure for oneself more than one is prepared to grant as due to
others—to war and unceasing danger. But that Hobbes even at
this juncture still sees the root of all evil in the striving after
reputation is shown plainly enough by his opposing the due
evaluation of one's own powers, reason, desire for security, fear of
death by violence to the *inanis gloria et falsa virium aestimatio*.[118]

False evaluation is overvaluing. Undervaluing one's own
powers is not taken into consideration at all. The reason for this is
plain. The man who underestimates his own power, the meek and
the poor in spirit,[119] is not a danger to others. Hobbes' political
theory takes into account men seen only in respect of how they
imperil others. Those human inclinations that are favorable to
peace between men (e.g. fondness for the pleasures of the senses
and love of knowledge) are assumed to be, in the fundamental
analysis of the state of nature, weak and of small account.[120]
This amounts to stating that Hobbes' political *theory* is determined
by the same motive as the one he has already recognized as the
sole reason for the foundation of enduring states: fear and distrust
towards (other) men.[121] The purpose of the state is peace and
security. Peace and security—and not pure theory—are also the
aim of Hobbes' political theory. In the "Preface to the Reader" in
De Cive, his most purely theoretical exposition of his theory of the
state, he announces that the work was written *"pacis studio."*

Anthropology (*philosophia moralis et civilis*) works toward an
aim other than that of physics. Physics sets out to serve man's
dominion over things, but anthropology serves peace. Now,

without peace, science is impossible, culture is impossible. The purpose of anthropology is more urgent than the purpose of physics. Furthermore, the aim of physics cannot be clearly established except by starting from the aim of anthropology. For effort directed towards mastery over things, toward *commoda hujus vitae*, does not contain within itself its own measure and restraint. By its very nature it leads to mastery over men, leads to hate and strife, to the war of all against all, which it cannot of itself bring to an end, and thus it brings about its own undoing. It becomes limited, and justified within limits, only through the most radical consideration, through regard for the fragility of the human body, through fear of death by violence and through our desire for security. Only thus is the unambiguous distinction between good and evil to be ascertained.[122] With this is also given the peculiar character of Hobbes' criticism of religion. Religion is rejected as a creation of vanity, desire for status and reputation, overestimation of one's own powers, the tendency to over-tender self-assessment. When Hobbes enunciates this view, he is not merely continuing the traditional hostile arguments against priests who are set on gaining wealth and advancement for themselves. It would be more natural to assume that the antithesis *gloriatio-modestia* as the ultimate antithesis which is the basis of morality, represents the secularized form of the antithesis *superbia-modestia*. If the root of all evil is *gloriatio*, then the religious illusion is not contested as illusion in the sense corresponding to the spirit of physics, as an attempt made with insufficient means; it is contested for the reason of its origin in *gloriatio*. Judged from the standpoint of physics, physics and religion surely spring from the same root: they differ only in that one has method and the other has not. Not until we come to anthropology, which is animated by the spirit of peace and civil society, do we find reason and religion opposed one to the other, from beginning to end.

Hobbes distinguishes between the "natural seed of religion" (anxiety and dreams), and the "culture" which religion took on within paganism and then revelation. The culture of religion takes as its aim the education of mankind to obedience, peace, love and ordered society. For the pagans, religion was a part of politics. The pagan legislators and founders of states brought it about, by the establishment of suitable institutions, that the populace should never even contemplate rebellion, but remain content with bread and circuses. The powerful Romans tolerated every type of religion within their city with the exception of Judaism, in which obedience to a mortal king was forbidden. The view which is here thus referred back to the Jews is contested by Hobbes as rebellious and likely to lead to rebellion.[123] Obedience to the established power is never sin. Rather, rebellion against established authority is sin. Revelation, the second path opened to the culture of natural religion with its basis in fear and dream, makes politics a part of religion. It thus, if we understand Hobbes aright, reverses the natural relationship which was realized in paganism.[124] However, with his formulation he indicates the way in which he seeks to counter the threat, contained in revealed religion, to public peace; politics is to be a part of religion; religion can never and must never contradict politics; the distinction between the spiritual and the temporal power is absurd. This distinction, which in paganism was in principle avoided, and was introduced only by the Jews, originates in the belief in spirits, which is part and parcel of natural religion. This distinction entails that within the realms of the Christian kings there is yet another realm, a realm of ghosts and spirits that walk in darkness. Religion thus leads to the absurdity that every citizen within the realm must obey two powers. It is a threat to the stability of the state that some subjects obey the temporal power, which is visible, and on which plays "the fierce light which beats upon a throne," while other subjects maintain their allegiance to the spiritual power, in whose favor there speaks the greatest fear, the fear of spirits and of eternal damnation. Only when the fear of spirits is well and truly expelled from men's minds is peace assured, as well as the loyalty of the citizen to his country. The duty of obedience and allegiance is confronted, indeed, not only with the natural human inclination to believe in spirits. When men find themselves in darkness and confusion on account of their un-tutored questing after causes, and have become alarmed and anxious, not only do they take as true and proved causes suggested to them by their own imaginations, but they lay themselves open to suggestion as to causes put forward by those whom they take to be superior, and because of their natural credulity accept the causes suggested as true. There are two forms of madness: one, which disposes to baseless anxiety because it stems from impaired vitality, consists of over-great modesty and self-depreciation; the other, which arises from an all too compelling craving, is over-weening self-confidence. What conduces to the madness of the second type is any form of marked self-confidence, in particular the belief that one is directly inspired. This belief abuses the belief in spirits held by simple people. The "spirit" to which the inspired make claim, is nothing other than their *gloriatio*. One who says that he speaks on the basis of inspiration says in effect that he feels a burning desire to speak, or has a high opinion of himself, for which he can adduce no natural or sufficient reason.[125] *Gloriatio* is the basis of prophecy, of the claim to revelation. Now, as has already been shown, according to Hobbes' doctrine, *gloriatio* is the root of all evil. Thus the criticism of revelation arises from Hobbes' central motive. Taking this into account, it is not difficult to recognize the inner bond uniting the two elements which we have distinguished in his critique of religion. Reason is common to all men, and is one and the same in all men. The difference among men consists only in the difference regarding the methodical training and development of this natural disposition which they have in common.[126] Method, by in fact doing away with this natural equality, recognizes it, whereas prophecy as *gloriatio* denies it. Reason is modesty. This formulation sums up the spirit of Hobbes' philosophy.

C. The Theoretical Critique and Hobbes' Attitude to Religion

"True (that is, accurate) Philosophy professedly rejects not only the paint and false colors of language, but even the very orna-ments and graces of the same. The primary bases of all science are not only not alluring, but actually unattractive, dry and almost repulsive" (*De Corp.* I, 1). It is in this spirit that Hobbes takes up arms against the "all too facile observation of human nature," on the basis of which most political philosophers take their stand, that man is a *zoön politikon*, that the state originates in mutual goodwill (*De Cive* I, 2). The principle from which *he* starts is indeed not in any sense alluring, but almost repulsive: it is mutual fear. In order to lead political theory back to infallible rules of reason and thus to raise the discipline to the rank of true or exact philosophy, "it is needful to take as basis such principles as desire does not distrust and does not wish to displace (*Elements*, Ep. ded.). The truth, i.e. the exactness of the political theory, is defined with respect to the dangerous enemy of the state, which is to be fought against, and won over. Hobbes' abhorrence of rhetorical eloquence, of embellishment, has thus unquestionably a particular reason, and this reason is born of his impelling motive. Subsidiary to this, and separable from it, there remains the general one, which is given with the philosophic intent as such. After he has made his point that the basis of any science is not alluring, but almost repulsive, he continues: "Attamen cum sint aliqui certe, quamquam pauci, quos in omne re veritas et rationum firmitudo *per se* delectat, paucis illis operam hanc navandam esse censui" (*De Corp.* I, 1). The contradiction here with the remark which follows soon after is only an apparent one: . . . ut quis de rerum dubiarum difficultate superata, vel de abditissimarum veritatum detectione, apud se tacitus gaudeat et triumphet, tanta operae quanta Philosophiae impendenda est, pretium esse non judico" (*ibid.,* I, 6). For here the philosopher is speaking of the universal function of philosophy, not of the specific interest, which the few who are philosophers know as the motive which impels them to undertake and continue their inquiries. Of himself he says that he has concerned himself with philosophy *animi causa*: ". . . and quite after the mode of Plato, he thinks of the infinite delight which lies within the commerce which the soul may have with the high beauty of the cosmos."[127] If he who has known the profoundest pleasure from theory does not allow his anthropology to culminate in the analysis and glorification of theory, the reason is in the very function of anthropology, which compels exclusive focusing of attention on what impels and activates the majority of men.[128] Therefore anthropology and those parts of physics which are legitimated by anthropology would permit only of a one-sided understanding of his criticism of religion. What can be separated from his moral criticism (born of an interest of the heart) is the independent theoretical criticism, which can be understood in itself.

The question, to what extent Hobbes' theory (apart from his anthropology) is conditioned by that interest cannot be treated here[129] nor can the theoretical thoughts as such which underlie the theoretical criticism of religion. Mere mention of the relevant elements must suffice here. From the limitation of philosophy to investigating efficient causes arises the exclusion of theology: God is not generated (*De Corp.* I, 8). The regression from cause to cause, any profound investigation of natural causes inclines men to believe that there is a First and Eternal Cause, and this Cause they call God. Any idea of God is impossible, for we are not capable of imagining anything which we have not already perceived through our senses, or alternately which is not itself composed of elements which are known to us through our senses. Knowledge of the infinite is not accessible to the finite questioner.[130] For us there can be no more than a premonition of God, but no knowledge. Critique of the traditional conception of God is directed against the concept of spirit, of incorporeal substance. Everything which is independent of our imagining fills some part of space, is thus, however ethereal and invisible, a body. Now, just as the sensuous qualities of things appear to us in dreams, so also do spirits, no less than in waking. They are therefore not external things, existent in themselves, but phantasms of our minds.[131] Hobbes does not venture so far as to deny the possibility of miracles, but he allows the denial of miracles to shimmer through. A thing is admired when it is rare and at the same time cannot be explained by natural causes. And so men believe—and believe the more readily, the more ignorant they are of natural causes—in miracles. It is of the essence of miracles that they happen when there is need of evoking faith, or of strengthening faith already existing. Thus we read in Mark 6:5 that Jesus could perform no miracles ("no mighty work") in the town of his birth, because his fellow-citizens had no faith in Him. The interpreters who understand "could not" as "did not wish to" do this without any other example in Greek. The passage is to be understood rather in the sense that he could not, because he had been sent only for the conversion of the elect. If one mark show much importance Hobbes attaches to this conception that it is the ignorant and inexperienced who incline to belief in miracles, it becomes clear which people he had in mind as the "elect." After he has retailed the miracles worked by Moses, and which the Egyptian magicians could not imitate, he raises the question whether words have the power to evoke effects; words have an effect only on those who understand them. If therefore a staff appears to be a serpent, or blood appears to be water, or some other miracle seems to occur by magic, then if this does not occur so that the minds of God's people may be lifted up, neither the staff nor the water nor anything else is transformed except the onlookers, and the magician's whole miracle consists in the fact that a deceiver deceives a man

—and that is no miracle. For men, especially those who are ignorant of natural causes and of human tricks, are easy to deceive. If two men come to an arrangement that one of them will feign lameness, another will heal him by charms, they may deceive many people. But when many come to an agreement that one of them will appear to be lame, another will heal him, and all the rest of them will bear witness, they will deceive many more. This goes to prove that a miracle is not a criterion of revelation, as is indeed taught in Holy Writ itself (Deut. 18). The criterion for the truth of a religion, and in accordance with that for its miracles, is the will of the government. The private individual always has this choice—for thought is free—of giving his faith to acts which are alleged to be miracles, or of withholding his faith. Yet when it is a matter of public profession of faith, private reason must subordinate itself to public reason, i.e. to the will of the government (*Lev.* xxxvii).

If, to these and similar utterances, one adds the definition: fear of invisible powers regardless of whether these powers are figments of the imagination or known by hearsay is called religion if the fear is publicly sanctioned; and if the fear is not publicly sanctioned and accepted, it is called superstition, then it would appear that in the matter of Hobbes' attitude to religion, there is not ground for uncertainty or doubt. However, to the definition quoted (*ibid.*, vi), there is this continuation: If the power thus demonstrated is as it is represented to be, then fear of that power is called "true religion." It is possible to doubt the sincerity of this gloss, for in each case it is the will of the government, and that will only, that lays down which religion has authority.[132] But independently of this concept of religion which is dictated by regard for peace, Hobbes makes a distinction between religion springing from fear and from dream (superstition), and the religion which has its source in contemplation and in investigation of the universe, uninfluenced by fortune and misfortune, the divination of God (*Lev.* xi f.). It is in this divination of God and in the connected tendency to see a relation of right in the indubitable superiority in power of the universe to man,[133] that one may justifiably seek that final residue which Hobbes recognized in his heart as "true religion." This minimum claim at least one must assert. An atheist in the theoretical sense of the term Hobbes is not. However, his "true religion" is no more than a fringe-phenomenon, which exercised no great influence on his way of thinking and feeling. The positive mind, for which reason itself is modesty, is content with those matters which are truly accessible to the finite mind. Only *this* world yields some answers. His mind and imagination do not go roaming into the infinite and eternal. From an agnosticism such as that of Hobbes, it is only a step into atheism, a step which this philosopher himself however never took. Furthermore, his extensive and penetrating preoccupation with theological themes is not to be understood as due to some residue left within him by millennial modes of thought and feeling, but exclusively to the necessity of bringing out the thesis of disbelief in the face of prevailing belief: it is in every sense a compromise, in characteristic contrast to the theory of religion put forward by Spinoza, whose break with the immediately preceding tradition was much less radical than that of Hobbes.[134] Whereas Spinoza, who is in this respect fully in line with the Averroist tradition, indeed takes the trend of this tradition to its ultimate conclusion, could not but recognize religion as an essential means for the maintenance of the state, in Hobbes' theory of the state there is no point of union which could serve for a similar defense of religion. That science and religion (i.e. the Scriptures) are essentially different, that the association of science and religion is harmful to both, is taught by Hobbes quite as definitely as it is by Spinoza.[135] But Hobbes advances to a position beyond that of Spinoza with his belief that the political allegiance of all the subjects of the state is a bond whose origin lies in reason alone. According to Spinoza, the command "thou shalt love thy neighbor" takes its force as commandment for the multitude only from the belief that the commandment is the directly "revealed" word of God, but from Hobbes' position this commandment is sufficiently binding upon men by virtue of the fact that God has created men as reasonable beings. The distinction between the wise men and the vulgar does not enter into the matter at all. *Because* that distinction does not come into consideration, there is no necessity for recourse to religion.

D. The Critique of the Bible

Hobbes' attitude towards the Bible is conditioned by the conviction that conflict between science and religion, and also between the State and religion, would never arise if the clergy kept strictly to the teachings of the Bible. For in the first place, "Scripture was written to shew unto men the kingdom of God, and to prepare their minds to become His obedient subjects; leaving the world, and the Philosophy thereof, to the disputation of men, for the exercising of their naturall reason" (*Lev.* viii) and in the second place, the behest of the Bible is unambiguous that obedience must be given to the temporal power. In this way, both philosophy(or science) and the State are secure from any appeal to Scripture, indeed theirs is a position of complete independence in regard to Scripture. But this assurance is not of itself sufficient. Hobbes finds himself forced to cast doubt on the authority of Scripture itself, and to make that authority dependent on the authority of the State. After he has derived the basis of temporal power from purely natural principles, he treats (in opening a long discussion on the nature and the rights of the Christian State), of the particular principle which is fundamental to this discussion, namely revelation, Scripture. "And to that end, I shall speak in the next Chapter, of the Books, Writers, Scope and Authority of the Bible" (*ibid.*, xxxii). The principle first to be established is that unconditional obedience must be given to God, King of kings, and this, if need be, in opposition to the command of temporal kings; it is not obedience to God which is called into question, but the problem of when did God speak His will, and what was His command. Since men who have no supernatural revelation can know nothing of this revelation, they must recognize as revealed those writings which are laid down as such by the legitimate power. This is in accord with natural reason, which demands that for the sake of maintaining peace they obey the legitimate power. It is to this statement that Hobbes appends his investigation of the authorship of various books in Scripture. The implicit aim of this investigation is not to be mistaken. He sets out to demonstrate that the authority of Scripture is grounded not in Scripture itself, but exclusively in the command given by the temporal power, and is dependent on the temporal power.

The Pentateuch was not composed by Moses. For in Deuteronomy 34:6 we read "So Moses the servant of the Lord died there in the land of Moab . . . but no man knoweth of his sepulcher unto this day," that is, down to the time when these words were written. These words are thus written after Moses' death. For it would indeed be a curious interpretation of the text if one were to say that Moses spoke as it were as a prophet about his grave, that it was not to be found on the day of writing, when Moses himself was still alive. One could put forward the view that only the last chapter was written by another hand. But this is contrary to Genesis 12:6, "and the Canaanite was then in the land." This passage was written at a time when the Canaanites were not in the land, and therefore not in the time of Moses. Furthermore, in Numbers 21:14 the author cites an earlier book, ". . . the book of the wars of the Lord," in which Moses' own deeds were recounted. This clearly cannot have been written by Moses. Moses is the author of only those parts of the Pentateuch whose authorship is expressly attributed to him, i.e. the deuteronomic Book of the Law (Deut. 11:27). To the Jews of the time before the Dispersion it was this book and this book only that was accounted as the Word of God. Moses gave it into the hands of the priests and elders of Israel to be kept within the Ark of the Covenant, and for reading at appointed times. Later the book was lost. It was found long afterwards by Hilkiah, and sent to Josiah the king, who renewed the Covenant between God and His people. (Sources: Deut. 31:9, 26; II Kings 22:8; 23:1–3.) The frequent use of the phrase "unto this day" and the quotation from source-writings which occur in the historical books of the Old Testament, go to show that these books were written long after the events of which the books report. Job, as is shown in Ezekiel 14:14 and in the Epistle of James 5:11, was an historical person. But the Book of Job itself is not an historical work, but a treatise on morals. There is further proof of this in the fact that it is written mainly in verse, and verse is not the usual style of those who are suffering or of those who offer consolation, but much more the style of moralizing philosophers. The Psalms were in great part written by David, Psalms 137 and 126 after the return from captivity, and Psalm 79 at the time of Antiochus, which clearly shows that the Psalms in the form in which we know them were compiled after the return of the Jews from captivity in Babylon. Since the Book of Proverbs contains proverbs that were coined not only by Solomon but also by Agur and by the mother of King Lemuel, it is to be assumed as probable that the book was compiled by one who lived in a later age than these three persons. Ecclesiastes and the Song of Songs are, the titles excepted, the work of King Solomon. Of the prophets the oldest are Zephaniah,

Jonah, Amos, Isaiah and Micah. The Book of Jonah is not a compilation of his prophesies but an historical account of his contumacy, so we must take it as highly improbable that he himself was the author if it. Hobbes sums up his verdict on the origin of the Old Testament as that the book was given the form in which we know it, after the return of the Jews from captivity in Babylon, and prior to the time of Ptolomaeus Philadelphus, who had the book translated into Greek. If one accepts what is said in the Second Book of Esdras (Fourth Ezra) 14:14, 21, 22, and ch. 45, it was Ezra who compiled the canon (*Lev.* xxxiii; *De Cive* xvi, 12).

The facts thus established by Biblical critique harmonize in the main with the corresponding arguments put forward by La Peyrère and Spinoza. There is, however, this important distinction. These arguments were not conditioned, as were the latter, by the conception of a science of the Bible. Hobbes is much less interested than is Spinoza in a specific Bible *science*. For him, the political preoccupation plainly predominates. Hobbes' political interpretation of Bible history is set on its specific path, understandably enough by his own particular conception of what is political. It is indicative that he begins his treatise with Adam and Abraham, whereas Spinoza begins with the people of Israel. Hobbes gives specific attention to the particular nature of authority prior to Moses because, for Hobbes, the difference between the *civitas institutiva*, arising out of social contract, and the patriarchal authority is important. This importance stems from the central position accorded to the social contract—a matter which Spinoza lets pass by default (*De Cive* xvi, *Lev.* xl).

PART TWO

SPINOZA'S CRITIQUE OF RELIGION

INTRODUCTION

THE QUESTION which we put to critique of religion in general and to Spinoza's critique of religion in particular would seem to have been proved inadequate by the preceding argument. It has become manifest from the examples of belief in God and belief in immortality that religion and critique of religion may both arise from the same motive. If this is the case, then the reason which causes men impelled by this motive to turn to critique of religion, instead of, by that very motive, to adopt religion—either choice is equally possible—must be sought in the theory and not in the motive itself. Let us put the question in a more general form. Can the Epicurean motive (let us stay with this particular example, which is more than a mere example) not satisfy itself with any or every theory? In the view of Epicurus himself, not all theories are equally apposite to his purpose. He lists a series, in order of decreasing appropriateness to his purpose: Epicurus' own theology and physics; the tales of active and effective gods; the determinism of the physicists. This last-named theory seems to Epicurus to be completely incompatible with his motive. It is in fact undeniable that the stringent determinism of mechanistic physics—which views man and his world as the latest and all-but powerless product of extra-human concatenations, which in their harsh indifference to man now favor and now impede him—offers little to our longing for tranquillity and consolation. Most of those who made use of this mechanistic theory for the purpose of critique of religion—and to popularize that critique—hid its inherently despairing character from themselves and from others by adventitious pantheistic adornments. This is not to say that these proponents were so full to overflowing with hatred of religion and rebellion against it that they were utterly incapable of reflecting on the consequences of their doctrine for man's self-awareness. We must assert that, at any rate, mechanistic physics is beyond the range of the Epicurean motive. Nevertheless, by comparison with the orthodox Arab theory which negates all inherent causality in events, and by so doing denies any possible prediction of events, asserting as the one and only ground of being and happening the momentary and arbitrary act of the divine creative

force—by comparison with this, the physicists' theory of inexorable law and inexorable doom is ground for some comfort. But
the very comparison with this extreme, through which any consideration of the motive seems to lose all foundation, re-establishes
in a more radical form the opposition which filled the mind of
Epicurus and of Lucretius: the opposition between the scientific
world-view, which is guided by the principle of continuity and
hence is comforting, and the mythical-religious world view, in
which everything is traced to the arbitrary action of divine
powers, and which therefore destroys all peace of mind. This
justifies a return to the question which was our point of departure.
Does the theory which is bound up with critique of religion, and
which is in character metaphysical, arise from the dialectics of
theoretical consciousness, or from a basic and ineradicable interest
springing from the heart? This question has become ambiguous
through the fact that more than a few religious positions did in
actual fact not only satisfy the Epicurean motive but also intended
to satisfy it. This fact loses its importance as soon as positions of
this kind are recognized as insufficiently radical and to be excluded
from the range of radical reflection.

But this exclusion cannot so easily be justified. We cannot hope
for a decision on this point and thus on the answer to the question
regarding the condition of possibility of radical critique of religion
until we have investigated the critique of religion in its act or
exercise. It does not suffice to consider the position of the attacker
only. For critique of religion transcends that position. Hence the
position under attack must be seen as it is in itself. Furthermore,
we must observe which assumptions come into play on both sides
by virtue of the conflict. It is with this focus that we approach
Spinoza's critique of religion, as it develops particularly in the
Theologico-political Tractate.

In this work, Spinoza expressly turns against two positions
taken up on behalf of revealed religion, positions that are diametrically different, even opposed to one another. On the one
hand stand the "skeptics, who deny the certainty of reason,"
and demand the subordination of reason to the authority of
Scripture, and on the other the "dogmatists," who adopt the
opposite position, and seek to make of Scripture the handmaid of
reason. Both these positions can be identified in history. To
Maimonides is attributed the origin of "dogmatism" within

Judaism, but according to Spinoza, the majority of the Jews adopt the "skeptical" approach, and by so doing, diverge from their teacher Maimonides (*Tr.*, pp. 166 f.). This limitation of attention to the conflict within Judaism, which takes its origin from the recollection of the highly important controversy for and against Maimonides in the early thirteenth century, is easily to be understood from the story of Spinoza's own youth.[136] But the opposition within Judaism is used only as provisional representation and only to facilitate the investigation of the opposition between skepticism and dogmatism that was universal throughout Europe. This is clearly to be seen from the fact that Spinoza treats the doctrine of original sin as part of the "skeptical" position (*Tr.*, p. 168). Taken as a whole, the *Theologico-political Tractate* is aimed much more directly at Christian than at Jewish orthodoxy;[137] "the greatest part" of the Jews means then in fact orthodoxy in general. The Christian orthodoxy, which Spinoza primarily attacks, is in particular Calvinism. The ultimate assumptions underlying the critique of orthodoxy will not come fully to light until the radical (Calvin's own) position underlying that orthodoxy is understood as the target imposed by the existing situation. The following order imposes itself then for analysis of the critique which Spinoza carries out in the *Tractate*:

  a) Critique of orthodoxy
  b) Critique of Maimonides
  c) Critique of Calvin.

CHAPTER V

THE CRITIQUE OF ORTHODOXY

THE CRITIQUE is directed *against* the theologians. However, it addresses not these but the "more prudent sort" whose minds are to be freed from the prejudices of the theologians (*Ep.* 30), those "who would philosophize more freely but for the one obstacle, the belief that reason must serve as the handmaid of theology" (*Tr.* praef., p. 30). The position against which the *Tractate* is chiefly directed is thus, following Spinoza's own distinction, the "skeptical" one, that of Christian orthodoxy.

In order to make plain the critique that Spinoza applies to orthodoxy, let us set out from Spinoza's own statement of the aims he had in mind in writing the *Tractate*. He writes in 1665 to Henry Oldenburg (*Ep.* 30): "Compono iam tractatum de meo circa scripturam sensu; ad id vero faciendum me movent, 1) Praejudicia theologorum; scio enim, ea maxime impedire, quo minus homines animum ad philosophiam applicare possint: ea igitur patefacere atque amoliri a mentibus prudentiorum satago.

2) Opinio, quam vulgus de me habet, qui me atheismi insimulare non cessat: eam quoque averruncare, quoad fieri potest, cogor.

3) Libertas philosophandi dicendique quae sentimus; quam asserere omnibus modis cupio, quaeque hic ob nimiam conciona-torum authoritatem et petulantiam utcunque supprimitur."

It may be said of the second aim that this led Spinoza into frequently softening and obscuring his opposition to revealed religion. Taken as a whole, his defense against the charge of atheism is that he unmasks as superstition the officially accepted teachings of the theologians, on the basis of which his teaching is bound to appear to be atheistic. The second aim thus essentially leads back to the first aim. There remain then two different aims, and these two aims differ very much in weight. The third aim intends freedom of speech, freedom to publish. The philosopher claims freedom publicly to accept what he recognizes to be true, and publicly to reject what he recognizes to be false. The legitima-tion of this claim presupposes the critique of the theologians' prejudices, and therefore the realization of the first aim is the precondition underlying the realization of the third aim. The first aim is however earlier, not only in respect of realization, it is also in itself more radical than the third. Spinoza is not so much concerned for freedom to spread abroad truths already discovered, but for the liberation of men's minds from those prejudices which the theologians have implanted. His concern is with the freedom of philosophizing. This therefore is the primary and the ultimate purpose for which Spinoza wrote the *Tractate*.

Critique of the theologians' prejudices is for Spinoza not a matter external to philosophy, a subsequent application of results derived from philosophic inquiry to the critique of false opinions, chance errors. He himself assures us that it is in no sense his habit to bring the errors of others to light (*Ep.* 2). The critique of the prejudices of the theologians is the necessary prolegomenon to philosophy as such. Not until the theologians' prejudices have lost their power over men's minds will the field for philosophy be unimpeded. A certain liberation of the will must precede philosophic liberty. And if philosophy is possible only within freedom of mind, then freedom to pursue philosophy is not yet philosophy, but propaedeutic for philosophy. This liberation for philosophizing requires a peculiar method, adapted, of necessity, to the pre-philosophic standpoint.

Spinoza had already had sufficient experience of the need for this introduction and guidance. In the very year in which he began work on the *Tractate*, there took place his correspondence with Willem van Blyenbergh, who demonstrated this necessity to Spinoza, and may well not have been the first to do so. The course of the correspondence leads to the precise point at which the analyses of the *Tractate* become needful. Blyenbergh had applied to Spinoza with the question of how the moral freedom of man can be compatible with the omnicausality of God. If God is the first cause of all events, and as such also the first cause of every stirring of human will, then it would seem to follow either that in human willing there is no element of evil, or that it is God Himself who brings about the evil in man (*Ep.* 18). Spinoza's answer runs: the judgment that something is imperfect, that an action is evil, pre-supposes the application of a standard. Within the thought of God, Whose knowledge of individual objects is not by means of universal ideas, but Who sees all things as they are in themselves, without any abstraction by comparison, there is no place for

judging a thing as imperfect, or an action as evil. When Scripture
nevertheless speaks of God's commands and prohibitions, it is
speech after the manner of men, so that it should be intelligible
to the people. The prophets, taking into account the small capacity
of the multitude, have taught the connection between causes and
effects as the connection between law and retribution (*Ep.* 19).
At this point Blyenburgh finds himself obliged, *before* he enters
into the substantive difficulties, to formulate the *general rules*
which he follows in his philosophizing. These rules are:

   1) The clear and distinct notion of his understanding.

   2) The revealed Word of God.

Should it occur after intensive examination that natural reason
seems to run counter to Scripture, then for him Scripture has so
much authority that he is readier to suspect that his own clear
ideas are erroneous than that Scripture is erroneous. For it is his
intent to hold fast to the faith that Scripture is the word of God.
This he at this point only assumes, since proof is here not in place,
or would require too much time, *and* further he is uncertain in his
own mind whether he might not, by a persisting error, have
deprived himself of a better position, in the sense of one permitting
perfect knowledge. He admits that, following only the light of
natural reason, he would have found himself obliged to accept
the truth of many of Spinoza's expositions, but that, by reason of
his belief in Scripture, he had been compelled to accept the other
view (*Ep.* 20). In the light of this letter, Spinoza recognizes that
Blyenbergh and he adopt opposite views on "the first principles
themselves." For Spinoza, the first principle is "Omnino in eo,
quod mihi intellectus monstrat, acquiesco sine ulla suspicione,
me ea in re deceptum esse" (*Ep.* 21). In other words, he places
full trust in the findings of his own intelligence. This trust is
"the first principle," the pre-condition of all philosophizing,
preceding all substantive considerations. Before philosophizing
can even be begun, belief in revelation, which calls trust in human
reason into question, must itself first be questioned. In this sense
the critique of revealed religion is not the achievement, but the
very basis of free science.

A. The Critique on the Basis of Scripture

Who then is to exercise this critique, if not the philosopher? First
of all, the Biblical exegete. The opponents appeal to Scripture

against reason. They demand that human reason, corrupted by the Fall, be subject to Scripture. This claim made by the opponents must, by reason of that claim itself, be measured by Scripture, and only by Scripture. Spinoza takes up this claim. In his critique of orthodoxy, he takes Scripture as his authority. He takes as the basis of his critique the doctrine that Scripture is a supra-rational revelation. His argument runs: according to the intent of supernatural revelation itself, it is needful to go back to the un-adulterated, the literal meaning of Scripture. For what can we, of ourselves, know of matters which transcend the range of our intelligence? Every human interpretation is as such false and falsifying: mere figments of the human mind, which set themselves up in the place of the pure word of God.[138] In this, Spinoza's critique sets out to perform no other task than to re-establish the genuine authority of Scripture. By so doing, he seeks to limit the authority of Scripture to its own realm, and thus to make philosophy independent of the authority of Scripture.

From the outset, there is mingled with the first task, which Spinoza recognizes clearly in its full significance and in its necessity, a second task, one of a quite different nature: that of establishing what it is that the Scriptures do actually teach, so that the teachings of Scripture may be measured by the standards of objective truth, and by establishing this to arrive at a judgment of the truth of the Scriptures.[140] This admixture of aims is made possible by the fact that both tasks demand recourse to the pure and unadulterated meaning of the Scriptures.[141] It is from this that there spring so many apparent contradictions in the *Tractate*. The resolution of these anomalies in detail is not of great import. But comprehension of Spinoza's whole criticism of religion requires in principle a separation of the criticism *based* on Scripture from the criticism *of* Scripture. The criticism *based* on Scripture is guided by the concept that the "*old* religion" is the perfect religion; and for that reason, recourse to the Scriptures is needful. But criticism *of* Scripture will pin down the opponent to the obvious "prejudices of an *ancient* people," and here the word "ancient" carries the overtone of "barbaric and without culture of the mind"; and for that reason recourse to the Scriptures is needful.[142] In the first case, the only standard is the text itself. In the second case, the only standard is reason itself.

The field within which the criticism will be called upon to work is first of all the Scriptures, the literal meaning of the Scriptures. On the assumption that the Scriptures have the character of revelation, the object submitted to critical judgment is the assertion "The Scriptures are throughout and in every respect true and divine."[143] If it is to the Scriptures alone that we are to refer in the last analysis for a decision on truth or untruth, if reason is subject to the Scripture, and therefore it is not reason which is to sit in judgment and decide, then the teachings of the Scriptures must be in full harmony with one another and devoid of all contradictions. Were it otherwise, we should be called upon to accept and to reject the same statement in one breath. The assertion that the Scriptures are throughout and without exception true and divine compels us, in direct consequence of this character, to make the assertion that the Scriptures at no time and in no place are in contradiction one with another. This conclusion was drawn in orthodox hermeneutics.[144] The orthodox postulate has no basis in Scripture itself. For in the first place, there is no word in the Scriptures themselves that asserts that these Scriptures contain no contradictions, and in the second place, there are in fact very numerous contradictions within the Scriptures. Spinoza takes as his chosen example: Samuel denies, and Jeremiah asserts that God repents of His decisions: "*Utraque sententia universalis est et utrique contraria: quod una directe affirmat, id altera directe negat. Adeoque ipse* [sc. Rabbi Jehuda Alpakhar, the representative of orthodoxy] *ex ipsius regula, hoc ipsum tanquam verum amplecti et simul tanquam falsum rejicere tenetur*" (*Tr.* p. 170). The contradictions cannot be eliminated by means of allegorical interpretation, for the literal meaning of Scripture, by reason of the fact that Scripture communicates supra-rational teachings, can in no sense be meddled with. The conclusion to be drawn is that the Scriptures cannot be true and divine *in every instance*, but only in what is throughout taught *without contradiction*.[145] The Scriptures teach throughout entirely without contradiction, that obedience to the Divine commandment "Love ye one another," manifested in works of justice and charity, is sufficient for salvation. This teaching is in truth suprarational; hence it was needful for man's salvation that it should be revealed. It is in the light of this doctrine that the whole of the Scriptures, and in particular all its contradictions, are in principle to be understood. In order that men should find their way to salvation, God revealed to each the

way to that salvation, and revealed it in the manner required by
the power of comprehension present in those to whom the
revelation was made. God gives reasons for His revelations in
accord with the character of the recipient of God's revelation.
So for the reader of the Scriptures it is not a matter of concern
that the reasons given vary. His concern is with the unvarying,
ever-identical purpose. The purpose is piety, obedience to God's
will, the fulfillment of the divine commandment to justice and
charity.

The Scriptures are the foundation of piety, only of piety. The
Scriptures are not the foundation of philosophy, for philosophy
seeks not after piety, but truth. Thus theology, which has its basis
in the Scriptures, and philosophy are in their bases and in their
aims entirely different, so different that there is no transition and
bridge from one to the other. It is therefore all the more absurd
that theologians, who must not have before them any other goal
than teaching humanity the doctrine of justice and love, should
persecute philosophers with anger and hatred. Thus on the basis
of Scripture, philosophy is liberated from the tutelage of theology,
and in this way philosophy is no longer in bondage as the hand-
maiden of theology.[146]

This much about the nerve of the criticism exercized by
Spinoza, using Holy Writ as the basis of his criticism of orthodoxy.
It is now in place to inquire into the assumptions which did not
come to the foreground in the general survey. The first assumption
is that the Old Testament and the New Testament are equal in
value and in validity. Jewish orthodoxy can invoke against
Spinoza the law of Moses, whose obligatory power is annulled by
Spinoza's restriction of religion to "piety": that restriction
patently runs counter to the teaching of the Old Testament. And
similarly Christian orthodoxy can invoke the "Word of the
Cross."[147] If the writings of the Old Testament and the writings of
the New Testament are in principle to be accepted as of equal
value, then all emphasis shifts to those parts which the two
collections of sacred writings have in common. Those elements in
which the two Testaments diverge—the Law and the "Word of
the Cross"—are now relegated to the realm of indifferent, varying
reasons adduced for the real purpose, varying in accord with the
capacity for comprehension exhibited by the recipients at a given
time. The one and the same religion was revealed by the prophets

before the birth of Christ, by virtue of the Covenant on Sinai, and by the Apostles after the Advent by virtue of the Passion of Christ (*Tr.*, p. 149). On the other hand, although it is not difficult to argue against Mosaic law and Jewish orthodoxy if the New Testament is recognized as the authority, nevertheless Christian orthodoxy can and must take its stand against the equivalence of the Old Testament and the New Testament through which the "Word of the Cross" is brought to naught in favor of the neutral command for obedience. Yet it was indeed Protestant Christian orthodoxy against which the *Tractate*. first leveled its shafts, that orthodoxy which asserted the complete identity of Old Testament and New Testament teachings, the concordance of prophets and Apostles,[148] but in the sense that "the Word of the Cross" was already to be found in the Old Testament. Against this Spinoza could without difficulty find counter-arguments, by recourse to the unadulterated literal meaning of Scripture. The orthodox Protestant doctrine of the complete harmony between the teachings of the prophets and of the Apostles is however only the very derivative result of a conception which has its basis in the "Word of the Cross." That the "Word of the Cross" should take a place subordinate to what is common to both the Old and the New Testaments could in no sense have been imposed on Protestant orthodoxy. In actual fact, Spinoza's assumption has but little to do with any seemingly similar orthodox Protestant thesis. This assumption is only a particular version of the rationalist principle that *consensus* is a criterion of truth. This principle was applied by Spinoza as a means of bringing out the truth contained in Scripture. He takes it in the sense that men are capable of agreement only in so far as they are guided by reason (cf. *Ethica* IV, 35). Immediately there appears the difficulty that the teachings of Scripture as a whole which are in harmony with one another are supra-rational. Full light cannot be cast on this anomaly until Spinoza's analysis of religion has been interpreted. But the critique based on Scripture leads of itself to the finding that what is common to the *whole* of Scripture is rational morality.

By assuming that the Old Testament and the New Testament are of equal value, Spinoza does then not reach the orthodox Protestant (still less the orthodox Jewish) position. He takes his stand against orthodoxy on a peculiarly Christian principle, the spiritual understanding of the Scriptures: "*Christiani omnia quae*

Judaei carnaliter, spiritualiter interpretati sunt" (*Ep.* 75); for Christians
are precisely those upon whose hearts and minds the Word of
God is imprinted, and who therefore have no need, as have the
Jews, to fight for the Law written on tables of stone (*Tr.*, p. 145).
He demands from his Christian opponents as Christians that they
should cease "to worship the letter and to be greatly concerned
with it" (*Tr.*, p. 148). What is needed for salvation is not knowledge of Christ according to the flesh, but knowledge of Christ
according to the spirit, in other words, knowledge of the eternal
wisdom of God made manifest in all things, especially in the
human mind, and most excellently of all in Christ Jesus. The dogmas of the Church are not merely incomprehensible, but even
absurd. The Resurrection is to be interpreted in the spiritual
sense only.[149] The injunction that the Scriptures are to be interpreted "in spirit and in truth" does not veto the steady striving to
penetrate to the literal meaning of the text. At least there is no
contradiction in the cases in which the tenor of the text itself
excludes literal, sensual, carnal understanding. This holds, in
Spinoza's opinion (*Ep.* 75), in particular for the central passage in
chapter 15 of the First Epistle to the Corinthians, from which, in
his view, the right of spiritual and allegorical interpretation of the
Resurrection is cogently derived. The teaching that is revealed
to spiritual interpretation of the Scriptures is, however, not in
any sense the supra-rational doctrine of obedience to God as the
way of salvation, but the very teaching of reason itself. The spirit
that understands Scripture in the spiritual sense, that grasps the
spiritual intent of the Scriptures, is reason. Not only is Scripture
far from asserting that the human mind has been corrupted by
reason of original sin, it must indeed on the basis of Scripture be
asserted that the law revealed by God to mankind by the mediation of prophets and Apostles is nothing other than the law that is
taught also by human reason (*Tr.*, praef., p. 6). On the basis of
this assertion it would seem, in the most extreme formulation,
that the view peculiar to revealed religion—the conception
of God implied in the behest of obedience to the command of
God—is an *innovation* which contradicts Scripture and quenches
the spirit of at least the most weighty parts of the Scriptures.[150]
Thus by showing Scripture to be authority only for piety, investigation of the Scriptures leads not only to the liberation
of philosophy from all theological tutelage, but over and beyond

this, to the corroboration of philosophic truth by the Scriptures.

It is not the Scriptures as a whole which provide the corroboration for philosophy, but only those *parts* of the Scriptures which are themselves philosophic. Taking these portions as point of departure—these portions which lend themselves to strict, spiritual, adequate exegesis—the remainder of the Scriptures are to be understood and dismissed as "spoken only after the manner of men." Now criticism of orthodoxy, in so far as this criticism has recourse to Scripture, must refer back to the harmonious doctrine taught in the Scriptures as a *whole*. That criticism must therefore disregard the difference between the philosophic and the unphilosophic parts of the Scripture (those parts designed to remain within the range of vulgar understanding). According to Spinoza's statement, what precedes this differentiation and is the doctrine common to all part of the Scriptures is the demand that obedience shall be given to God through works of justice and loving-kindness (*Tr.*, p. 164). But obedience requires that we "know" God to exist as the fount of all justice and mercy, and this "knowledge" is not true but adapted to the mental range of the vulgar, and—this is of major import—indeed runs counter to the real meaning of the philosophic parts of Scripture.[151] The concern of the Scripture as a whole can therefore only be to bring about active obedience to God, and this obedience expresses itself only in works of justice and charity. This obedience may be justified in two ways, which stand directly opposed to each other: philosophically, or vulgarly. But what counts is not the justification; but the works. The justification peculiar to the Scriptures in contradistinction to philosophy, hence the justification peculiar to the unphilosophic part of Scripture, but according to Scripture as a whole not obligatory, contains the idea of a just and merciful God. We are free to interpret this idea as we will—for instance, as merely vulgar—provided the interpretation adopted does not serve to make unjust and uncharitable conduct possible and justifiable (*Tr.*, p. 164). Scripture is exclusively concerned with obedience to God in *acts*.

Spinoza reaches this conclusion in the first place by treating the Old Testament and the New as equal in value. Given this premise, the specifically Jewish and the specifically Christian elements are reduced to a minimum; but this premise is arbitrarily assumed over against Judaism and Christianity alike. If Spinoza

recognizes the preeminence of the New Testament for Christians
—and this he manifestly does in numerous passages of the *Treatise*
—then it is only by "spiritual" interpretation of the Scriptures
that he can save himself from the positively Christian element.
But such understanding of the Scriptures must be understanding
of the literal meaning of the words, i.e., the literal meaning
must have a spiritual intention. For this purpose it is sufficient
that *within* the Scriptures there are passages whose primary
intent is spiritual. For these parts then *contradict* the positively
Christian teaching, so that *the* doctrine of the Scriptures is no
longer to be sought in the positively Christian teaching, or
indeed in the philosophic teaching, but in the neutral behest to
active obedience, be that obedience sprung from faith or from
philosophic insight. Spinoza's critique of orthodoxy based on the
Scriptures depends then upon the fact that the teachings of Paul
diverge from the teachings of the other apostles.[152] It is dependent
in the first place on his interpretation of Paul's doctrine. That this
interpretation is in full accord with Spinoza's sincere opinion will
not be doubted in the slightest by anyone acquainted with
Spinoza's writings. What gives his recourse to Scripture its
passionate character is his conviction that he comprehends Paul
and agrees with him, whereas of the Scriptures as a whole he says:
"plane et sine ambagibus profiteor, me S. Scripturam non
intellegere" (*Ep.* 21). On the adequacy of his exegesis of Paul's
teaching depends the significance of that critique of orthodoxy
which is based on Scripture, i.e. which is based on the basis of
that orthodoxy itself.

The core of this critique is the concept: the Scriptures teach
nothing on those matters on which they make conflicting statements. At the points where the Scriptures teach *nothing*, reason
may teach *anything* that it can answer for to itself by its own
standards. The Scriptures provide conflicting teachings on all the
theological tenets over which revealed religion and philosophy are
in conflict. The Scriptures cannot or rather—since God can do all
that He wills—the Scriptures are not intended to tell us anything
about the essence of God. Knowledge of God's essence—since
God in his loving-kindness reveals all things that are needful
for man's salvation—is not necessary for salvation. Speculation
on God's essence is therefore entirely liberated from any tutelage
to theology. Cosmological investigation is freed on the same

ground. The philosophical parts of the Scriptures—here Spinoza
has recourse not to Paul, but to Ecclesiastes, the book of the
"philosopher" Solomon[153]—teach that nature maintains a
fixed and unalterable order, and hence that there are no miracles.
Thus, the assertion of miracles is not a doctrine of *the* Scriptures.
Thus, belief in miracles is not necessary for salvation. No bound is
set to the seeking after natural causes.

But, we may ask, has not Spinoza by his assertion that there are
contradictions contained in the Scriptures already left the plane
which he has in common with his opponents, the plane on which
he must in the first place try to liberate men for philosophizing?
Is he not already by making that assertion denying the authority
of the Scriptures? Assuming the fact that the Scriptures are
revealed, he demands unqualified acceptance of the literal meaning of the Scriptures, and abstention from any arbitrary interpretation. Only after this can he prove that the Scriptures do
contain contradictions. But does it not follow from the revealed
character of Scriptures and thus from their truth that they are *not*
self-contradictory, that therefore one of the contradictory statements must be given an allegorical interpretation? Spinoza might
tranquilly grant that the contradictions are only apparent. He
needed to do no more than to urge that every allegorical interpretation is a falsification of the pure Word of God. He might
have been content to let the matter rest on the assertion that the
teachings of the Scriptures are, it is true, obscure on those questions
that are differently answered at different places within Scripture,
and therefore, if the Scriptures are sufficient guidance for finding
the way to salvation, then these matters cannot in themselves be
necessary for salvation. But what would he gain from so doing?
At most a refutation of orthodox dogmatics. He would be reminding orthodoxy on its own ground that what Scripture requires of
us is not theoretical disquisition, but active piety. To the extent
however that he himself recognizes the authority of Scripture,
he must forbid to himself all pursuit of speculation, as he forbids it
to the orthodox, for active obedience is the one thing needful.
Thus it is not on the basis of Scripture that Spinoza can bring
about the liberation of philosophizing—his real aim.

If the Scriptures are self-contradictory, then no dogmatics can
be based on the Scriptures. That stands beyond doubt. But
equally there can be no free pursuit or philosophic investigation.

That the Scriptures do not offer a single and unambiguous answer to the problem of whether and in what sense God is "free," means no more than that, assuming the recognition of Scriptural authority, this theologem is a mystery, which God has neither unveiled nor wished to unveil to the eyes of man. Then theology cannot extract from Scripture any unambiguous answer with which to oppose the philosophers. On the other hand the philosophers are not justified in venturing in a spirit of punishable pride beyond the limit which God Himself has set.

Spinoza forcibly frees philosophic inquiry from its trammels by *interpreting* the Scriptural utterances which contradict one another as not binding, because adapted to the capacity of the men addressed in the passage in question. This interpretation is not as clearly founded in the Scriptures as is the proof of the contradiction itself. Thus Spinoza cannot take from the Scriptures themselves his reply to the orthodox who counter his interpretation with the argument that it contradicts the veracity, the goodness and the omnipotence of God to leave the prophets in erroneous opinions.[154] The question, Is it fitting for God to adapt His revelation to the false opinions of men, and, if it is indeed fitting, within what limits is He to adapt that revelation? must be decided by the light of reason, before the matter can be argued on the basis of the Scriptures.

But even assuming that the orthodox opponent would be ready to grant this assumption, it would not yet be conceded to him, that even though the Scriptures may in principle prove self-contradictory on matters of speculation, they speak always with one voice in full accord on matters of practice. The divergence between rational morality and the prescripts laid down in the Sermon on the Mount is admitted by Spinoza himself, by the very fact that he is at pains to explain this divergence away. He asserts that in the mind of the speaker these prescripts are intended for men living in a political order already in decay and soon to pass away (*Tr.*, p. 89). Without this forced interpretation Spinoza would not have been able to establish the existence within Scripture of any tenet that runs uncontradicted throughout the whole text, even among such tenets as relate only to practice. He himself therefore proceeds after the manner of believing interpreters, who, in order that the consistency of Scripture shall not be endangered, "falsify" the meaning of the text. His interpretation of the Sermon on the Mount does at least as much violence to the text as does the orthodox interpretation of Paul's teachings on the Resurrection, an interpretation which brings down in ruins the whole edifice of the criticism which Spinoza builds up on the Scriptures. By this it is made clear in decisive examples how little power to convince inheres in this criticism, even if one concedes to Spinoza the benefit of an assumption which is by no means self-evident, i.e. not to be accepted as actually founded in Scripture.

Finally, and above all, the critique based on Scripture assumes that the meaning of the Scriptures, by reason of which orthodoxy may be refuted, is the literal meaning, that is, a meaning which is accessible in equal measure to the devout reader and to the unbeliever. This assumption is a *petitio principii* in the face of any opponent who asserts that genuine interpretation of the Scriptures is possible only on the basis of faith.

B. The Critique on the Basis of Reason
(Critique of Scripture)

1) *Critique of miracles*

If the pursuit of philosophy rests on the self-confidence of reason, on one's readiness to come to rest, "without any suspicion," at what one grasps clearly and distinctly, then we must divide critique of religion into pre-philosophic critique, a critique that sets men's minds free to philosophize, and philosophic critique, which presupposes the freedom to philosophize. Pre-philosophic critique has as its task the awakening or re-awakening of reason to confidence in its own powers. Since reason's confidence in itself is shaken by the prejudice that reason must subject itself to Scripture, it is the task of pre-philosophic critique to do away with this very prejudice. It is in the first place critique on the basis of Scripture. As such its task is to show that the Scriptures do not mean to set a limit to philosophizing. Full subjection to Scripture, the return to the pure word of God, a return well and truly performed, will bring about liberation from the dominance of Scripture. But pre-philosophic critique is not only critique based on Scripture. It can show not only that the authority of Scripture is not of a nature to shake the self-confidence of reason. It can also shake the authority of Scripture. This second task falls within the field of the philosophic critique only in the case where that critique presupposes the constitution of philosophy, but not if through its exercise the constitution of philosophy, liberation to philosophy, is accomplished.

Since it is only men who already have confidence in their own judgement, to whatever results it may lead them, who can begin to philosophize freely, that critique is indeed pre-philosophic, whose aim is limited to the task of providing encouragement. This critique is nothing other than the awakening of reason from its slumber by the clarion call: *sapere aude!* It requires the man, who holds that he must submit his power of reasoning to contra-rational revelation, to awake and make clear to himself what he is about. For what he is doing cannot be made clear. What he does is in itself confused. The reflection shows the absurdity of what he does. For—so runs Spinoza's central argument, which is then more than a mere argument—we subject ourselves to contra-rational revelation either *without* any rational ground for so doing, and then we are acting foolishly and without judgment, or we act on a rational ground, and then we contradict ourselves by recognizing and rejecting reason in one breath; the subjection of reason to the contra-rational is thus completely absurd.[155]

The disjunction "without reason—with reason," on which Spinoza's central proposition rests—characteristically formulated in a single sentence—is complete only if subjection to revelation must have its ground in man himself, in his reason or his unreason. Spinoza's Protestant opponents however assume that true recognition of the authority of revelation rests on "the inner witness of the Holy Spirit," in other words, that its origin is not in man but in God. Therefore they are not reached by Spinoza's argument. True, they concede that apart from the faith wrought by God there exists a "human faith" resting on human thought and reflection, infinitely inferior to the former in its certainty. According to Calvin's *Institutes* human reflections are of value only on the basis of that God-given certainty, and even then only as "very appropriate," but still merely "secondary supports for our weakness." They suffice for refuting arguments against the revealed nature of Scripture. They are insufficient for manifesting the revealed nature of Scripture to unbelievers.[156] Since human arguments are in any case secondary only, and devoid of relevance to the certainty of revelation, Spinoza, by using these, would not, even by a complete refutation, reach the goal at which his critique aims.

Spinoza reckons with the central objection, namely, that recognition of reason is necessary only in argumentation with unbelievers but not for providing the basis for faith itself, which is brought into being by "the inner witness of the Holy Spirit." He says against this that the Holy Spirit of which Scripture speaks bears witness only to good works, and not to subjects of speculation. The Holy Spirit is not a source of theoretical insight.[157] This argument strikes home only in the case of those theologians for whom speculation is not incompatible with faith. The following argument is of more general validity. The supernatural light which vouches for the divine nature of Scripture and which opens up understanding of Scripture is said to be granted to believers only. But the prophets and the Apostles spoke not only to the faithful, but for the most part also to unbelievers.[158] This other statement, equally founded on the Bible, is only another expression of the same thought: the prophets required, as corroboration of the revelation made to them, a *sign*; in other words, the revelation is corroborated by the occurrence of a predicted event. Not only through the sign thus understood, be it said. For in certain circumstances an event may occur which was predicted by a false prophet. Mosaic law therefore requires of the prophet that, apart from the sign, his teaching should be in full accord with the doctrines recognized as divine. An essential characteristic of the sign is that it should be of such a nature as to stir the imagination of men in such a way that they find themselves impelled to wonder and thus to piety, and in particular to recognition of the prophet through whom the sign is given.[159] Since in most cases prophets are addressing themselves to the disbelieving, it is then assumed in Scripture that the sign is a means, even though not in itself a sufficient means, of convincing unbelievers, or in other words, that the decision in the conflict between belief and unbelief is given by the event predicted by faith. The gulf between faith and unfaith is bridged by sensory perception of the event which was predicted by faith, and which has now occurred. Spinoza not only does not say, but expressly denies (*Tr.,*p. 64) that Scripture requires that historical credence be given to signs and wonders occurring in previous ages, or even teaches that such credence is meritorious. But even though the gulf between faith and unfaith in regard to

merit and justice may remain unbridged in all eternity, the
miracle that occurred, the sign that was fulfilled, can be seen
by believer and unbeliever alike, the believer who wishes to see
it, and the unbeliever who is compelled to see it. On this seeing,
which cannot be gainsaid, rests the proof-value, which is asssumed
in Scripture, of the sign. Spinoza has recourse to this assumption in
Scripture, in order to refute the self-evidence of Scripture, the
witness borne by God Himself to Himself, in His sacred book.

By establishing that the prophets address unbelievers as well as
believers, and indeed especially unbelievers, and that the prophets
are successful in convincing unbelievers, Spinoza proves that faith
and unfaith have some ground in common. By further establishing
that signs are necessary, even though not sufficient, criteria of
prophetic revelation, the common ground is demonstrated as such.
This common ground is "mere experience."[160] The choice of this
designation is partially conditioned for Spinoza from the outset
by his bearing in mind the nature of philosophic knowledge,
measured against which mere experience is rejected in advance.
Through this rejection revealed religion, as founded on mere
experience, is also condemned in its entirety.

If therefore one bears in mind from the outset this rejection of
revealed religion in its character of merely empirical certainty,
any detailed analysis of Spinoza's critique of religion will be
superfluous. However, Spinoza by no means contents himself with
this summary rejection of the certainty of revealed religion. He
provides a detailed critique of revealed religion, precisely on the
ground of mere experience, without having recourse to the
condemnation in principle of empirical certainty. This critique
must be understood in itself, in its intention, its justification and
its bearing.

Revealed religion is *positive* religion, grounded in experience.
The critique devoted to it is therefore positive critique. On the
basis of experience, this critique opposes the attempt to found
revelation on experience, and it opposes not only the particular
empirical basis of the particular Biblical revelation, but also—by
becoming self-conscious of empirical awareness (which thus
becomes positive consciousness)—it contests any empirical
foundation of revelation at all. Therewith, since revelation in the
sense prevailing in Scripture is empirically founded, the critique
contests revealed religion itself.

Scripture justifies its assertions by "mere experience." This does not amount merely to stating that the authority of the prophets is corroborated by the occurrence of signs. It states generally that in Scripture all teachings, the teachings referring to creation and to providence, are based on experience only.[161] To convince the heathens that the visible gods to whom they paid worship (sun, moon, elements) are powerless and insubstantial, and that they are subject to the rule of an invisible God, the Jews told their miracles. Scripture therefore makes miracles the basis of its theologems. It is by miracles that the existence and essence of God, and therefore God's providence are most clearly to be known. To the theology founded on the experience of miracles, Spinoza opposes his theology which stands rooted in awareness of the stable and unchanging order of nature. He sets out to prove: that God's essence and existence, and consequently His providence, cannot be known from miracles but can be much better perceived from the fixed and immutable order of nature (*Tr.*, p. 68). Here we meet again the opposition we saw in Lucretius' confrontation of the religious and the scientific world-view: the world as the work of spontaneously and suddenly appearing, discontinuously willing, working forces, and as such not surveyable by man, causing anguish and confusion; and the world as fixed and unchanging eternally identical order, thus in principle within the range of human conceptions, and as such not disquieting but rather offering tranquillity of mind.

The first task of Spinoza's critique is thus an investigation of what power of proof resides in miracles. Can God be known from miracles? Is a theology founded on miracles possible at all? To answer this question requires that the Biblical concept of miracle be defined. In this concept Spinoza sees these moments:

1) God and nature are to be distinguished as two powers. So long as God acts, nature remains inert, and vice versa, even though God had in a particular sense determined nature, or even created nature.

2) The two powers, God and nature, stand in such a relation one to the other, that God exercises a kind of dominion over nature, that "the power of nature has as it were been subjugated by God."

3) Therefore miracles demonstrate to a higher degree than the order of nature does, the existence, the power and the providence

of God. "Miracles" and the "works of God" are one and the same: at least miracles are to a higher degree the works of God than is the order of nature.

4) The original aim served by the assertion of miracles is to prove that man, and in particular the Jews, are the final cause of all creation (*Tr.*, p. 67).

The historical characterization of this conception of miracles as Biblical is contradicted, however, by what Spinoza expressly teaches in the same context in which he expounds this conception of miracles: Scripture understands by God's action nothing other than the order of nature, which necessarily results from eternal laws. In proof of this, he adduces the following points:

1) Some of the miraculous occurrences that are recounted in Scripture can be explained naturally, by taking into account other circumstances that also happen to be recounted in the same text: from this we can assume—since it is only by chance that accompanying circumstances have been recounted—that in the case of all other miracles matters would stand no differently.

2) Scripture refers to natural events as works of God.

3) In some passages, Scripture uses parabolic expressions.

4) Scripture teaches "in some passages about nature in general that it maintains a fixed and immutable order."

5) Nowhere does Scripture expressly teach that anything occurs which contradicts the laws of nature (*Tr.*,pp. 68, 75–77, 81–82).

The four arguments first adduced offer obviously inadequate proof. The first and the third arguments merely prove that many events traditionally interpreted as miracles are not regarded by Scripture as miracles. The second argument proves only that Scripture regards the natural events, not only the miracles, as God's works. The fourth argument, characteristically enough, rests mainly on evidence drawn from Ecclesiastes, by the "philosopher" Solomon, and hence on the philosophical part of Scripture, and, according to Spinoza himself, the philosophical part offers no possible material for conclusions to be drawn regarding the "vulgar" part of Scripture. The fifth argument proves more than the four which precede it. But even it does no more than prove that Scripture does not know the *traditional* conception of miracles, which presupposes the development of the concept of nature, even of "laws of nature." It does not prove that, once the concept of nature has developed, Biblical accounts may not be interpreted in the sense of the traditional concept of miracles. How little Spinoza finds himself at ease in this critique of miracles which is based on Scripture is made apparent by his remark (*Tr.*, p. 77) that those passages in Scripture that unhesitatingly report on miracles as contra-natural or supernatural events must have been interpolated in the holy book by sacrilegious men. This remark directly opposes his whole principle of interpretation, that objective truth may not be used as the key for interpreting Scripture. By making that remark, Spinoza is regressing to the stage of da Costa's critique of the Bible, in which all portions of Scripture which conflict with reason are to be excised as late additions, as forgeries. But quite apart from the fact that the critique of miracles on the basis of Scripture is in direct contradiction with Spinoza's principle, he expressly states that the conception of miracles, on which he expatiates at the beginning of this critique, "originated in the earliest Jews" (*Tr.*, p. 67), by which none other than the Biblical teachers can be meant. He means nothing else when he says (*Tr.*, pp. 73 f.), also in the context of his critique of miracles, that almost all prophets had no more than a very confused conception of Divine providence.

The observation that the traditional conception of miracles cannot be derived directly from Scripture remains important. On the basis of the traditional conception of miracles, contemporary apologetics turns against the conception of miracles as expounded by Spinoza.[162] The traditional concept of miracles presupposes the conception of nature, i.e. the constitution of philosophy. Therefore from the outset Spinoza can contest this conception on a ground which he cannot occupy when contesting the Scriptural conception of miracles. The inadequacy of "mere experience" is, as it were, granted to him from the outset. The common ground from now onwards is *reason*.

Revealed religion interprets the revelation recorded in Scripture with more or less express, but always effective regard for philosophy, which exists independently of revelation and which is the work of unassisted human reason, as either rational or contra-rational or supra-rational. The interpretation of revelation as rational is characteristic of the "dogmatists"; for the time being we are concerned with the "skeptics," with those who demand that reason shall be subject to contra-rational or supra-rational revelation. The interpretation of revelation as contra-rational is

possible only if there is a ground for the authority of revelation
that is independent of reason, independent of man; otherwise
Spinoza's central argument, according to which rational justification of contra-rational revelation is absurd, comes into force;
the second alternative is proved to be actual by the peculiarly
Scriptural manner of establishing its theologems. Spinoza's central
argument is of no avail against the rational justification of
supra-rational justification, and orthodoxy assumes that revelation
is supra-rational, not contra-rational.[163] Orthodoxy thus in
principle concedes the right of reason. Spinoza has then from
the outset the possibility of constructing his philosophy on the
basis of reason, of course on the assumption that he does in
fact construct his philosophy in accord with the dictates of reason.
By his philosophy the possibility of revelation is excluded. The
denial of revelation is the result of the system developed in the
Ethics. Compared with it any other critique of revealed religion is,
it seems, superficial, superfluous and confusing. This was certainly Spinoza's conviction. In constructing his system, *he* was
not confused by dogma or by texts from Holy Writ. But others
were, even the "the more prudent sort," to liberate whom into
the freedom of philosophy was his chief concern. He was therefore
bound, as a first step, before he began to propound *his* philosophy
which was naturally for him philosophy *tout court*, to undermine
the authority of Scripture on the basis of reason, but not as yet on
the basis of reason developed into philosophy, i.e. his philosophic
system—in a word, on a basis of "common sense."

The conviction that there exists a revelation to which reason
must bow has, for Spinoza, the character of a prejudice. Liberation
of the mind from prejudice is accomplished by a free, in other words,
an unprejudiced examination of prejudice.[164] Is freedom from
prejudice therefore the prerequisite of liberation from prejudice?
Between the freedom which is the prerequisite of criticism, and the
freedom which is the result of criticism, there remains the distinction that the former is void and open: it does not even exclude
the possibility that the content of the theological prejudices will
withstand examination. But once they are examined, "prejudices"
are no longer prejudices. The first prerequisite for free investigation is thus not rejection of revelation, but a farewell to all that
has been taken over as truth without critical examination. The
prejudice-free test of prejudice is "free of presuppositions" in

the sense that its presupposition, the resolve to apply reason when facing an opponent who himself recognizes the right of reason, stands in no need of justification.

The opponent who in principle recognizes the right of reason has another conception of miracles than the one which Spinoza discovers in Scripture. With his assertion of the existence side by side of nature and of miracles, he does not intend that nature is as it were only subsequently conquered and made subject to God. According to his doctrine, nature itself exists only by virtue of God's will. Not only the miracle, but all natural events whatsoever manifest the power of God. God, in His perfect wisdom and in His perfect freedom, established the order of nature. Therefore He and He only is able to set aside the order of nature. All creation has its ultimate ground in the power of the Creator: but the power of the Creator is not exhausted in creation. If God could not perform miracles, He would not be free and omnipotent. Miracles are therefore events which do not originate in the power which God has made inherent in nature, they originate directly in God's action which does not employ the natural forces created by Him. Miracles are acts of God against the natural order, or external to the natural order (*contra vel praeter naturam*). If therefore miracles are real, if, in addition, it can be known that the occurrences which are then to be characterized as miracles cannot have arisen out of any finite cause, then by the fact of miracles we directly infer the existence of God. The miracles which are possible by virtue of God's freedom and omnipotence become actual in the context of "special providence": the miracles are a means of turning men's minds to the truths of salvation, of making the truths of salvation enter into the hearts and minds of men. Thus miracles on their side confirm the truth of revealed religion. They must be knowable as miracles also and in particular for this very purpose. But there are facts—such as recalling the dead to life, the path through the Red Sea, Joshua's miracle—which are evidently supernatural.[165]

Whatever may be the difference between this and the Biblical conception of miracles, they have in common two decisive moments: 1) the assumption that God rules the world or nature like a king, that He treats the world with more than kingly freedom, and can intervene how and when He will;[166] 2) the assertion that the miracle carries in itself its power to prove, even where there is no pre-existing faith. This agreement is the justification for Spinoza to content himself with a summary criticism that all but disregards the points of difference. We must also not take it amiss that he asserts without qualification that miracles are the foundation of revealed religion. For, apart from the fact that in central passages of Scripture the miracle occurs as the necessary and sufficient proof for the unbelieving, his devout opponents raise the objection to his critique of miracles that miracles and miracles only are capable of corroborating revelation.[167] It is only to this objection that Spinoza returns the answer, summarizing the result of his critique, that the certainty of revelation can be established only by the inner truth of the doctrine revealed, but not by miracles, i.e. cannot be founded on ignorance: ignorance is the basis of superstition (*Ep.* 73). Here we must recall that Spinoza throughout the whole *Tractate* always co-intends under "superstition" the traditional revealed religion. In a word: when Spinoza asserts that miracles are the basis of revealed religion, or when he formulates this more precisely, that the common run of men believe that there is no clearer proof of the existence of God than miracles, he is, in so doing, striking home at the position which he is contesting.[168]

If anything is to be proven from miracles, then the miracle as miracle must be knowable to reason unguided by faith. Reason must be able to establish that a particular occurrence could not have come to pass as a result of natural causes. In other words, the limits of the power of nature must be fully known. How should these be fully known? Certainly not by the failure to uncover the natural causes of an event. For what is thereby proved is that the laws of nature as known to us, *so far* known to us, are insufficient for the explanation of the event in question. And it is indeed the case that not all the laws of nature are as yet known to us. Hence no conclusion whatsoever can be drawn from the fact that the natural causes of an event are unknown to us. Rather is it the case that we cannot from this conclude that the cause sought is supernatural. From a determinate effect it is at the most only permissible to assume as cause one which has greater power than the effect brought about, but there is no ground for assuming a cause of infinite power. The alternative remains open that the event which is marveled at as a miracle arises from the effect of many causes of smaller power which work in unison (*Tr.*, pp. 71 f., *Ep.* 75). For reason, no proof can then be adduced that a miracle has occurred. Rather is it characteristic of reason, which knows nothing of supernatural acts of God, but which has knowledge of many natural causations, to assume in each case that a natural causal nexus of a kind hitherto unknown is in operation, rather than to assume the presence of a miracle. Even the recall to life of a corpse already in process of decay—contemporary Catholic theology still makes use of this example[169]—would be for Spinoza nothing other than a *problem.* From his insight into "human weakness" there follows for him indeed *not* a readiness to assume miracles, but rather suspension of judgment.[170]

The assumption on which the traditional conception of miracles rests is the possibility of final and conclusive judgments on what is possible within nature. This possibility seems to be rejected in principle by Spinoza. However he does not hesitate to assert in regard to certain events reported in Scripture that, as one can apodictically demonstrate, they contradict the laws of nature, or could not have followed from them (*Tr.*, p. 77). Thus even in spite of all the inconclusiveness or even the changeability in results of scientific investigations, there are certain fundamental facts established by natural science which are not subject to concrete doubt, and which remain unimpaired, whatever may be the further progress made in scientific knowledge. At least Spinoza assumes this to be the case. He therefore cannot but come to the conclusion that certain events reported in Scripture are recognizably in contradiction with the natural order, or stand outside that order.[171] His criticism of the knowability of miracles as miracles is then defective. This defect is remedied by the following consideration: If the natural causes known to us do not suffice as explanation of an occurrence which is asserted to be a miracle, nothing can be inferred from this. It is rather a case for suspending judgment. Miracles do not happen at the present time, at least not for the Jew or the Protestant. According to the view of all those who believe in revelation, the exceptional events recorded in Scripture were real occurrences. But to us they are known only as reported. We know something of the manner in which men report on events which have beyond doubt actually occurred. Their preconceived opinions, their emotions, their interests exercise an influence on their reports. These factors must be taken

into account when we interpret reports on miracles, so that we
may arrive at sharp discrimination between the matters of fact
which underlie the account, and the prejudices which influence
the account, which are not founded on the matter of fact recounted
(*Tr.*, pp. 77 f.). The miracles we know from the Bible thus give
us no ground to consider the natural causes known to us, and still
less natural causes in themselves as inadequate for the explanation
of these miracles, since it is not even established to what extent
the miracles actually occurred and to what extent they are
figments of imagination.

Does this amount to asserting that only historical criticism
makes criticism of the knowability of miracles compelling, and in
so doing, destroys the demonstrative power of miracles? Yes and
no. No, to the extent that it is not necessary to test each miracle
by historical and philological criticism. For then there would
remain open in principle the possibility that miracles are recognizable as such, and therefore have value as proof. This possibility
is excluded by the fundamental historical reflection that is entirely
independent of all detailed historical and philological criticism,
namely that Scripture embodies (is adapted to) "the prejudices of
a people living in *ancient* times" (*Tr.*, p. 166), that the idea of
miracles seems "to originate among the *earliest* Jews" (*Tr.*, p. 67).
The fact that miracles do not occur in present times—which fact
can be made readily comprehensible within revealed religion on
grounds of theology and the economy of salvation—is interpreted
on the basis of living experience of progress in knowledge of
nature as follows: miracles cannot occur in the present time,
because they would not be capable of withstanding present-day
precise observation and exact analysis. The fact is interpreted on
the basis of living experience of progress in the natural sciences,
from which standpoint the matter not understood appears to be as
not *yet* understood. No living experience of miracles opposes this
type of experience. Experience of miracles proves to be linked
with the age in which exact scientific investigation was unknown,
with the age of "ignorance" and "barbarism." In that age,
thought is dominated by imagination and by passions, and not
ordered by clear and distinct insight and rational planning. On
the basis of this essentially historical self-awareness, the positive
mind finds itself—independently of all secondary, inconclusive
philological and historical criticism applied to miracles and which,

in principle, leave the question open—unmovable by all reports on miracles, and therefore by all experience of miracles. To the positive mind it is plain that the prophets and the apostles did not view and analyze the events which they report with the same sobriety and severity which that mind brings to bear on events observed.

Up to this point stress has been laid only on the fact that in Spinoza's interpretation experience is the appropriate field for argument on the part of the Biblical teachers, because, in the main, it is the unbelievers who are to be convinced. Now we must note that the unbelievers whom the Biblical teachers attempt to convince are the ignorant, the unschooled, or those belonging to the vulgar. The method of argument peculiar to Scripture is not scientific, but vulgar. For vulgar thinking, a matter is understood if it is familiar, ordinary, and therefore not astonishing. Vulgar explanation proceeds, therefore, by recalling a resemblance between the matter that is striking by reason of its unusual character, and something else that is familiarly known, and, as such, in no sense astonishing. In this unmethodical haphazard method of thinking and explaining we have the root of the Biblical conception of miracles, in accord with which any fact is to be called a miracle, if there is no analogy for it in facts already known by familiarity. This vulgar conception of miracles is that of the ancients.[172] The historical characterization has a twofold meaning: old, in the sense of "original," "genuine," "pure," and as such the standard for revealed religion, which has as its sole reason the message of revelation; and old, in the sense of pristine, original, primitive, raw, untutored, and therefore to be rejected by the educated scientific consciousness.

This historical characterization, and therewith the critique, is corroborated and confirmed by a comparison between the miracles of the Bible and the miracles of the heathen (Tr., p. 82). Either the improbability which is attributed to the pagan miracles compromises also the Biblical miracles; or, if the reality of the pagan "miracles" as works of magicians or demons is recognized, the area of attack is broadened. Skepticism in regard to the reality of magic, witchcraft, devils and angels (such skepticism has subsequently become so commonplace that it can be described as characteristic of modern consciousness) increased skepticism in regard to miracles. For of such "miraculous" beings Scripture and tradition spoke in much the same manner as of miracles. Was it not an objection against experience of miracles that there existed also an "experience" of witchcraft? Once skepticism had found an entry there was no foreseeable end to the working of skepticism. The authority of Scripture was shaken prior to all historical and philological criticism, but also prior to all metaphysics, through the establishment of the positive mind, through the disenchantment of the world and through the self-awareness of the disenchanting mind.

In order to bring out the character of the positive critique of miracles which is already substantially present in Spinoza, we have taken into account elements of that criticism which are beyond those found in Spinoza's argument. It must be noted that in Spinoza that critique is built on denial of the possibility of miracles on the conviction that he can demonstrate the impossibility of miracles. But that critique does not depend on this metaphysical support.[173] Taken only by itself, that criticism does not and cannot prove the impossibility of miracles. It merely proves that miracles are not recognizable as such by the truly unbelieving mind which does not openly assume—or surreptitiously smuggle in—an element of faith. Reason devoid of faith, engaged in the pursuit of scientific inquiry, shows itself as immune to miracles. The assertion of miracles, as trespassing beyond the bounds set to strict experience that can be tested, is rejected as asserting too much. To speak more precisely, miracles can be rejected only on the ground that these events are seen as occurring for a state of consciousness which is not capable of strict scientific investigation of experience. So it is not the advancing positive method, proceeding from point to point, but only the reflection of the positive mind on itself, the recognition by the positive mind that it represents a progress beyond the previously prevailing form of consciousness (a finding that first takes the form of the crude antithesis between superstition, prejudice, ignorance, barbarism, benightedness on the one hand, and reason, freedom, culture, enlightenment on the other) which creates a position impregnable to proof by miracles.

2) *The critique of the teachings of Scripture*

Spinoza's free examination of Scripture, taking place on the plane of reason, is still a critique of Scripture even if it should lead to full recognition of its authority. It may be divided into the critique of the mode of establishing the authority of Scripture (the critique of miracles) and the critique of the teachings thus founded.

The critique of miracles is by intention the more radical critique. As critique of the foundation it includes a critique of what has been founded, a critique of the teachings of Scripture. The teachings founded on miracles lack a foundation, are baseless. It has already been shown that the positive critique of miracles becomes conclusive by the proof that Scripture is "vulgar." Thus the critique of miracles proves to be itself part of the critique of the teachings of Scripture. The relation between the critique of miracles and the critique of the teachings of Scripture must therefore be more precisely determined. Within the limits set by the positive critique of miracles, for proof that Scripture is vulgar, it is sufficient to take into account those Scriptural passages which relate to nature. Spinoza takes as typical the miracle accorded to Joshua. This miracle is founded on the vulgar prejudice that the sun revolves round the earth, and the earth remains at rest. By this observation, the suspicion is engendered that the experience presupposing the vulgar prejudices is itself vulgar. In order to engender that suspicion it is then sufficient to measure those passages of Scripture that contain statements on nature against scientific insight methodically acquired. The theological teachings of Scripture may therefore be left entirely out of consideration. This distinction is not an arbitrary one. In two different passages of the *Tractate*, Spinoza analyzes the account of the miracle ascribed to Joshua as typical, and with the same intention in both cases: first, in connection with the general proof that the prophets were in possession of no more than vulgar insight into matters speculative (*Tr.*,pp. 21 f.), i.e. in connection with the critique of the teachings of Scripture, and then again in connection with the critique of miracles (*Tr.*, p. 78). In the second discussion the report in question is expressly quoted as the single example of how prejudices condition the accounts given in Scripture. And it is not a matter of chance that the only example that Spinoza treats in the context of his critique of miracles should be one that demonstrates a clash between natural science and Scripture. Above all, in the first discussion the criticism of the scientific (and mathematical) insight of the Biblical teachers is clearly and expressly differentiated from the subsequent criticism of the theological teachings of the Bible.[174] For the positive criticism of miracles, criticism of the scientific views advanced in Scripture is then sufficient. Positive criticism of miracles then on its own part undermines the theological teaching of Scripture, since it is especially by miracles that God is to be shown as the *Lord* of the world. From "miracles" nothing whatsoever can be proved, and hence in particular not the central theologem of Scripture. This does not amount to asserting that the teaching based on miracles is false, or that the teaching could not be unimpeachably proved in some other mode. Therefore direct criticism of the theological teaching contained in Scripture is not superfluous.

Spinoza's assertion that the opinions of God held by the prophets were very vulgar, is aimed at the anthropomorphisms and anthropopathisms of Scripture (*Tr.*, pp. 23–28). To the extent that in the present context we are concerned only with that critique which does not presuppose the constitution of philosophy, i.e. the system of the *Ethica*, this first argument must be understood to mean that it measures the opinions advanced by the prophets on the subject of God by the traditional theology, that it discloses the contradiction between the theological tradition, which is based on Scripture, and Scripture itself. The proof of this contradiction has in this context of the critique of Scripture a sense opposed to the one it has in the context previously treated, of the critique based on Scripture. In the first case, Spinoza emphasizes those elements of Scripture which he prefers to the opposed opinions put forward in the tradition, those portions which he can demonstrate to be in complete contrast with tradition, i.e. the "ancient religion." In the present case he is concerned to lay bare the "prejudices of an ancient people," which contemporary orthodoxy cannot subscribe to in any way. Spinoza's mode of procedure is therefore not self-contradictory, since both of these occur in Scripture, "pure doctrine" and "prejudices," quite apart from the fact that in each of the two cases his argument proceeds on a different plane. The second argument of the critique of the teaching of Scripture runs: the prophets contradict each other in their opinions of God (*Tr.*, pp. 35–44). Taken as a whole, the assertion of this critique amounts to stating that there is in revealed religion no teaching on the subject of God that could guide and hold in check speculation on God, since there exists no single-voiced teaching within revealed religion. Scripture and the tradition contradict each other, the various prophets contradict each other.

Furthermore, the various revealed religions contradict each other. The Jews make their appeal to tradition, which is said to go back to the prophets themselves. The Catholics refer to the authority of the Pope. The Jewish tradition is denied by the *oldest* sects of the Jews, the authority of the Pope is denied by *earliest* Christians. Therefore both authorities are questionable.[175] The arguments adduced for the truth of revealed religion always speak, and must always speak, for the truth of a *single* revealed religion. Therefore in fact these arguments speak for *no* revealed religion, since they never speak for one and for one only. Does the consensus of an unaccountable number of men speak for the Catholic church, as does the uninterrupted tradition, and the great number of martyrs? The same reasons may be adduced with at least equal weight for Judaism. Does the fact that untutored and ordinary men have converted almost the whole world to Christianity speak for the Catholic Church? So it speaks for all Christians, but this means, as Christendom is itself divided into many sects and confessions, all of which fight one another with the greatest possible bitterness, that it speaks for none. If it is not argument, but faith itself that is to have the last word, the same decision is inescapable. Each revealed religion considers its own faith to be the only true faith, and each of them is equally justified, in the sense that no single one offers a sufficient reason. Before what tribunal shall this conflict be resolved? Scripture? But so many and so completely opposed sects, which persecute each other as enemies of God, have their recourse to Scripture (*Tr.*, p. 159; *Ep.* 76). Revealed religion is essentially particular. Each revealed religion therefore regards that element in which it departs from the other revealed religions as the most important. The individual revealed religions call each other into question, they refute each other. There is therefore no need for reason to refute them individually. Reason is not opposed by the majesty of one single revelation, but by a number of theological systems, each of which is believed by its adherents to be the only true religion, and is defended against all other religions with narrow-minded zeal.

But what here speaks against belief speaks also against reason. The argument put forward by Spinoza in the above-mentioned letter to Albert Burgh (*Ep.* 76) against the Catholic Church, against all churches, is only an answer to Albert Burgh's own objection to Spinoza's philosophy, and to all philosophies: each philosopher has recourse to reason, and not one of them succeeds in convincing the other (*Ep.* 76).[176] Are there not, within philosophy, just as many sects, which are unable to convince each other, as in revealed religion? In principle, the philosophic have the intent to convince each other and may have in principle the possibility of doing it for they make their appeal to "what is common to all men" and to no other tribunal; nevertheless they do not in fact convince each other. If the conflict of the revealed religions among themselves represents an objection to revealed religion itself, then the "anarchy of systems" is quite as compelling an argument against systematic philosophy itself. Only positive science has a right to make this objection, since, unlike systematic philosophy it has not only by claim but in actual fact the power to convince all those who are in any sense open to science. Only to the extent to which Spinoza is determined to construct his system in the spirit of positive science, and as itself strictly scientific, and subjects himself to scientific scrutiny in consequence, is he with greater right entitled to raise this objection than his opponents who believe in revealed religion. This objection thus precedes essentially the constitution of his philosophy, as appears also from the fact that it is common to the whole radical Enlightenment. Spinoza makes it more acute on the plane of positive criticism only by not leaving matters at the contradictions of the various revealed religions—the proof of this contradiction plays only a minor role—but by laying bare the contradiction between the individual prophets, the contradictions within Scripture itself.

3) *The philological-historical critique*

Positive criticism, as criticism of the supra-rational teaching justified by miracles, is independent of philological and historical criticism. The criticism of the basis (critique of miracles) and the critique of the teachings of Scripture (proof of the contradictions between the teachings of the various prophets, and between Scripture and traditional theology) is independent of whether Moses is the writer of the Pentateuch, or whether the text of Scripture has come down to us uncorrupted and without spurious additions. It is thus not a matter of chance that Spinoza comes to

treat philological and historical criticism only in Chapters VIII–
X, after the critique of the teachings of Scripture in Chapter II
and the critique of miracles in Chapter VI.

Critique of the teaching of Scripture does not require that it be
completed by philological and historical critique. Its aim is to
prove that there is no teaching in Scripture, since there is no
single unanimous teaching. Therefore that critique is complete in
itself. For either the contradiction has been proved, or it has not
been proved. The proof is not a matter of probability, of such a
nature that its validity might be strengthened or weakened by
argument from another side. The case of the critique of miracles
is different. Spinoza's critique of the knowability of miracles leaves
some openings. This critique presupposes that the limits set to
nature are not known to us, even though Spinoza himself must
admit that many events reported in Scripture cannot be understood as the results of what is naturally possible. The formal
contradiction makes the formal conclusion questionable, but
does not make the intent of the critique questionable: the spirit
of examination, the spirit of accurate observation, reminding us of
the factual limitation of our knowledge of nature, warns us against
drawing a facile conclusion, because an event cannot *at the
time* be explained by natural causes, that this impossibility is
absolute; by so doing, that spirit attains to consciousness of itself,
of its essential difference from the vulgar mind, which is far from
sharing its concern with observation and analysis, which does not
conscientiously distinguish between what is experience and what
is imagined—in a word, from the spirit which he believes is the
one found in the Scriptural accounts of miracles. Thus it follows
that miracles are indeed formally recognizable as such; but the
miracles in question are known to us only as reported, as reported
by unscientific minds, by men who performed their "miracles"
or recounted them so as to give guidance to a people lacking
scientific culture. Therefore it is very much to be doubted whether
the miracles actually occurred. This proof has no more than the
character of probability. As such it can be corroborated or undermined by arguments of a different kind. Miracles are known to us
only as reported. Who reports these miracles? Eyewitnesses, or
men of a much later age? Were they persons of authority, whose
utterances carry weight, or unimportant scribes, perhaps completely unknown, whose credibility is very slight considering the

fact that they transmit to us matters which are so hard to believe.

The question thus couched, one understands why orthodoxy, Jewish and Christian, attached so much weight to the view that Moses is the author of the Pentateuch. It becomes understandable that casting doubt on whether Moses was in fact the author of the Pentateuch, the foundation of revealed Scripture, was taken as tantamount to doubting that the Law was revealed.[177] What was at stake was not only to safeguard miracles, but prior to that and above all to safeguard revelation itself. Spinoza's relevant critique will be treated in detail in the chapter on his Bible science. Here we do no more than inquire into the principles of the critique which comes to its climax in the proof that Moses is not the author of the Pentateuch, that the text of Scripture has not come down to us pure and unadulterated.

When Spinoza raises the objection (*Tr.*, ch. viii) that neither Moses' authorship of the Pentateuch, nor the inspired character of every word, nor the uncorrupted character of the text, can be asserted on the basis of Scripture, and in accord with the meaning of Scripture, he fails to recognize the inner necessity that leads from Scripture itself to those very "prejudices" which he is attacking. The validity claimed for Mosaic Law is dependent on its having been transmitted by Moses on God's command to the people as God's command. The Mosaic origin of the law proper must therefore remain certain beyond all doubt. Further, the revelation on Sinai is not to be separated from the previous miraculous freeing of the Israelites from bondage in Egypt, nor from the history of the Patriarchs. The historical parts of the Pentateuch must therefore claim the same certainty and truth as the purely legal parts. In particular, numerous events of Moses' own time and of post-Mosaic times are presented as the fulfillment of promises and predictions occurring in the times of the patriarchs. If the Pentateuch in all its parts is no more than the production of a much later age, in which the events promised and prophesied had already occurred, then these "promises" and "prophecies," on which the "fulfillment-character" of the events is based, are forgeries. If it were possible in principle to consider specific passages of the Pentateuch as interpolations of a later age, then the concrete prophecies—and these in particular—would be exposed to the suspicion that they came into being at a later time, *ex eventu*. From the fact that not only the truth, but the veracity[178] of Scripture depends on whether the utterances accepted as prophecy are indeed prophecies, we immediately understand the necessity and the meaning of the assertion that the actual text of Scripture has come down to us pure and entire from its source in revelation.

In the circumstances, the proof that the Pentateuch goes back in the main to Ezra, "a man of only average intelligence"[179] (or even to some entirely unknown, and therefore by no means authoritative author), amounts to annihilating critique of the claim made for the validity of Mosaic Law. But what is Spinoza actually proving? In fact, nothing more than that it is not *humanly* possible that Moses wrote the Pentateuch, and that the text of a book should come down to us through the centuries without any corruption of the text at any single passage. This is not denied by the opponents. They actually admit it by assertions that God verbally inspired Scripture, and that God, by His providence, has preserved Scripture uncorrupted and entire.[180] Philological and historical critique cannot undermine the principle of verbal inspiration, nor, for the same reason, the teaching that Moses is the writer of the Pentateuch, by way of direct argument; for on the assumption that Scripture is revealed, it is more apposite to assume an unfathomable mystery, rather than corruption of the text, as the reason for obscurity of a particular passage. Given the interest in revelation, interpretations that seem to the "objective," "unprejudiced" readers arbitary and far-fetched, are preferable to doubt of revelation with all its unforeseeable consequences for life. The importance of philological and historical critique therefore consists only in displacing the core of the argument to very remote, if necessary, consequences. What, for instance, has it to do with the core of revealed religion, that the town which did not receive the name Dan until the time of the Judges is already called Dan in Genesis (cf. *Tr.*, p. 107)? In this manner the decision on the most important matters is made dependent on trifles. The omnipotence, the wisdom, the unfathomable mystery of God must be called on for aid, in order to avoid the admission that the text of Scripture is at any point corrupt. From this point of view it is easy to understand how mockery came to play so great a role in critique of religion in the Age of Enlightenment. The Enlightenment, as Lessing put it, had to laugh orthodoxy out of a position from which it could not be driven by any other means. For the assertion that God is omnipotent cannot be refuted, but the contrast between divine omnipotence and the use of that omnipotence to inspire Moses with the name of a town or a mountain, which that town or mountain will bear only long after the death of Moses, is matter for laughter. The assertion that God's wisdom is unfathomable cannot be refuted. But the contrast between the unfathomable wisdom of God and the obscurity of Scriptural texts, which lose their mystery through (humanly speaking) the obvious, unobjectionable, even necessary admission that the text is corrupt, is matter for laughter. The assertion that God can perform miracles and did perform miracles cannot be refuted. But the resemblance between the fantastic feats of Samson and the fantastic ascent of Elijah into heaven in a chariot of fire, with the deeds of derring-do of Orlando Furioso or the story of Perseus, as told by Ovid, has a comic effect.[181]

C. The Premises and the Limitation of the Critique of Orthodoxy

The critique of orthodoxy is a critique of the "prejudice" that reason must subject itself to the supra-rational revelation laid down in Scripture. Its task is to liberate men's minds, held fast in that prejudice, so that they may philosophize freely. Therefore this critique cannot presuppose the constitution of philosophy (in other words, of Spinoza's philosophy). This critique is in the first place critique on the basis of Scripture, and afterwards critique of Scripture. In the second case, the basis is experience, empirical reason, the methodically proceeding experience of positive science. We shall denote the critique carried out on this basis as *positive* critique, to distinguish it from metaphysical critique, which presupposes the constitution of the system set out in the *Ethics*.

The critique of orthodoxy stands or falls by resolutely keeping the opponent to the literal meaning of the text of Scripture. Only after this has been accomplished can Spinoza undertake to prove that Scripture is vulgar (the critique of miracles depends on this proof), that Scripture contradicts itself, that the text is corrupt or spurious, that Moses is not the author of the Pentateuch. Since however his opponents do not recognize as their authority the merely literal meaning of Scripture, the whole of Spinoza's critique of orthodoxy, in so far as that critique seeks to refute orthodoxy, rests on a *petitio principii*.

It is another matter, if and to what extent orthodoxy claims to be able to convince the unbeliever, on his own ground, of the revealed nature of Scripture. Proof of miracles functions as the most excellent means to this end. The positive mind, which keeps within the limits of unbelieving experience and which is conscious of itself, is quite capable of warding off, in all superiority, this attack on its own position. Positive critique is legitimate only as *defensive* critique.

Yet what is the significance of this limitation, self-imposed on the positive mind, to a field which is open to accurate observation and strict analysis? Is that limitation not a deed of human defiance, of convulsive closing-in on itself? Is not the insensitivity to the command and the grace, to the Law and the blessing, a matter of will? The defensive attitude in face of (real or alleged) revelation is then not a matter of course. It is called in question again and again by belief in revelation. If the positive mind denies that it closes itself in defiance against revelation, it must confess that it does not itself experience revelation. In so doing, does it not admit that it lacks an organ, that it is blind? This is not a reproach that can be volleyed back against the opponent, for the believer sees everything that the unbeliever sees, sees it also exactly as the opponent sees it, and yet nevertheless sees *more*. But does not assumption the whole world over justifiably speak for those who see rather than for those who do not, for those who see more rather than for those who see less? Is the unbeliever then to resign himself to being, as compared with the believer, "ungifted in the matter of religion," just as the unmusical are ungifted in the matter of music? By accepting this, he would be granting recognition to revelation. Merely defensive critique against revelation is thus in no sense possible. Reserving judgment in the matter of revelation is mistrust, suspicion of revelation. One rational ground for this misgiving is supplied by the positive critique. It points to the connection, the contrast between the central assertion of revealed religion and the assertions, peripheral, it is true, but necessary assertions that Scripture is verbally inspired, that Moses composed the Pentateuch, that the text of Scripture has come down to us without corruption and without falsifying modifications, that the miracles recounted in Scripture actually happened. This critique has a prospect of success, not by direct argumentation, but only by virtue of the mockery that lends spice to the arguments, and lodges them firmly in the hearer's mind. Reason must turn into "esprit" if reason is to experience her more than royal freedom, her unshakable sovereignty, and to realize it in action. Through laughter and mockery, reason overleaps the barriers that she was not able to overcome when she proceeded pace by pace in formal argumentation. But all the self-consciousness of the Enlightenment cannot conceal the fact that this critique, peculiar to the Enlightenment—historically effective as it was—does not reach the core of revealed religion, but is only a critique of certain consequences and is therefore questionable.

CHAPTER VI

THE CRITIQUE OF MAIMONIDES

A. The Divergences between Spinoza and Maimonides

1) *According to Spinoza's own view*

FOLLOWING Spinoza's own distinction between the "skeptical" and the "dogmatic" conception of the relation between reason and Scripture (*Tr.*, pp. 166 f.) we divided his critique of religion into the critique of orthodoxy and the critique of Maimonides. Since Spinoza has not followed this division in constructing the *Tractate*, but has in almost every chapter chosen to discuss or analyze orthodoxy and Maimonides, historical and critical interpretation has no choice but to take responsibility for itself using that division. If it evades this task it will not pass beyond idle repetition of what Spinoza has surely himself stated better. The external structure of the *Tractate* cannot be binding on the interpreter, since it is partially conditioned by the two subsidiary aims that Spinoza is following, apart from his primary and highest aim in composing the *Tractate* (defense against the allegation of atheism, and ensuring freedom for the public expression of opinion). In accord with the primary and highest aim of the *Tractate*, the interpretation must look at each position criticized, as that position presents itself, and thus bring to light the problematic nature of Spinoza's critique of religion as an attempt to liberate "the more prudent sort" from their imprisonment in revealed religion, so that they can philosophize.

For the sake of that liberation, the "prejudice" that reason must subject itself to the supra-rational or contra-rational revelation contained in Scripture is to be eliminated. In the face of "dogmatic" theology, the task is to be differently defined, since this theology does not subject reason to Scripture but Scripture to reason. The most general definition of the task of the *Tractate* reads: radical *separation* of philosophy (reason) from theology (Scripture). Since the "dogmatists" recognize as the meaning of

Scripture only what the text means as interpreted in the light of rational truth, argumentation on the ground of the letter of Scripture is not possible. In the case of Maimonides, the plane available from the outset for the criticism is that of reason. On the plane of reason, the compatibility of reason and revelation is to be questioned. However, with this the aim of the critique is not yet fully defined. Maimonides does not merely assert that revelation and reason are mutually compatible, but above all that revelation is necessary for salvation, or that reason is insufficient for such conduct of life as leads to beatitude. These two assertions are brought into union by the contention that only such fulfillment of the Law is pious and assures "a share in the future world" as takes place in obedience to God's revealed will, although the Law be by content in accord with reason (the seven Noachidic Laws) and binding on all men (*Tr.*, pp. 65 f.).[182] It is at any rate in this way that Spinoza understands Maimonides' position. We must now ask whether, and within what limits, this reading of Maimonides' position corresponds to that position itself. At the same time, the real and ultimate divergence between Spinoza and Maimonides must be established and analyzed.

Maimonides defines his position by two frontiers. In the face of orthodoxy he defends the right of reason, in the face of philosophy he directs attention to the bounds of reason. Under orthodoxy we are to understand in the first place the standpoint of those rabbis who invoke only the authority of the Bible and of the Talmud, without making any effort to find a philosophic basis for their teachings. Maimonides' verdict on these "vulgar" theologians is no less harsh than is Spinoza's corresponding verdict. His reproach against them runs: because of their stupidity and ignorance, they accept the impossible as possible by standing to the letter of the text, when that text is intended as allegory or analogy. They concern themselves exclusively with the outer shell of the "secrets of the Torah," hinted at in certain passages of the Talmud and of the Midrashim, and do not heed that these have a hidden kernel. In the face of this orthodoxy, Maimonides defends the right of reason by taking as his hermeneutic principle: "All passages which contradict rational insight when taken literally are to be interpreted allegorically."[183] In the second place we must understand by the orthodoxy which Maimonides is contesting, the orthodoxy of the Arabs, the so-called Kalâm, which influenced certain Jews. Maimonides defends the right of reason against the Kalâm in the main by two principles:

1) What exists does not adapt itself to opinion, but right opinions are those that adapt themselves to the existent. Science must take its bearings not by what *might* be, but by what is real, visible, manifest.

2) Only on the basis of thorough investigation of what is, as it really is, hence only on the basis of Aristotelian natural science, is theology possible.

This distinction permits delimitation not only from the Kalâm but from philosophy as well. Characteristic of the philosophers is the doctrine of the eternity of the world. Against this, Maimonides sets out to defend the doctrine of faith, that God freely created the world, freely bestowed on the prophets His gifts and His grace, and freely judges mankind. He is aware that in so doing he is at one with the aim of the Kalâm. But Maimonides wishes to prove on the basis of solid science what the Kalâm sought to prove under the actual but unclear assumption of what it intended to prove, and further in total disaccord with the real visible order of the world. Science leads to the complete disjunction: creation of the world or eternity of the world. Science cannot settle which member of this disjunction represents the truth. The question whether the world is eternal or was created stands at the frontier where reason must halt. This frontier must be shown to be such to philosophy. Now on the assumption of the eternity of the world—this was demonstrated by Aristotle—and also on the assumption of the creation of the world, it follows that God exists, that He is one, and that He is incorporeal. These three basic theologems are thus strictly demonstrable. However, the Kalâm, which set out to support these theologems by the doctrine of creation, makes the theologems questionable, since the creation of the world is not strictly demonstrable. In opposition to the Kalâm, Maimonides intends first—in view of the fact that the creation of the world is not provable—to set the three fundamental theologems beyond all doubt, and then and then only to treat the question to which philosophic thinking is impotent to give a decisive answer— creation of the world versus eternity of the world. In favor of the creation of the world and against the eternity of the world, he sees as a first line of argument, that the doctrine of creation is handed down to us by the prophets, and as a second line of argument, the objective probability.[184]

2) *As contrast regarding the central theological assumption*

According to Maimonides' exposition, the first two metaphysical assumptions of the Kalâm run:

1) All bodies are composed of atoms, atoms are the substance of bodies.
2) The void exists.[185]

The striking agreement between this metaphysics and Epicurean metaphysics facilitates understanding of the meaning to be ascribed to Maimonides' critique of the Kalâm. Epicurean and Lucretian atomism belongs to the context of thought constituted by the intention to free the mind from the fear inspired by religion. "This disturbance of mind and this darkness cannot be dispersed by the rays of the sun, the shining arrows of the day, but only by the contemplation of nature, and by investigation of nature." The principle of this natural science lies in the proposition: never, even by the action of the gods, can something be created out of nothing, for in that case anything and everything could come into being from anything, unneedful of seeds; nothing would then be required to remain within its own order, within the definite and continuous mode of its arising. But it is manifest that reality has a definite and continous order. Since in the realm of the manifest there is not only definite, continuous order, but also indefiniteness and discontinuity, it is necessary to assume that underlying the manifest order there is another order, atomism, as the real order of things, if we are radically to exclude the operation of divine powers.[186] At the furthest pole from Epicurean metaphysics is the metaphysics of the Kalâm as the result of faith in the sovereign power of God, who every moment creates all things out of nothing. For the Kalâm, according to the teaching of which the atoms are in each moment of time being created out of nothing, according to the sovereign and arbitrary will of God, atomism is the correlate of a radical denial of the manifest order of nature as an inherent, continuous nexus. Both these forms of atomism deny the solidity of the manifest order. That of Epicurus, so that he may eradicate faith in gods who act; that of the Kalâm, by reason of faith in the acting God. Both diverge from the manifest order in

opposite directions. Between these two extremes, which touch
one another, stands Aristotelian science. It stays fast within the
manifest order. In express adherence to Aristotelian science,
Maimonides appeals against the Kalâm to the manifest order.
On this ground he sets out to prove that the world is created out
of nothing. To achieve this, he cannot but understand the
Divine creative will as an ordering and rational will. His metaphysics therefore centers on the problem of the relation between
reason (understanding) and will in God.

On the basis of the manifest order, on which Maimonides
seeks to prove the creation of the world as possible, even probable,
the philosophy which Maimonides contests and rejects as incompatible with Judaism, that of the Arab Aristotelians, arrives
at the opposite conclusion, at the doctrine of the world as eternal.
Thus the contest between belief and unbelief takes place on the
plane of Aristotelian science. To this extent, we may at the outset
ignore the difference between the teleological metaphysics of the
twelfth century and the mechanical physics of the seventeenth
century. By adopting the doctrine of Ibn Roshd, Spinoza would
already overstep the boundary drawn by Maimonides. Spinoza
teaches, as do the Arab philosophers, the eternity of the world, in
contradiction of the doctrine of creation laid down by revealed
religion. That those philosophers considered themselves believers
in revelation, and actually were believers in revelation, need not
concern us here, when we are investigating only the opposition of
Spinoza to revealed religion as understood by Maimonides. The
first formulation for this opposition is thus: doctrine of the eternity
of the world versus doctrine of the creation of the world.

With the doctrine of the eternity of the world the denial of
miracles is given, with the doctrine of the creation of the world the
possibility of miracles is admitted.[187] In the context of the
Tractate, Spinoza justifies his denial of the possibility of miracles
by means of the proposition: "Dei voluntas, et Dei intellectus in se
revera unum et idem sunt; nec distinguuntur, nisi respectu nostra-
rum cogitationum, quas de Dei intellectu formamus" (*Tr.*, p. 48).
It follows from this proposition that God wills all things which He
knows, that thus the distinction between the possible and the
actual has no ontic significance. There is nothing possible except
or beside the actual: the actual is of necessity such as it is; the rules
of actual events are necessary laws, eternal truths; the modification

of nature, the annulling of a law of nature, the miracle is an
absurdity (*Tr.*,pp. 68 f.). A scholar believes he has shown that the
proposition that in God intellect and will are one and the same is
to be found in the work of Maimonides also, and therefore that
there is a basic agreement between Maimonides and Spinoza;[188]
the conclusion was surely agreeable to Spinoza himself, who not
unintentionally, and particularly in the *Tractate*, adopted such a
formulation for his central assertion as echoes traditional teachings. If one were justified in assuming this agreement, then
Spinoza's doctrine—not despite, but on account of, his denial of
miracles and of creation—would then be seen as the consistent
further development of Maimonides' theology, which is considered to be the culmination of Jewish theology.

   Maimonides concludes from the unqualified oneness and simplicity of God that it is impossible that God should have positive
attributes. Each positive attribute would posit a manifold in
God. Thus it is in particular impossible to attribute intellect and
will to God, to distinguish God's intellect and God's will from His
essence. For this reason the distinction between intellect and will
in God loses the significance it has in precise speech. Were Spinoza
to have adopted this assertion of identity in meaning and not
merely in words, he would then have been obliged to assert the
identity of thought and extension in the same way as the identity
of intellect and will. Even by so doing, he would not have achieved
a genuine concord. For Maimonides, the proposition means a
reality which is higher than all human understanding: since God
is indeed one, nothing positive can be said of Him. His being is
ineffable, uncompassable. We grasp only the That, not the What
of God, if by the What more is to be conveyed to our minds than
by the That.[189] So the human comprehension is transcended by
the conclusion drawn, namely that the intellect of God and the
will of God are not distinguishable from God's essence, and therefore not distinguishable one from the other, for we grasp will and
intellect only as clearly different from one another. Spinoza,
however, makes the claim of understanding the identity of will
and intellect, as in his doctrine the identity of will and intellect
indeed holds for man as well as God. Whereas for Maimonides,
the identity-proposition cannot but be incomprehensible for the
very reason that it negates in regard to God the duality known to
us from the observation of ourselves. Spinoza's proposition of

identity does not express opposition to the positive attributes, but exclusively opposition to will as distinguished from intellect.

Spinoza can therefore draw from the proposition of identity conclusions for understanding created things only because this proposition is comprehensible to him, and is not merely the limit set to all comprehension. Maimonides on the other hand sees himself compelled by his understanding of the created thing, to attribute to the incomprehensible creator intellect and will distinguished one from the other, in improper speech. For the analysis of "things created" provides the probability-proof for the creation of the world. The creation of the world can, however, be asserted only if intellect and will are differentiated in God. One of the "philosophers'" arguments against God's being Creator runs: If an *agens* acts at one time and at another time fails to act, the cause on the one occasion is that there is a stimulus to action, or hindrances are not present, whereas another time that stimulus is lacking or hindrances are present, which one time cause the will to act, another time to refrain from action—in other words, which change the will. Now God is not moved by stimuli to action, nor by hindrances to refrain from acting. Thus it is not possible that on the one occasion He acts, and on another occasion refrains from action. Rather is it the case that He, who is pure actuality, necessarily acts always. Maimonides replies: there are in fact no stimuli and no hindrances which at one time determine God to act, and at the other to refrain from acting. His will determines itself spontaneously now in the one way, now in the other. It is peculiar to the will, now to will and another time to refrain from willing. Since the essence of will is spontaneity, God may on the one occasion will to act and therefore act, and on another occasion will not to act and therefore not act. It is not an imperfection, but the essence of will that it wills and does not will. The matter is obviously very different in the case of the intellect. Non-understanding is obviously less perfect than understanding. It is therefore impossible that God should on one occasion know and on another occasion not know.[190] Thus with a view to the creation of the world, will in its peculiar character is attributed to God, and thus, and as a matter of fact, a distinction is drawn between will and intellect in God. Thus there is no basis for saying that Maimonides and Spinoza both assert that will and intellect are one and the same. It must indeed rather be stated, taking into account the immediate connection between the assertion of creation and the attribution to God of will in its peculiar character, that this is the very opposition between Maimonides and Spinoza: identification of intellect and will in God versus distinction between intellect and will in God.

One might think that the contradiction between Maimonides' denial of all positive attributes to God and his attribution of will to God entitles Spinoza to his "development" of the identity-proposition. In fact no contradiction is present. The denial of positive attributes is to be understood from the assertion that God's essence is incomprehensible. The attribution of will to God —possible only in improper speech, but necessary in such— is the surpassing means of adumbrating the incomprehensibility of God. The very proof that establishes the volitional character of God at the same time establishes the incomprehensibility of God.

The preceding definition of the opposition between Maimonides and Spinoza can suffice to cast light upon the opposition regarding dogma. The connection existing between the judgment passed on miracles as possible or impossible and the central theological assumption has already been mentioned. Spinoza further concludes from the identity of intellect and will in God that revelation of a Law is impossible. A law presupposes the possibility of transgression. If God wills everything which He knows, and if, being omniscient, He fully knows human action, then human action against the will of God is impossible; hence a law revealed by God is impossible. Maimonides on his side—holding fast to the impossibility of attributing to God either intellect or will in proper speech—is obliged by the fact of the revealed Law to make the distinction necessary in improper speech between intellect and will in God; "since the whole sacred legislation, what it commands and what it forbids, rests on this base: that God's fore-knowledge does not lead the possible out of its nature" (i.e. make it actual). Not everything which is possible, which God knows, is simultaneously willed or made actual by Him. In particular, God's knowledge of possible human actions does not call forth these actions into actuality, neither those which conform with His will nor those which contradict His will.[191] From the central theological assumption it follows that sin as sin against God is impossible according to Spinoza and possible according to Maimonides. This consequence in its turn is the condition for

THE CRITIQUE OF MAIMONIDES

tolerance in principle on the one hand, or for the persecution of enemies and haters of God on the other. Maimonides expressly holds fast to the assertion that there are inexcusable rebellions against the Torah, carried out "with hand upraised" and blasphemies against God, whereas Spinoza holds that even the devil, and precisely the devil, as the most excellent of all rational creatures, cannot rebel against God.[192]

In his critique of Maimonides' theory of prophecy, Spinoza does does not explicitly apply the proposition of the identity of God's intellect and God's will. His express critique, however, presupposes the critique which follows from that proposition. Only a God who is free and unfathomable wisdom can truly reveal Himself. It is an essential character of revelation that it should be a free gift bestowed by God, and that it cannot be acquired by human talent or training. The Islamic philosophers, in whose footsteps Maimonides followed, recognized revelation, and so conceived the natural pre-conditions of revelation that Maimonides could adhere to their views. Spinoza's critique is linked to these views which Maimonides shares with the philosophers. But Maimonides must in the name "of our Torah and of our religion," make one reservation: that a man endowed to receive prophecy, and properly trained for it according to the philosophers' correct specifications, may nevertheless be restrained from prophesying by the miraculous intervention of God's will. Since God acts with unfathomable freedom, selective revelation is possible. But Spinoza, by reason of his central theological assumption, must deny the possibility of selective revelation.[193]

If God's essence may be sufficiently known by the natural light particular revelation is deprived of urgency, if not of meaning. For under this condition there is sufficient knowledge of God "common to all men," which cannot be complemented or surpassed by revelation, nor does it require to be vouched for by revelation. If God's essence is hidden and unfathomable, if all human knowledge of God is fragmentary and intermittent, then there cannot but be a genuine interest in revelation; if God is hidden from us by the world and by our preoccupation with that world, if our knowledge of God is comparable to the occasional flash of lightning in a night of profound darkness, if then there may be gradations in the clarity of this vision, from almost unceasing illumination to complete benightedness, and if the zenith of

clarity was attained only by Moses *the* prophet, and if all other
human knowledge of God remains in varying degree far below
that zenith: then acceptance of the unsurpassable teaching of
Moses, far transcending the knowledge of all other men, is due
and binding. If God is a hidden God, then theology is not a
discipline like the other transparent, methodical disciplines; if its
object is not open to sight always continuously, but manifests
itself only from time to time, then the only fitting way in which to
speak of God is by recourse to parables and enigmas.[194] Thus
the interest in the Torah as both the document of revelation and
at the same time the mode of its interpretation (the allegorical), is
based on Maimonides' central theological premise, just as
Spinoza's central theological premise leads to the consequence that
he can set up a theology *more geometrico*, sufficient unto itself,
unconcerned with the teachings of others, and especially unconcerned with the opinions of the Biblical teachers, is perfectly
clear and distinct, and that he sees no reason for speaking in
riddles and parables, and therefore tolerates no such form of
speaking, and recognizes no other meaning than the literal meaning of the text itself.

3) *As contrast regarding the conception of man*

From the opposition in regard to the central theological presupposition there necessarily follows adoption of the opposed
position toward revelation. Yet is the central presupposition in
fact the first presupposition?

From Spinoza's theological presupposition the decision on
allegedly actual revelation directly follows: revelation is not
actual, because it is not possible. Maimonides on the other hand
requires as a justification for revelation, apart from the assumption
of the possibility and the urgent need for revelation in general,
also the historical justification of the particular revelation made to
Moses. The historical justification is by its nature open to historical critique. Thus it is open to Spinoza, independently of any
denial of the possibility of revelation itself, to apply historical
critique to the allegedly actual revelation. The historical critique
does not differ essentially in meaning and limits when directed
against Maimonides' position than when directed against orthodoxy. When Spinoza proves, following an allusion made by
Ibn Ezra, that Moses could not have written the Torah, he does

not strike Maimonides. For "He who says: the Torah is not given by God: he who says, and be it only of a single verse, of a single letter, here Moses spoke only out of his own mind—denies the Torah."[195] In principle, no critique of Scripture can touch Maimonides' position, since such critique is capable of no more than establishing what is *humanly* possible or impossible, whereas his opponent assumes the divine origin of Scripture. But to the extent that this assumption is historically justified by recourse to allegedly reliable tradition,[196] critique of that tradition is in principle possible. It is only cursorily that Spinoza applies criticism to Jewish tradition as such, to the tradition as distinct from the matter transmitted by that tradition. The only actual instance is his recalling the Sadducee polemics against the Pharisees (*Tr.*, p. 91). His fundamental critique of the Jewish tradition is contained in his argument against the Catholic Church, which he uses in his answer to Burgh (*Ep.* 76). He inquires of Burgh whether he believes that all the arguments adduced by him—even assuming that all the reasons adduced by Burgh speak for the Catholic Church, and only for that Church —can be *mathematically* proved. No historical legitimation can meet the standard of certainty that Spinoza here sets. But it is equally true that the same applies to any historical refutation. Therefore the concern lies essentially with philosophic critique, which does not—as does historical criticism—stop at undermining belief in revelation, i.e. in a particular revelation, but eradicates this belief altogether, by cutting away any possible interest in revelation.

Yet is not belief in revelation the source from which interest in revelation springs? Is the interest in revelation not grounded in the knowledge conveyed by revelation that God is a hidden God? Or has this interest in revelation a prior reason? The basis of Maimonides' theory is Aristotelian physics, the analysis of the actual order of the world. Stringently pursued, science leads to the question, creation of the world or eternity of the world? But the answer to the question transcends the range of that science. Unguided human reason finds itself exposed to error when faced with the central question on which being or non-being of revelation depends, according to Maimonides' unmistakable declaration. What is truly accessible to man is only his world, the sublunary world. Even Aristotle, *the* philosopher, has himself progressed no further than to knowledge of this world.[197] In the face of this limitation upon all human understanding, Maimonides demands caution and mistrust in regard to the inclination of human thinking, and points to the Jewish tradition founded by Moses' prophecy.[198] Thus according to the inner structure of Maimonides' science the interest in revelation precedes the belief in revelation. The insight into the insufficiency of the human understanding—an insight gained on the basis of Aristotelian science, in principle prior to the introduction of the central theological presupposition—motivates the recourse to revelation; this insight inclines man to the acceptance of revelation. The difference between Maimonides and "philosophy," and therewith between Maimonides and Spinoza, comes to light first in the assertion that human reason is inadequate for solving the central problem. In the conviction that human *reason* is inadequate lies the reason for concern with revelation. Concern with revelation precedes belief in revelation.

This is evident independently of the preceding reasoning, which took its bearing by the structure of Maimonides' science. If revelation is believed in, without the belief being supported by interest in revelation, the belief in revelation becomes a piece of knowledge alongside other knowledge, from which the most weighty conclusions for knowledge may result, indeed must result. For example, for the philosopher who reasons from the fact of revelation to the attributes of God, revelation is devoid of significance except as fact, like any other fact which in its character of fact is only an object. Spinoza does justice to this state of things by providing for the *Tractate*, which devotes its basic part to critique of revealed religion, a Preface which contains a critique of interest in revelation, i.e. of the assertion of human insufficiency. There he integrates the critique of the belief in revelation and of the content of that belief into the most fundamental critique, that of the interest in revelation.

Since for Maimonides, as for Spinoza, the human perfection pre-delineated in human nature consists simply in knowledge of God, the assertion "human understanding is inadequate to answer the central theological question" means for Spinoza no less than "man is unable to direct life to its goal, *beatitudo*." To the question "is purely human capacity sufficient for the conduct of life?" the answer given by Maimonides is contradicted and completely opposed by Spinoza: "nihil enim lumen naturale exigit, quod ipsum lumen non attingit, sed id *tantum*, quod nobis clarissime indicare potest, bonum, sive medium ad nostram beatitudinem esse." It is essentially on this ground that Spinoza denies that fulfillment of Mosaic law is necessary for attaining *beatitudo*; for this law requires observance of "ceremonies, i.e. actions which are in themselves indifferent, and which are binding only by virtue of having been posited" (*Tr.*, p. 48). Even Maimonides who, be it said, takes the greatest pains to demonstrate the rational character of Mosaic law, admits that the individual regulations of that law are binding only by virtue of having been posited. With reference to certain regulations for sacrifices, he suggests that no one will ever be able to discover a reason for them.[199] Since, however, Maimonides considers Mosaic law as *the* divine law, as *the* way to *beatitudo*, Spinoza is justified in the following view: "At Judaei contra plane sentiunt; statuunt enim veras opiniones, veramque vivendi rationem *nihil prodesse ad beatitudinem* quamdiu homines eas ex solo lumine naturali amplectuntur, et non ut documenta Mosi prophetice revelata: hoc enim Maimonides cap. 8. Regum lege 11 aperte his verbis audet affirmare" (there follows a quotation from Maimonides—*Tr.*, p. 65).

The whole structure of Maimonides' science corroborates Spinoza's judgment. Revelation beyond all doubt guarantees more than reason can of itself guarantee. Reason needs revelation, reason desires the solution offered by revelation. We may now define the contrast between Maimonides and Spinoza in the formula: Human inadequacy versus human adequacy. One may raise the objection that belief in human inadequacy, distrust of human capacity for reasoning, is in point of fact not characteristic of Maimonides. This objection derives its force from a comparison of Maimonides' position with other positions based on belief in revelation. But this consideration is inappropriate when the question concerns the characteristic difference existing between Spinoza, who denies revealed religion, and Maimonides, who affirms it.

The position which Spinoza is contesting, the compatibility of reason and Scripture, assumes the inadequacy of human intellect for attaining perfect knowledge of God. What is true for Maimonides is true of all believers in revelation who are confronted with the claim raised by independent human reflection developed into philosophy to guide life. If independent human reflection, if man's capacity in his quality as human being, is adequate for the guidance of life, revelation is dethroned; there may perhaps still be belief in revelation, but certainly no longer interest in revelation. Spinoza, convinced as he is of the adequacy of human capacities for the guidance of life, turns not only against Christianity with its doctrine of original sin, but also against Maimonides and against Judaism in general, in so far as this latter fosters, or even merely tolerates, the concern with supernatural guidance of human life.

4) *As contrast regarding the attitude toward Jewish life*

The definitions so far established in the matter of the divergence between Maimonides and Spinoza are insufficient. The opposition of the central theologems is called into question by the fact that it is not the central theologems, but the assertion of insufficiency which is the first word from Maimonides that distinguishes his view characteristically from that of the "philosophers." In the context of Maimonides' science the declaration of insufficiency precedes the central theologem. If Spinoza's assertion of human sufficiency were the genuine contrary of Maimonides' assertion of insufficiency, then that assertion must precede his central theologem in the context of Spinoza's science. It does not, however. It is impossible that it should do so, since for Spinoza there is no physics preceding theology, so that at the frontier of physics, along with the theological problem, the insufficiency of human intellect comes to sight. Nevertheless, the opposition "insufficiency-sufficiency" is serviceable, and justified at least as provisional description of the pre-scientific difference. It will become clear that this second definition comes nearer to the root of the opposition than does the first, which was limited to opposition in the field of dogma. We cannot, however, limit ourselves to the dogmatic element, because Spinoza's critique of Maimonides has so wide a range.

Maimonides sees as the indispensable basis of revealed religion, more precisely of Judaism, the doctrine that the world is created, not eternal. In confirmation of this he does not simply refer to passages from Scripture in which the creation of the world is specifically taught. For these passages are, in his opinion, even more easily to be interpreted as in favor of the doctrine of the eternity of the world than are the no less numerous passages which attribute corporeality to God, and which he has already interpreted in the sense that God is incorporeal. Two reasons bring him to his decision to adhere strictly to the literal meaning of the Scriptural passages that tell of creation. In the first place, the eternity of the world is not proved, whereas it is already proved that God is an incorporeal being. In the second place: "To assert that the world is eternal, as does Aristotle, i.e. to assert this as a necessity in the sense that nature does not change and that nothing ever departs from its customary course, would amount to destroying the Torah root and stock, to accounting all miracles as fictions, and to declaring baseless everything for which the Torah makes one hope and of which it makes one fear."[200] This coordination of the two reasons would seem to rob the second of all weight. For assuming that Aristotle had proved the eternity of the world, would Maimonides have let himself be influenced by the second reason? In fact, the two reasons are most closely connected. Maimonides asserts not merely that the eternity of the world has not been proved, but rather that it is unprovable.[201] Contradiction between the two reasons is therefore impossible. Yet this leaves unclear the relation between the two reasons, between the philosophical reason and the conclusions drawn from the presuppositions of Judaism. The relation becomes clear if one assumes that the inference of basic tenets of Judaism is also scientific in character. The part played in the first reason by the fact of the actual world-order is taken in the second reason by the fact of the Torah. The second reason therefore involves no *metabasis eis allo genos*, since it too is based on fact. By the fact of the Torah is meant the fact of the revealed character of the Torah. Even though this fact is not as obvious as is the actual world-order, it can nevertheless be unimpeachably proved by historical tradition and by reflection. Maimonides' context of thought may then be summed up as a nexus of scientific reasoning. Scientific reason shows first of all the limits set to itself (critique of the philosophic proofs adduced for the eternity of the world); that same scientific reason then shows the possibility of revelation; and finally, by arguments taken from history, it demonstrates that the foundation of Judaism was by a genuine revelation, and in so doing shows that the conditions of such revelation are actual.

The inference from the fact of revelation leads up to the condition of possibility of revelation. This condition is, however, fully expressed in those theologems which are recognized even by the "philosophers," the unity and incorporeality of God.[202] As is shown by the circumstance that Maimonides derives his theory of prophecy from the "philosophers," the fact of revelation as such does not, in Maimonides' view, presuppose the creation of the world. It is therefore not inference from the fact of revelation that proves the creation of the world, but inference from miracles, which accompany the period of revelation generally, from the nexus of providence postulated throughout Scripture—providence which includes the miracles, and shows itself most plainly in the miracles. It is not revelation but creation that is vouched for by miracles. Maimonides' corpus of doctrine presupposes the reality of miracles, to the extent that it contains within itself more than doctrines grounded in physics, i.e. the proof for the three fundamental theologems (the existence, the unity, and the incorporeality of God) and the critique of the proofs adduced for the eternity of the world, and to the extent that the theory establishes the doctrine of creation strictly, and not merely as probable. In other words, that part of his doctrine which for Maimonides is most important, is exposed to Spinoza's superior critique of the knowability of miracles and has been discussed before. The source from which that critique draws its strength is the spirit, conscious of itself, of natural science in a stage of high progress. Under the assumptions of the twelfth century Maimonides' body of theory is scientifically possible, to the extent that the science of the twelfth century has the character of an essentially completed discipline, and does not live within a horizon forever receding, in which an infinite series of questions and answers to questions will follow one another. It is possible for Maimonides to defend against the philosophers of his time a view that can no longer be defended over against Spinoza.

Strictly speaking, the inference from the fact of miracles is usable as proof only against the doctrine of the eternity of the world, i.e. of the eternity of the actual order of the world, and not for the Biblical teaching on the creation of the world. Maimonides expressly states that from the Platonic doctrine according to which God created the world from matter co-eternal with Himself according to His will, there follows the possibility of miracles. He nevertheless decides in favor of creation out of nothing against the Platonic doctrine since the latter doctrine he alleges, is not proven.[203] This implies: the literal meaning of Scripture is valid as binding truth, so long as the contrary remains unproved.

Scripture is acknowledged as true on the basis of the assumption that Scripture is revealed. This assumption is based on proof from history. As soon as "unprejudiced examination" is begun, controversy breaks out along the whole unsurveyable line of combat. An infinite abundance of instances and counter-instances begins to accumulate. What is to happen in the time before this question is resolved? How meantime, until the matter is settled once and for all, is the Jew to live? Is he justified even in pleading, let alone zealously fighting, for the continuance of Judaism, if its title-deed stems from a tradition, the reliability of which is to be tested by historical examination of boundless extent, perhaps never to be decided by a final verdict? To place the burden of proof on him who contests the reliability of that tradition, to take it that it suffices to ward off attack, would mean admitting that one holds one's position not by virtue of historical proof, asserting the pre-emptive rights of hitherto-accepted opinion as such; it would amount to committing a *petitio principii*. But even if the most compelling historical considerations are taken as finally establishing the central event on Sinai, the revelational character of this event is still far from established. On the premises acceptable to the positive mind, the factual character of revelation is as little to be established as the factual character of any other miracle as such. Here too it is the case that what Maimonides could adduce in opposition to the philosophers of his own time can no longer be convincingly adduced against Spinoza.

Were one to leave the matter at this point, one would be failing to do justice to the basis of Maimonides' position, which remains unimpaired by all the changes that have occurred in the time that separates Maimonides from Spinoza. One would, therefore, fail to do justice to the problematic character of Spinoza's critique of religion. The inference leading back to the premises of the Torah is only formally comparable with the ascent from the actual order of the world to the First Cause. What is introduced by an inference is in truth originally familiar, corroborated by daily life as lived. It is not possible for any interpretation of the *Guide of the Perplexed* to disregard the fact that this book is not addressed to philosophers of another faith, nor to unbelieving philosophers, but exclusively to believing Jews, and, be it admitted, particularly to those believing Jews who have, by reason of their training in philosophy, fallen into doubt and perplexity, into a conflict between the views that they have taken over on the basis of the tradition and their philosophic insights. The assumption of the traditional faith is expressly declared: the stage of intellectual formation that necessarily precedes the stage of philosophic knowledge is obedience in act to the Torah; knowledge of the truths embodied in faith on the basis of tradition is necessarily prior to proof of those truths, that is, to philosophy. Maimonides is not setting up a pedagogic program by virtue of sovereign philosophy. He himself had in his own life followed this advice given to the young. He also was brought up as a Jew, before he turned to philosophy. As a Jew, born, living and dying with Jews, he pursued philosophy as a Jewish teacher of Jews. His argumentation takes its course, his disputes take place, within the context of Jewish life, and for that context. He defends the context of Jewish life which is threatened by the philosophers in so far as it is threatened by them. He enlightens Judaism by means of philosophy, to the extent that Judaism can be enlightened. He elevates Judaism by means of philosophy once again to the height it originally attained, so far as Judaism had descended from that height as a result of the disfavor of the times;[204] Maimonides' philosophy is based in principle and throughout on Judaism.

Spinoza also was born and brought up as a Jew. However matters may stand with the cogency of the critique by means of which he justifies his apostasy from Judaism, the result, at the least the result, is the radical and continuing distance from Judaism. The actual distance from Judaism creates an entirely new situation for the critique. It is no longer needful for Spinoza to justify his apostasy from Judaism before the tribunal of Judaism. On the contrary, he requires of Judaism that it should justify itself before the tribunal of reason, of humanity. He casts off the onus of proof from his own shoulders, and sets it on the shoulders of his opponent. The justification which Spinoza can require is not merely defense of Judaism. The best defense of Judaism would be powerless. What is demanded is the positive justification of Judaism on grounds that are external to Judaism, and before a judge who, perhaps devoid of hatred, certainly devoid of love, tests with inexorable severity the arguments advanced—with "a free mind." To take one's bearings by Judaism, as Maimonides had done, seems to him to be remaining imprisoned in *prejudice*; his Jewish upbringing seems to him to have been a process of becoming imbued with prejudices; distance from Judaism seems *freedom from prejudice*.

If, in the polemics of the previous age, and still to some extent in Spinoza's own polemics, the weightiest suspicion that could be cast on an opponent was the reproach of innovation, from now on the *jus primi occupantis* is denied. Doctrines or institutions can no longer be defended on the ground that they are prescriptive and generally recognized. All prejudices are questioned. The more radical the doubt, the greater the assurance that one becomes free from prejudices. Innovation, apostasy, arbitrariness as terms of reproach have finally lost their capacity to strike terror to the heart.

Thus the free mind becomes free. It becomes what it is. It brings its potential into actuality. It presupposes itself, as faith presupposes itself. If faith cannot keep down unbelief, unfaith cannot cast down faith. On what ground is critique to take place, if faith and unfaith have no common ground? Critique of religion such as Spinoza has in mind, radical critique of religion, refutation of religion is possible only if faith and unfaith have some ground in common. Otherwise the critique never reaches the position under criticism.

B. Spinoza's Critique

1) *The critique on the basis of Maimonides' science*

Spinoza's critique of Maimonides becomes possible only by virtue of the fact that Maimonides trespasses on scientific ground, and endeavors to erect his structure of theory on that ground. Since that theory is presented as a *reconciliation* of reason and revelation critique becomes possible first as the proof that reason and revelation, understood in the sense in which Maimonides understands them, are irreconcilable. This primary critique does not call Maimonides' assumptions into question at all; it merely questions the consistency of his position. Our first task is to isolate this primary critique.

Maimonides reconciles reason and revelation most fundamentally by identifying the distinctive aim of the Torah, divine law, with the aim of philosophy. The characteristic difference between divine law and human law is that the purpose of the latter is to serve the perfection of the body, whereas divine law is directed to the perfection of the soul as well as to the perfection of the body. Perfection of soul consists in the perfection of theoretical intellect. For the theoretical intellect is peculiar to man, this intellect is his, regardless of all relations with whatever is external to him. Perfect knowledge of being in its actual order, recognition of being as created, the knowledge of God as Creator, thus conveyed, is the pre-condition and the element of man's whole relation to God, which therefore is pre-delineated in man, as his proper perfection. Bodily perfection is health; the means necessary for health cannot be secured by man living as single individual. For the sake of his bodily well-being, man seeks life in community with his kind. Life in community presupposes prevention of acts of violence, and moralization on the part of each member of the community. The true perfection of man, the perfection of intellect, is on the other hand essentially non-social. Essentially, it exists and persists not by virtue of life in community, nor for the benefit of the community, in contradistinction to moral perfection. The Torah, the divine law, thus has three objects: 1) the prevention of acts of violence, the external order of life in community; 2) the moral training of mankind; 3) the perfecting of knowledge.[205]

Spinoza's teachings on the legitimate aims of human desire bear a close resemblance to those of Maimonides on the aims of the Torah.[206] There are three aims of human desire: 1) to understand the nature of things by their first causes; 2) to keep the passions in check, or to acquire the habit of virtue; 3) to live in security and with a sound body. In the perfection of our understanding lies our proper perfection. Understanding leads of itself to knowledge of God and to love of God, as the final goal of all human action. Determination of the means that are required for the attainment of that goal is the task of divine law. The distinction made between understanding and virtue falls away on closer scrutiny. In the wise, understanding and virtue are one. The distinction is appropriate only in reference to the multitude, since the multitude can be induced to tame its passions even without understanding. Seen in this light, virtue is nothing more than civilization in Maimonides' sense, social perfection. Social life is essentially founded in the concern with security and health, the means of attaining which are not within the capacity of man as single individual, whereas the proper perfection of man depends only on such means as belong to the individual human being.[207]

Maimonides and Spinoza thus have the same conception of the end peculiar to divine law.[208] Spinoza concludes from this conception that divine law, which brings about the highest and hence non-social perfection in man, has no bearing on society. In the first place, it is not addressed to societies, but to the individual as individual: in other words, to every human being as human being. Therefore it is addressed not only to certain men, to a particular group, as is Mosaic law, which is plainly addressed only to the Jews. Secondly, it is directed at each man as individual, whether he lives among men or as a hermit. It is obvious that the greater part of the precepts contained in Mosaic law are to be observed not by the individual, but by society in its entirety. So Spinoza deduces from the conception of divine law which he holds in common with Maimonides that Mosaic law is not divine law.[209]

In this argumentation only the critique of the particularist character of Mosaic law is really cogent from Spinoza's point of view. This critique may easily be rejected by referring to the universal function of the particular-Jewish law: to educate mankind in true worship of God through Israel.[210] However, what is very strange, because in direct opposition to Spinoza's own intent, is the critique of the social function of Mosaic law. The realization of the highest aim of man (knowledge of God) is bound up with the realization of the lower aim (security in living), hence with life regulated by law, in society with others (*Tr.*, p. 59). Now, means are to be determined with regard to the aim, to the final aim; therefore the standards of political life are to be determined with regard to knowledge of God (*Tr.*, p. 46). From the relation between the realization of the higher and that of the lower aim, Maimonides too concludes that divine law must determine the means which serve the aim of human law with a view to the proper aim of the divine law.[211] How then are we to understand that Spinoza completely severs divine law and human law: ". . . per humanam [legem] intelligo rationem vivendi, quae ad tutandum vitam, et rempublicam *tantum* inservit; per divinam autem, quae *solum* summum bonum, hoc est, Dei veram cognitionem, et amorem spectat" (*Tr.*, p. 45). [212]

In this part of the *Tractate*, Spinoza's critique of the Law is a critique of the significance of the ceremonial law for salvation. What he is concerned with is the question whether the ceremonies stand in *immediate* relationship to the highest aim of life, to the

love of God, as Maimonides had held.[213] Spinoza not only does
not contest the political value of ceremonies, in other words, the
value which is only mediate in relation to *beatitudo*: he in fact
asserts this value polemically with the utmost emphasis (*Tr.*,
pp. 59 ff.). In this connection, and only in this connection, *lex
humana* and *lex divina* must stand opposed. Facing the question of
the immediate value for salvation of the ceremonies, Spinoza
adopts the Christian position towards Mosaic law as a whole, in
comparison with the "new law" (or, as the case may be, with the
New Testament) as a whole. The Christian cleavage made
between the Old Testament and the New (or the old Law and the
new Law) stresses the same characteristics, which are also used in
the distinction made between *lex divina* and *lex humana*: the former
regulates external actions; it derives its force from fear of punishment; it promises worldly goods.[214] Starting from this point,
Spinoza adopts the Christian conception of the relation between
the divine law and the human law, which can by no means be
reconciled with his own conception of the relation between
beatitudo and the State.

The discussion between Spinoza and Maimonides thus seems to
hinge on the question of what place is to be allocated to ceremonial
law: or—since the political interpretation of ceremonial law is
not in conflict with Maimonides' fundamental definitions of the
divine law—on the question of the political value of this body of
law. Meanwhile there is the question of whether it has binding
power. In Spinoza's view, law that is binding is set up by the
supreme power in a given state at a given time. He does distinguish
between the actual state and the best state. For the time being,
the possibility remains open that Mosaic law politically interpreted contains the constitution of the best state, especially since
Spinoza asserts that his theory of the state contains no element that
has not already long been seen by the politicians (*Tr. pol.* I, 3–4),
and he has every appearance of placing Moses in the first rank of
rulers notable for their shrewdness. That Mosaic law is a model to
be followed was particularly asserted by orthodox Calvinism,
with which Spinoza is compelled to dispute in the *Tractate*.
In this debate therefore Spinoza must once more justify his falling
away from Judaism.[215] In his rejection of the assertion just made,
he shows himself as completely conditioned by regard for the
situation in the Netherlands (or, as the case may be, in Europe

in general) for the claims of the Christian churches, and for the dangers to peace arising from these. No power on earth seemed at the time less capable than religion of fulfilling the primary need for peace. Thus the difference existing between Maimonides' views and those of Spinoza regarding the value of the Mosaic law would seem to be reducible to the different social and political situations obtaining in the twelfth and in the seventeenth centuries. But before Spinoza could find access to the political stresses weighing on the Netherlands and on the whole of Europe, and therewith to the sovereign secular state entirely independent of both Scripture and tradition, and this in such a fashion that he could then make decisive objections against the value of Mosaic law, it was necessary that he should first have cut himself away from Judaism. In this process, denial of the importance of Mosaic ceremonial law for salvation together with the political interpretation of that law plays a decisive part.[216] That interpretation was not from the first supported by the political interest, and indeed differed but little from the inclination of contemporary *libertins* to place kings and priests in the same category. But what are we to think of the denial of the direct importance of ceremonies for salvation?

For Spinoza as for Maimonides, the significance of *lex divina* is determined without regard to the particular character of Mosaic law, but by reason of a general reflection on the essence of man. With a view to the aim thus discovered, the ways which lead to that aim, the content of *lex divina*, are to be determined. Assuming that several different means conduce to the same end, that no single one of these means is more highly justified by the end than others, then the choice of the means may be left to the arbitrary decision of the individual. Therefore, from rational insight into divine law, there is no reason to prefer the means laid down in Mosaic law to other equally good means. On the other hand, there is also no reason for preferring these other means to the traditionally accepted ones. The deciding factor therefore is the attitude to revelation, to the Jewish tradition. Spinoza's position is determined by his fundamental alienation from Judaism. Thus it is to this alienation (the "freedom from prejudice") that the rejection of Mosaic law is to be traced. However Spinoza may try to justify this alienation, by proving the impossibility of revelation or by casting doubt on the reality of the revelation made to Moses, our present concern is simply to show that his attempt to prove the incompatibility of the two elements, which according to Maimonides' view are united in the Torah, is indefensible on the basis of his own theory. This attempt reveals itself to historical reflection as belonging to an intermediate stage, in which Spinoza has already freed himself from the social nexus of Judaism but has not yet found his home in the liberal secular state. But if the irreconcilable character of the contrast existing between *lex divina* and *lex humana* has not been demonstrated, it will never be possible to demonstrate from Scripture that Mosaic law is a purely human law. For Spinoza can do no more than assert by an unjustified exaggeration, which he himself cannot continue to sustain,[217] that the ultimate aim of *lex divina* is not revealed also in Mosaic law. The compatibility of *lex divina* and *lex humana*, however, necessarily follows from the relationship between *beatitudo* and the state.

A similar judgment must be passed on Spinoza's attempt to prove that philosophy and theology are irreconcilable by assuming that philosophy is a matter for the wise minority, and that socially intended revealed religion is a matter for the unwise majority. This attempt too belongs to the context of the critique of Maimonides. According to Maimonides, the precepts of Mosaic law convey two groups of articles of faith: first, the fundamental truths as such, and second, propositions that must be believed for the sake of maintaining order in human communities.[218] Similarly Spinoza makes a distinction between true and pious dogmas (*Tr.*, p. 162). If *beatitudo* requires living together, and thus demands the state, and therewith general recognition of such pious dogmas, then the comprehensive unity of *lex divina* must be granted, since this law conveys fundamental truths as well as merely pious dogmas. For it is only the wise elite who, by their insight into the fundamental truths, are directly induced to conduct themselves in a manner favorable to social life. The majority, the unwise, need quite other methods of education. They must be brought to believe in God's mercy and punitive justice. But is the general run of men ever concerned with the fundamental truths? Spinoza, at first in opposition to Maimonides, answers with a negative. He takes recourse to the impossibility of a knowledge of *intelligibilia* that is not founded on one's own insight, on demonstration.[219] This reasoning is not far removed from Maimonides, who intimates that the knowledge of God of which the general run of men is capable, and which is sufficient for them, has no cogitive significance whatever.[220] It must be conceded that Maimonides recognizes as an intermediary stage between unmeaning automa-ton-like speech and genuine philosophic understanding such an understanding of the fundamental truths taken by themselves which indeed remains dependent on trust in the wise men who possess true knowledge.[221] That the multitude should adopt such an attitude to the wise man seems Utopian to Spinoza: the multitude would be more likely to ridicule than to honor the philosopher who ventured to claim authority in matters spiritual (*Tr.*, p. 100). This critique comes from considering as typical the philosopher living "cautiously" remote from the crowd, whereas Maimonides, by a standard by no means Utopian, has in mind the philosophically enlightened rabbi, who feels himself re-sponsible for the guidance of the multitude and who enjoys the people's confidence. Thus this critique too has already its root in Spinoza's alienation from Judaism. Furthermore, Spinoza himself requires acknowledgment by the multitude of certain fundamental teachings which clearly must be understood if they are to fulfill their function of inculcating piety. To these *pia dogmata*, which are to be believed for the sake of piety and not for their truth, belong some propositions of which the intent is in full accord with the truths which Spinoza himself recognizes (e.g. the oneness, uniqueness, absolute knowledge, absolute right of God).[222] By this the intermediary stage, postulated by Maimon-ides, between total lack of understanding (or ignorance) and genuine philosophic knowledge is conceded. The difference shows itself only in the fact that Maimonides requires recognition of the fundamental truths (existence, unity, incorporeality, knowledge, power and eternity of God) for their own sake, and expressly distinguished from the socially required articles of faith (the punitive justice and the mercy of God). Recognition of *one* truth is to unite all men, the wise and the foolish. For faith given to untruth is idolatry, *sin*. Those who go astray on matters of faith are inexcusable; for even if they themselves are incapable of independent thinking, there is nothing to prevent them from seeking guidance from the wise.[223]

Spinoza's critique of the law is critique of sin, as sin against God. Does there exist, apart from all humanly constituted law, a law plainly imposed on all men, and of which transgression is sin? Is there human action which contravenes the will of God? For Spinoza, *this* is the question regarding the *lex divina*, and to the question understood in this sense his answer is No. However much he may agree with Maimonides on the purpose of the *lex divina*, according to him the means necessary for the highest aims of human life *may* be called "God's commandments" (*Tr.*, p. 46); i.e. they are only improperly so called; for it is against reason to consider God as Law-giver (*Tr.*, pp. 48–51). On the critique of God as law-giver depends then the critique of the compatibility of philosophy and theology, of truth and piety, in one body of doctrine on revelation. The attempt made to prove a direct contradiction between the elements which Maimonides treats as united in Mosaic law comes to grief on this issue also. The same is true of Spinoza's critique of Maimonides' theory of prophecy. This doctrine also assumes the compatibility of two heterogeneous elements. For various reasons, Maimonides must distinguish between outer and inner meaning in Scripture, between the literal and the real meaning.[224] He must therefore present the act of prophetic perception in such a way that the co-existence of inner truth and expression by imagery becomes understandable. He therefore teaches that in the act of prophetic perception imagination and understanding work together, that the necessary condition for prophecy is the utmost perfection of both imagination and understanding in the prophet.[225] Spinoza, on the other hand, taking his stand on the unambiguous evidence of experience and of reason, denies the possibility of such cooperation of intelligence and imagination, that is, a cooperation of both in perfection: the stronger the power of understanding; the less the power of the imagination, and vice versa (*Tr.*, p. 15). Maimonides does not deny that imagination, when it influences understanding, may impair and inhibit it. But he asserts that apart from the pernicious effect of imagination on understanding, there is the highly beneficial effect of understanding on imagination. If man is entirely dominated by desire for knowledge, his imagination busies itself day and night with the object of his knowledge. So, this cooperation of imagination is far from impairing the dignity and power of prophecy, or robbing prophecy of all cognitive value; it vouches all the more for the prophet's being completely gripped by "active understanding," which is the pre-condition of all human knowledge.[226] Spinoza's critique thus presupposes the proof that understanding does not influence imagination as imagination influences understanding. This proof is contained in the critique of the conception of imagination shared by Maimonides with others, a critique which is a result of Descartes' revolution of science.

The critique of prophecy has the incontestable advantage over the critique of divine law, that it is immediately given with Spinoza's own doctrine, whereas the critique of divine law contradicts Spinoza's own doctrine. But even for the former the same result holds at which one arrives if one traces the critique of divine law back to its root: it presupposes the constitution of Spinoza's philosophy. The attempt to demonstrate that there is an inherent contradiction in Maimonides' doctrine has failed. This attempt had to be made, if the opponent was to be driven *ad absurdum* as far as possible on his own ground.

Now it might be said in particular of the critique of the doctrine of prophecy—and a corresponding comment might be made on all other parts of the critique of Maimonides: no more is needed than the proof that the opinions of various prophets contradict each other in their assertions on God, and that these opinions are vulgar; for with this proof, independently of all critique of the concepts of understanding and imagination, it is established that the words of the prophets have no cognitive value. In other words what seems to be immediately available as the plane of the critique is not only Maimonides' philosophy but also Scripture. But Spinoza's critique of Maimonides on the basis of Scripture presupposes that the literal meaning is the true meaning of Scripture. This presupposition is however rejected in principle by Maimonides, since it would lead to conclusions that would contradict the revealed character of Scripture. Therefore, before argument can be taken up against Maimonides on the basis of Scripture, his hermeneutics must be called into question. In his explicit and coherent critique of Maimonides' hermeneutics (*Tr.*, pp. 99–102), Spinoza argues to some extent on the basis of findings from his own Bible science. This line of argument presupposes the critique of Maimonides' hermeneutics, and is therefore circular. For that reason, we shall not consider it. We shall further disregard the argument based on the assumption that the multitude is incapable of directing its life by the precepts of philosophy, and thus, as has already been shown, presupposes the alienation from Judaism. There then remain two arguments which require more precise scrutiny.

Spinoza calls up against Maimonides' principle of interpretation an insight, sharpened by the Reformation and by humanism, into the actual meaning and purport of the Scriptural *text*, which must be allowed to stand, and which may not be turned or twisted, or highhandedly and arbitrarily interpreted. Spinoza sees as lacking from Maimonides' exegesis the requisite prudence and caution, exclusion of his preconceived opinions. He voices his astonishment over the lack of scruple with which Maimonides disregards the most obvious counter-instances, and the headlong license with which he adapts Scripture to his preconceived opinions. Spinoza's scientifically trained mind forbids the allegorical interpretation of Scripture. The scientific, "unprejudiced" attitude towards Scripture, to which he makes claim, and by virtue of which he has the possibility of rejecting Scripture, is however in itself not so much a presupposition as a consequence of radical critique of revealed religion. Maimonides' interpretation of Scripture, even in its most venturesome moments, and particularly in these—through which the original meaning of Scripture is apparently or in fact put aside in favor of philosophemes, i.e. doctrines totally alien to Scripture—is nevertheless guided by concern with Scripture. This concern springs from concern with the conduct required of man, required of the Jew, by Scripture. On the other hand Spinoza's scientific approach to Scripture presupposes total absence of any concern with Scripture, of any need for Scripture; in a word, freedom from prejudice, i.e. alienation from Judaism.

The second argument against Maimonides' hermeneutics to be considered here runs: if the true meaning of a passage in Scripture can be brought out only by the interpretation of the passage with a view to the truth of the matter spoken of in the passage, then that objective truth must have been established beyond doubt.[227] Spinoza robs this central objection of some of its substance by the comment which he adds to it, that the objective truth on the matters mentioned in Scripture is never capable of being established by the light of natural reason. This comment does not amount to a great deal. For to Spinoza the fact that "almost everything which is to be found in Scripture can not be deduced from facts known by the natural light," amounts to nothing less than stating that the greater part of Scripture is indubitably in conflict with objective truth—and in so doing Spinoza implies that objective truth is established and at our disposal. The objection under consideration has a meaning almost entirely hidden by Spinoza's explanation, the same meaning as the critique of the knowability of miracles. This meaning of his objection is, in fact, that Maimonides' interpretation of Scripture in regard to objective truth is essentially interpretation guided by the teaching of Aristotle. For Aristotle is the philosopher *par excellence*. Admittedly, Aristotle is not infallible: it is to be conceded that in astronomy and mathematics for instance he has been superseded by later investigations. His science applies truly only to the sublunary world.[228] Nevertheless his investigations essentially span the whole realm accessible to human reason. Only on the assumption of such a completion of science is the principle of interpretation adopted by Maimonides capable of application. As long as reason is not yet in full possession of the truth, as long as reason must have doubts and is therefore imperfect, it cannot bring to light the (assumed) perfect truth of Scripture; it would draw Scripture into its own uncertainty and incompleteness. Not until science is completed and perfect can it unlock the mysteries of Scripture. The final interpretation of Scripture, therefore, is an impossible undertaking on the basis of the essentially progressive, hence always imperfect new science. The type of theory with which Maimonides is confronted refuses itself far less to the identification with revelation than does the opposite type which Spinoza has in mind. This holds quite apart from the difference in the substantive assertions. The emergence of positive science living in the limitless horizon of future tasks and discoveries makes Maimonides' principle of interpretation impossible of acceptance. Accepting it would have the absurd consequence, for instance, that the account of creation would have to be interpreted anew with each advance made in geology, palaeontology and other relevant sciences.

Even the critique of Maimonides' hermeneutics is thus not in the first place critique on Maimonides' own ground. It presupposes the constitution of the new, ever developing science—assuming that this critique does not demand scientific reserve in interpretation of Scripture as a matter of course, and that it therefore presupposes the alienation from Judaism. Therefore the constitution of the

new science is presupposed also in the critique on the basis of
Scripture, a critique rendered possible by the critique of Maimonides' hermeneutics. Critique of hermeneutics is part of that
critique which sets out to demonstrate on Maimonides' own
ground the incompatibility of the elements, namely, philosophy
and revelation, which Maimonides believes to be compatible. This
critique becomes possible, as has been shown now regarding all
its parts, only because Spinoza takes his conception of philosophy,
or even his critique of *Deus legislator* or his alienation from Judaism,
for granted. Therefore Spinoza's critique of Maimonides is not
to be understood as at bottom an attempt to separate philosophy
and theology from one another. It is not worth wasting a word on
this separation, if "philosophy" is understood in Spinoza's sense.

2) *The Critique on the basis of modern metaphysics*

Spinoza's critique of Maimonides is carried out on four different
planes of argument:

1) On the basis of Maimonides' science, as critique of the
   inherent untenability of that science;
2) On the basis of the literal meaning of Scripture, as critique
   of Maimonides' conception of revelation;
3) On the basis of history, as critique of the revealed character
   of the Torah;
4) On the basis of philosophy, as critique of the possibility of
   revelation as such.

The critique on the basis of Maimonides' science, and even
more the critique on the basis of Scripture is to be put aside as
untenable. As far as the historical critique is concerned, this is
possible against Maimonides only as critique of the Jewish
tradition regarding the revealed character of the Torah. But,
as has already been mentioned, Spinoza criticizes the Jewish
tradition only casually. From his point of view, the critique of the
Jewish tradition is of only slight importance. Thus the main
weight of the critique is brought to bear on the possibility of
revelation as such. This critique is not exposed to fundamental
objections, since Maimonides has attempted to construct his
doctrine on scientific grounds.

The question, Is revelation possible at all?, is in the nature of
things not the primary question within the philosophic critique,

which—with a view to its final and complete result—can be taken as providing the answer to the question posed. That question does not stand out as the primary question if we bear in mind what Maimonides' position was. The basis of this position is the analysis of the actual order of the world. The problem of revelation becomes necessary only when one faces the limiting question: creation of the world or eternity of the world?

Therefore, after eliminating the three other stages of the critique, the first question to be faced on the plane of the philosophic critique is:

Is it possible to ascend from analysis of the actual order of the world to theology and to revelation? This question, which Spinoza treats most clearly in his critique of whether miracles can be known as such, is the central theme of the positive critique, which is to be distinguished from the metaphysical critique by the fact that metaphysical critique casts doubt on the legitimacy of starting from the analysis of the actual order of the world and therefore seems to be more radical than the positive critique. Since the positive critique has already been treated in the analysis of the critique of orthodoxy, we shall here do no more than investigate the metaphysical critique. The essential difference between the two kinds of critique becomes manifest from the clear difference between the two assertions which Spinoza adduces in order to contest the knowability of miracles:

1) No good reason suggests that we should attribute limited power and force to nature.

2) The power of nature is infinite, and no event occurs that does not follow from the laws of nature (*Tr.*, pp. 69, 76).

The second assertion assumes Spinoza's metaphysics, as appears from all the reasons adduced by Spinoza; the first assertion is independent of this metaphysics, of any metaphysics. It is grounded exclusively in the insight that not all the laws of nature are known to us. It therefore stands clear of the two diametrically opposed "dogmatic" assertions: "the power of nature is limited," "the power of nature is unlimited." Now one may doubt whether positive science, living within a limitless horizon of questioning and questing, could ever have arisen at all, had not the concept of infinity in modern metaphysics opened the way. But on the basis of the development, which found its first completion in

Kant's discussion of the antinomies of pure reason, one cannot doubt that the completely open character of positive science is in itself independent of the "dogmatic" assertion of infinity. Indeed, if this assertion otherwise is indeed "dogmatic," then positive science is not only independent of that concept, but actually, as soon as positive science has arrived at a sufficient understanding of itself, is seen to be incompatible with that assertion. In spite of the ultimate opposition between the positive mind and the spirit of modern metaphysics, the content of modern metaphysics is more favorable to positive science than was the content of earlier metaphysics; and, moreover, the positive mind is itself the basis of modern metaphysics.

a) *The concept of prejudice and modern metaphysics*

The word "prejudice" is the most appropriate expression for the dominant theme of the Enlightenment movement, for the will to free, open-minded investigation: "prejudice" is the unambiguous polemical correlate of the all too ambiguous term "freedom." True, the Enlightenment itself introduced other prejudices, which took the place previously occupied by the prejudices which the new had dislodged. The Enlightenment never in fact completely freed itself from the very prejudices which it set out to eliminate and destroy. But this means no more than that the Enlightenment was itself only imperfectly "enlightenment"; it is no radical objection to the intent of the Enlightenment because the objection is itself made in accordance with that intent, but above all since every age suffers the same fate. Each age can judge only on the basis of its own experiences, and therefore it judges, whether expressly or tacitly, on future experiences, and in so doing also on those past experiences which will themselves become comprehensible only in the light of future experiences. But since every age has its own experiences, and, in principle, the capability of holding strictly to its experiences in its judgments, the admonition to freedom from prejudice is meaningful. The particular character of the Enlightenment is due primarily to the unforgettable insistence with which it first of all proclaimed this admonition.

From the will to pursue knowledge, to see things with one's own eyes, to submit judgment unconditionally to observation and reflection, comes the struggle against prejudice. This struggle is in no need of justification over against the human inclination to take the easy way. Because the Enlightenment understood its struggle against prejudice as a battle against taking the easy way and against inertia, and fought the battle on these terms, it failed to recognize the questionable character of its fight. The justification—and at the same time the questionable character of "prejudice" as a category—does not come to light until revealed religion is taken into consideration. No one denies that the traditions of revealed religion have brought down from past ages many "prejudices," in the common usage of the term, in their train. But this important obvious fact is external or, at the most symptomatic. What is important is that revealed religion essentially appeals to a fact that is prior to all human judgment, to the revelation made by God, the King of the world. However spacious the field in which the judgment of later generations is permitted to range in approaching this event, what counts in the final instance, according to the meaning of revelation itself, is what is written: "Not with our fathers did the Lord make this covenant, but with us, who are all of us here alive this day." The present of revelation is quite other than the present of experience, in which the positive mind lives, and this by reason of the fact that the latter experience is and wishes to be immediate experience, to be as close as possible to the experienced, whereas the immediate hearing of revelation quenches the will to immediacy, and calls forth the desire for non-presence, for mediacy. Those who indeed hear revelation cannot will that they hear it immediately: "They said unto Moses: speak thou with us, and we shall harken: and let not God speak with us, for we shall surely die." They cannot summon the *will* to approach so close as to see with their own eyes: "the people saw, then trembled and stayed afar." If the will to mediated hearing of revelation is grounded in actual hearing of revelation, then the tradition of revealed religion, and with this the obedience to the tradition and the fidelity to that tradition, is grounded in the actual hearing of the present revelation. Then all critique of prejudice, and even more, all critique of the "rigidity" of the tradition from the point of view of "experience," cannot touch the seriousness and the depth of the *will*, grounded in immediate hearing, to mediacy.[229]

When the prophets call their people to account, they reproach them not only on account of this or that transgression, but they

recognize as the root and the meaning of all particular transgressions the fact that the people had deserted their God. It is
on account of this falling away that the prophets reproach the
people. At one time, in the past, the people was faithful; now it is
fallen away; in the future, God will restore it to its original state.
The natural, original, pristine is *fidelity*; what has to be accounted
for, and what is not accountable for, is the falling away.

If what is required of man in relation to God is fidelity, trust
and obedience, then above all what is required is trust when all
human assurance fails, obedience when all human insight fails.
In this spirit Abraham ibn Daud, Maimonides' forerunner,
justifies the superiority of the revealed commandments, which are
beyond human understanding, to the rational commandments.
The high example is the obedience of Abraham who made ready
to sacrifice his son at the command of God, even though God had
promised him that his son should be his heir, even though
Abraham, had he wished to pretend to wisdom, could not but
find that command absurd.[230]

The attitude of obedience, if it allows inquiry at all, limits
inquiry, not from without, but by permeating inquiry itself. In
the beginning was the revelation. Inquiry is nothing other than
making the revelation fully one's own, elucidating it. As such, it is
limited. At these limits, the living obedience, which is effective
throughout, becomes visible. Obedience does not arise at the end
of the inquiry as a makeshift but precedes all inquiry.

Defection can be spoken of only if fidelity is primary. The
perfection of the origin is the condition that makes sin possible.
If sin is actual, the forgiveness and the restoration into the pristine
state is of the future, and then there is suffering for the past which
is present, and there is hope for the future.

The positive mind, which rebels against revealed religion, is
characterized precisely by this: that it looks toward the future,
not merely hoping for it, but rather using its own powers to build
the future, and that it does not suffer from the past. The positive
mind is incapable of suffering from the past, since it has not lost an
original perfection by a Fall, but has by its own effort worked itself
out of the original imperfection, barbarism and rudeness. What is
felt from within as fidelity, as obedience, appears to the positive
mind as stupidity, imprisonment in prejudices. To that mind,
"rebellion" is "liberation," "to become an apostate" is "liberty."

The contraries prejudice–freedom correspond strictly to the contraries obedience–rebellion, and strictly contradict them.

From the attitude of obedience, rebellion can never arise. Every rebellion presupposes readiness and capacity for rebellion, liberty to reject Scripture, "as we reject the Koran and the Talmud," hence rebellion itself. There is no gradual transition in this. Apostasy as such is not to be justified. Therefore it is of no account which particular grounds Spinoza adduces for his own apostasy. The critique in its entirety is contained in the question: is what is called apostasy indeed apostasy? Is not what is given prior to inquiry in fact prejudice?

With a view to the radical meaning of revealed religion it must be said: there exists *the* prejudice pure and simple. Therefore freedom—falling away from revelation—also exists. Therefore the struggle of the Enlightenment against prejudice has an absolute meaning. For this reason the age of prejudice and the age of freedom can stand opposed to one another. For the age of freedom it is essential that it be preceded by the age of prejudice. "Prejudice" is an historical category. This precisely constitutes the difference between the struggle of the Enlightenment against prejudices and the struggle against appearance and opinion with which philosophy began its secular journey.

What has been said so far is valid for the positive notion of "prejudice," from which the metaphysical conception of "prejudice" is derived, and from which it diverges. The peculiar meaning of the metaphysical concept is expressed in classic style, in its simplest and strongest form, in Descartes' resolve to doubt of everything in order to free himself once and for all from all prejudices. Once in one's life, one must doubt of everything if one desires to liberate oneself from all prejudices—this is what Descartes demands. Once in one's life—the fresh beginning once made, the entirely primary and entirely decisive beginning once found, when the domain of truth has been measured by paces absolutely certain, when the structure of science has been erected on foundations absolutely certain, there is no longer any place left for doubt. One makes a beginning so as to arrive at the end. And the end is reached when in principle all questions, all questions of principle, have been answered. In this way philosophy is intended as completed science, while the positive open science is being founded.

Descartes' metaphysics is connected with the positive mind not only through the fact that his *Meditationes de prima philosophia* expressly excludes everything "which bears on faith or on the conduct of life," and pursues the goal of "finally establishing something fixed and permanent in the sciences," but also by the explicit divergence in the treatment of the very metaphysical problem from scholastic metaphysics. This divergence is an essential moment in Spinoza's critique of Maimonides. When Descartes is asked why he had departed from the way carved out by Thomas Aquinas and by Aristotle, he first adduces these two reasons: 1) the existence of God is far more evident than the existence of any object of sense; 2) by following the chain of causes I can but come to a knowledge of the imperfection of my understanding, but from such knowledge nothing follows regarding the existence of God; therefore, knowledge of God is not possible on the basis of analysis of the actual order of the world. This result of positive critique is thus the presupposition underlying Descartes' founding that kind of metaphysics which liberates positive investigation of natural causes from all limitations, which replaces the traditional ascent from physics to theology by the descent from theology to physics; knowledge of God is possible only on the basis of my knowledge of myself, not so much by asking myself from what cause I came forth in the past, but rather by what cause am I preserved in the present.[231] The foundation of metaphysics is to be what is present, what is available as present. The "liberation from every sequence of causes" and "liberation from all prejudices" have the same, positive intention as basis.

In this sense Spinoza constructs his system. This system does not begin with the analysis of the actual world-order, but with elements that are beyond all doubt, i.e. with "certain very simple concepts" with which what relates to the nature of God is connected. Thus it is proved that God necessarily exists, is omnipresent, that everything that exists has the ground of its being in God, and that all our conceptions involve in themselves the nature of God, and are conceived through it.[232] Thus it is proved that nothing could have been produced by God in any other manner and in any other order than that in which it was in fact produced. Therefore any reasoning based on analysis of the actual order of the world is in principle impossible against Spinoza.

b) *The critique of prophecy*

With Descartes' fundamental doubt, through which the final liberation from all prejudices, the final foundation of science is to be achieved, the notion of knowledge is posited from which Spinoza's critique of Maimonides' doctrine of prophecy follows. It has already been mentioned that the decisive element in this doctrine is the conception of the imagination. Maimonides presupposes the Aristotelian analysis of imagination (*De anima, Gamma* 3) by which the relation of imagination to sensory perception and to intelligence is thus defined: in the first place, imagination is inferior to sensory perception and to the intellect, in that the latter are as such truthful, whereas imagination is in most cases deceptive. Secondly, imagination is superior to sensory perception in that imagination is capable of functioning without sensory perception, for instance during sleep. Imagination is thus essentially distinguished from sensory perception. Therefore critique of imagination is in no sense critique of sensory perception. Maimonides' critique of sensory perception is exclusively directed against the sensory conception of what is supersensory, against the conception of the incorporeal as corporeal, or necessarily linked to the body. This false conception is however not due to sensory perception, but to imagination.[233] Further, since imagination can function independently of sensory perception, there exists the possibility that the intellect may force imagination into its service for perceiving the super-sensory: hence the possibility of prophecy.

Spinoza's critique of this doctrine of prophecy follows from the conception of knowledge posited by Descartes' radical doubt. Radical doubt is directed as much against whatever is not fully certain and indubitable as against what is manifestly false. What is accepted as true on the evidence of the senses is from the outset liable to come under doubt, and therefore to be rejected. In this step it is taken as decisive ground for dubiety that everything which is perceived by the senses in waking life may equally well be encountered in dream. Anything perceived by the senses might equally well be the work of imagination. Otherwise expressed: the knowledge proved beyond all possibility of doubt must stand beyond the difference between waking and dream, between sensory perception and imagination. Only mathematically certain knowledge fully meets this supreme demand. Judged by this demand, the difference between sensory perception and imagination loses its weight. In our context, it is of no importance that from this point of view the fear of *Deus deceptor* besets even mathematical certainty, and that, in order to counter this most radical of all suspicions, the *cogito, sum* is discovered as fundamental fact. The assessment of imagination is not modified by these considerations. Even after the discovery of the *necessario sum* and of the *sum res cogitans* there still remains: *fieri posse ut omnes istae imagines, et generaliter quaecumque ad corporis naturam referentur, nihil sint praeter insomnia.*[234] It is true that certainty of the existence and of the goodness of God guarantees in principle the truth of sensory perception, the difference between waking and dreaming; yet the definition of true knowledge as not to be impaired by the fact that it may have occurred in dream, is retained: *nam certe, quamvis somniarem, si quid intellectui meo sit evidens, illud omnino est verum.*[235]

Spinoza draws the conclusion. He no longer distinguishes, in his division of forms of perception, between sensory perception and imagination. The lowest form of knowledge, *opinio vel imaginatio*, is in principle liable to error, whereas rational and intuitive knowledge are in truth (*Eth.* II, 40, *Schol.* 2). This means indeed immediately that it is sensory perception rather than imagination which falls to a lower rating. But since the distinction between sensory perception and imagination thus loses its importance at the same time, legitimate co-operation between imagination and intellect in an act of perception can as little be conceded any more as previously, on Maimonides' assumptions, co-operation could be conceded between sensory perception and understanding in the knowledge of incorporeal being. Imagination and understanding exclude each other. All the more is the heightened activity of imagination, which is evident in all the prophets (and admitted by Maimonides also) an unmistakable sign that the prophets were particularly poorly endowed for purely intellectual activity (*Tr.*, p. 15).

The matter does not however rest at this stage, that sensory perception and imagination are rejected together, in such a way that the difference between them becomes in the final issue a matter of indifference. But to the extent that the undeniable difference between perception and imagination, as the difference between *waking* and *dreaming*, is taken into account, the rejection of perception and imagination together reflects the *absolute* preference for waking as against dreaming. Whether and to what extent this preference is not already an essential motive in the Cartesian proposition of philosophic doubt cannot be investigated here. For Spinoza in any case it is a matter of course—so much a matter of course that he mentions it only in passing—that dream-perception is altogether valueless. On the other hand, the evaluation of dream, as in certain respects superior to the waking condition, is characteristic of the position which he is contesting.[236] Thus the outcome for Spinoza is that prophetic perception is cognitively inferior to sensory perception—or, at the most, of no greater value.

Midway between the critique of Spinoza the renegade and that of Maimonides the believing Jew, there stands the new founding of science by Descartes the Catholic. In other words, from Descartes' assumptions, Spinoza's radical critique of religion does not inevitably and immediately follow. Nevertheless it must be stated that once Maimonides' position is adopted, once the union of faith and knowledge peculiar to his position is accepted as the point of departure, adoption of Cartesianism cannot but lead to critique of religion. This shows most plainly in Spinoza's critique of Maimonides' theory of prophecy. Maimonides, by not accepting, as do the Christian theologians,[237] an essential difference between the natural dream, and the dream that is bestowed by grace, but by understanding prophecy as potentiality only from what is essential to man as man, binds up his theory of prophecy so closely with his own conception of man, and in particular with the Aristotelian conception of sensory perception and of imagination, that his theory stands or falls according to acceptance or rejection of that Aristotelian conception. Spinoza could therefore all the more easily start from Jewish theology rather than from Christian theology, adopt Maimonides' view rather than the view advanced by Descartes, in order to demolish with Cartesian means the unity which Maimonides had attempted to establish between knowledge and faith.[238]

c) *The critique of miracles*

Descartes has before him at least the possibility of discriminating clearly between the sciences and all that relates to faith and the conduct of life. This possibility does not exist for Maimonides, nor for Spinoza, since in their view love of God is the single aim of human life, but science, scientifically founded knowledge of God, is the presupposition and element of love of God.[239] Spinoza's critique of religion in so far as it is more than positive critique can be understood at a deeper level if one starts from this central harmony between Maimonides and Spinoza than if one starts from Cartesian science. That this is the case is seen when one compares Spinoza's critique of miracles with Maimonides' doctrine of miracles. Exhaustive consideration of Maimonides' theory of miracles is not required for this purpose.[240] It will suffice to indicate the tendencies in Maimonides' theory which, if thought through, lead to Spinoza's critique of miracles.

We have already seen (*vide* p. 162) what importance Maimonides attributes to miracles. The inference drawn from Biblical miracles is a highly important argument for the creation of the world, as opposed to the eternity of the world. Given the fact of the creation of the world, the possibility of miracles is posited. The urgency with which recognition of the possibility of miracles is put forward seems out of keeping with Maimonides' tendency to weaken and to limit the bearing of the Biblical accounts of miracles. How does it come about that a theologican who enters the lists full of zeal for the assertion of creation is made ill at ease by the actual miracles? Can it be, in the final instance, that we must see the reason for resistance to miracles in the assertion of the creation of the world?

Creation of the world is the pre-condition of miracles. Thus miracles cannot controvert the assertion that the world is created. Although the creation of the world is not strictly demonstrable, nevertheless, the analysis lays hold on those characteristics of the world that make the doctrine of the world as created more probable. The possibility and the limits of miracles are pre-indicated by the characteristics which indicate that the world is created. In the first place, the reason why the world has the character that it possesses does not lie in the world itself. The world might be quite other than it in fact is. The world is what it is by virtue of having been determined by the will of a being who wills, and who as such can will that the world can be different. Miracles are therefore possible. In the second place, the actual order of the world, the visible harmony of the world as a whole, shows that the ground which determines that world must be a rational will:

God will therefore not undo the order of the world through miracles, the order which He in His wisdom has placed in the world. Miracles are "changes of nature," that is, changes of the particular natures: for instance, of water into blood, of the stave into a snake. These transformations do not imperil the harmony of the whole, they do not endanger the broad character of the universal order, because God foresaw them prior to the creation of the world, but above all because they are only transient and not permanent modifications, because they occur only rarely, not frequently.[241]

Maimonides' doctrine of miracles assumes the distinction between the enduring and the transient, between what always occurs and what occurs rarely, as an ontologically relevant distinction. If this distinction is called into question, if the order of the world is also, and in particular, determined with consideration of events that happen rarely and outside the normal course of events, then the possibility that miracles should be spoken of in Maimonides' manner falls to the ground. Even though it happens but rarely, and only transiently, that water changes into blood, in so far as it occurs at all, it belongs in the same sense to the order of the world as those events which occur regularly and which persist. In that case, the rule that water does not change into blood is only provisionally significant, as opposed to the universal law, which embraces within itself the regular and the rare. On the assumptions of the modern conception of nature therefore, miracles, in their character of deviation from rule, are distinguished from the regular occurrences only "in relation to the imperfect character of our understanding." Therefore, a rare and transient change of nature, a change, as Maimonides says, "only in some particularities," is as much a subversion of the natural order as would be the falling of the stars.

How legitimate this critique is from Maimonides' own point of view appears from the fact that Maimonides tends to deny changes of the sempiternal. This reveals the dependence of his doctrine of miracles on certain cosmological assumptions. This doctrine assumes a qualitative difference between heaven and earth.[242] To these assumptions Maimonides links the conception of miracles. He does so in order to be able to maintain the assertion of miracles as a scientifically possible assertion. By so doing, he exposes this conception to criticism from a more advanced stage in knowledge of nature.[243] He defines miracle as a change of nature, and he denies changes of the sempiternal. The moment the conception of nature is modified so that the distinction between "always" and "as a rule" (more often than not) loses its meaning, indeed even in the moment when the distinction between heaven and earth loses its significance, denial of miracles in heaven must lead to the denial of miracles altogether. If the attitude to miracles alters on the way from Maimonides to Spinoza, this occurs not in the first place as the result of a change in the attitude to revelation, but already in consequence of change in attitude to Aristotelian physics. Modern science was not needed for evoking skepticism regarding miracles. The reason that induced Maimonides himself to forsake the natural philosophy contained in the Kalâm, induces him to weaken and limit the assertion that miracles occur: consideration of the actual order of the world; the same reason, but adducing the modern conception of nature, leads to Spinoza's critique of miracles.

An essential of miracles is that they occur without human intervention in non-human things, for the sake of men. Maimonides denies that the purpose of miracles is to evoke faith in the prophets "for in the heart of the man who believes because of miracles there remains doubt." But the greatest miracles, those granted to Moses, which are distinguished from those of other prophets in essence and not only in degree, happened "according to the need," in relation to the imperilment of the children of Israel.[244] The assertion of miracles therefore includes in itself the more general assertion that God cares for men, and for the well-being of men. What makes miracles possible is not only creation but, more immediately, providence. The Jewish conception of providence, which is Maimonides' point of departure, asserts that all good or evil that may happen to men happens justly, as reward or punishment.[245] The miracles, which rarely occur, which occur only in particularities, and do not persist, have their place in the continuous, always equal context of providence. They differ by their miraculous nature from the universal context of providence, but they presuppose it since they presuppose that God does indeed concern Himself with men, and does not leave them to chance.

Maimonides explains the assertion: to each man occurs what he merits by his works, by the closer definition that Divine providence follows the emanation of Divine intellect, that man partakes of

providence in accordance with the participation of the human
intellect in the divine intellect. Providence is not equally concerned with all men. Providence protects the individual according
to his perfection, according to the degree of his knowledge of
God and of his love of God.[246] Thus the reward of virtue is the
consequence of virtue, the punishment of vice is the consequence
of vice. Maimonides resolves the difficulty that remains—that
the just suffer and the unjust live in happiness—in his interpretation of the book of Job. The happiness with which Job is preoccupied is the happiness which consists in possession of external
goods, (wealth, children, health). Hence his suffering. He suffers
from the loss of these goods. Job, as is clearly to be seen from
Scripture, prior to the revelation at the end, through which he
attains to true knowledge of God, is not wise, but only morally
perfect. The just man suffers—this means that the morally perfect
man suffers from the loss of external goods. But moral perfection
is not the genuine perfection of man: it is a perfection that exists
only in community life, by virtue of community life. Therefore
it does not make man immune to external happenings. What is
entirely a man's own is perfection of knowledge, which is fulfilled
in knowledge of God, which can and must be the only desire of
man in order that he may become impregnable to all external
happenings.[247] Maimonides expressly states that providence
watches over the well-being of the pious, over every step they take.
He is far from asserting that the highest perfection of man is a
matter of indifference for his external fate, but he asserts that this
perfection *makes* for indifference to external fate. But if *interest*
in all external things dies away, then the interest in all help from
without also dies away, and therewith dies all interest in miracles.

The only interest—which absorbs all other interests into itself,
or robs them of all value—is to be the desire to draw close to
God. Entry into the "inner court of God's house" may be gained
only by scientific knowledge of God, and this in its turn is based
on natural science. Thus theory is only a means, but an indispensable, immediate and most important means of attaining
beatitudo. The final bound set to knowledge is the knowledge of
God as creator, the knowledge of God as unfathomable, a
knowledge obtained through recognizing the mysterious character of things created. Contemplation of created things, however,
leads directly to lessened interest in miracles, in the modifications

made in the existing world-order for the benefit of man. Maimonides finds, as does Spinoza, that given man's insignificance
compared with the universe, man's claim to be the end for
which the world exists is untenable. Thus we understand Maimonides' effort to weaken and limit the bearing of the Biblical reports
of miracles. His mind, accustomed to seeing the free, creative
Divine will of God in the grand, eternally unchanging order of the
universe, has no spontaneous interest in direct intervention by
God, as exemplified in miracles.

Light is cast on the relation between the assertion of creation
and the assertion of miracles by the following argument, typical
of the Enlightenment.[248] The world, as created by God, is perfect;
by intervention into its order, by miracles, the perfect world
becomes of necessity less perfect; it is unthinkable that God should
will this. Thus the impossibility of miracles is inferred from the
presupposed creation of the world. But by the creation of the
world the possibility of miracles is posited beyond doubt. If the
possibility of miracles is denied, then the creation of the world is
also denied. The line of argument adopted against the possibility
of miracles is, then, formally not tenable if the creation of the world
is asserted. Maimonides does not attribute any contradiction to
the writer of Ecclesiastes, when he finds in one and the same verse
of this book (3:14) a denial of change in the order of the world
(the purpose of change would be a further approach to ultimate
perfection, but the world is already perfect, since it is created)
—and a justification of miracles.[249] If Maimonides' interpretation
is elaborated according to its own tenor, it is plain that no contradiction occurs here. The world is not modified, even in the
smallest particular, on account of any imperfection. For the world
is perfect, by reason that it is created. God intervenes in the
natural order not for the sake of nature[250] but for the sake of
man.[251] This amounts to stating that from the assertion of creation,
with which, as has been shown, the possibility of miracles is
posited—from this assertion as a theoretical assertion, founded on
analysis of the world, there is no immediate way to the assertion of
miracles, to the assertion of miracles as having actually occurred.
In point of fact, the assertion of creation as a theoretical assertion,
by its immanent tendency, if one carries it to its conclusion, bars
the way to any assertion of miracles. For the theorist who sees his
goal, or the last stage before reaching his goal, in the contempla-

tion of the order of the universe, rejects as absurd the claim that man is the final end of the world. He can not will that the natural order shall be changed for the sake of man. To him it seems petty to assert the interest "only" of man, in the face of the universe. Thus the ground is cut away from any interest in miracles. The conclusion from creation against miracles—an untenable conclusion—has its basis in the genuine clash of interests on which the assertion of creation of the world on the one hand, the assertion of miracles on the other hand, is based.

The decline of interest in miracles does not refute the assertion of miracles. If the assertion of miracles is to be refuted, the assertion of the creation of the world must be refuted. In Spinoza's case, this assertion follows from his system. Prior to the system, prior to the metaphysical critique founded on the system, there is the positive critique which remains on the same plane as did Maimonides' attempted justification. Positive critique is unable to refute the assertion that the world was created. It limits itself to examining the reasoning underlying that assertion. But by finding the reasoning defective positive critique gains the right to reject the opposed assertion of creation as unfounded. For the assertion was made on allegedly scientific grounds: positive critique rejects it as an unfounded assertion, as an over-hasty hypothesis. This critique is scientific critique, and in principle not question-able, since the assertion called in question is itself intended as a scientific assertion.

3) *The limitation of this critique*

In his controversy with Maimonides, Spinoza can fight on his own ground, on the basis of science. He has no need first to con-quer the territory, and establish his right on it. But if Spinoza's critique of Maimonides is in fact not critique of religion at all, but philosophic critique of scholastic philosophy, the term critique of religion, applied as designation of Spinoza's critique of Maimonides, is erroneous in principle. It makes no differnce to this finding that Maimonides does not himself from the outset build up his position on the basis of science, but merely defends on that basis his pre-given Jewish position. For the pre-givenness may be understood as the outcome of some reasoning, i.e. of a historical proof for the fact of revelation. It was our belief that we could justifiably assume that the pre-giveness had a more radical significance, but Maimonides himself casts no light on this more radical significance.

The critique carried out in the *Theologico-political Tractate* is directed less at Maimonides' "dogmatic" position than against the "skeptical" position of the orthodox, and in point of fact less against Jewish orthodoxy than against the Christian orthodoxy of the Reformation. This latter orthodoxy understands the pre-givenness of its position as already vouched for by the doctrine of "the inner witness of the Holy Spirit." If one examines Spinoza's critique of this doctrine, the critique, formally considered, turns out to rest on a *petitio principii*. Nevertheless, Spinoza's critique of orthodoxy has great potentialities—not only as defensive critique of the scientific foundations of the orthodox position, but also as critique for attack on the consequences flowing from the orthodox position. We may assume justification in principle for that critique despite its formally questionable character because this opponent too in principle acknowledges the right of science. For that very reason, the essentially problematic character of Spinoza's critique of religion could not as yet be brought into full light. This problematic character becomes manifest only when the radical critique of religion is brought to bear on a religious position which is as radical as Spinoza's critique. As such a position we must recognize that taken by Calvin. It is highly probable that Spinoza knew this position directly.[252] Whether he did or not, Calvin's position, as the foundation of the orthodox position which Spinoza is contesting, is the predestined object of the critique.

CHAPTER VII

THE CRITIQUE OF CALVIN

A. Calvin's Position as Immune to Spinoza's Critique

CALVIN's CHIEF theological work begins with an exposition of what knowledge of God is. In that exposition, the content of knowledge of God, primarily God the creator, maintainer and ruler of the world, the omnipotent God, the just judge and the merciful father of mankind—in other words, the Biblical conception of God—is taken as true, and in no way the matter of any discussion. For Calvin, knowledge of God thus understood is implanted in the heart of man, and furthermore it is manifest to man from the structure of the world and from the constant governance of that world. If men refuse this conception of God, it would be a sign—as is also, in Calvin's view, "the shameful multiplicity of philosophies"—that the natural knowledge of God may all too easily be obscured, that human understanding is insufficient for the knowledge of the true God. Man is therefore in need of better support than that of the natural light. He needs the Word of God, as the witness borne by God about Himself, which is offered in the Old and the New Testaments. Man is convinced of the authority of Holy Writ by the inner testimony of the Holy Spirit. The same Spirit that spoke through the mouth of the prophet vouches, by being effective in us, for the truth of Scripture. Illuminated by the Holy Spirit, we believe that Scripture is from God, and we believe this with a faith that makes any form of proof superfluous, and that indeed cannot be supported by proofs, since Divine authority cannot be based on human testimony, although even human reflections are supports well adapted to prove that Scripture surpasses all the books in the world. The living unity of Scripture and spirit convinces us of the truth of that conception of God which Spinoza contests (*Inst.* I, 3–8).

Calvin does not leave the matter at this statement that the human understanding is insufficient ever to attain to knowledge of the true God, and therefore requires guidance from revelation. His skepticism does not remain on the plane of theory. He proceeds to contest the legitimacy of theory as such. He waives investigation of *quid sit Deus*. He does this not because knowledge of the *essentia Dei* far transcends the capacity of the human understanding, as Maimonides and Thomas Aquinas, but because such "chill speculations" are not salutary for man. There are matters more important. There is but one thing needful. Knowledge of God is not the knowledge by which we comprehend that there is a God, but the knowledge which serves to honor God. Where there is no piety, there is no knowledge of God. That a knowledge of God which is content with mere insights, which does not consist of life being radically determined by God avails nothing—indeed, that such knowledge of God is impossible—is Spinoza's conviction also. But the basic determination of life by God, in the sense of *amor intellectualis Dei*, has its basis in theory for Spinoza, whereas *pietas* in Calvin's sense, indeed Calvin's theology itself, dispenses with all theoretical basis, and deliberately so. Calvin is not minded to say anything about God that does not serve the purpose of man's learning to depend utterly on God, to fear God, to trust and obey God. The conception of piety which finds expression in this definition of the purpose of theology assumes a particular conception of God: how could man put his trust in Spinoza's God? how could one obey Him? What is decisive with respect to what is to be thought and said and taught about God is the function of those thoughts, words, doctrines for piety, their *utilitas*. It is not conceded that the first step is to establish what God is, or, at the least, what the relationship is between God and man, what God requires of man; the first step, i.e. a step preceding one's living piously, is to ask the question, Does it obey God? As is man's whole life, so theory also is subjected from the outset to God's judgment and to that question. Theory, allegedly stripped of presuppositions and prejudices, theory which seeks first of all to examine cautiously and suspiciously, is thus viewed as in actual fact full of presuppositions: in the place of the fear of God, which is the beginning of wisdom, it puts disobedience. For God has revealed to man by Scripture all that is needful for piety: *non longa nec laboriosa demonstratione opus esse ad eruenda, quae illustrandae asserendaeque divinae maiestati serviunt, testimonia* (*ibid.*, I, 5, 9). It is headstrong curiosity, disobedience, ingratitude, defiance, blindness, in any case *sin*, if man disregards revelation, if man presumptuously takes it upon himself to judge the witness borne by God to Himself (*ibid.*, I, 5, 15; 6, 2).

The first assumption of Spinoza's critique of religion is that he acquiesces on each occasion in what the understanding reveals, without in any way suspecting that he might be deceived (Ep. 21). All concrete objections to the doctrines of revealed religion are founded in the last resort on man's trust in his own reflections, on faith in man and in reason as man's supreme power, the capacity and readiness to acquiesce in human capacities.[253] It is against this very readiness that Calvin's radical critique turns. Correlative to knowledge of God is man's self-knowledge. The one is impossible without the other. The characteristic obstacle to self-knowledge is man's tendency to flatter himself, his more than blind self-love, which all too easily persuades him that there is in him nothing that deserves hate. From this sinful tendency stems the conviction held by almost all men: "hominem sibi abunde sufficere ad bene beateque vivendum" (*Inst.* II, 1, 2). Men are inclined to acquiesce in their gifts, to be at peace with themselves, to be satisfied with themselves. Satisfaction with oneself is possible only for the man who does not know himself, whose conscience is not tender enough and who does not prostrate himself before the majesty of God, in confusion and distress of mind (*ibid.* I, 1; II, 1). Calvin recognizes this incapacity and unwillingness to being radically shaken in one's conscience as the basis of self-confidence, of the faith in man's self-sufficiency which is the presupposition for disinterestedness in revelation.

For his theology Spinoza appeals to "the natural light," as Calvin appeals, for his theology, to Scripture as vouched for and opened by the "testimony of the Holy Spirit." The contrast between them is not bridged by the fact that Calvin also recognizes in effect the natural light for, quite apart from Spinoza's opinion that science can be constituted and maintained only by a complete break with the modes of understanding peculiar to everyday life, the contrast between belief and unbelief is maintained in the exercise of reason by believers and unbelievers. Believing exercise of reason is set apart from unbelieving exercise of reason by the same gulf that yawns between belief and unbelief in general. It is a *petitio principii* if the critic takes as his point of departure that he is applying his critique to the teachings of human beings, that the character which he shares with his opponent, "what is common to all men," is the only possible ground for the critique.[254] Still less may the critic invoke Scripture. For Scripture cannot be divested of that operation of grace by "the Holy Spirit," without which there can be no genuine understanding of Scripture.[255] Yet the principle which Spinoza applies to Scripture assumes that very divestment.

Thus Spinoza's position and that of Calvin stand directly opposed to each other, without being able to arrive at agreement or even at mutual toleration. These positions are not defensive positions, impregnable by virtue of a fundamental circle and on that very account inadequate for attack. Rather, the passionate faith in the justice and truth of his cause compels each of the two opponents—it could indeed not be otherwise—to the attack! To the opponent's position every right is denied. One is not yet satisfied by a smooth and clear-cut severance of religion from theory. But revealed religion and theory fight, on the same plane of the one and eternal truth, their life and death combat.

Earlier in this study, Spinoza's critique of the knowability of miracles was stressed as his central achievement in the critique of religion. The limitations of this critique stand out sharply when Spinoza comes face to face with Calvin's doctrine of miracles. Spinoza's shafts strike home only to the scholastic doctrine of miracles, which sharply distinguishes miracles from natural events, and in so doing presupposes the concept of nature that is theoretic in origin. Calvin on the other hand understands what is commonly called natural as miraculous. Admittedly he does not deny that there inheres in all created things a characteristic being due to their creation. But he holds all the more strictly to the view that created things are none the less tools with which God works His will, as seems good to Him. The so-called miracles of God's making are not any more miraculous, nor any more immediate than His ordinary activity. "When He desired that Jonah should be thrown into the sea, He sent forth a whirlwind. Those who deny that God holds the reins of government will say that this was contrary to ordinary practice, whereas I infer from it that no wind ever rises or rages without His special command."[256] Thus the miracle is dislodged from its exceptional position, the distinction between the miraculous and the natural is reduced to the distinction between the unusual and the usual, between the unfamiliar and the familiar activity of God, and is by this process leveled out. Yet not even the slightest shadow of doubt is permitted, as though it were a matter of limiting or weakening the assertion of miracles with a view to theoretical difficulties. For in the case of Calvin such difficulties cannot exist. His superbly sweeping doctrine of miracles, which is nothing other than his doctrine of Providence, is no theoretical assertion. It is essential to it that it is wholly inaccessible to "carnal" understanding and the doctrines on Providence which are meant to be theoretical stem from "carnal" understanding. His doctrine is to be understood only on the basis of faith, and on the basis of faith it is necessary. It is true because it does justice to God's honor, and therefore at the same time it provides the man who ponders it with the "best and sweetest fruit."[257] The truth thus to be understood—what God vouchsafes about Himself by means of His word, what serves to honor Him and is fruitful for men—suffers no other truth beside its own, no theoretical truth beside the religious truth.[258] Any other view of the world is rejected as "carnal." Any critique arising out of a "carnal" world-view is from the outset bereft of significance.

If thus the assertion of miracles, identical with the assertion of providence, is founded in faith and understandable only by faith, then faith itself cannot be founded on miracles. The spiritually effected certainty of the authority of Scripture needs no support from human reflection. And the proof from miracles is a proof on the basis of human reflection. It can be of value only on the basis of the certainty brought about by the spirit. On the basis of this certainty, the proof from miracles is admittedly "a highly appropriate support." In any case, for this very reason— because faith stands not on miracles, but on the contrary, the assertion of miracles stands on faith, and since obedience of faith depreciates from the outset all theoretical objections as stemming from carnal understanding, from disobedience—the assertion of miracles stands impregnable: God in His limitless power and freedom can use the things created by Him as tools, at His will; He was able to make plants grow before the creation of the sun, thus without the apparently necessary sunshine; he could stay the sun in its course at the prayer of Joshua.[259]

The controversy that was carried on in the seventeenth and eighteenth centuries on miracles presupposes a clear and unambiguous distinction between miracles and nature. It follows from this that Spinoza's critique of miracles in particular falls wide of Calvin's conception of miracles. For, according to Calvin's doctrine, miracles are not at variance with natural events by reason of their essence, and by reason of their being brought about by an agent. They are in fact not more genuinely, essentially works of God than is nature. Even in regard to human knowledge, in regard to the clarity and plainness with which they bear testimony to God's working, miracles are not distinguishable from non-miraculous events. Immediately after the quoted interpretation of the miracle granted to Joshua, Calvin says "Nothing is more natural than for spring in its turn to succeed winter, summer spring, and autumn summer. But in this series the variations are so great and so unequal as to make it very apparent that every single year, month and day is regulated by a new and special providence of God" (*ibid.*, I, 16, 2). Thus the action of God shows itself manifestly and unambiguously not only in miracles but in every manifest inequality, irregularity, discontinuity that affects the manifest order.

God's working is more easily to be recognized from the discontinuous than from the continuous. Here we again find exemplified dichotomy of approach of which we became aware first, but from the opposite side, in Lucretius[260] and which we could then observe from the opposing use made of atomism in Epicureanism and in the Kalâm.[261] By invoking the manifest order of the world, the Epicurean contested the tales of active gods. But because irregularity, discontinuity, disorder are also manifest in the directly given, the Epicureans could attain their aim only by making the manifest discontinuities derive from unmanifest continuities. For the sake of the aim, they had to step back from the manifest order; nevertheless they claim that this departure from the manifest order is made in accordance with the manifest order. Their starting point is the manifest order. In opposition to this we note in the case of Calvin a predominant tendency to set out from the manifest *inaequalis diversitas*, which bears more manifest witness to the momentary action of the living God than does the no less manifest order and regularity.

The issue here is not between a "rational" and an "irrational" *philosophy* but between the unbelieving and the believing manner of experiencing the world. What bears this assertion out is that Calvin in principle puts forward his teaching on God's working not as a theoretical assertion but as an enunciation of faith. On the other hand, what seems to contradict our assertion is that the devout Jew Maimonides invokes the manifest order of the world against the Kalâm. This invocation is directed however mainly against the specific doctrine by which the Kalâm deviates from the manifest order, absurdly denies that manifest order in the face of the evidence. He leaves the intent of the Kalâm unchallenged. Maimonides is himself setting out to prove the same point as the Kalâm, that is, the creation of the world by God's sovereign will. The strongest proof of the fact that God acts as will is seen by him also in the manifest *inaequalis diversitas*, in particular in the manifest variations in the movements of the spheres.[262] This proof with its particular intent is not to be viewed as scientific reasoning, as is indicated by Maimonides' express statement that the proof in question is only a probable proof. The non-scientific character of the proof becomes clearer when one reviews Maimonides' position in its entirety. For Maimonides, science serves the purpose of defending the pre-given teaching which was originally revealed and has been handed down in the tradition; but starting from revelation is primarily not starting from a fact established by historical proof. The positive meaning inhering in the pre-given character of revelation is not illuminated by Maimonides. In this respect there is an essential difference between him and Calvin. The difference between these men's positions, both based on revelation, against which Spinoza directs his critique, must be taken into account if that critique is to be understood. But attention to be given to these divergences must be guided by a previous glance at the fundamental community in the face of which the fundamental meaning of the critique of religion first comes into prominence. This community opens up before us if we follow Spinoza when he directs his critical gaze on revealed religion, when we in fact look at the matter through Spinoza's eyes. He sees as the characteristic of the Biblical view of providence, that Scripture "lets one realize" the providence of God only from the *dissimilar* states of human circumstances, and from the *unequal* fate of men" (*Tr.*, p. 74). From this remark we can clearly determine both the agreement and the difference between the positions adopted by Maimonides and by Calvin, for Spinoza's remark means two things:

1) Religion is focused on man and his fate, it intends only what is of service to mankind. Unlike science, it does not focus on the order of nature seen in its entirety (cf. *Tr.*, p. 185). In rejection of

the anthropocentric aspect in favor of the cosmocentric aspect, Maimonides and Spinoza are at one. This rejection is made *via* recognition in principle of theory, or rather of that theory which for Maimonides and for Spinoza is identical with theory in general. All the divergences between Maimonides and Calvin have their root in the opposite attitude to theory.

2) Religion in the main focuses not on the identical, regular and similar, but on the irregular and the dissimilar: in this, Maimonides and Calvin are of the same mind. We are therefore justified in seeing in this a characteristic of the revealed religion against which Spinoza takes his stand.

Calvin does not assert that from the *inaequalis diversitas* he can prove the providence of God to the unbelieving. He merely states that by virtue of his faith he recognizes a more compelling and more fruitful witness to the acts of the living God in the mysterious quality of the world than in its regularity and surveyability.[263] Calvin thus creates for himself a position not to be controverted by explaining for instance the irregularity of the seasons, by tracing the deviating to the recurrent, or the exceptional to the ordinary. This is a position which it is impossible for Spinoza to attack on account of its fundamental presupposition, since that position is the result of having, in principle, rejected theory.

B. The Illusion of the Critique

If one denies the existence of any ground common to revealed religion and to Spinoza's philosophy, on the basis of which Spinoza could apply his critique, and by this denial questions the meaningful character of Spinoza's critique, then one must make intelligible the illusion which Spinoza cherishes in regard to his critique. By understanding the conditions of this illusion one will see more clearly than before the original opposition existing between Spinoza and Calvin.

Spinoza did not believe that he was rebelling against God in judging God by the verdict of his reason. The so-called personal judgment or verdict of reason, as contrasted with alleged revelation, is identical with God's immediate self-communication which is far above all mediated revelation (assuming that such mediated revelation is possible). God's revelation by means of the natural light is in itself sufficient, clear, indubitable, common to all men, and unsurpassable in every respect. The opponents, with their faith in revelation, have never themselves experienced the only possible self-communication from God, God's own word speaking within us.[264] The assertion that human reason is insufficient for the perfection of theory, and that therefore caution and suspicion must be applied to human reasoning, is rejected as skeptical (*Tr.*, p. 166). Skepticism is however nothing more than pusillanimity of the understanding. Pusillanimity (*abiectio*) is for its part an enhanced form of humility (*humilitas*), and closely akin to this humility. Spinoza rejects both affects as forms of dejection. To humility Spinoza opposes composure of mind as the joy that springs when man contemplates himself and his power of action.[265] Spinoza feels himself secure against the objection that arises here, that it is to man and not to God that he is paying honor; that he is attributing to man the possibility of being righteous by his own powers and thus admitting that man can apply a form of compulsion to God. Nothing could more strongly confirm him in his belief that he is in harmony with the real teaching of revealed religion than the fact that he, on the strength of his own premises, found himself obliged to adopt the doctrine most abhorrent to all the freer minds—the doctrine of predestination in its harshest and most extreme form. He had no need for the infra-lapsarian alleviation of the *decretum horribile.* He was unconcerned with the objections raised by the Arminians. Everything that man does, out of what are called his own powers, is done by the power of God acting through man's powers. On God's decree, and not on human works, depends the righteousness or unrighteousness of men. God extends His mercy to whom He will, and hardens the heart of whom He will. All men are in the hand of God, as clay in the hands of the potter who may make from the same lump a vessel of honor or a vessel of dishonor.[266] Spinoza might believe that he made God much less dependent on the works of man than did Calvin (and Paul). For according to his teaching, election and damnation are completely independent of man's merit and guilt. Calvin sees in the corrupt nature of the human race the manifest reason, the reason "nearest to us," for damnation. He asserts that this is the sole reason to which importance is to be attached. He demands that we should disregard the hidden and completely incomprehensible reason in the will of God (*Inst.* III, 23, 8). Spinoza cannot but see in this—that man is thus made responsible for his own damnation, even though it be in one respect only—

an inconsistency, an arbitrary act. He cannot but believe that he
is the man to make consistent and complete the doctrine of
predestination, and to cast out completely the "Pharisaic"
justification by works. According to his doctrine, all things are
exclusively determined in every respect by God, whereas his
opponent attributes to man no more than the capacity to choose
the evil, but in so doing still retains human acts as an essential
reason. Thus it becomes comprehensible how Spinoza sees in the
love of fate, in the *amor Dei intellectualis* , the least limited, the most
perfect recognition of the honor due to God, the total eradication
of "Pharisaic" salvation by reason of works. It would be to mistake
the pathos peculiar to Spinoza altogether, were one to seek to
understand it in the light of his "mysticism" rather than in the
light of his sympathy with the doctrine of predestination. In view
of this profound concord with one of the most radical positions
in the whole of revealed religion, the opposition at a deeper level
becomes clear. Spinoza forcibly severs the concern with the *gloria
Dei* from the fact with which the *gloria Dei* stands in inseparable
connection, i.e. from the consciousness of human sinfulness as
stated by Calvin: "ex ignorantiae, vanitatis, inopiae, infirmitatis,
pravitatis denique et corruptionis propriae sensu recognoscimus
non alibi quam in Domino sitam esse veram sapientiae lucem,
solidam virtutem . . . atque adeo *malis nostris* ad consideranda Dei
boni excitamur; nec ante ad illum aspirare possumus, quae
coeperimus nobis ipsis displicere" (*ibid.*, I, 1, 1). The human
correlate of the majesty of God is for Spinoza not man's sinfulness,
but the fact that he is perishable and only a part. Only with the
denial of sin does Spinoza's opposition to revealed religion come to
unambiguous expression.

Spinoza does not halt at denial of man's sinfulness. If all things
are exclusively determined by God (and thus the "sinner" is not
guilty of his "sin"), then it cannot but seem that God is also the
originator of "sin." Spinoza eludes this difficulty by a total denial
of the positive nature of sin. Such action or such attitude as seems
in men's thoughts to be sin with a view to the perfection pre-
delineated by nature, is in its actual being quite as much the work
of God's power, in every respect as perfect as everything else that
is. Therefore Spinoza—who in an earlier letter to Oldenburg (*Ep.*
75) had attempted to adopt and adapt the utterances of Paul on
the inexcusability of man—cannot, when Oldenburg parries him

close, do other than admit: *"possunt quippe homines excusabiles esse"* (*Ep.* 78). But this form of expression is far too weak for Spinoza's real view, in accord with which every man and every being has a natural right to everything: the state of nature knows no law and knows no sin. The natural human striving, the striving after self-preservation, man's self-love, are unconditionally recognized and affirmed (*Tr.* xvi). From self-love arises the attempt to dwell to the greatest possible extent on that which gives pleasure, and to turn away from that which awakens distaste. Human nature rebels against the sadness that arises whenever man contemplates his weakness or his lack of power; in other words, when man rebels against humility. Humility is for that reason a very rare affect.[267] This is a noteworthy confession on the part of Spinoza, who at other times can find no expression too strong for the vulgar character of religious affects, a confession which is surely made no less significant by the fact that it is made with polemical intent. It is a noteworthy confirmation of Calvin's critique of the belief in human sufficiency: striving after self-preservation, human self-love rebels against contemplation of human impotence and weakness. But it is precisely Spinoza's resolute derivation of all human phenomena from egoism that provides him with his most potent hold for his critique of religion, and at the same time puts into his hand the key to the analysis of religion. It is striving after self-preservation that first causes the passions to manifest themselves, and in those very passions striving will run aground, and will sublate itself. The passions imperil our being. From the situation in which the striving after self-preservation loses itself in the striving after pleasure of the senses, after temporal good, there arises religion: the most excellent example of this is prayer (*Tr.* praef., p.5). The man who seeks his real advantage must disregard —"since one cripple cannot carry another"—the uncertain transient good, and, for the sake of his own self-preservation, seek after union with the only certain and imperishable good. He must love God; but he who loves God cannot direct his striving into an aspiration that God should love him. For that would be indeed to wish that God should not be God, and man would then be acting contrary to his own intention.[268] Thus self-love, thought and lived to its final conclusion, is transformed into the most selfless love of God. Thus self-love, radically understood, makes its *salto mortale* into a fundamental relinquishment of all regard for human advantage—in which, according to Spinoza, religion has foundered.[269]

It is certainly not without significance, it is certainly more than a sign of "caution," that Spinoza so often harks back to the saying that man in his relation to God is "as clay in the hand of the potter." But it is not from this fact that Spinoza's critique of religion is to be understood. There is no continuous transition from Scripture, from the spirit of Scripture, to denial of sin. From the outset, Spinoza understands the dependence of man on God in the sense that from this dependence denial of sin directly follows. Therefore he understands that dependence from the outset in an unbiblical manner. But—whether biblically or unbiblically—Spinoza is convinced that denial of sin, and the theological premises which bear out this denial, are capable of being demonstrated by strictly scientific means. Calvin's radical doubt of theory undermines this position. Even if all the reasoning adduced by Spinoza were compelling, nothing would have been proven. Only this much would have been proven: that on the basis of unbelieving science one could not but arrive at Spinoza's results. But would this basis itself thus be justified? It was Friedrich Heinrich Jacobi who posed this question, and by so doing lifted the interpretation of Spinoza—or what amounts to the same thing, the critique of Spinoza—on to its proper plane.

C. Systematic Critique of Religion
(in principle possible, and proving in fact impossible)

Yet such a critique is not immediately convincing. The characterization of Spinoza's science as that of an unbeliever, which is beyond doubt justified, is as little to be taken for granted as is that science itself. The doubt cast by Calvin on theory can be ignored by Spinoza, since this charge is leveled on the basis of unproved assumptions. Furthermore, Calvin's principle of cognition is called in question on his own plane, by reason of the great divergences between those who also take "the Holy Spirit and Scripture" as their authority. Spinoza can set out on his path undeterred by the protest raised by faith. But he does not rest content with this. He is minded to refute his opponent. And he cannot but be so minded. He must go over to the attack, since the defensive critique of revealed religion succumbs to the second attack from the side of revealed religion.

The positions against which Spinoza's critique turns presuppose that God is unfathomable will, that God is a hidden God known to man only from time to time and in fragmentary fashion, only to the extent that He reveals Himself, at the times and in the ways which He wills—who is therefore a terrible God and, as such, an object of hatred to all Epicureans. How is such an assumption assailable?

Positive critique cannot prove anything beyond the statement that the ascent to God from the world, from its obvious order or its obvious enigmas or from the miracles, is made by reason of an unjustified over-hasty closure of the investigation. Further, that critique can make plausible the relativity of the accounts of miracles, or, more generally, the relativity of an anthropomorphic understanding of non-human events to the pre-scientific, "primitive" stage of mankind. The critique can make men inclined to grasp how inadequate the reports of miracles are to manifest what revealed religion primarily and ultimately intends. Nevertheless, these efforts and others similar to them in principle can do no more than show that the most fundamental assumption of revealed religion is, at best, improbable. But is not that assumption "improbable" even in its intention, so that any effort made to prove its improbability is vain?[270]

The next stage in the critique is critique on the basis of the principle of contradiction. Quite apart from the fact that this type of critique often disregards the more subtle distinctions made by theologians, and therefore more often asserts contradictions than proves them, that type of critique is inapplicable in principle. Is it of any importance whatsoever that men are unable to understand, for instance, how the omniscience of God is compatible with human freedom? If God is unfathomable, is it not necessary that human statements about God contradict each other? Can any statement about God be made except analogically? Does therefore the assertion that two statements about God contradict each other, not rest on an unintelligent or unspiritual "understanding" of these statements? As long as it remains unproved that God is not unfathomable, the principle of contradiction fails as an instrument of the critique. But how can it be proved that God is not unfathomable? Let us rather put the question, What would be gained by such a proof? There would still remain the possible and indeed more than merely possible answer, that *this* God, the God penetrable by the human mind, is not the God in whom the faithful believe, that *this* God is the God of Aristotle, and not the God of Abraham. At this level of the critique it is impossible to bridge the gap, and the objections raised by the believer in revealed religion remain in force. The proof that "God" is not unfathomable does not suffice—for what is here meant by "God"? Even the internal contradiction in the notion of an unfathomable God (but how should one in this connection prove a contradiction?) would amount to nothing. Rather would it be needful to prove that in the universe of beings there is no place for an unfathomable God. In other words, the possibility for critique of revealed religion depends on the possibility of the *system.*

Admittedly, Spinoza's system too is based on the principle of contradiction, or at least persists in accord with this principle. But it is not on this that its power in regard to critique of religion is founded, but rather on its comprehensiveness. Its intention is to offer a guarantee that no being whatsoever fails to find its place within it. If this claim is justified, there is no longer any possibility of argument at cross-purposes, for instance, in the sense that revealed religion intends by its God something quite other than the systematist intends by his God. For if revealed religion intends by its God something other than does the systematist by his, that "other" has its place in the system, dependent on the ultimate ground of being.

Of necessity, critique of religion is driven from defense to attack, from positive critique to systematic critique. Systematic critique alone has the possibility in principle of excluding all argument at cross-purposes. Has Spinoza realized this possibility? How little insight he has into the position which he sets out to refute is shown by his objection to the doctrine of the "inner witness of the Holy Spirit," to the effect that the Holy Spirit bears witness only to good works, but not to subjects of speculation (*Tr.*, pp. 173 f.). As if Calvin had left any possible doubt that the "inner witness of the Holy Spirit" not only does not bear witness on matters of speculation, but actually excludes any possibility of the speculative attitude of mind as such! Similar considerations apply to Spinoza's critique of Maimonides and of orthodoxy. Spinoza is convinced that he can explain revealed religion, the interest in revealed religion, the fear of the wrath of God, prayer and much else from the emotions that produce superstition. Quite in accord with the Epicurean tradition he derives the central facts of religion (which his critique considers only in the case of revealed religion), from fear and dream (imagination); interest in revelation from fear, and the content of revelation from imagination. Now throughout the literature of revealed religion, a distinction is drawn between true fear of God and superstitious fear of God, between fear of God and a slavish state of mind, between fear of God and profane fear, and so on.[271] This distinction may be untenable or unimportant, but if it is so, surely the first task of adequate critique would be to show it. Spinoza never showed it. This is not a chance omission, but an indication of the objective impossibility of conceiving of the interest in revealed religion, understood as what it is in terms of superstition. Spinoza's admission that he does not understand Scripture is true in a stricter sense of the statement than he himself is likely to have intended. He understands only the alternative: freedom as self-determination—obedience as fear of punishment (*Tr.*, p. 45). Because ceremonies are a means of training in obedience, they can, to his mind, have no other purpose than to produce the well-being of the body (*Tr.*, p. 62). For him, the will to mediated hearing of the message is merely the outcome of fear implanted in the minds of the people by clever deception (*Tr.*, pp. 191–193). That he does not understand the revealed religion which he has "refuted" becomes an important indication against the system from which his critique of religion and his conception of religion follow.

Spinoza's incapacity to grasp revealed religion as it presents itself has been established often enough. Any unprejudiced reader of the *Tractate* will observe this for himself. We mention it in order to proceed from it to a further question. The connection between Spinoza's judgment on revealed religion, and especially on Biblical Judaism, and his system makes it completely impossible to explain this judgment by "tendentiousness" in the ordinary sense of the word, however "tendentious" many of his individual utterances in the *Tractate* may be. It makes sense to speak of his "tendentious" judgment on revealed religion in general, and on Judaism in particular, only if one means by

"tendency" the *motive* of the whole system. It was in this sense that
Hermann Cohen meant his critique of Spinoza. If Hermann
Cohen calls Spinoza's attitude to Judaism—to which his judgment
on Judaism belongs—"a betrayal which surpasses human understanding,"[272] he means not so much a merely "psychologically"
relevant slip, but, carefully disregarding "all subsidiary circumstances," he believes that he is able to find the explanation of this
betrayal in "the very foundation of Spinoza's mind."[273] Cohen
thinks that he has discovered this mind in Spinoza's equation of
evil with other "defects" (the ridiculous and the absurd—cf.
Tr., p. 177), in the denial of sin, of responsibility, or responsibility
for the future of mankind. Cohen characterizes this spirit as
"pantheism" or also as "mysticism." But what then is "mysticism"? The mystics are those "who do not rest content with the
transcendency of God." It was thus that Spinoza saw himself,
for instance when he reproaches the scholastics with the fact that
they recognize God only from the created things, whereas he himself believes that he possesses adequate and immediate knowledge of God. In what way does the desire for "proximity to God"
—to disregard for a moment the radical difference between
"proximity to God" and "unity with God"—understand itself
while opposing itself to the spirit of Judaism, to the spirit of the
Law? To the "carnal" attitude of *fear* Spinoza opposes the
"spiritual" attitude of love. He understands only the absolute
antithesis: fear—love; he does not understand the fear of God,
which is the precondition and an ingredient of love of God. The
battle he fights against Judaism is a battle against fear of God.
Great as is the difference between the gnostics, Marcion, the
Socinians, the English deists among themselves, and however
wide a gap may yawn between all these and Spinoza, there is one
element which all of them have in common: a revulsion against
the jealous God of Wrath shown in Scripture, in favor of the God
of Love. With this truly world-historical opposition to Judaism
that occurs partly within Christianity and partly only as a stirring
on the borders of Christianity, Spinoza's critique converges—
that critique which, not by chance, becomes a critique of Judaism
even though (or because) it is directed primarily against Christian
believers in revelation. The attitude that finds expression in this
opposition to the spirit of the Bible was characterized as Epicurean
as early as Tertullian, who defended the "Old Testament" in his

critique of Marcion, within Christianity, and for the sake of Christianity.

D. The Motive of the Critique

Both Epicurean critique of religion, and the critique more or less closely connected with Christianity and directed against the Jewish conception of God, have this in common, that they intentionally, or only by their effect, further consolation and tranquillity of mind, and security and amelioration of life. Interest in security and in alleviation of the ills of life may be called the interest characteristic of the Enlightenment in general. This movement sought in every way open to it to assure greater security and amelioration of life, and it waged war, in every way open to it, on "persecution"—at first only on religious persecution, then consistently on every form of persecution, indeed on every infringement of full freedom for expression of opinion. Nothing could be more odious to the Enlightenment than the conception of God as a terrible God, in which the severity of mind and heart, the spirit of the Book of Deuteronomy, finds its ultimate justification.[274] Therefore Max Scheler is wide of the mark when he writes "In *all* previous atheism (in the broadest sense of the word) of materialists, positivists, etc., the existence of God is taken as desirable in itself, but either as *not provable*, or else as not directly or indirectly conceivable, or as refutable by the course of events in the world."[275] The exact contrary is the case. All previous atheism—in the "broadest" sense of the word, which sets out not from the formalized concept of God, but from the concrete Biblical conception, and which is current in the seventeenth century—did indeed also consider the existence of the God of the Bible as "refutable," but in the first instance as "undesirable."[276] Looking back on this tradition, and looking forward to the later evolution of critique of religion, the motive peculiar to Spinoza must now be more precisely defined.

In Spinoza's critique of religion, two traditions converge; in their battle against religion in itself or against revealed religion or against Judaism in particular, both traditions fight against fear. Against fear the one tradition sets love, the other sets happiness. How the two traditions may unite has been seen in da Costa's critique. Happiness is ensured by following the divine command, by following the natural law of love between men. Even from a

first glance, Spinoza's critique is immediately distinguishable from
the critique current in the popular Enlightenment movement—
which critique is however recognizable in his critique as background and ingredient—by the characteristic predominance of the
scientific intention. The same is true of the critique of Hobbes,
whose deserts in founding the new science were surely not smaller
than those of Spinoza. The conceptions of religion held by these
two thinkers agree in the element which both of them had been
able to take over from the Epicurean tradition. The divergence
between their conceptions of religion has its basis in the profound
opposition which will be more explicitly treated when we come
to the exposition of Spinoza's political teaching. Here all that is
needed is to bear the most general elements in mind. Hobbes
rejects the conception of *beatitudo* propounded by the ethical
thinkers of antiquity, and replaces it by the prospect of endless
progress from desire to desire, from power to ever greater power,
and establishes, by reason of this conception of happiness, positive
science as foundation of technology. Spinoza stands incomparably
closer to original Epicureanism, since he holds fast to the classical
view of *beatitudo* and sees science as a means of attaining to
beatitudo, a stable condition complete in itself. This amounts to
stating that Spinoza's conception of science is basically different
from the conception that Hobbes has in mind: the preoccupation
with ever greater power of man over nature, not only does not
demand, but actually precludes the conception of a completion
of science, of observation and analysis of the causal connections
within nature; equally this preoccupation cannot but exclude all
interest in "metaphysical" questions. On the other hand, Spinoza's
interest (since for him *beatitudo* presupposes final and unconditional
certainty on particular "truths") demands attainment and final
consummation in knowledge at least of these central "truths."
Spinoza expressly demands that all sciences should be directed
to one purpose, to achievement of the perfection of man, *beatitudo*
in this sense. Everything in the sciences that does not bring us
nearer to this goal is to be rejected as valueless (*Tract. de intell.
emend., in princ.*). Spinoza's conception of *beatitudo* can with equal
justice be recognized as Stoic or as Epicurean. If one disregards
the admittedly quite different bases, a profound harmony is
seen to exist between the concrete conception of *beatitudo* as
envisaged by Epicurus and that of the Stoa.[277] As far as the bases

(pleasure and self-preservation) are concerned, the divergence was bridged before Spinoza's time by Telesio[278] and by Hobbes. In Spinoza's own *Ethics*, pleasure and self-preservation are inseparable one from the other—as little to be separated as previously hédoné and hygieia in the teaching of Epicurus.[279] The ideal of *beatitudo* held by the post-Aristotelian Greek schools of thought (for which *beatitudo* does not consist primarily in scientific investigation, but rather requires the sciences as a means) characterizes Spinoza also.

The "true good," which is the object of Spinoza's science, is the eternal enjoyment of enduring and supreme joy.[280] This aim demands certain knowledge, which brings peace of mind. We emphatically endorse von Dunin-Borkowski's judgment: for Spinoza "it was essential to set his mind at rest. This unquenched longing arose from a basic characteristic of his being. As others find their happiness in seeking and in incessant excitement, to his mind his own lay in peaceful possession and satisfied knowledge. His mental and spiritual life, when he came to turn his thoughts upon himself, was ruled by the one axiom: only that knowledge is true which logically excludes any possibility of any disquiet of mind."[281] This "axiom" is sufficient in itself as starting-point for critique of religion. Spinoza demands that truths established shall be of a nature to bring peace of mind because they are absolutely certain, because to doubt them is impossible. Be it conceded however, that he does not—and this is a characteristic difference between him and the original Epicureans—require knowledge that brings peace of mind in that it is by nature comforting. He rejects any and every regard for "advantage to man." The "true advantage" for man consists in the disinterested contemplation of "the whole nature." The inexorable necessity of events, from which Epicurus recoils, is unconditionally accepted and affirmed. This *amor fati* underlies the attitude to religion characteristic of Spinoza. Religion is not rejected originally because of its capacity to awaken fear—this character is only an indication—but as the creation of wishes, of an impotence that is incapable of controlling chance, of loving fate. Love of fate presupposes indeed unconditional certainty that there exists a necessary concatenation of causes, presupposes that in the infinite series of causes there works the necessary ground of all being, which can be loved in intellectual love. For that reason, *amor fati* is Spinoza's last word, but not his first word.

E. The Justification and the Precondition of Positive Critique

Spinoza's critique of revealed religion, the basically problematic character of which becomes most plainly manifest when brought face to face with the position upheld by Calvin, is not immediately—or it may be, is only too immediately—to be understood by its setting up love against fear. The certainly intentional echo in the *Tractate* of the traditional polemic against the Jewish conception of God masks the peculiar meaning attached to the word "love" in Spinoza's thinking. Spinoza's critique of religion belongs to an order other than that of this tradition and the kindred tradition. His conception of Judaism remains in any case symptomatic of his incapacity simply to comprehend Judaism in particular, and revealed religion in general. His critique thus becomes an indication of the limits of his system. Having reached this point, we must now inquire what is in fact the meaning of Spinoza's critique, if his systematic critique does not meet the purpose for which it was brought into being.

The central assumption of revealed religion, namely, that God is unfathomable will, cannot be refuted by positive critique but only by systematic critique (*vide* p. 205 *supra*). Positive critique finds itself face to face with this central assumption in particular when it contests the reality of miracles, for miracles are asserted on the basis of this assumption. Critique of miracles is the central part, the weightiest part of positive critique. What is at stake in this dispute over miracles?

The outcome of Spinoza's critique of miracles is the proposition: miracles exist only in relation to human opinions (*Tr.*, pp. 69 f.). This proposition is met with the counter-proposition: miracles occur not only according to the opinions of men, they are not in the first place constituted by men's interpretation, they occur as miracles, they are "in themselves" miracles.[282] However, this assertion might be construed in the sense that miracles occur without any action on the part of men but essentially as happening to men, to the souls of men. The subject of critique of miracles is however not the miracles which can be thus understood, the miracles of salvation, but miracles as works of God occurring within the corporeal world, and affecting the corporeal world. If miracles are denied, then the relation of God to the corporeal world, to nature, the sovereign power of God over nature becomes suspect. Yet the efficacy of God in and over the natural course of events is the pre-condition that man in his human existence can know that he is truly in the hands of God. Trust in God, obedience to Him, discerns in each cosmic process (not only in the stirrings of the human heart), the hand of God at work. This attitude sees no reason to discriminate between "miracles" and "nature." It is not bound to concede this distinction to the scientific mind. Certainly, in asserting and glorifying Divine governance, it is not bound to observe the limit of what appears to the unbelieving understanding as possible. It does not hesitate to assert the acts of God vouched for by the authority of Scripture—even though these events so markedly deviate from the regular mode of His acting—with the whole force of faith unimpaired, a faith quite different from the faith that owes its existence to a longing for faith. The assertion of miracles remains, in its essence, untouched if it is subsequently articulated by means of the scientific conception of nature. For this reason, contesting the possibility of works of God that are not "natural" is an attack on the very core of revealed religion.

Positive critique does not merely prove that miracles are not knowable for the unbelieving understanding. It simultaneously detects, by virtue of the self-consciousness of the positive mind, the relativity of the accounts of miracles to the pre-scientific "vulgar" stage of mankind. But is the assertion of miracles not more completely undermined by this than by any fruitless demonstrations that miracles are not possible? When one considers the final result from all the efforts made in the course of seventeenth and eighteenth century critique of miracles, one cannot but conclude that positive critique of miracles, which at first sight appears to be so inconspicuous and which does no more than inquire how miracles are to be recognized, is of more enduring significance than the attempt, at first sight so attractive, made in the metaphysics of the Enlightenment, to prove the impossibility of miracles. Positive critique demonstrates that the positive mind, applying precise observation and stringent analysis, is incapable of perceiving miracles. Previous to this, positive critique establishes that miracles must be accessible to that mind if they are to be indubitably established. But are miracles—understood as primarily meant—"established"? Are not miracles looked forward to, implored in prayer and supplication? In Spinoza's sense, one may say against this, that according to the testimony of Scripture miracles were experienced also by those who did not await them in trust and faith. These unbelieving "spectators" were however not convinced by merely *seeing* the miracle, but by a form of seeing which had a peculiar pre-supposition. They see—after waiting, not in faith, but in doubt, in uncertainty, to see whether the event announced will occur, by which the question, "Jahveh or Baal" will be decided. Can the man who has understood the meaning of this question even wish to "establish" anything? Just as the assertion of miracles is called in question by the positive mind, positive critique of miracles is called in question by the mind that waits in faith or in doubt for the coming of the miracles. The weapon which the positive mind believes in has discovered in the fact that the assertion of miracles is relative to the pre-scientific stage of mankind, is taken away from the positive mind by the observation that this fact permits the opposite interpretation. Is the will to "establish," which needs only to have become victorious for experience of miracles to become impossible, itself something to be taken for granted? Does not man come to his most weighty and impelling insight when he is startled out of the composure of observation by which facts are "established," when he finds himself in the condition of excitation, in which alone miracles become perceptible at all? Positive critique of miracles, the foundations of which are already to be found in Spinoza's work, has in the course of its evolution made miracles more and more improbable; but this development does not seem to be of any significance, for the reason that improbability is the essence of miracles, and the difference of degree between more probable and less probable therefore can have no effect on the prospects for critique of miracles. Nevertheless, the fact remains that, in the course of the last three centuries, the assertion of miracles has more and more lost ground, even among believers. This change has been effected to a considerable extent by the moral attitude which expresses itself with special clarity in Spinoza's analysis of revealed religion.

CHAPTER VIII

THE ANALYSIS OF REVEALED RELIGION

THE DOCTRINES of the *Ethica*, according to Spinoza's view, stand in the same relation to the doctrines of revealed religion as do the truths on God, the world and man to the typical errors on God, the world and man. The errors of revealed religion are interconnected. They all follow from one basic error. They are prejudices. Men are bound to them by habit, and the habit itself is founded in an original inclination of human nature. The basic human prejudice, on which all the other errors of revealed religion depend, is the assumption that all things, and even God Himself, act as men do, according to purposes. This assumption necessarily follows from the joint action of two human characteristics: 1) ignorance of real causes; 2) men's knowledge of their own instinct of self-preservation.

Men find inside and outside themselves numerous means which serve their self-preservation. Men are therefore prone to consider all things in nature as means to their own advantage. Since men find these means ready to hand and since they make inferences by analogy from the means which they make for themselves, they believe someone else has prepared the means not made by themselves. From the understanding of things as *means* there arises the conception of creation and providence. Belief in providence is contradicted, however, by everyday experience. Thereupon the men who are fallen a prey to superstition close their minds against the truth, asserting that the judgments of the gods are beyond the grasp of human intelligence (*Eth.* I, App.). Belief in providence comes to carry the terrible weight that it has because the interest of men clutches at this belief, uses it and gives it life. It is therefore not a merely negative condition that is meant by "ignorance of causes." The human mind, so long as man remains in a state of ignorance, so long as he does not yet know the true causes, is not entirely without conceptions. Man then considers things rather according to the random order in which they come into his field of vision. This mode of seeing and considering —the term for it is "*imaginatio*"—is in the most favorable case unconflicting sensory perception which has a probability-character sufficient for ordinary living, but, on account of its radical uncertainty and lack of completeness, must be excluded from the realm of true knowledge, i.e. of knowledge absolutely certain and comprehensive. *Imaginatio* is the totality of random and isolated "images" in our waking or dreaming mind, which correspond to the effects which bodily things have on our own bodies.[283]

If the effects which man's own body experiences from without, and to which inadequate thoughts correspond, exercise a favorable or unfavorable influence on the body's capacity for self-preservation, then passions arise from them, or rather from the inadequate thoughts corresponding to them. There is a strict correlation between the inadequate thoughts and the passions. From inadequate thoughts only passions can arise, and passions arise only from inadequate thoughts. Thus the concrete context of imaginative-affective life—which is only imperfectly defined by the two assumptions which Spinoza gives in the Appendix to Book I of the *Ethica*[284]—is the breeding-ground of revealed religion.[285]

The devaluation of imaginative-affective life takes place not only with regard to the falsity, to the paucity of truth, in the inadequate thoughts, but also and in particular in respect of the dangerous and deleterious affect of the passions on self-preservation. The harmony between comprehension of objective truth and self-preservation in man is here presupposed. Accordingly the condemnation of the cognitive value of religion implies a verdict on the value of religion for human existence. It is impossible fully to grasp Spinoza's critique of religion as Spinoza himself intended it, if one keeps only to the incontestable fact that Spinoza sees in the teachings of revealed religion theoretical errors, demonstrably false assertions.

Man has two diametrically opposed courses open to him: theory and revealed religion (*sapientia* and *superstitio*). Both are founded in the nature of man, in man's one and only basic drive, the drive to persist in his being. Man, essentially a particle of nature, determined in every respect by the laws of nature, is exposed to manifold impingements which affect him, i.e. his body. His desire for self-preservation directs him to the bodies about him, to his chance environment. He gives his love to what preserves his being, to

what furthers or increases his power. He hates whatever en-
dangers his being, lessens or limits his powers. Men's natural
tendency to consider wealth, honor, and the pleasures of the
senses as the highest types of good is grounded in the context and
the structure of the passions. Striving after these goods is necessary,
but it is necessarily self-vitiating. The striving for self-preservation,
which brings forth the passions of greed, ambition and lust, and
which runs aground in these passions, is sublated in them. The
man dominated by these passions does not preserve, but rather
imperils, his being. Experience teaches one man and another, but
at any rate only very few men, that these apparently certain goods
are in truth certain evils. They endanger our being. Their pursuit
and enjoyment enforce on us a life of misery, expose us to mortal
dangers, and hasten our end. The perilous character of these goods
is in the final instance grounded in their transience: they are the
extreme instance of transient goods. Since we are weak and
vulnerable we must, in order to exist at all, draw strength from a
being outside ourselves, by entering into union with it: we must
"love" something outside ourselves. This strengthening of our
selves can receive no help from perishable goods, since they themselves are liable to fail, and one cripple cannot carry another:
therefore for the sake of our self-preservation we must love an
immortal, intransient, imperishable good (*Tract. brev.* II, 5). The
condition and the element of our love for the eternal being, which
is based on our existential need of the intransient, of the enduring,
is knowledge of the eternal. Since the transient stands in a strict
relationship of dependence to the eternal, and therefore knowledge of things transient points to knowledge of the eternal, the
original interest of man in the preservation of his being turns
into concern with knowledge. Radically understood striving
after self-preservation evolves into interest in theory.

These definitions, taken mainly from the anagogic meditation
that starts out from common consciousness, with which the
Tractate on the Improvement of the Understanding begins, give a mis-
leading picture of Spinoza's intention, to the extent that they
incline us to the view that Spinoza intends by the preservation of
being the preservation of life, of temporal existence. Admittedly
he intends this also (*Eth.*IV, 20 schol.), but he does so only in a
subsidiary sense. In the last analysis, he is not concerned with the
latter. This is shown by the fact that, in Spinoza's opinion, the

man who genuinely understands his interest in the preservation of his being does not find himself dismayed by the thought of death. The interest in self-preservation is interest in self-determination. I preserve my being, I continue in being myself, to the extent that I am essentially determined by my being, to the extent that I am active. My being is imperiled to the extent that I am determined from without, to the extent that I am passive. I am transient only to the extent that I am passive. It is therefore essential to the active element in us that it be enduring, eternal. This eternal, active element is mind. The life which radically comprehends its original intention and which radically pursues that original intention frees itself from the passions and becomes pure understanding. It follows the path from the perishable and partial to the imperishable and total, from the temporal to the eternal, from the carnal to the spiritual, from passivity to activity, from impotence to strength and virtue, from bondage to freedom. Spinoza's conception of the relation between theory and revealed religion is completely defined by these pairs of contraries. Theory, the concern of the few who are free and strong, lives for the eternal and in the eternal. Man's innate power, and nothing else, leads to theory. Revealed religion, the concern of the many slavish and impotent, lives for the temporal and in the temporal. It has its basis in man's essential insufficiency of power in regard to the temporal: "si homines res omnes suas certo consilio regere possent, vel si fortuna ipsis prospera semper foret, nulla superstitione tenerentur." True as it is that human direction and vigilance can greatly contribute to attainment of security and health, the legitimate temporal goods, there are nevertheless limits to the efficacy of human planning: it is not possible for man to carry out all his projects according to an assured plan.[286] The free and strong man, whose mind is open to fate in intellectual love tries to command fortune as far as possible and to direct his actions according to the certain plan of reason (*Eth*.IV,47 schol.). And in each case therefore, even in cases when his own powers fall short, in the cases when he can not apply any plan, he knows how to bear his fate, love his fate as a man. In contrast to this, those who live as prey to their passions more frequently and more easily bring themselves into impassable straits, and then in particular, take refuge in superstition (in other words, in revealed religion).

Revealed religion is a product of the imaginative-affective life.

Imagination and the passions work together in this manner: passions can flourish only on the basis of the imaginative way of thinking, and on the other hand the function of imagination in the context of religion depends on the passions, by which this context is supported.[287]

Since the striving to preserve himself is the essence of man, there inheres in the human mind the striving, to dwell as much as possible on those thoughts and images that increase or further his power. On the other hand, he spontaneously turns away from anything that lessens or limits his power. In other words, man is inclined by nature to wishful thinking. Thus the foretelling which is the function of prophets is nothing other than wishing. Since man is concerned with imagining his power, he is prone to recount his own deeds to all comers, and to display the power of his body and mind. From this comes the inclination to recount matters not as they actually were but rather as he wishes they might have been. Thence comes the effort to distinguish oneself above other men, and to have at one's disposal some advantage not available to other men. This explains the concern with election, the concern of the Jews with their election. For election is surely predominance of one over another. He who wishes to be elect wishes to be superior. With this is connected the liking for recounting tales of out-of-the-way things that surprise and astound other men. Hence arises the depreciation of whatever is common to all men. Thus the multitude despises the natural light which is common to all men, and prefers the ravings of imagination. The interest in the extraordinary is objectified by relating all unusual or exceptional things, or whatever may be astounding, unknown, or ununderstood, to God.[288]

Men, driven headlong on their way by their elemental and single-hearted effort, in limitless greed and vanity, do not know, of course, how to plan. From pure self-assurance—bragging, boasting and puffed up with vanity as they are—they believe that an injustice is being done to them, if they are offered counsel. Such a mode of conduct can thrive only when fortune smiles. What will men of such nature do when they find themselves beset by ill-fortune? They will turn to faith.

In its cognitive status, faith is nothing other than opinion or imagining. In the realm of imaginative thinking, unambiguous, consistent sensory perception proves relatively justified. True, it is uncertain and incomplete; nevertheless it shows a certain order and consistency. But it is essential to faith that it be faith in anything and everything. What is understood under faith, in contrast to knowledge, is credulity, incapacity and unwillingness for stringent examination. But faith is more than mere levity. Belief has a definite function. Men cannot avoid finding themselves in sore straits from time to time. When this happens, they are irresolute, not knowing which way to turn, driven hither and thither, and willing and ready then to believe anything and everything. *Faith begins where planning ceases: faith takes the place of planning.* Men imperiled, thrust into circumstances from which there seems to be no way of escape, are to the highest possible degree interested in the issue. When they are uncertain of the issue which is not controlled by a firm plan, they can feel only inconstant joy from imagining a favorable issue, and only inconstant sadness from imagining an unfavorable issue: they vacillate in misery between hope and fear. Faith is not a disinterested guessing, but is hoping or fearing. The free and strong man has no faith, because he does not hope and does not fear: he loves fate, he takes joy in contemplation, which is the certain good, in possession of which he knows unceasing joy. But the foolish multitude, which does not merely strive after uncertain good but strives after it boundlessly, must believe, cannot but hope and fear. By nature men are more inclined to hope than to fear (*Eth.* III, 50 schol.). Their situation must therefore indeed already be extremely grave, or at the least seem so to them, before they even begin to feel fear. Once they have been driven, against their natural inclination, into a state of fear, when fear predominates over the hope which is inseparable from fear, and hence fear borders on despair, then religion arises.

When man finds himself in a situation from which he believes it is impossible to extricate himself, not knowing which way to turn, he follows any counsel, even the most foolish and the least appropriate, and at such times he is prepared to give credence to anyone and to anything. His self-confidence and his conceit—these passions which come to the fore when man finds fortune smiling on him—are profoundly undermined. His despair comes to a climax if at such a time and in such a state of mind he encounters anything unfamiliar. The familiar which he encounters is seen by him, according to whether it reminds him of a favorable or an unfavorable event, as a good augury or as an evil augury. The

familiar permits him then to hope, in certain cases. But the encounter with the unfamiliar merely heightens his fear. He takes
it as a miracle that announces the anger of the gods, or of the
Supreme Being. The unfamiliar, the unwonted, the unaccus-
tomed, alarms by its strangeness. This alarm then turns into fear
of God in the man already fear-ridden. God is imagined as a king,
who becomes terrible when one insults Him (cf. *Eth.* I, app.; II,
3 schol.; *Tr.*, p. 79). Man seeks to placate the wrath of God by
sacrifices and by vows. He supplicates God for His aid, with vows
and womanish tears. Prayer, vows, sacrifices are measures taken
to placate the wrath of God, in other words, illusionary measures
taken against an illusionary peril. What is the meaning of these
illusions? They serve desire, the desire for self-preservation. Men
believe because of their unlimited desire. If one desires the unattainable—and salvation out of overwhelming difficulties is
unattainable, or at least uncertain—then man falls a prey to
despair. The way out of despair is prayer and casting aside,
as blind and idle, all rational reflection that stands in the way of
the wishes being cherished. For this reason then—because revelations give scope for wishing—the multitude takes the ravings of
imagination (read: prophecy) as answers from God. For this reason
then, the multitude believes that God turns His face away from
the wise, and inscribes His decrees not in the mind of men but in
the entrails of beasts (not in the mind of men, but in the letter of
Scripture, paper and ink—*Tr.*, p. 145); or that simpletons, fools
and birds foretell God's decrees by divine inspiration or impulse.
Despairing of being capable of achieving their salvation, of
attaining to what they desire by their own power, altogether
despairing of their own capacities, men reject reason and clutch
at "revelation." Faith is thus nothing other than wishing, than
hope of something uncertain or even of something unattainable—
but certainly wishing and hoping heightened and made more
acute through the torments of fear and despair.

The interest in revelation, the mistrust of reason, are thus explained and judged. This interest, and the mistrust which corresponds to that interest are the offspring of the complex of the
passions, which vacillate between overweening self-confidence
and dejection, which are slavishly subject to the good or evil fortune which may befall, and which are completely devoid of any
inner equilibrium. However variously this complex of passions

may react to good or evil fortune, it is invariably incapable of
reflection and foresight. It always rejects reason. And the most
potent of all the passions is fear.[289] If man finds himself imperiled
and thus becomes aware of his impotence and weakness, and
especially if as a result of his encounter with some hazard entirely
unfamiliar, his fear, his natural fear is heightened into fear of the
wrath of God, then man puts his trust in others rather than in
himself, rather than in his own powers of rational reflection, and
he sees in any application of reason a sign of frowardness and of
overweening pride. He comes thus to despise human reason, and
takes dreams and the ravings of imagination as revelations.

Spinoza's analysis thus derives religion from the two basic
facts which were emphasized again and again in the Epicurean
tradition: fear; and dream (or phenomena akin to dreaming).
In so doing he makes considerable modifications in the traditional scheme. Dream appears as a source of hope rather than of
fear. Man, once his self-confidence is undermined and fear
befalls him, reaches out to dreams (as revelation), since it is only
by this means that he can hope to attain to the goal of his desiring.
Further, in Spinoza's analysis of religion, fear and dream are
understood in the light of his complete conception of man; besides,
religion in the sense of revealed religion, the conviction that
human reason is inadequate for the conduct of life, and that man is
therefore bound to have recourse to belief in revelation, is the
actual object of his analysis.[290]

The multitude of those in bondage to their passions, and for that
very reason prone to adopt faith, falls a prey to the passions of
the few, to the lust for power and glory on the part of kings and
priests. These "tyrannize over the minds of the simple, by offering
them as eternal oracles a world of false thoughts, and by propound-
ing the figments of their imagination as testimonies of God (*Tr.*,
praef.; Freudenthal, *Lebensgeschichte*, p. 19). Strictly speaking
these men do not so much invent as exploit the *natural* products of
superstitious fear ("Omnes homines *natura* superstitioni esse
obnoxios"). From Spinoza's presentation it is not possible to
deduce beyond doubt whether to his mind these men are themselves, like the multitude, a prey to superstition, or whether they
merely adapt their utterances to the superstitious notions of the
multitude for the sake of their own ends.

Both the multitude, which by reason of superstition is in subjection to kings and priests dominated by their thirst for power and glory, and their rulers are remote from the supreme aim of human perfection, which is the man strong and free, whose love is given to fate and to the contemplation of the eternal order of nature. Nevertheless there is more gain than loss from the fact that the multitude is led by any man who knows how to exploit its passions, and from the existence of men who by their insight into the human mind well know how to sway the multitude to do their will, and who devote themselves to this purpose, whatsoever may be their reasons for so doing. For the multitude is not to be kept within bounds except when it is dominated by fear. Thus the passions of humility, repentance, fear and hope—though these are, strictly speaking, bad—have a relative value. If however it happens that the (unwise) leaders of the multitude are themselves influenced by the passions of compassion and benevolence, those leaders then, by the guidance which they give to the multitude, actually carry out a task of exceptional and even indispensable value (cf. *Eth.* IV, 50 schol.; 54 schol.; *Tr. pol.* I, 5). Seen in this aspect, qualified recognition may be granted to religion. Although for radical consideration, the unbridgeable gap between the wise and the foolish remains, a distinction taking into account the requirements of human life in society must be drawn within the group of the unwise between the "superstitious" and the "pious." Under this secondary aspect, theory and "religion" even stand in some alliance against "superstition." Closer definition of religion thus understood becomes possible only by the indication of the necessity of "religion" that emerges from analysis of Spinoza's political theory.

CHAPTER IX

THE STATE AND THE SOCIAL FUNCTION
OF RELIGION

FREEDOM AS independence of all external events, as self-determination, life in disinterested contemplation, love of fate, freedom from prejudices (all of which have their source in lack of freedom) and freedom in the political sense of liberalism and democracy—is there a necessary connection between these two meanings of freedom? For Spinoza the necessary connection between the inner freedom of the individual and the external freedom of society and in society is as certain as the corresponding manifest alliance between spiritual and political authority.[291] It is therefore possible to elucidate his conception of the State by starting from his *ethos* which contains a political *ethos*. However, if one adopts this direct path, one will fail to grasp the character of his political doctrine, which as doctrine, as theory, presents the real and indispensable connection between the theory and the state. For the doctrine of the state is based on the decline of natural right, and this doctrine in its turn is based on the proposition that intellect and will are one and the same in God. This proposition is the formulation preferred by Spinoza in the *Tractate* for his innermost thought. We must start—if we are to reach deeper comprehension of the complex relation between political theory and political ethos—not from the sections of the *Tractate* devoted to political theory but from the more rigorous and lucid fundamental reflection which is to be found in the *Political Tractate*.

That the *Political Tractate* goes more to the roots is evident from the fact that that work has an important Introduction, in which Spinoza develops the program of his political doctrine. This chapter is based on two models of very different origin—on the Preface to Book III of the *Ethica* and Chapter 15 of Machiavelli's *Principe*. A comparison of that Introduction with its two models will enable one to recognize the particular tone of Spinoza's political doctrine.

A. The "Realism" of Spinoza's Political Doctrine

A comparison of the Preface to Part III of the *Ethica* with the introduction to the *Political Tractate* lets us see that Spinoza revised that Preface with a view to the political theme. The theses advanced in the Preface to Part III of the *Ethica* are now to serve as introduction to political theory. In the two texts the same theses are asserted to some extent literally in the same terms.

1) Human emotions are not arbitrary trespasses, vices, which might well never have come into being; they are necessary, in accord with the universal laws of nature.

2) Therefore they are not to be loathed or bewailed but simply to be understood.

In the face of this general concord between the texts, the divergence in tendency and in tone to be recognized in the polemics of the two passages stands out all the more sharply. The preface to Part III of the *Ethica*, which treats of "the origin and nature of the emotions," directs its shafts first against those who look upon man in nature as a state within a state by attributing to him a power over his actions independent of universal causality. The Preface then turns against the Stoics and Descartes, who also, despite their other merits, did not set forth an adequate theory of human passions. The tone adopted towards opponents is cool and peremptory. That tone takes on a note of respect when he comes to the Stoics and to Descartes. The note struck is that of a philosopher concerned to attain to knowledge who finds himself facing on the one hand a kind of moralist who has never understood what the quest for knowledge is, and, facing truly philosophic precursors on the other hand, whose views are to be contested but who are to be respected. In the *Political Tractate* this tone has become much sharper. Here Spinoza opposes philosophers as such. It is not difficult to recognize in the philosophers the moralists whom he opposes in the Introduction to Part III of the *Ethica*. But now Spinoza does not look over and beyond these with the subtle contempt of one who is concerned with knowledge, but charges full tilt against them with the whole-hearted scorn of the realist free of illusions who knows the world. He reproaches them not so much for their assertion of freedom of will, but for their imperfect awareness of reality. He does not speak as a philosopher engaged in argument with other philosophers, but, as it were, blushing for and disclaiming the fact that he is a philosopher, he speaks against the philosophers in the name of the statesmen, these acute, wily or sly men who are generally taken as more inclined to deceive than to keep faith, since they are past-masters of the craft by which it is possible to circumvent and guard against human badness and baseness, who are indeed not wise, but who, instead of wishing or dreaming, recognize what is real and what is effective. In this way a mood expresses itself which, in part thanks to Spinoza's own direct influence, became predominant in the nineteenth century against the "ideologues" and the "idealists." Already the sense is clear in which this attitude of mind is distinguished from the apparently similar one of the politician proper, and to which the victory of that state of mind in the coming age is due: the loathing of Utopias is conscious of its basis in more stringent intellectual discipline, in a deeper intellectual probity.[292] The opposition to Utopia is thus nothing other than the opposition to religion. For religion too was rejected because it was held to have its foundation in wishing.[293] Not wishing, but recognizing what is; not waiting for good fortune, but commanding fortune; therefore not making claims on fate, but loving fate; hence not making claims on men, on other men.

What is to be set up is a *realistic* doctrine of the State. This doctrine consists in nothing other than the strict deduction of what statesmen—men of penetrating understanding of man as he is—have discovered or invented, from the ultimate facts of human nature. The political philosopher learns from the politician and the statesman. The political theory justifies politic which follows its own laws, and remains independent of theory. Here Spinoza describes the procedure which he actually followed. His analyses of political facts take their bearings partly by actual institutions of various states, and partly by the political reflections of the "most ingenious" Machiavelli[294] (and of other publicists). Even Spinoza's realistic program came into being under the influence of the art of the Florentine of which he thought so highly, and which gave the decisive impulse to Spinoza's political theory—indeed, one may even trace that program directly to the programmatic statement of Machiavelli in Chapter XV of *Il Principe*. It would seem that Spinoza was impressed by the opposition there established between what is imagined and what is factual, between life as it is and life as it should be, and by the equation of moral demands with the unreal, which is, as such, unworthy of consideration. But what is the significance of this "dependence" of Spinoza on Machiavelli?

If one considers the chapters in which the two thinkers set out their programs, one immediately comes up against the striking fact that Spinoza's tone is much sharper than that of Machiavelli. Machiavelli expresses himself coolly and lucidly, with no trace of that bitterness with which he inveighs, say, against the Church. His theme seems to him too serious to permit of any pre-occupation with the figments of imagination remote from reality; he therefore thrusts those figments out of his way. He is unconcerned with them. By warning his readers against them, he shows that he has in mind a reader who must be helped to discard more or less effective scruples, that he is conscious of being the teacher of his reader. None of these Utopias is his concern, but they are—for the time being—still the concern of his readers, men engaged in political activity. Spinoza on the other hand is convinced from the outset that Utopias do not exist for political men, and that they are of no concern to his reader, in so far as his reader is a political man. Nevertheless he himself is concerned with them, deeply concerned. He contends much more hotly against them than does Machiavelli. The reason is that the Utopias concern Spinoza. Unlike his precursor, he says no word on their perniciousness or their impairment of political practice. Spinoza sees them only under their ridiculous aspect—and he sees in this the disgrace of philosophy. His opposition to Utopia is then not so much in the interest of politics as in the interest of philosophy. In these circumstances, what is the meaning of Spinoza's political realism?

In the final analysis that realism is not at all political. At most it is a modified version of unpolitical realism founded in Spinoza's ultimate assumptions. That unpolitical realism which consists in the unqualified affirmation of reality and which is born of motives entirely unpolitical, is modified secondarily with a view to politics. The situation in which Spinoza finds himself in his political theory cannot be grasped except in the light of that fundamental character of his philosophy, which one may describe, in agreement with Dilthey, as "two-sided," or with Cohen, as "ambiguous." It is thus that he comes to a dual judgment of the *passions*. It is open to him to see in these the humana *impotentia*.

He can equally well see in them the communis naturae *potentia*, the naturae necessitas et *virtus* (*Eth.* III pr.). The second possibility, which Spinoza unmistakably adopts in the passage quoted from the *Ethica*, is even more ruthlessly actualized in Chapter I of the *Political Tractate*. It is plain that the interest in the problem of the State is the reason for the more ruthless realization of the possibility which does not itself stem from the interest in the State. The serious, non-Utopian justification or deduction of the State must start from the factual predominance of the passions as the basic fact, uncomfortable, but not to be swept aside either by talk or by indulging in dreams. The politician who dared to count on good faith among men would indeed be building his house on sand. He would prepare his own destruction. This Spinoza could affirm in full accord with Machiavelli. But recognition of the factual predominance of the passions is far removed from affirmation of the passions. To *resign* oneself to the incorrigible folly and wickedness of men is one thing. It is quite another matter to *affirm* this folly in its positive being, with a view to the natural necessity which brings it forth. And on the other hand: if affirmation of the passions is taken as having a political meaning, then the state must be founded for the sake of the passions, whereas Spinoza assigns to the statesman the task of counteracting those passions. As for instance, Machiavelli's recognizing the highest *virtù* and at the same time the source of *virtù* in all other men in the *virtù* of the legislator and founder of the state: Machiavelli admires that *virtù* while enthusiastically accepting and affirming the wickedness going with it. For Spinoza however it is established that the precipitous path of virtue is closed to the common run of men, and also to the statesmen. He retreats from the literal meaning of *Il Principe* (*Tr. pol.* V. 7). Thus he is further from an affirmation of the passions than is Machiavelli—the dangerous passions of course included—as a positive foundation for the state, and yet, or perhaps therefore, his affirmation of the passions is much more extreme. This affirmation emerges prior to *any* consideration of politics, and it is fundamentally indifferent to this consideration. The possibility which Spinoza has, thanks to his ultimate assumption, namely, to see the *virtus* of nature (of God), even in the life of the multitude, swayed as it is by passion, slavish and unworthy of the *vir fortis*, and to rejoice in the contemplation of that life, is identical with the realism of his political theory. The inner anomaly of his position is obvious: he affirms for others what he rejects for himself; and therewith he constructs the political world from the distance of contemplation, affirming the powers which form it, "loving" them after the manner of "amor fati," but expelling them from the sphere of his own life. The cool statesmanship for which Spinoza makes a claim against the philosophers is not the spontaneous outcome of political life, political interest, political responsibility. In the last instance, it is nothing other than that pure understanding, by which man consciously shares in the imperishable whole. His interest in the state is mediated by his interest in theory. His political theory presupposes that theory is the one thing needful—even though only as the sole means of attaining perfect happiness. For on this assumption the gulf between the few wise and the multitude is given, and political theory is unconcerned with the wise and concerned only with the multitude. The abyss, created by interest in theory, between the wise and the multitude, makes the wise essentially spectators of the life of the multitude. For the wise, the multitude becomes an object of theory.

B. The Theory of Natural Right and the Critique of Theocracy

Spinoza's political theory, and in particular his theory of natural right, is to be understood as the outcome of his remoteness from the multitude. Thus his theory is *toto coelo* different from the theory of Hobbes, with whom his name is often coupled. This state of things cannot be overlooked except by superficial observers: by people who see Spinoza not in himself, but as a son of his time, or who take their bearings not by the motives but by the dogmas. Whereas Spinoza's theory of the state rests on the recognition of *tranquillitas animi* as the legitimate aim of life, Hobbes' theory of man and hence also his theory of the state involves the rejection in principle of that *summum bonum* of the "ancient moral philosophers" which contradicts the nature of (this) life (*Lev.* xi). True, both philosophers see self-preservation as the essence of man, but they mean very different things by the same term. Self-preservation, truly understood according to Spinoza, compels to theory; according to Hobbes, it compels to assuring the future, to peace and to the state. Therefore the essential content of Hobbes' moral philosophy is the peaceable attitude. For this reason, his theory of natural law and his moral philosophy are essentially the same.[295] Similarly, from Spinoza's ultimate assumption it follows that there is no immediate bond of union between his moral theory and his theory of natural right: he must refrain from enjoining the precipitous path to *his* goal in life on the common run of men, or even considering it as open to them (*Tr.*, p. 176; *Tr. pol.* I, 5). Since Spinoza's political theory cannot possibly be understood if it is confused with Hobbes', which has influenced the formulations adopted by Spinoza, the bases of the two doctrines must now be contrasted.

Hobbes' point of departure is man in the condition he is in before the founding of any government, namely, the state of nature. He has no positive interest in this condition. He draws a clear picture of it in order to show his contemporaries what a state worthy of the name, the absolutely sovereign state, does for men, how it serves men's advantage. Taking account of such genuine experience of the state of nature as is to be gained from living through any civil war, the possibility of the state of nature is radically analyzed so that, in light of the genuine human needs which make the war of all against all necessary, the state may be shown as justified. Hobbes' description of the state of nature is a passionate and adroit polemic. It arises from the interest in peace, which is itself given with the concern for self-preservation, the interest in peace being primary for the preservation of bare life. From his notion of man's pre-political experience, Hobbes defines natural right. As the source of all right, natural right is not identical with the actual behavior of men, and in particular not with the behavior of men living without a state. For this behavior is to a large extent contra-rational. Natural right is however the rational human behavior in the state of nature.[296] It is the characteristic of the state of nature, however, that in it the war of all against all arises not only from men's contra-rational but from their rational behavior. For since to each his own self-preservation is the primary good, and the primary evil is death, and in particular death by violence (*De Hom.* xi, 6; *De Cive*, ep. ded.), men are not to be blamed if they look out suspiciously on all the dangers which threaten each of them, as a result of the natural desire animating several men at the same time to possess some objects which cannot be shared. "It is thus not contrary to reason and not contestable and not against right reason, if a man takes all pains to protect his body and limbs against death and pain, and to preserve them. But what is not against right reason is said by all to be justified and justifiably performed. For the word 'right' denotes nothing other than the freedom which each man possesses to use his natural capacities in accord with right reason. Therefore the first basis of natural right is that each man defends his life and limbs to the extent of his powers" (*De Cive* I. 7). Reasonable behavior in the state of nature, in other words the right of nature, is the protection of life and limb. Hobbes does not proclaim the right of the stronger with the fire of a Callicles; for him there is no "stronger" individual, since in principle any man may kill any other, and *therefore* all men are equal: but he understands the state of mind of men in the condition before the founding of the state. It is important to note the cautious, exclusively negative bases adduced for natural right as the understandable and indispensable claim which each man has to defend himself: there is no room for blame or recrimination, it is not absurd or against right reason to defend oneself. Hobbes has in mind not only a multitude to which he does not belong, but also himself: "cavere sibi adeo vituperandum non est, ut aliter velle facere non possimus" (*ibid.*). The conception of the state of nature, and the natural right based on it, are unaffected by the difference between defensive and aggressive actions, for he who does not anticipate his opponent or competitor is himself undone.[297]

In Spinoza's case, matters stand quite differently. In the first place, he starts from natural right, and defines the state of nature by reference to natural right. In the second place, he does not define natural right in terms of man, but only applies to man a concept of natural right otherwise gained.

Every individual—not only every human individual, but every individual simply[298]—has just so much natural right as it has power. For the power through which individuals exist and act is not their own nor does it arise out of their essence, but it is the eternal power of God himself. In God, in the original source of all power and of all right, power and right are one and the same, and since all natural things are determined by God to exist and to act in the peculiar manner in which they exist and act, since the eternal power of God is effective in their power, power and right are one and the same in all natural things too: "Hinc igitur, quod scilicet rerum naturalium potentia, qua existunt et operantur, ipsissima Dei sit potentia, facile intelligimus, quid ius naturae sit" (*Tr. pol.* II, 3; *Tr.*, pp. 175 f.). Since it is the supreme law of nature that each thing strive, so far as in it lies, to continue in its condition without regard for anything other than itself, therefore every individual and in particular every human individual, by having the power, also has the right to use such means as it has to self-preservation, without regard for others. Thus it is not immediately from the human situation, from the necessities of man as man, that Spinoza derives man's natural right, but from God.

It could seem that the gulf between Spinoza's metaphysical natural right and Hobbes' positivistic natural right is bridged by the connection established also by Spinoza—although in a way exactly opposite to that of Hobbes—between natural right and the striving for self-preservation. However, so simple a reconciliation between such different, even opposed approaches is not possible.

From the metaphysical proposition: *Jus Dei nihil aliud est, quam ipsa Dei potentia*, it follows that men who do not know right reason but are in bondage to their passions have a right to whatsoever those passions may urge. With the general definition, that carrying out self-preservation by all available means and without regard for others is the natural right of man, the fundamental assumption on which Spinoza's political theory is based has not yet been reached. There are two ways of human striving after self-preservation: the way of the multitude guided only by their passions and the way of the wise who are led by reason. Both ways have the same natural right. Politics, however, in so far as it is not prepared to start from Utopian assumptions, may take only the first way into consideration. To the multitude and to the politicians the way of reason is forever barred. This fact is not so much accepted with resignation as it is justified as founded in the *jus naturae*, affirmed, "loved"; not, however, understood. Hobbes had understood his natural right, given the human situation, given the elemental necessities of man, to be incontestable. For Spinoza this possibility is not open. For he defines natural right by starting from God, from the order and the laws of nature in its entirety. The natural right of the passions, and therewith the rule, founded in natural right, of conflict, hatred, anger and so on is against reason in respect to *our* nature, but not against reason in respect of the laws of nature *as a whole*.[299] All disharmonies in the human realm—all things derisible, contra-rational or evil—are resolved in the harmony of the universe. But in the human context, as tacitly conceded by Spinoza, the war of all against all, natural right, is not to be justified.[300] In the face of this, one must remind oneself of the almost prolix way in which Hobbes makes appeal to our *understanding* in his founding of natural right, which precisely from the human point of view is "not to be controverted, is not absurd, is not against right reason." Hence natural right, as seen by Hobbes, is truly adapted to the founding of right and the State: it is itself a legal concept. When he teaches that justice and injustice, and right and wrong, have no place in the state of nature (*Lev.* xiii; *De Cive* I, 10 n., III, 4 n.), he is saying neither more nor less than that, *on the basis* of natural right as of a reasonable and intelligible claim, every man may, as he thinks fit, use all means for preserving his life, that every man may *rightfully* apply any act to any other. The difference in value between damage done to another "in accord with right reason," i.e. in self-defense, and such damage done "for the sake of vain-glory and a false estimate of power"—the difference in value between the root of justice and the root of injustice—is not can-celed by the authorization, founded in natural right, to do anything whatsoever to anyone whomsoever. Rather than being canceled, it is asserted.[301] Spinoza's theory of natural right, on the other hand, offers no immediate handhold for the foundation of right as right. For one must never forget that natural right understood in Spinoza's sense legitimizes, in principle in the same way, both reason and the passions, and as the passions so also idiocy and thunderstorms. That the passions are of higher import-ance in the foundation of the state than imbecility and thunder-storms is beyond doubt. But this inheres in the character of the passions, and not in the "right" which hallows them. As a result of carrying the concept of "rational action" on to the *ratione duci* of the wise, the specific form of "reason" that prevails in the average social sphere is not grasped by Spinoza. In this sphere he sees only the limitless dominance of the passions. Natural right as reasonable conduct on the part of poor devils defending their skins, and natural right as *summum naturale jus*, as the power of the imperishable whole which produces and thus consecrates even the irrational, and which is higher than all human reason, certainly differ enough to justify speaking of an opposition between Hobbes and Spinoza precisely in regard to their theories of natural right.[302]

Hobbes, as we have seen, in contrast to Spinoza, starts from the state of nature and legitimizes natural right by the "right reason" of the men living in this state of nature. This natural right is however entirely illusory, as it leads to the war of all against all, in other words to a state in which the preservation of life and health becomes impossible. For this cause, it is a command of right reason to seek peace. And this is the fundamental "law of nature" as distinct from the right of nature. The meaning of this distinction[303] is that natural right is the expression of human behavior in accord with reason in the state of nature, while the laws of nature are the expression of the conditions which underlie the transformation (required by reason) of the state of nature into the civilized state. Here we must bear in mind that natural right is not subjected to a law of entirely different origin, but *one* right brings forth both natural right and the law of nature: the right to preserve life and limb. It is the logic of this right itself that leads to the war of all against all: for one cannot preserve oneself unless one increases one's powers, and in so doing, conflict with others becomes necessary. For this very reason, that right is transformed —negating, sublating itself—into the obligation of keeping the peace. All "laws of nature" therefore contain nothing other than ingredients of the will to peace. The most important of these laws states: "Covenants must be honored." The social contract stands or falls by the validity of this rule of natural law. Let us consider the instructive example which Hobbes uses. He sets himself the question: if I, in fear for my life, promise to give a robber a thousand gold pieces on the next day and to refrain from doing anything by which he might be brought to justice—am I bound by this promise or am I not? He answers: I am bound, and for the following reason: Were I not to keep my promise, it would follow that the robber acted unwisely in trusting a promise of ransom given to him by a captive. In other words, the chance of saving one's life would be lessened in future as a result of the breach of contract, general insecurity would be increased, life would be more at hazard, to the extent at least that that robber would never again allow himself to be fooled, but would in every case become a murderer. Now the social contract is understood on the analogy of this example: even the social contract is a matter of blackmail, in so far as it has arisen from fear, but it is for all that by no means invalid (*De Cive* II, 16; *Elements*, Pt. I, xv, 13;

Lev. xv). For—thus are we to understand Hobbes—fear is the expectation of future evils and at the same time the care for avoiding cause for fear (*De Cive* I, 2n.). Therefore fear leads to interest in peace. The social contract is the measure that opens up the way to peace.

Now Hobbes leaves no room for doubt, that in the state of nature we are pledged only to the attitude in favor of keeping the peace, not to putting this attitude of mind into practice. Were we to behave peacefully in the war of all against all, we should be acting altogether against reason. Not peace, but certain and premature death would be the outcome. Peace therefore requires, in addition to the peaceable attitude, the coercive power of the state which ensures security (*De Cive* III, 27; V, 1 ff.; *Lev.* xv). But the peaceable attitude, the attitude of trust and faith of itself tends by itself toward a situation in which it can become fully active. The power of the state, which protects the performance of contracts, does not merely come from without as supplement to the peaceable attitude but is the fulfillment of that attitude's own intention. The pacific attitude and the power of the state support each other in turn.[304]

From what has been established regarding the opposition between Hobbes and Spinoza, it follows that Spinoza has no possibility at all of understanding, after the manner of Hobbes, the germination of the pacific attitude, of honesty, from men's concern to preserve their lives, thus no possibility of understanding the social contract. Spinoza too discusses the case adduced by Hobbes—the promise extracted by the robber. His decision is entirely different. Since the right of a man is identical with his power, he has a perfect right to break every promise, if breaking his promise seems to him advantageous. The right to break a promise is given with the power to break it (*Tr.*, pp. 177 f.; *Tr. pol.* II, 12). In his discussion of the natural right of contract, Spinoza does not enter at all into the value of honoring contracts in principle. He simply denies the obligation to honor a contract apart from the utility of honoring it. Hobbes of course does not advocate any such fidelity to contract apart from utility. But he denies precisely that, all consequences weighed, in principle the breach of contract may have higher utility than keeping the contract. The greater utility of fidelity to contract in principle is the inner bond between the natural right of self-preservation and the civil condition. Spinoza severs this bond. Thus he is only apparently more realistic than the actually much more concrete-minded and sober Englishman, with his regard for sound common-sense.

Once the natural right of the passions and the natural right to break contracts is established, the inner bond between the multitude and the state becomes questionable. Naturally even the unwise would prefer to live in security rather than in enduring fear. But security of life requires that men relinquish violence and cunning, and live together in concord. This is beyond the powers of most men, for the very reason that they are not wise, but are ruled by their passions. The evils of insecure and barbaric life obviously do not sufficiently alarm them. They obviously require a still more massive compulsion: the threat of punishment. Fear of each other does not suffice to move the multitude to peaceful behavior. They must be driven into a state, like a flock of sheep into their pen by their shepherd, the shrewd and cunning politician, by force and threats. Nevertheless, fear of the misery of life outside the state is great enough to keep alive all men's interest in the state (*Tr.*, p. 177; *Eth.* VI, 37, schol. 2; *Tr. pol.* VI, 1 ff). But that fear is not great enough to produce the attitude of the citizen.

A superior reason must bring order into the play of passions. What induces this power to take over the function of ruling? Usually the passion for ruling. The interplay between the duller, less shining passions of the multitude and the will to dominate in their leader brings about peace. Even though the man who rules because of his craving to rule is no wiser than the multitude, nevertheless, since he disposes of the power to rule, he is far superior to the multitude. He has more power, and therefore he has a greater right, than has the multitude. By cunning and deceit he rules over the souls of his subjects, and therefore also over their bodies. The specific intelligence of the ruler is cunning. The able politician knows how to work on those passions of the multitude which best induce to obedience. He will therefore not wish merely to be feared. For when the multitude fears or mainly fears its ruler, they will rejoice in his misfortune, will wish him all ill and will do him all the ill in their power. The prudent ruler will therefore prefer to bind his subjects to him by promises rather than to alarm them by threats. The ruler must further be tender of the vanity of his subjects. Men do not readily tolerate having to serve their equals. The ruler is therefore well advised to convince his subjects that he is superior to the common run of mortals—whether by claiming that he is a descendent of the gods, or that God speaks to him directly and gives him counsel. As a consequence one can imagine men who believe, love, hate and despise according to the will of their ruler, and who believe that they take care of their own advantage whereas they are merely serving the purposes of their ruler, doing battle for their servitude as though it were their salvation and holding it no dishonor, but rather as the highest honor, to sacrifice their blood and even their life for the presumption of one man (*Tr.*praef., p. 3; *Tr.*, pp. 59 ff., 188 ff., 193, 200 ff.; *Tr. pol.* I, 2, 5; II, 10 f.; V, 6; VII, 4).

Such rule is possible only as a theocracy. For men can be completely enslaved only if their minds are sold into bondage, bound by superstition. But since superstition is deep set in human nature, and is therefore more or less alive in every age and in every nation, theocracy may well persist for ever. Theocracy is thus the form of state that best corresponds to imaginative-emotive life. In theocracy this life, which would otherwise perish in the war of all against all because of its lack of moderation, takes on a certain measure of order and security. The pre-condition for this efficacy of theocracy is indeed that the prevailing superstition, which is the foundation of the theocratic regime, be sheltered from every form of doubt by the prevention of free thought. This proviso obviously cannot be fulfilled, for no one can do away with whatever capacity for judgment he has. The subjects who do not permit themselves to be duped by their ruler set a limit to that ruler's power. There is ineradicable resistance to the predominance of a single individual, and ineradicable suspicion that the ruler recognizes his own interest and that of his family to the detriment of everyone else. Men who are not entirely barbarians cannot be duped so manifestly, nor allow themselves to be transformed from subjects into slaves, useless to themselves. Theocracy necessarily becomes rule by force, and no one has ever maintained rule by force for long (*Tr.*praef., 3; *Tr.*, pp. 59, 191, 205, 207, 211, 225 ff.; *Tr. pol.* II, 11; VI, 4).

Theocracy is the typical possibility of safeguarding life available to the life of the passions. From what has been said it follows that passion-dominated life can not safeguard itself by its own power.

The passion-dominated life has then no consistency, no enduring being. To the extent that it is inferior to rational life, in the sense of having less reality, less power, it also has less right. The natural right of man becomes the right of reason, since reason and reason only founds and constitutes consistent human life (*Tr. pol.* IV, 4 f.; V, 1; VIII, 7).

C. NATURAL RIGHT AND RATIONAL RIGHT

If we are to understand the problematic character and therewith the actual presuppositions of this critique of theocracy, we must first cast another glance back at Spinoza's doctrine of natural right. This doctrine states: no being can be criticized: there is no absolute norm for beings; there are only efforts, *conatus*, which of necessity arise from each and every being. The efforts and the actions of beings cannot be criticized, any more than the beings themselves. Only that man whose being impels him to transcend the emotive-imaginative life can and must judge that life in relation to himself, and must reject it. He would be acting foolishly if he were to apply such criticism to other men who, by their own being, are not called to the higher life of reason. He would be acting as foolishly as if he were asking of a cat that it should live according to the laws that govern the nature of a lion. To this extent, then, all beings have the same right. Now, each being in its own specific nature is a result or an element of the One Being; hence the different beings become comparable—they become comparable in regard to the fact that they express the One Being to different degrees, that they all *are* to different degrees. The equal right of all beings—because this right is founded on the conditioning of each being by the One Being—becomes the higher right of the being which "is" to a higher degree. To call this right the right of the stronger would be to expose Spinoza's intent to a grievous misunderstanding. Even though Spinoza may say that the wise man is the truly strong man, he cannot but concede that this type of strength and power is of minor significance for the foundation of the state. This is so because the multitude of men enslaved by their passions is so much superior in power to the wise man, that the latter must bow to them. If one were to understand power in a different, more refined sense,[305] one would conceal the problem. In accordance with Spinoza's doctrine of natural right one must say that the multitude, to the extent that it possesses more power than does the wise man—and the multitude *has* greater power in the sense of that word relevant to the constitution of the state—also possesses more right. Only if the power of the wise man proves to be quantitatively the greater power might one speak of the higher right of the wise man.

To eliminate any possible ambiguity from the equation of power with right, let us distinguish that equation, drawn as it is from the prior equating of greater power with the greater right, from the doctrine properly so-called of the right of the stronger. (In passing, let us also once more recall that Hobbes too does not assert the right of the stronger, for in his theory, all men are equally strong.) Natural right, in Spinoza's sense, is not on the side of the stronger as a personage to be contemplated, feared and admired because of his vitality, but on the side of the greater quantum of power, and this without regard to whether this power exists in one or in a number of individuals (cf. *Tr. pol.* II, 13). The tyrant who by violence and cunning becomes the ruler acts—according to Callicles as well as according to Spinoza—in full accord with the highest right of nature. The mob of slaves, which conspires and enslaves the man of excellence, sins against the right of nature, according to Callicles, but according to Spinoza by the very fact of its gaining the victory acts justly. Spinoza's doctrine of natural right is free from any consideration of the specifically human; it is conceived in terms of the cosmos alone. Only by attributing to man cosmic relevance can it lead to the understanding of human right. Man is only a particle of nature. But this particle of nature which is man must, in an eminent sense, be nature, be power.

Man as man is superior to all the other animals in wiles and in cunning, and therefore in power (*Tr. pol.* II, 14). He therefore has more right than has the beast. Now men, for the very reason that they are so wily and so cunning, are dangerous in the highest degree one to another. The war of all against all, and the correlative necessity of the state, is given, thanks to the distinctive characterization of man who *is*, on the plane of quantitative comparability, in a higher degree than the beasts *are*. Man's need of the state, of government, is thus already in itself a sign of greater inherent power.

The power of each man in the state of nature is equivalent to zero in the face of the cunning and duplicity of all other men. The power of two men united is greater than the power of each of them singly, and the power of many united is correspondingly greater than the power of many who remain disunited. The right of society in the face of the individual is identical with the power of the many united in the face of the many who remain in isolation (*Tr. pol.* II, 13, 15, 16). Therefore the power of man exists as such only as the power of society, of the state. It exists as the power left by the state in the hands of the individual, as residual power, or rather, as a power created by the state. Right in the narrower sense, in the human sense, is the power-relation predelineated by human nature. This power-relationship however is the reason of the state, the rational state. For the state which is not directed by reason has no permanence.

By its nature, affective life requires guidance from reason. Affective life exists only in so far as it is rational. Therefore the state is not a demand, but a pre-condition that is always met, even though in differing degrees. What is the *locus* of the reason of the state? The multitude, who are in bondage to their passions, are guided by their own interest into life in common with others; but only by their own interest properly understood. They themselves are incapable of seeing what is to their own interest: they stand in need of compulsion, of the state. Whether by chance or by reason of natural endowment, some men take the task of government upon their shoulders, and these men are guided by their own interest, though usually, indeed, not by their true interest. The reason of the state lies not in the governing nor in the governed, but in the capacity of the ruler to rule, and in the capacity of the ruled to be ruled. Even if the reason of the state lies mainly in the government, it does not lie in the governors as human beings, but merely in their function of governing. The reason of the state lies in no human being as such, not even in the wise. It is admittedly true that the wise, and they especially, seek—and also find—their true advantage in the state. But no man can live as a wise man, in other words, live purely in accord with the dictates of reason, when he is distracted by the claims of public business (*Tr. pol.* I, 5). Thus the wise man, who is most profoundly interested in the state, and who recognizes most clearly the advantages of the state, stands apart, in his very capacity as wise man, from the direction of the state, from the specific reason of the state.[306]

What guarantee exists for the reasonableness of the state?

Who or what brings the needed harmony into the unregulated play of the centripetal passions? The logic of events themselves does it. For only the rational state endures, or maintains its reality with any permanence. The reason of the state is identical with that harmony of passionate life which is the outcome of living-out the affective life. For the means by which the multitude may be guided have not been thought out by philosophers but by the politicians, as a result of their efforts to take suitable measures against the badness of men. And the politicians themselves are dominated by their passions.

D. THE CONCRETE PRESUPPOSITION FOR THE CRITIQUE OF THEOCRACY

The critique of theocracy would seem to have established that life lived under the sway of passions is incapable of safeguarding its own continuance. However, this critique rests on a particular presupposition which we have not yet taken into full account, because of the need first to understand the relationship existing in principle between natural right and rational right. This presupposition is the drive on the part of the people toward freedom. A case in point is the Turkish Empire. No other empire endured as long and as securely. But on the other hand, never have there been more disturbances and unrest than in democracies, which, according to Spinoza, are the most natural and the most rational form of government. The Turkish Empire however is founded on superstition, hence on unreason (*Tr. pol.* VI, 4; *Tr.*praef.,p. 3). Of a people that refuses to endure such a regime and that compels the theocracy, or the monarchy based thereon, to rule openly by force and thus to bring about the downfall of this irrational regime, it is presupposed that that people is not entirely barbaric, that it cannot be duped as to its real advantage by cunningly fostered illusions, that it is not willing to tolerate enslavement. It is therefore presupposed that the people is more than the vulgar (sanctified as are all other beings by natural right) which frightens as soon as it is not itself in fear, and which falls an easy victim to the cunning wiles of priests and kings. Once the eyes of the people are opened, it will no longer allow itself to be cheated by illusory good and evil, of the real good and evil—albeit of second rank— which are its real concern. Then and then only will it throw off theocracy. It was for the people concerned with its freedom, and vigilant of that freedom, that Spinoza composed his political doctrine. He reflects on the means, means not of his invention but thought out by politicians, for safeguarding that freedom (*Tr. pol.* VII, 31; V, 7).[307]

It is not the passions in general that move the people—how easily could many passions be manipulated in the interest of theocracy—but the will to freedom, naturally the will to freedom for the people's own life of the passions, for its striving after temporal goods. Whereas Spinoza, in profound opposition to Hobbes, initially deprives himself, by his sharp distinction between the wise and the multitude, of the possibility of seeing the kind of reason that is active in average social life, he does understand the natural love of freedom in a people, and through sympathy with that love he gains the possibility of supplying a theoretical basis for the state and the law. Only in conjunction with this human fact does Spinoza's natural right take on a human politically fertile meaning. But the connection does not seem to be necessary. Between the state of the free multitude and the state founded in violence and conquest, there exists no essential difference (*Tr. pol.* V, 6). But does there not exist a difference of degree which is of the utmost importance? Is not a people, when it is defending its freedom, fighting for hearth and home, more powerful than an army of mercenaries called on to fight for the glory of a ruler and impelled only by the hope of booty? Indeed it is so (*Tr.*, pp. 198 ff.; *Tr. pol.* VII, 22; VIII, 9). Thus, only if we take into consideration the concrete elements of power within the "free multitude," does the rational state show itself to be more powerful than the nation ruled by force, whatever may be the trappings of that force.[308] Without this consideration, the assertion of the higher right of the free liberal state would make the conception of natural right uncertain and ambiguous.

To just such an ambiguity are we led by the interpretation of the state of nature as a state of complete freedom and complete equality (*Tr.*, p. 181).[309] The proposition asserting the natural right of the passions contains a relic of the view according to which the natural life, uninfluenced and unchanneled by political, human compulsion, or man as he comes from the hands of God, is perfect. In this context, natural right does not mean the right of everything that is, but the right of all that is natural, divine, free, in contrast to the legal, to what depends on human arbitrariness.

This conception of natural right brings forth a political goal, a directive for the institution of law and of the state: the society of the free and equal. But there is no need to argue further in order to demonstrate that this conception of natural right, which is indeed present in Spinoza's work, conflicts with his philosophic premises, since that conception manifestly assumes that an alienation from nature—and a guilt-fraught alienation at that— is possible. For Spinoza however, theocracy, since it is founded on a combination of passions, that is, of natural forces, is essentially as natural as democracy. Not in the beginning, not previous to the founding of the state, but in the end, in the rational state, freedom and equality become actual: by the fact that the rational state proves to be the most natural, and also the most powerful.

The preference for the free state may, it is true, be combined with the doctrine of natural right, but the preference follows from that doctrine only if the abstract opposition between the multitude and the wise is relinquished, or, more accurately expressed, if it proves possible that the people can free itself from superstition. Otherwise theocracy can not be reduced *ad absurdum*. If we disregard the antinomic-naturalistic conception of freedom, which is annulled by Spinoza's ultimate assumptions, then, as has already been shown, neither the democratic, nor, as we are about to show, the liberal conception of freedom is an immediate consequence of natural right. Man—thus reads the reasoning adduced in this connection—may relinquish all things except his humanity: his freedom to judge, and to think what he pleases, cannot be taken from him (*Tr.*, pp. 187, 225 ff.; *Tr. pol.* IV, 4). The rights of man are inalienable. But Spinoza finds himself forced to concede that there may be men whose thoughts and feelings are completely regulated by ingenious measures taken by the sovereign; and this is not merely a possibility. Historical experience shows that an enduring and mighty empire may be founded and maintained by enslaving the minds of the multitude in superstition. A certain degree of inner freedom must already be present before the rights of man can be claimed at all, and can become a power.

Spinoza's doctrine of natural right takes on political meaning only after Spinoza has ceased to see in the multitude the passion-ridden vulgar, the inevitable prey of its abominable seducers, who shrewdly turn to their own account the illusions of superstition that fill the minds of that multitude. Only when he has begun to see instead a free people seeking after freedom and its real advantage by means of common sense, does his theory of natural law become meaningful as political theory, and the identity of natural right with rational right demanded by this theory becomes provable. In this way Spinoza becomes the equal of Hobbes as regards the understanding of the state after having been his inferior since his doctrine of natural right is primarily metaphysical or cosmological whereas Hobbes is throughout positive or limited to man. In addition, Spinoza possesses an insight inaccessible to Hobbes because of the latter's preoccupation with the preservation of bare life, a preoccupation which puts all other considerations into the background. Spinoza knows that the advantage of the people, if properly understood, does not unqualifiedly command to seek the quest for peace—a peace which even theocracy and absolute monarchy may guarantee, and which, nevertheless, thus understood, would be no more than the desolate peace of the desert—but the peace in which the people lives its own life, and not for the sake of someone else.[310]

There is no right distinct from might. But there are degrees of power, and therefore also degrees of right. Human power, human existence are possible only in the state. Even the "mightiest" individual, the wise man, can exist only in the state. The natural right of man—in other words, the pre-condition of human existence—is the state. The mightier the state, the greater is its right. The state of the free multitude is mightier than the state ruled by force. The rational state is the state that is real in higher degree. Here we need not assume that the word "real" is ambiguous. At the level which is the only one relevant here, of political discussion in terms of power, the power that wins the day is the greater power of the free multitude which sets its forces against the hirelings of tyrants. What is the attitude of mind that animates the citizens of the free state? They are concerned with their private advantage. If this is in fact their concern, at the very least they will not permit themselves to be turned into slaves, unprofitable to themselves. But the exclusive preoccupation with one's own advantage leads only to hatred and strife, and does not allow a peaceable attitude to develop. Men must be in a position to anticipate more gain to themselves from peace and order than they can anticipate from war and rebellion. But this is not sufficient, for it would amount to no more than a condition free from war, and not a condition of true peace. What is the power that forges a stronger and more intimate bond among men? Reason. But reason exercises only little influence on the majority of men. Not reason, but *religion*, teaches the multitude to love one's neighbor.

E. Vulgus and Nation, Superstition and Religion

The part played by philosophy in the life of the wise, and by superstition in the life of the vulgar, has its correlate in religion for the life of the nation. Since Spinoza asserts that an unbridgeable gulf separates the multitude from the wise, he is obliged to attribute to religion, as distinct from superstition, a function and significance. He cannot elude the question: How is the multitude, trapped as it is in the life of the passions and the imagination, to be induced to adopt behavior not indeed guided by reason but to some extent conformable to reason, socially useful, supporting not merely any state—for superstition would suffice for this—but a free state. How is the passionate-imaginative life to be protected from falling into superstition? Hobbes, if one disregards the concessions which he had to make to the powers prevailing in his time, set off on his philosophic inquiry from a starting-point of quite different character, and therefore had no call to face the necessity of such considerations. But Spinoza who, in accord with the "philosophic" tradition sees a perfect condition as attainable by man by virtue of powers inherent in man, is compelled by that tradition to seek a particular norm befitting the multitude composed of men incapable of perfection.[311]

Now the antithesis between philosophy and superstition corresponds to the fundamental distinction drawn throughout Spinoza's anthropology—a contrast that ultimately rests on the ontic opposition between the total and imperishable which is *in se*, and the partial and transient which is *in alio*. Between these there is no middle term. It has been shown earlier in this study how the difference between imagination and perception, on the assumption of which Maimonides bases his theory of prophecy and therewith his whole conception of religion, loses its force through the Cartesian conception of knowledge which Spinoza adopts. For Spinoza there remains only the abrupt antithesis of reason and imagination. The Cartesian conception of knowledge never-theless gives Spinoza a new possibility of understanding and justifying religion. The idea of God is "better known," more fundamental than knowledge of the world. There is therefore an original knowledge of God, common to all men. This is the *one* basis for philosophy and for religion.

It could with equal justification be said that the imaginative-passionate life, the life of the multitude, is the *one* basis of religion and of superstition. Religion stands midway between philosophy and superstition. How shall we understand this intermediary position? Spinoza defines the frontiers of philosophy and religion in the following way: the aim of philosophy is truth, the aim of "faith and theology" is obedience and piety; the basis of philos-ophy is the common notions, the basis of faith is Scripture (*Tr.*, p. 165). The "fundamental dogma of theology" is the doctrine that men may attain to salvation only by way of obe-dience, without insight. This dogma is not accessible to reason, it is known only through revelation. Nevertheless, it is possible for us to understand this dogma, once revealed, with moral certainty. We can observe in particular how much consolation for the multitude and how much support for the state accrue from belief in this dogma (*Tr.*, pp. 170–173). Spinoza thus expressly forgoes every attempt to reconcile religion—as he understands and recognizes it, and believes he finds it in Scripture—with his principles, which simply exclude all possibility of revelation. The interpretation must attempt to make good what Spinoza has omitted, to show how, from his principles, his theory of religion is to be understood.

Religion is primarily a postulate of reason. All men are by nature a prey to superstition. Only the few, who take it upon themselves to climb the steep path of reason, free themselves from superstition. Since superstition is a product of "passive" life, since its content depends therefore not on eternal, universal and integral truths of reason, but on transient and partial experiences undergone by transient and partial individuals, there necessarily exist side by side very many forms of superstition, and each form claims for itself exclusive truth. Therefore superstition is a center and source of never-ending unrest. If, in order to put an end to this evil, any particular form of superstition were to be declared the religion of a state and all other opinions suppressed by violent means, the evil would only be increased. In all times and in all lands, superstition is a power making for hatred and dissension. Religion on the other hand is required as a power productive of love and peace.

The actions required by religion are identical with the actions required by reason: works of loving-kindness.[312] On the level of works, works of love and peace, the free man and the multitude can and must meet and agree. Works of this nature are the only signs of piety. Piety is not directed toward something holy which is independent of piety. On the contrary, those things which are conducive to piety are called holy. The means to piety are different in different men. Therefore, according to prevailing circumstance, the most varied actions and objects may be holy (*Tr.*, pp. 146 f.). Since, however, in the case of the multitude, the command to render obedience to God proves itself to be the best means of achieving piety, there is a more particular norm set, a framework of fundamental dogmas, which must in all cases be observed and recognized, since without them no obedience to God is possible.

This foundation is however to be taken as wholly inaccessible to reason, a statement which on Spinoza's lips amounts to the assertion that it is contra-rational. If however the demand for obedience were in reality only positive, in every respect only positive, there would then be no possibility of understanding how it can be the foundation of the *fides catholica sive universalis*, how it is that "all can obey."[313] A possibility so universal must be based on human nature itself. The nexus of superstitious thoughts corresponds to the life of all men. Men of necessity assess and explain things in the first place according to the chance order in which those things were encountered and in particular according to the utility which the things have for those men. This anthropocentric, teleological mode of consideration leads to the conception of God as a king, acting according to purposes, ruling the world, concerned in particular for humanity, meting out punishment and rewards. To this conception there is connected the demand for loving one's neighbor in such a way that this behest is seen as the only command of a God who requires of men unqualified obedience, and who watches over the fulfillment of His behests. This connection has no inner, objective necessity but merely a "moral certainty," which certifies the opinions which lead to good works as pious.

Even though religion is more in accord with reason than is superstition, religion has no rational means to prove its superiority over superstition, for it is grounded in "mere experience." If religion wishes to defend itself against superstition, it cannot invoke truth, take its stand on the inner right of love over against hatred, but only on the will of God.[314]

Religion thus presents itself as a combination of elements that stem from reason and from superstition. Its aim stems from reason but its means stem from superstition. The bond between these remains obscure. In order to make the connection clear, let us first consider the not yet discussed lack of grounding for love of one's neighbor, which is possible on the basis of superstition. From the statement, "All men are by nature liable to superstition" (*Tr.* praef., p. 2), we try to understand the universal possibility of religion, in other words, to understand how it is that "all can obey." Men, dominated by the tendency to consider everything they encounter as a means, must conclude that there is a God who directs nature and whose supreme care is for mankind: in order to understand the facts which speak against providence (earthquakes, diseases and so on) men must proceed to the notion of the wrath of God on account of human sins. Are these natural thoughts, which arise from the primary reflection on the world, not identical with the foundations of piety? This question, to Spinoza's mind, is to be answered in the negative. Piety requires, for instance, belief in one God, whereas consideration of things as means makes both the monotheistic and the polytheistic view possible.[315] The former requires works of justice and mercy: the latter, cult, sacrifices, rites. Yet, even though we need to bear in mind that, according to Spinoza's principles, the prophets themselves, as men who both were not themselves philosophers and preached exclusively to the unphilosophic multitude, were necessarily dominated by the teleological view, and that the teleological view was the basis of their arguments (*Tr.*, p. 74), we must also bear in mind that their preaching is not to be understood from the teleological view alone. For whence did they draw the criterion, which taught them how to distinguish between the thoughts which were necessary and favorable to piety and those which were unfavorable, and to do this with unerring certainty? Reason and Scripture alike agree that God's eternal word is graven on the hearts of men (*Tr.*, p. 144). When the prophets teach this, must they not also have experienced it? The voice of the eternal word of God in their hearts showed them the true standard for life, although not in clear concepts. When they desired to adduce a reason for that standard, they had to start from the data of sensory experience (*Tr.*, pp. 62 ff.), which as a result of the natural tendency of men to view all things teleologically, are always already interpreted in such a way that they *may* lead to faith in a God who is law-giver and judge. What is decisive for the realization of this possibility is the eternal word of God in the human heart: it chooses from the prejudices those that are favorable to piety. The doctrine of God as law-giver and judge, to whom obedience is due, is thus by no means *known* exclusively from Scripture. It requires no more than to be vouched for by Scripture, since in itself, like all inadequate ideas, it has no consistency.

From this point of view, the general possibility of religion becomes understandable. Essentially, the prophets had at their disposal no knowledge of God surpassing the knowledge of God possessed by the multitude itself; they "had very vulgar opinions about God" (*Tr.*, p. 23). They spoke not to believing and learned men but, essentially, to the multitude. They spoke to the multitude of the word of God which is written in the hearts of men. Did they not appeal in their preaching to the word of God in the hearts of their hearers?

Spinoza's conception of religion cannot be reconciled with his principles so long as it is assumed that the passive (passionate-imaginative) life is the basic stratum of human life, in such a manner that in only a few men does reason rise above this stratum and against it. However, what is acted upon must be, be in itself, act. Being acted upon is only the counter-effect of an original agent, to effects produced from without. The being of man is in the spirit, which is eternal and one. All men are aware in themselves of the eternity of their spirit (*Eth.* V, *prop.* 34 schol.). Since therefore the scintilla of spirit is alive in every man, although in most men kept down by effects from their chance surroundings and by reaction to those effects, there thus lives in all hearts the conception, however dimmed, of spiritual life. God has graven His eternal word in all human hearts. This word requires of us love and righteousness, and nothing beyond these. This is the true, universal, natural religion (*Tr.*, pp. 144 f.).

Thus the eternal word of God, the one and only source of love of God and of love of one's neighbor, is the original fact. Now men who are constantly exposed to the impression of the world around them can scarcely avoid the dimming of their conception of God. They then represent God to themselves in the manner of the corporeal things (*Eth.* II, prop. 47, schol.).[316] But even this dimmed representation, which is necessarily very variable, can still suffice to support a life lived in the spirit of love and righteousness. The eternal word of God, which is still at work in this dimmed conception, guides toward that inadequate conception of God which is of a nature to make possible a life of piety.

CHAPTER X

SPINOZA'S CONCEPTION OF THE BIBLE AND BIBLE SCIENCE

A. Spinoza's Indifference to Scripture, and His Historical Consciousness

SPINOZA, disciple of Maimonides as he was, never doubted the legitimacy of science. His scientific efforts led this son of the seventeenth century to results essentially different from the doctrines put forward by Maimonides. At first, Spinoza seemed to have the possibility of maintaining the connection with Judaism by interpreting Scripture, as Maimonides had done, in the light of what he thought to be true. This possibility was closed to him when he gained insight into the peculiar and obstinate meaning of the actual text of Scripture, in the face of all the artful ingenuities of interpretation, i.e. when he applied the elements introduced into the consciousness of his time by the humanists and the Reformation. The result could not but be an awareness of the *distance* which separated his mind from Scripture. Once he had gained insight into the formal and material "vulgarity" of Scripture—in other words, into its total lack of scientific thinking—awareness of the superiority of the scientific mind to Scripture followed. This superiority, in an age in which science was felt to be not essentially completed but constantly progressing, could not but appear to him as belonging to a more advanced stage of human thought.

But is it not the case that Scripture itself calls science into question? Does not Scripture reveal an end of life, a task of life quite different in kind from science, namely, obedience to God's revealed Law? But the mind convinced that it clearly recognizes the aim of life, and also that it itself disposes of the means to that end, lacks all interest in guidance by authority, and hence all interest in Scripture. Because for him human perfection consists in freedom, and freedom consists in man's own sovereign self-determination, he rejects as a form of bondage the attitude and conduct required by Scripture. He looks down on the morality required by Scripture. Indifferent, not heeding it, unconcerned, sure of his own mind, Spinoza confronts Holy Writ.

This does not mean that he rejects Scripture in its entirety. He finds the most important truths in Scripture. But, and here he cancels the step toward Scripture, he finds these truths not only in Scripture. He asserts the immanence of God, as he says with Paul—however not only with Paul, but also with all the ancient philosophers and all the ancient Hebrews (*Ep.* 73). The utmost that he finds himself able to say in praise of Scripture as a whole is that on the subject of morality Scripture teaches nothing other than what the light of nature, which all men hold in common, teaches us of itself. The truths contained in Scripture are eternal truths. Understanding of these is in no wise furthered by our knowledge in which age, by which men, or within which nation they were perhaps first discovered or expressed.[317]

Spinoza's historical consciousness is conditioned by two facts, which are independent of one another, or if they are interdependent, this is as yet not fully clear to us. The first of these is the constitution of the new science, and the second is the Reformation. The discrepancy between these two currents of thought emerges in the contrariety of meaning in which the category "ancient" is applied to Scripture from each of these two points of view:

1) "the prejudices of an ancient people," in opposition to views reached by applying rational insight and resting on methodical investigation.

2) "the ancient religion," in contrast to the contemporary decline of the churches into a merely external cult, into credulity and prejudices, and into intense hostility to all who think otherwise.

The two contrasting meanings attached to the word "ancient" have their complement in the two meanings which the word "superstition" has for Spinoza. "Superstition" means different things according to whether it is being understood as the opposite of philosophy, or as the opposite of religion. In the first case, "superstition" is the product of imagination and of passion, which antedates intellectual freedom,[318] and liberation from which can be achieved only by the effort of reason. Superstition, understood in this sense, "teaches men to despise reason and nature," and to admire and venerate only such things as oppose or hinder reason and nature (*Tr.*, p. 83). In the second case, "superstition" is the decayed form of the old, original and true religion,[319] which has been brought about by the striving of priests after power. Here superstition stands revealed in a piety reduced to outward show and by the introduction of more and more new ceremonies and mysteries (*Tr.*praef.,4, *Tr.*, pp. 83, 208). What justifies Spinoza's tacitly ignoring this variance in the meaning attached to the term "superstition," which may be crudely distinguished as the positivist (Epicurean) and that of the Reformation? In the first place, "superstition" means in both cases the same objectionable facts. But above all the imaginative-passionate life and therewith superstition are original and primary only in the sense that the dominance of these precedes the dominance of reason. For the imaginative-passionate life itself rests on reason, the active man's true being. Thus superstition—even when it is understood as the opposite of philosophy, not of religion—is to be considered as a decline from an original condition. If we now further take into account that Spinoza equates *lex divina*, the standard by which the philosopher lives, with that religion which is common to all men (*Tr.*, p. 148), then we must insert into the formulation: superstition is decadence of original religion, also the philosophic conception of superstition. The original religion is in the one case the pure revelation, free of all deformation; in the other case, it is the pure word of God within us. Regardless of the sense in which the origin is understood, the power of the "flesh," the servile attitude (the striving of priests after possessions and honor or the immoderate striving of the multitude after uncertain good, and the fears and desires based on that striving) leads to decadence in the original and pure. Therefore all the efforts made by Spinoza serve one and the same task: the restitution of the original freedom.

But the priority of the self, the active, the intellectual or spiritual to the imaginative-passionate life is not to be taken in any temporal, historical sense. Indeed, to Spinoza's way of thinking, the imaginative-passionate life and both the world-view and the social order belonging to that form of life are historically primary. How is this view, according to which the ancient is in principle the primitive, raw and barbaric, to be reconciled with the return to the pristine religion as the pure doctrine? The only way open is to equate superstition with heathenism. From heathenish superstition there leads on the one hand the Biblical religion of the spirit, and on the other hand, modern science based on mathematics. But superstition is ineradicable[320] Even today the multitude is still a prey to the superstitions of the heathen. Therefore it was possible for the priests, spurred by their ambition and their thirst for power, to falsify the original, ancient religion into superstition. The Reformation has restored the original religion. But there now arises the peril that the ministers of the reformed religion "will again force everything back once more into bondage."[321] Spinoza composed his *Tractate* with a view to averting this peril, led by the wish rather than the hope that he might see at last improved what had deteriorated, that he might see his age free from all superstition.[322] By setting himself this task, he could not but take over a view of history which is not in keeping with his own intent.

"Antiqui vulgi praeiudicia" has been translated here as "the prejudices of an ancient people" in order to avoid a linguistic difficulty. The translation is not accurate. In the context in which the phrase is applied, the translation was incapable of causing misunderstanding because all weight lay on "prejudice" and "ancient." It is not by chance that Spinoza used the term "antiqui *vulgi* praeiudicia," and not, for instance, "antiquae *nationis* praeiudicia." The matter for concern is the *vulgaritas*, the popular character of the prejudices which are laid down in Scripture, and not their national characteristics, because there are no national characteristics as ultimate, natural facts. Nature does not create nations, nature creates individuals. Individuals are distinguished as nations in respect to differences of language, laws and customs. Only laws and customs bring it about that each nation has a spirit peculiar to it, a particular set of conditions for living, and finally, its own particular prejudices (*Tr.*, p. 203). Spinoza thus does not deny that there exist prejudices nationally conditioned, which must indeed be taken into account if Scripture is to be understood. But in so doing he is actually asserting that what is conditioned by nationality is no more than prejudices, not truths nor the discovery of truths, and further that the national spirit is not natural, pristine, original, but only the product of customs and law. The nations are the product of chance, chance products of particular laws, which were figured out by particular law-givers. Nothing national is as such by nature, nothing natural is national, i.e. peculiar to any one nation. If there were natural differences among nations, national advantages of one nation over another, then nature would have brought forth different kinds of men—which is obviously absurd. There is only one human nature. This one human nature is inalterable, always identical throughout the whole human race (*Tr.*, pp. 32 f.).

The nation is constituted by its laws. The laws are to be traced back to the law-giver. These laws differ according to whether the law-giver was wise and vigilant, so as to anticipate and guide those drives within his subjects which might endanger peace. The task of the law-giver may be performed in various ways, in accord with the character of the subjects—raw and barbaric as a nation, or trained and disciplined. In the first case, absolute monarchy, or absolute monarchy in the trappings of theocracy, is the suitable constitution, in the second case democracy. Thus differences exist among nations, at least in relation to their state of civilization or of barbarism, in relation to what is within the range of conscious human effort, and not in relation to what the natural endowment may happen to be—differences which are prior to the differences brought about by divergences in the laws, the capacities and the inclinations of the law-givers. There are no natural differences among the nations, but there are indeed differences in respect of the cultivation of human nature. In what sense is it true that there is an historical development from barbarism to culture, from superstition to freedom? The question must be put in a more pointed form in relation to the subject of the *Tractate*: how does Spinoza understand the evolution from Judaism to Christianity, from Moses to Paul?

Spinoza reshapes the Christian conception of this development so that it is in conformity with the positivist viewpoint. Mosaic law was intended for the early stage of development. But in the fullness of time, the place of the written law was taken—as Moses and the prophets had foretold—by the law which is inscribed on the hearts of men.[323] Yet Spinoza takes the "infancy" of the Jewish nation as barbarism. He measures the stage of development of the Jewish nation, at the time when Moses promulgated the law, by a standard entirely profane. He measures it not only by the conditions brought about by Christianity, but also and in particular by the state of the Macedonians at the time of Alexander the Great (*Tr.*, p. 191). The Israelites, accustomed to the

superstitions of the Egyptians, untutored and exhausted by miserable bondage, were incapable of rational understanding of God,
incapable also of grasping the inner necessity of moral teachings.
After the Exodus from Egypt, when Moses presented them with
the Law, he therefore propounded the moral teachings to them in
the form of laws, the observance of which he ensured by reward
and punishment. He took into account the slight culture and
power of comprehension of his nation, and therefore prudently
promulgated his Law as revealed to him by God. In particular,
he elaborated the ceremonial law in order to train his people to
unconditional obedience, since they were not ripe for freedom.
"Divine legislation" is a contradiction in the light of reason, but
is understandable as the subtlest *arcanum* of monarchic policy.
Whatever may be the reasons for which Moses composed this
fiction, it ensured that the fulfillment of the ceremonial law,which
is fully dispensable, and even absurd for rational men, was
accompanied by fulfillment of the rational moral law (*Tr.*,pp. 24 ff.,
48 ff., 55, 59 ff.). No more was needed than severing the tie
uniting the two bodies of law, by recognition that ceremonial law
is of purely temporal, purely positive validity, and what then
remained was, that obedience must be given to the God-given
moral law. By the idea of *Deus legislator*, Moses created the en-
duringly valid basis of piety.

The severance of the moral law, as the universal standard of
piety, from the particular ceremonial law was first opened up by
the prophets, and carried to its conclusion by the Apostles.
Mosaic law was valid only for the Hebrew nation, and indeed
only for their State (*Tr.*, p. 62). The office of the prophets was not
so much to teach the particular laws of their own country, as to
teach the moral law, the way to salvation. For this reason, the
prophets were sent not only to their own nation but also to many
other nations. That does not mean that the Hebrew prophets
were *kat' exochén*, the teachers of humanity. Prophets have arisen
in all nations. The pagans only gave them other names, such as
augurs or soothsayers. The pagan prophets too were men of high
and upright character, as is demonstrated by the story of Balaam
(*Tr.*, pp. 36 ff.). The prophets, because they speak not only to
their own nation, stand nearer to the Apostles, who were called to
preach to all nations (*Tr.*, p. 140), than they stand to the Hebrew
law-giver Moses. This position of the prophets between the

Law and the Apostles is shown also in the fact that Moses invoked Divine revelation alone for his teachings, and never made use of valid arguments, but the prophets do from time to time use valid arguments, whereas the lengthy deductions in the Epistle to the Romans makes appeal only to the natural light (*Tr.*, p. 139). The prophets stand midway between Moses and Paul; prophecy stands between pure "revelation" and the *lumen naturale*. This is not to be understood as though on the path leading from Moses to Paul the truth had been toilsomely brought to light: there is no indication of *evolution*. In essentials Paul teaches nothing other than what Solomon had already taught. The faith of which Paul speaks is the same as the understanding which is praised in the Proverbs of Solomon. Paul's doctrine of predestination has the same meaning for Spinoza as has the fatalism of the Book of Ecclesiastes. Solomon and Paul are philosophers. They are familiar with the *lex divina* in all its purity, free from all relation to the idea of obedience.[324] What they teach is wisdom, the eternal truth of the spirit, which thus was equally recognized in the time of the Old Covenant and of the New Covenant. Evolution occurs only on the periphery, in the doctrine of piety.

What is true of Paul is not directly applicable to the other Apostles. Paul is the most philosophic of the Apostles (*Tr.*, p. 144). In investigating the difference between prophets and Apostles, Spinoza takes Paul almost exclusively as his guide (*Tr.*, ch. xi). Spinoza's previously adduced definition of this difference can therefore be taken as valid only with limitations. He remarks in passing the contrast between Paul's Epistle to the Romans and the General Epistle of James. The latter forgoes the long disquisitions made by Paul on predestination, and compresses the whole teaching of religion into a few points. In contrast to Paul, James teaches that man may be justified by works (*Tr.*, p. 143). That means, even though Spinoza does not expressly say so, that the difference between Paul's Epistle to the Romans and the General Epistle of James coincides with the difference between wisdom and piety. Thus the difference between the Old Testament and the New Testament is not the difference between piety and wisdom. Both Testaments contain teachings of piety and teachings of wisdom. The core of the teaching of piety is rational morality, and in respect to this too, the two Testaments do not differ. The morality of the Sermon on the Mount, in so far as it

diverges from Mosaic morality, is to be understood only as interpretation of one and the same morality in relation to the distress-
ful political conditions of the age, just as Jeremiah under similar
circumstances taught on similar lines. The difference between the
Old Testament and the New Testament consists only in the kind
of reasons adduced for the teaching, which is the same in both.
The prophets take their authority from the Covenant granted to
Moses, and the Apostles take theirs from the passion of Christ.
Nevertheless the historical foundation peculiar to the New Testament has the advantage that in it the obligatory character of the
moral law is established for *all* peoples (*Tr.*, pp. 89 ff., 142, 149,
171). In this very limited sense, Spinoza does recognize a development from Judaism to Christianity.

B. Interest in Scripture and the Idea of Bible Science as Positive Science

Spinoza was not spontaneously interested in Scripture, and was
entirely devoid of any sense of need for Scripture. Yet because in
his age, freedom to philosophize was hampered by the as yet
almost unchallenged authority of Scripture, he finds himself
obliged to have recourse to Scripture. In the face of the intolerant
spirit of persecution alive in the minds of the contemporary
clergy, Spinoza sees Scripture as a document of humane, gentle
and conciliatory temper. As such, it is gratefully recognized,
especially since the gulf between the philosopher and the multitude
seems to be unbridgeable; with regard to the multitude the
authority of Scripture remains valid. But this is not the only nor
the weightiest reason why Spinoza, unconcerned as he himself is
with Scripture, nevertheless gives his mind to Scripture. He must
remove the prejudice that reason must be subject to the revelation
contained in Scripture, so that men held fast in their belief in the
authority of Scripture might be freed to philosophize. Thus it becomes needful to examine Scripture in regard to its truth. The
prerequisite for such scrutiny is to establish what it is that Scripture
does indeed teach. Only then is it possible to judge whether the
teaching contained in Scripture is true (*Tr.*, pp. 167 f.). Answering
the question of fact is the precondition for answering the question
of right. Thus Bible science appears to be the precondition for a
critique of the Bible, for critique of revealed religion. In actual
fact, the reverse relationship obtains, as the analysis of Spinoza's

critique of religion has established. The mere fact that Spinoza's Bible science is to become the foundation of a critique of revelation proves that in truth the critique of revelation is the precondition for the critique of Scripture. But this is not in need of any further proof. Spinoza comes to found Bible science as such only after completing his critique of religion. In chapter VII, "On the interpretation of Scripture," he refers back on almost every page to the findings of the previous chapters, which are devoted to critique of religion.

Spinoza understood his Bible science as positive science, and indeed as inductive science. He saw the possibility of Bible science as "objective" science which abstracts from any verdict on the truth of Scripture. He defined the method of interpreting Scripture by taking as his model the method of natural science.[325] Just as we must turn to nature if we are to understand nature, the only source for knowledge of Scripture is Scripture itself. Scripture does not, any more than does nature, provide definitions of the matters of which it speaks. Just as natural science (*interpretatio naturae*) infers from the data of natural history the definitions of natural things, so from the different narratives in Scripture on each of its subjects, definitions of these subjects can be inferred, and also the views held on them in Scripture. The difference consists not in the method, but in the aim of the investigation. Unlike natural science, which sets out to define the things themselves, Bible science is concerned with defining the opinions which the various Biblical authors hold on the things. The foundation for understanding of Scripture is knowledge of the character of the Hebrew language. The whole range of possible meanings in each single utterance occurring in Scripture is to be defined by knowledge of ordinary usage of the Hebrew language, and on this basis only, without adulteration by introducing our views or convictions on the truth of the matter contained. After this, the significance of each individual text must be derived from the context. The individual utterances, once so understood, are then to be arranged according to the subjects which they treat. If in the course of doing this we find speeches of an author which contradict what that author teaches in general, it must be concluded that either the contradictory or the habitual utterance is to be interpreted metaphorically. But first the question must be raised whether the usage of the language permits metaphorical interpretation of the passage in question. If it does not then the two texts remain irreconcilable, and judgment on the author's opinion must be suspended. For working out the meaning of Scriptural utterances it does not suffice to understand the utterances in their context. For to know, for instance, that an utterance has the character of a law or of an admonition, or in order to know whether it is permanently valid or valid only at a particular time we require knowledge of the circumstances in which the author lived, and out of which the utterance arises. Furthermore, one must investigate the history of the book itself, to gain certainty as to the authenticity of the individual statements. One must also investigate the history of the canon in its entirety. Only on the basis of a *historia Scripturae* as thus defined is interpretation of Scripture possible, and therefrom an answer to the question: What does Scripture actually teach? Exactly as in interpretation of nature, setting out from the thoroughly ascertained and methodically arranged data, once the most general structures common to nature as a whole are investigated, we progress step by step to the less and less general; so also in interpreting Scripture on the basis of data prepared by "the history of Scripture," we must first inquire what is most general, and what is the basis and foundation of Scripture as a whole, and then—and only then—proceed to the less general. What then is that most general element in Scripture, the understanding of which is prerequisite to the understanding of all other parts of Scripture, which stands in the same relation to Scripture as a whole as the phenomena of motion and rest stand to nature as a whole? What Scripture teaches *throughout, clearly and distinctly*, in such a way that its meaning is unambiguous. This is at the same time the *weightiest* matter, in the sense that it is what is always in the same sense enjoined on *all* men by *all* prophets, as the teachings *most* profitable to all men. The progress from the most general to the most particular therefore takes on the sense of disclosure of what is not the prophets' concern or not simply their concern, by the light of what is their absolute and ultimate concern. Only after this has been done, is it required to establish the reasons that bring forth those particular teachings on which the prophets do not always teach the same lesson; in other words, the reason for the divergence among the teachings of the different prophets. This task falls to the theory of prophecy and to the theory for interpreting the accounts of miracles.

The organ for understanding Scripture is the natural light, which by its nature interprets the obscurities by a process of correct deductions made from the parts which are clear. What counts as clear for "the history of Scripture" is the individual utterance which is easily intelligible from the context; what counts as clear for "the interpretation of Scripture" is the sum total of the utterances which have been found clear according to the standard of "the history of Scripture," the utterances which occur with identical meaning in all the books which make up Scripture. Thus the remnant which remains unclear in the sense of the interpretation of Scripture is such teachings as show divergence among the various books. Systematic explanation for this type of obscurity requires the theory of prophecy and the theory of miracles.

The obscurities which hamper even "the history of Scripture" are in part due to peculiarities of Hebrew as a language and as written language. These peculiarities are as follows:

1) In Hebrew, consonants are often interchanged for other consonants of the same class, for instance one guttural for another guttural;

2) many particles have several meanings, sometimes even contradictory meanings;

3) the tenses of the verbs are not sharply differentiated;

4) there are no vowels;

5) there are no punctuation marks employed to elucidate the meaning, or separate the clauses.

The obscurities affecting the "history of Scripture" are further due to our ignorance of the fate of all Scriptural books. Of many books we do not know who composed them, on what occasion, and at what time, nor do we know through whose hands they have passed, etc. All these obscurities thus have natural causes. They in no sense indicate that the natural light as such is inadequate for understanding Scripture.

These findings of Spinoza's do not immediately serve any purpose directly connected with critique of religion. They are necessary for founding Bible science. A comparison with La Peyrère's teaching on the obscurity of Scripture is appropriate here. La Peyrère asserts the obscurity of Scripture as an argument against Scripture being taken as a standard for science (cf. *supra*, pp. 75 ff.) Spinoza attains this aim, which he too intends to reach, by laying bare the contradictions among individual prophets, and the fact that Scripture was written for the vulgar. For this aim he has no need to demonstrate the obscurity of Scripture. Both critics find themselves compelled to limit their thesis, since the aims of both require that Scripture should remain the standard for piety. Both therefore assert that Scripture teaches with perfect clarity on whatever is relevant to piety. La Peyrère supports this assertion by recourse to the will of God, Spinoza adduces a reason inherent in the subject-matter itself. He asserts: whether an author is easy to understand or not depends on whether the matters he retails are easy to comprehend and to credit or not. For that reason, the passages of Scripture that speak of matters which are credible and easy to grasp are mostly safe-guarded from misunderstanding. But the moral teachings are particularly easy to grasp.

Spinoza demands of Bible science that it should be a means of unprejudiced understanding of Scripture. Unprejudiced under-standing is equivalent to historical understanding.[326] Scripture is not being understood if the interpreter is introducing his own insights or convictions into the text, if he is not taking Scripture as it presents itself. The analogy with natural science is not a matter of chance. Natural science and Bible science are alike concerned in the task of establishing "objective" knowledge. Spinoza's emphatic critique fights against that conception of nature which attributes to nature elements of human thinking, categories of purpose and value unknown to nature in its entire otherness. In accord with this, he defines the purpose of inter-pretation of Scripture to be the bringing about of knowledge of Scripture in so far as the message of Scripture is other than what the interpreter thinks, believes or feels. The demand for objectiv-ity, thus understood, is not bound up with Spinoza's metaphysics. Therefore it is to be expected that Bible science founded on that demand is not bound to that metaphysics.

C. CRITIQUE OF RELIGION AND BIBLE SCIENCE

We began by stating that Spinoza's critique of religion is the presupposition of his Bible science. It is now time to define the limits within which this is the case. The analysis of the critique of religion implies the answer. Critique of religion was to be divided into metaphysical and positive critique. Only the positive critique is the presupposition for Bible science as such. Were the matter to lie otherwise, it would not be possible to comprehend how Spinoza's scientific achievement could be taken up and accepted by men who were anything but Spinozists. The positive principle of Bible science amounts to stating: nothing may be asserted to be a teaching of the Bible which cannot be shown to be taught by the Bible by recourse to its literal sense. That amounts to stating that there is no other standard for the interpretation of Scripture than the standard which is regularly applied to every other written work. All attempts to interpret the Bible by principles other than those applied to other documents are based on the assumption that Scripture is revealed. Spinoza is at pains to undermine this assumption by his critique, the result of which may be summed up in the sentence: Scripture is a human book, thought out and written by men, in principle understandable by every man, and—as regards its origin—to be explained by the laws which govern human nature. Spinoza bases this result in part on the assumptions supplied by his metaphysics. but it is manifestly not bound up with these assumptions. How much a matter of course, how little in need of justification it is to Spinoza's mind, comes out in such statements as the following: " . . . unless indeed we believe, or rather dream that the prophets had human bodies but non-human minds, and therefore that their sensations and consciousness were entirely different from our own" (*Tr.*, p. 2). Spinoza's Bible science is "free from presuppositions" in the sense that it has fewer presuppositions than the Bible science which is based on the belief in revelation. It approaches Scripture as it would any other book. It places foursquare on the shoulders of the opponents the necessity of the more inclusive statement that the Bible is basically different from all the other books in the world—different in principle, because of its supra-human origin. This latter, just as any other miracle, is impossible to prove to the positive mind.

The Bible is a human book—in this one sentence we can sum up all the presuppositions of Spinoza's Bible science. For the meaning to be attached to the word "human" is here defined concretely by the view of man expounded in the *Ethica*. The later evolution of Bible science continues by reason of implicit or explicit critique of this view. The first step, perhaps the most important step, is taken by attributing a new value to imagination. The consequences of this transvaluation are drawn by Herder in his essay on "The spirit of Hebrew poetry." Herder's interpretation is based on what Spinoza took as the decisive result of his Bible science—that the Bible is a work of the imagination.

D. PHILOLOGICAL AND HISTORICAL CRITIQUE

The proposition "Scripture is a human book" implies that what is not possible to men is impossible. If implies therefore the possibility of historical and philological critique. The investigation of the authors, and of the times in which the books of the Bible were compiled, is not called upon within the *Tractate* to serve critique of religion directly. Spinoza states in the *Tractate* that if we are fully and truly to understand the books of the Bible, we must know who wrote them (*Tr.*, p. 87). That this investigation is of mediate service to the critique of religion is certain, since "the authority of the books of the Bible depends on the authority of the prophets" (*Tr.*, p. 171). Spinoza treats first, and by far the most extensively, the question "Who was the author of the Pentateuch?" What stands fast is the negative finding: the writer of the Pentateuch is not Moses. For proof of this, Spinoza makes use of all the arguments advanced by La Peyrère and Hobbes. He adds to these, partly in connection with an allusion made by Ibn Ezra, several further arguments of the same kind. The most important of these, according to Spinoza, are:

1) The author of the Pentateuch speaks of Moses in the third person, whereas in that part of the Pentateuch which, according to the Pentateuch itself, was actually written by Moses, Moses speaks of himself in the first person. Furthermore, the author speaks of Moses in a way that Moses would have been unable to apply to himself ("this man Moses was very humble," etc.).

2) Not only does the writer recount Moses' death and burial, and the mourning for Moses, but he also compares Moses with all the prophets who came after Moses, from which it is to be deduced that the writer lived many centuries after Moses.

3) He gives the names of localities which were thus named only after Moses' death.

4) He continues his narrative sometimes beyond Moses' lifetime. The conclusion is that the author of the Pentateuch lived many centuries after Moses.

Moses is the author of:

1) "The Book of the wars of the Lord," which is quoted in Num. 21:14, and which doubtless contained the history of the war waged against Amalech as recounted by Moses himself (cf. Exod. 17:14) and a list of the places where the Israelites pitched their tents (Num. 33:2);

2) "The Book of the Covenant" (cf. Exod. 24:3 ff.; Exod. 20:22 and 24:3);

3) "The Book of the Law of God," which was later supplemented by Joshua (cf. Deut. 31:9 ff. and Josh. 24:25 f.), but which was subsequently lost;

4) The "Song of Moses" (Deut. 32).

Reasons of similar nature speak against Joshua as having composed the Book of Joshua. In particular, Josh. 22:10 ff. certainly does not refer to Joshua, but only to the people of Israel as the decisive authority. The source of the Book of Joshua is the Book of the Just, cited in Josh. 10-13 ff. The end of the Book of Judges proves that this book was written in the time of the Kings, and by one author only (not by the many judges in succession). The Books of Samuel were written many centuries after Samuel, as appears from Sam. 9:9. The Books of Kings are summarized from the Chronicles of the Israelite and Judaic kings.

The books so far named are therefore not sources (*autographa*) but rather accounts which make use of sources (*apographa*). They form a unity, as is shown by the connection between the various books and the aim of the whole undertaking. They are in their entirety the work of *one* historian, who composed the work in accord with his intention "to teach the words and the commands of Moses, and to demonstrate them by historical events." Convincing reasons indicate that this historian was Ezra. The historian describes the history of the Jews approximately up to the time of Ezra, and, according to the Book of Ezra, no one in that age concerned himself so much with the law of Moses as did Ezra himself. On the evidence of Neh. 8:8 and taking into account the peculiarities of Deuteronomy, we come to the supposition that Ezra first wrote Deuteronomy as the "Book of the Law of God," and then allocated it a place in the large historical work which was composed later (*Tr.*, ch. viii).

Ezra's historical work forms a whole only in the sense that it was compiled by him, from a single point of view, out of material drawn from older historical works. These source-books were in some cases inserted *verbatim*. Thus for instance, the story of the miracle granted to Hezekiah, as given in Second Kings, is copied with very few deviations from the Book of Isaiah, which was contained in the Chronicles of the Kings of Judah (cf. II Chron. 32:32). The deviations prove to anyone who is not prepared to adopt fanciful explanations that there were different readings of the story as recounted by Isaiah. Similarly, chapter 25 of the Second Book of Kings stems from the Book of Jeremiah (ch. 39, ch. 40, ch. 52); chapter 7 in the Second Book of Samuel is to be found again in chapter 17 of the First Book of Chronicles, and Gen. 36:31 ff. (the genealogy of the Idumaean kings) occurs again in the first chapter of I Chronicles. Further, the lack of order, the frequent repetitions and especially the numerous contradictions in chronology plainly show that the historical work has been compiled from heterogeneous sources, the divergences of which were not reconciled. By reason of the chronological discrepancies we can deduce:

The story of Judah and Tamar, in the 38th chapter of Genesis, is drawn from another source than the story of Joseph, into which it is interpolated.

The story of Jacob and Joseph has been compiled from various sources, as has also the whole history of the time of the Judges and of the Kings. Ezra used his sources for his historical work without putting them in order and without reconciling them (*Tr.*, ch. ix).

The other books of the Bible are scrutinized in a manner similar to that applied to the great historical work:

a) The Chronicles were compiled very late, perhaps at the time of the Maccabees.

b) The Psalms were collected at the time of the Second Temple, and re-arranged. For according to the evidence of Philo, Psalms 88 and 89 were composed at the time of the captivity in Babylon.

c) The Proverbs were collected at the time of the Second Temple; cf. Prov. 25:2.

d) All the prophetic books are fragmentary. Many prophecies have been lost. In the Book of Jeremiah and the Book of Isaiah pieces from different historical works have been incorporated.

e) On the Book of Job, Spinoza passes the same judgment as does Hobbes, that the speeches contained in the book are not those of a man sore-tried and in the midst of his trials, but point rather to an author reflecting at leisure on his theme. He also considers it probable that Ibn Ezra is justified in asserting that the work was translated into Hebrew from another language, since the work seems to imitate pagan poetry.

f) The books of Daniel, Ezra, Esther and Nehemiah were all written by one and the same historian, using the chronicles of the princes and priests of the Second Temple. Neither Ezra nor Nehemiah can be the author, since the books named continue their account into much later ages. They may well have been written at the time of the Maccabees.

The result: the canon of the books of the Old Testament is not earlier than the time of the Maccabees, and was indeed only compiled on the basis of a decree of the Pharisees. The pharisaic character of the canon is proved not only by the fact that in the Book of Daniel the doctrine of resurrection (which was pharisaic) is taught, but this origin is also vouched for by some statements actually made by Pharisees in the Talmud. The authority of the canon therefore depends entirely on the authority of the Pharisees. If one is not prepared to set out from the unprovable assumption that the council of the Pharisees, which decided on the canonicity of the various books, was infallible, then one is obliged to demonstrate the authority of each single book of Scripture in order to prove the authority of Scripture as a whole (*Tr.*, ch. x).

In other words, even if it were granted that the Bible is based on an original revelation, it would still remain doubtful whether the text as known to us is identical with that original revelation. To this context belongs the statement, which is substantiated by various passages in chapter ix and chapter x of the *Tractate*, that the text has suffered numerous corruptions, e.g. in Gen. 4:8; I Sam. 13:11; II Sam. 6:2 and 13:37. The uncertainty of the text is particularly shown by the marginal notes to be found at sundry places in the Hebrew codices, and which are for the most part only variant readings of doubtful passages.

But Spinoza goes further and asserts not only that the text is of a later period, and corrupt, but actually that the text has been wittingly and intentionally modified by the Pharisees in their own interest, to bring it into concordance with their particular views. Spinoza does no more than indicate his supicion in this respect in the course of the *Tractate*. In conversation he openly stated this suspicion.[327] He must have considered as decisive ground for suspicion the fact which he brings out in the *Tractate* (p. 128), namely that the rabbis had intended to "hide," i.e. to suppress, the Book of Ecclesiastes and the Book of Proverbs; in other words, the only truly philosophical portions of the Old Testament.

NOTES

NOTES TO PREFACE

1. Consider Leon Trotzky, *The History of the Russian Revolution*, tr. by Max Eastman, The University of Michigan Press, I, 329–31 and III, 154–55.

2. Heinrich Heine, "Die romantische Schule," *Sämtliche Werke*, ed. Elster, V, 217. Cf. the discussion of romanticism in Hegel's *Aesthetik*.

3. Consider *Jenseits von Gut und Böse*, Chapter 8.

4. *Wilhelm Meisters Wanderjahre*, Bk. 3, ch. 11.

5. *Jenseits von Gut und Böse*, no. 251; cf. *Morgenröte*, no. 205.

6. *Einführung in die Metaphysik*, Tübingen, 1953, p. 152. This book consists of a course of lectures given in 1935, but as stated in the Preface "errors have been removed." Cf. also the allusion on p. 36 to a recent "cleansing" of the German univercities.

7. Cf. Gerhard Scholem, "Politik der Mystik. Zu Isaac Breuer's 'Neuem Kusari,' " *Jüdische Rundschau*, 1934, no. 57.

8. Cf. Yehezkel Kaufmann, *The Religion of Israel*, tr. and abridged by Moshe Greenberg, The University of Chicago Press, 1960, pp. 2, 233–34.

9. Maimonides, *Mishneh Torah*, H. teshubah VI, 3.

10. Ahad ha-Am in his essay "External Freedom and Internal Servitude."

11. Cf. Spinoza, *Theologico-political Treatise*, praef. (sect. 7 Bruder).

12. *Théodicée*, Discours de la Conformité de la foi avec la raison, sect. 3, and Vergil, *Georgica* IV, 86–87. The poet speaks of the battle between two rival queens for the rule of a single beehive. The philosopher seems to think of the question whether philosophy or revelation ought to be the queen.

13. Cf. Franz Rosenzweig, *Kleinere Schriften*, Berlin, 1937, pp. 354–98.

14. On the relation between Rosenzweig's and Heidegger's thought, see Karl Löwith, *Gesammelte Abhandlungen*, Stuttgart, 1960, pp. 68–92.

15. Rosenzweig, pp. 380, 387.

16. *Eclipse of God*, New York, 1952, p. 97; cf. the German original, *Gottesfinsternis*, Zürich, 1953, pp. 87–88. I have not attempted to bring the translation somewhat closer to Heidegger's German statement which, incidentally, is not quite literally quoted by Buber. Cf. Heidegger, *Nietzsche*, II, 320.

17. Hermann Cohen, *Ethik des reinen Willens*, 4th ed., p. 422: "Der Prophet hat gut reden: Himmel und Erde mögen vergehen; er denkt sie in seinem Felsen, den ihm Gott bildet, wohlgegründet."

18. *Eclipse of God*, p. 81; *Gottesfinsternis*, p. 71. I believe that the translator made a mistake in rendering "Führung einer Welt" by "conduct of the world," and I changed his translation accordingly, but I do not know whether I am right; it does not appear from the Preface that Buber has approved the translation.

19. Cf. the reasoning with which Wellhausen justifies his athetesis of Amos 9:13–15: "Roses and lavender instead of blood and iron." *Skizzen und Vorarbeiten*, Berlin, 1893, V, 94.

20. *Der Satz vom Grund*, p. 142; *Was heisst Denken?* pp. 32 ff.

21. *Gottesfinsternis*, pp. 143, 159–61; *Eclipse of God*, pp. 154, 173–75. Cf. Rosenzweig, pp. 192, 530. Cf. above all the thorough discussion of this theme by Gershom Scholem, *On the Kabbalah and its Symbolism*, Schocken, New York, 1965, chapters I and II.

22. Cf. *Gottesfinsternis*, p. 34 with pp. 96–97 and 117 or *Eclipse of God*, pp. 39–40 with pp. 106, 127.

23. Heidegger, *Sein und Zeit*, sect. 57. Cf. C. F. Meyer's *Die Versuchung des Pescara*.

24. Cf. *Fröhliche Wissenschaft*, no. 343.

25. *Jenseits*, nos. 45, 224; *Götzen-Dämmerung*, "Die 'Vernunft' in der Philosophie," nos. 1–2.

26. Letter to Overbeck of February 23, 1887. Cf. *Jenseits*, no. 60; *Genealogie der Moral*, I, no. 7, III, nos. 23, 28 beginning; Nietzsche, *Werke*, ed. Schlechta, III, 422.

27. *Fröhliche Wissenschaft*, no. 344; *Jenseits*, no. 227; *Genealogie der Moral*, III, no. 27.

28. *Jenseits*, I; *Fröhliche Wissenschaft*, nos. 347, 377. Thomas Aquinas *S. th.* 1 qu.1. a. 4. and 2 2qu.1. a. 1.

29. *Sein und Zeit*, pp. 48–49, 190 n. 1, 229–30, 249 n. 1.

30. *Kleinere Schriften*, pp. 31–32, 111, 281–82, 374, 379, 382, 391, 392.

31. *Ibid.*, pp. 108–9, 114, 116–17, 119, 155–56.

32. Nietzsche, *Also sprach Zarathustra*, "Of Thousand and One Goals."

33. Cf. also Kant, *Die Religion innerhalb der Grenzen der blossen Vernunft*, ed. Kehrbach, p. 43.

34. *Kleinere Schriften*, p. 154; *Briefe*, Berlin, 1935, p. 520.

35. *Ethics* V, prop. 25 and prop. 36 schol.; cf. *Tr. theol.-pol.* VI, sect. 23. Cf. Goethe's letter to F. H. Jacobi of May 5, 1786.

36. "Spinoza über Staat und Religion, Judentum und Christentum," *Hermann Cohens Jüdische Schriften*, ed. Bruno Strauss, III 290–372; "Ein ungedruckter Vortrag Hermann Cohens über Spinozas Verhältnis zum Judentum," eingeleitet von Franz Rosenzweig, *Festgabe zum zehnjährigen Bestehen der Akademie für die Wissenschaft des Judentums*, 1919–1929, pp. 42–68. Cf. Ernst Simon, "Zu Hermann Cohens Spinoza-Auffassung," *Monatsschrift für Geschichte und Wissenschaft des Judentums*, 1935, pp. 181–94.

37. *Jüdische Schriften*, pp. 293, 320, 325–26, 329–31, 343, 358, 360; *Festgabe*, pp. 47–50, 57, 61–64.

38. *Jüdische Schriften*, pp. 299, 306–9, 329, 360–62.

39. *Jüdische Schriften*, pp. 333, 361, 363–64, 368, 371; *Festgabe*, p. 59.

40. *Festgabe*, pp. 46, 47, 49–50; *Jüdische Schriften*, p. 344.

41. *Jüdische Schriften*, pp. 317–21, 323, 337–38.

42. *Jüdische Schriften*, p. 367; *Festgabe*, p. 56. Cf. *Tr. theol.-pol.*, I, sects. 35 and 37 with the titles of *Ethics*, I and II (cf. *Cogitata Metaphysica*, II, 12) and V, 36 cor.

43. *Tr.* xii, 19, 24, 37; xiii, 23; xiv, 6, 22–29, 34–36; xx, 22, 40; *Tr. pol.* viii, 46. Cf. especially *Tr.* xii , 3, where Spinoza takes the side of the Pharisees against the Sadducees. The contrast of *Tr.* xiv with Hobbes' *Leviathan*, ch. 43, is most revealing.

44. *Tr.* v, 7–9.

45. *Ibid.* v, 13, 15, 30–31; xvii, 95–102; xix, 13–17.

46. Cohen, *Jüdische Schriften* III, 333.

47. *Ibid.*

48. Cohen, *Kants Begründung der Ethik*, 2nd ed., p. 490, speaks of the "gewagte Spiel" of Kant in his *Die Religion innerhalb der Grenzen der blossen Vernunft*, a work according to Cohen rich in "ambiguities and inner contradictions."

49. *Ethik*, pp. 61, 64, 94, 439–58, 468–70, 606. Cf. *Kants Begründung der Ethik*, 2nd ed. pp. 356–57.

50. Spinoza, *Tr. pol.* i, 2. Cohen, *Ethik*, pp. 64, 269, 272, 285–86, 378, 384–86; *Kants Begründung der Ethik*, pp. 394–406, 454. Cf., however, Hegel, *Rechtsphilosophie*, sect. 94 ff.

51. *Pirke Abot* III, 2.

52. *Kants Begründung der Ethik*, pp. 309, 430, 431, 439, 446, 452, 511, 544–45, 554.

53. *Festgabe*, p. 44 (*Kleinere Schriften*, p. 355).

54. *Jüdische Schriften* II, 265–67. Cf. *Tr.* iii , 25, 33, 34, e.g. with Rashi on Isa. 19:25, Jer. 1:5 and Mal. 1:10–11, and Kimchi on Isa. 48:17.

55. *Festgabe*, pp. 64–67; *Jüdische Schriften* III, 345–51. Cf. *Tr.* v, 47–48.

56. Misreading his authority or Caro, Cohen erroneously asserts that Caro declares the reading "but to the wise ones" to be the correct reading.

57. Cf. also Manasse ben Israel, *Conciliator*, Frankfort, 1633, Deut. q. 2. (p. 221).

58. In one of the passages (*Edut* XI, 10) Maimonides says that the pious idolators have a share in the world to come; but how do we know that he does not mean by a pious idolator an idolator who has forsworn idolatry (cf. *Issure Bia* XIV, 7) on the ground that idolatry is forbidden to all men by divine revelation? In the other passage (*Teshuba* III, 5) he merely says that the pious Gentiles have a share in the world to come; the sequel (III, 6 ff., see especially 14) could seem to show that the pious Gentile is supposed to believe in the revealed character of the Torah.

59. *Jüdische Schriften* III, 240.

60. *Guide* III, 29 to end; Aristotle, *Metaphysics* 1003a33 ff.

61. Cf. *M. T. H. Yesode ha-Torah*, I, 1.

62. Cohen, *Die Religion der Vernunft aus den Quellen des Judentums*, p. 205.

63. *Festgabe*, p. 53; *Jüdische Schriften* III, 365; cf. II, 257.

64. *Jüdische Schriften*, pp. 335–36; *Tr.* iv , 17 (cf. 9–16), 21.

65. *Jüdische Schriften* III, 351; *Festgabe*, pp. 50–54.

NOTES TO TEXT

INTRODUCTION

1. The basic text for the references to Spinoza's writings is Gebhardt's edition of the *Opera*. The *Tractatus theologico-politicus* (abbreviated *Tr.*) is cited according to the pagination of the *editio princeps*, followed by Gebhardt.

CHAPTER I

THE TRADITION OF THE CRITIQUE OF RELIGION

2. An exhaustive presentation of the tradition is here neither possible nor necessary, as will be readily understood. The reasons for the choice made of elements within the tradition to be treated here will become apparent in the course of the study.

Criticism of religion can strictly mean only express criticism, actual contention against religion. Mere indifference to religion, even in the cases in which it leaves no room for religion at all, will not be regarded by us as criticism of religion. Nor does criticism of religion arise in response to religion as a pure negation, in the sense that this negative response is no more than "a free individual decision"; unbelief is not yet criticism of religion. The question is here left open whether indifference and unbelief, even the most severe skepticism, if they are seriously and consistently adopted do not necessarily develop into criticism of religion.

In order to maintain a distinction between criticism of religion as such and intra-religious criticism of particular forms of religion, we shall apply the term "radical criticism of religion" to such denial of religion as claims that its findings are valid for all superior men.

3. Epicurus, *Sententiae selectae* 10–13; Hermann Usener, *Epicurea*, fragmenta 219, 221, 227.

4. Diogenes Laertius, *Lives of Eminent Philosophers* x, 128 ff.; Usener, fr. 442.

5. Diogenes Laertius, x, 81; Usener, fr. 455; *Gnomologium Vaticanum Epicureum* 17; Cicero, *De finibus bonorum et malorum* i, 17, 55: *Tusculanae Disputationes* v, 33, 96.

6. Usener, fr. 242 f., 251. R. Philippson, "Philodem über die Frömmigkeit," *Hermes, Zeitschrift fur klassische Philologie*, Vol. 55, p. 240: Vol. 56, p. 403.

7. Diogenes Laertius x, 35, 36, 83–85; Usener, fr. 562; *Gnomologium* 41.

8. Diogenes Laertius x, 77, 133 f.; Usener, fr. 281; Hermann Diels, *Fragmente der Vorsocratiker*, Democritus A 50.

9. This is sharply brought out in antiquity: "Quae est anus tam delira quae timeat ista, quae vos videlicet, si physica non didicissetis, timeretis . . . ? Non pudet philosophum in eo gloriari, quod haec non timeat et quod falsa esse cognoverit?" (Cicero, *Tusculanae Disputationes* i, 21, 48).

10. What is said here is valid without proviso only on the assumption that the primacy of the motive in Epicurus' philosophy is fully established. If we accept it as established, the question arises whether the theory is to be derived from his motive. This question must be answered in the negative, if we take into account the possibility (which Epicurus himself indicates) that peace of mind and absence of fear may be attained by belief in kind gods, as well. In accord with this, theoretical and moral

criticism of religion must be kept strictly apart, even opposed one to the other. On the opposite assumption, on the assumption of the primacy of the theory, this distinction falls to the ground. For then the motive is, in principle, derivative. We cannot exclude the possibility that Epicurus, given his (naturalistic) theory, which by setting the independence of areté over against hédoné, at the same time cancels the independence of the theory in relation to arete, thus eventually reached the standpoint of attaching so much importance to the practical hedonistic purpose of theory. What he says on the purpose and the necessity of the theory need not necessarily be the program, they may indeed very well be the final result of the theory. In that case, they would not be the spontaneous expression of Epicurus' original intention, but the theoretically founded postulate for the only possible, the only legitimate intention—a postulate through which the primary interest in the theory for its own sake might be unmasked and discovered to be specious or erroneous. Thus it must be taken as possible that only in the course of pursuing his theoretical interest might Epicurus have arrived at renouncing that interest. Our presentation of Epicurus' critique of religion is thus to be taken as operating within the limitation that we interpret the criticism in accord with the point of view which the originator of that criticism wished to take. This limitation is justified as heuristic assumption, given the objective of casting light on the problems set by criticism of religion in the seventeenth century. For in this connection it is not of primary import whether Epicurus' actual intent is expressed truly and in full in the explication which he himself gives. The expressed intent is in and of itself understandable and viable as motive for criticism of religion.

11. Marx's doctoral thesis takes as its subject "The Difference between the Natural Philosophy of Democritus and that of Epicurus." Marx shows himself aware of the historical connection here mentioned (cf. *Literarischer Nachlass*, ed. Mehring, I, 73, 111, and also Mehring's comments, *ibid.*, pp. 49, 52 f.).

12. Which is only partially justified; what is said in the text applies without proviso only to the radical Christian-Averroist tradition. Cf. Ernest Renan, *Averroès et l'Averroisme*, 3d ed., Paris, 1866; Léon Gauthier, *La théorie d'Ibn Rochd (Averroès) sur les rapports de la religion et de la philosophie*, Paris, 1909; Julius Guttmann, *Religion und Wissenschaft im mittelalterlichen und im modernen Denken*, Berlin, 1922.

13. The earliest protagonist for this conception of religion is the sophist Critias (Diels, B 25). Cf. Aristotle *Metaphysics* 1074b and Cicero *De natura deorum* i. 42, 118.

14. Nicolo Machiavelli, *Discorsi* II, 2; Giordano Bruno, *Spaccio della bestia trionfante*, Dial. 2; Spinoza, *Tract. theol.-pol.*, p. 43: ". . . imo nisi fundamenta suae religionis eorum [sc. Judaeorum] animos effoeminarent, absolute crederem, eos aliquando, data occasione, ut sunt res humanae mutabiles, suum imperium iterum erecturos."

15. *Eroici Furori*, Pt. I, Dial. 3.

16. *Discorsi* I, 11–14.

17. Cf. the extensive indications in K. O. Meinsma, *Spinoza en zijn Kring*: historisch-kritische studien over hollandsche vrijgeesten, Hague, 1896 (German translation by Lina Schneider, Berlin, 1909); Stanislaus von Dunin-Borkowski, *Der junge de Spinoza*, Münster, 1910, pp. 475–91; Fr. Mauthner, *Der Atheismus und seine Geschichte im Abendlande*, Vol. II *passim*; Meinecke, *Die Idee der Staatsräson*, pp. 56 f., 104, 124, 252.

18. Lorenzo Valla, *De voluptate* I, 9, 11; III, 7 ff.; Pierre Gassendi, *Syntagma Epicuri* III, ch. i; Jaques Parrain, Baron des Coustures, *La morale d'Epicure*, avec des reflexions, La Haye, 1686, pp. 6 ff., 65, 92; Jacob Freudenthal, *Lorenzo Valla als Philosoph (Neue Jahrbücher für das klassische Altertum*, 1909, pp. 727, 735; Wilhelm Hasbach, *Die allgemeinen philosophischen Grundlagen der von François Quesnay und Adam Smith begründeten politischen Ökonomie*, Leipzig, 1890; on the "epikureisch-reformatorisch" conception of human nature, pp. 28 ff.; cf. pp. 94 ff.

CHAPTER II

URIEL DA COSTA

19. The text used is *Die Schriften des Uriel da Costa. Mit Einleitung, Übertragung und Regesten, herausgegeben von Carl Gebhardt*, 1922.

20. This happened under the impact made by the preaching of Vincent Ferrer and by the *Disputatio* of Tortosa. See Fritz Baer, "Probleme der jüdisch-spanischen Geschichte," *Korrespondenzblatt des Vereins zur Gründung und Erhaltung einer Akademie für die Wissenschaft des Judentums*, 1925, p. 23.

21. Which Gebhardt does, on p. xix.

22. Gebhardt, p. 106. This argument is traditional; cf. Judah Halevi, *Cuzari* I, 10; Joseph Albo, *Ikkarim* I, 11, 24.

23. "Thesen gegen die Tradition," Gebhardt, pp. 1–32. In this context belongs the formulation: "A text which has against it the testimony of other *Jews* is unworthy of credence" (Gebhardt, p. 85).

24. "A new custom, and therefore not good." ("2. These gegen die Tradition," Gebhardt, p. 5).

25. The author is indebted to Julius Guttmann for indication of the relationship between da Costa and Servetus.

26. Servetus refers expressly to the Jewish (and Islamic) polemics against the "triune God, which our people have introduced" (*Christianismi Restitutio*, 1553, pp. 34–36); when da Costa adduces in favor of Moses that Moses spoke "simply as intermediary" (simplicem internuncium, p. 106), this is to be taken, given the context, not as begotten Son of God.

27. Servetus, *ibid.*, p. 169: "In his omnibus est unius spiritus et lucis Dei energia." On p. 170: "Hinc dicitur anima esse in sanguine, et anima ipsa sanguis, . . . ut docet ipse Deus, Gen. 9, Lev. 17 et Deut. 12." On p. 178: "Ecce totam animae rationem et quare anima omnis carnis in sanguine sit, et anima ipsa sanguine sit, ut ait Deus. Nam afflante Deo, inspirata per os et nares in cor et cerebrum ipsius Adamae, et natorum eius, illa caelestis spiritus aura, sive idealis scintilla et spirituali illi sanguineae materiae intus essentialiter iuncta, facta est in eius visceribus anima, Gen. 2, Isa. 57, Ezek. 37, et Zech. 12." On p. 179: " . . . Idipsum probat litera Geneseos. Nam non simpliciter dicitur halitus ille Dei esse anima: sed inspirato illo halitu facta est intus anima vivens." On p. 216: "Nisi haec vis, ac eliciendae et producendae animae virtus elementis inesset, non dixisset Deus, Producant terra et aqua animalia." In da Costa, p. 65: "Thus the human soul, we assert, is and is called the spirit, by which man lives, and the said spirit is in the blood . . . In accordance with this, the soul of the beast is his spirit-filled blood, as the Law states, and it is in the blood that the soul dwells." On p. 76, da Costa refers to Gen. 2:7 to prove "that Brutes have the same spirit of life as has man, for when God created them He said: Let the earth bring forth the living creature; and later, when He created man, who was already endowed with spirit, which God breathed into him, Man became a living creature, so that He used the same word in the one passage and in the other . . ." On p. 77: "If Adam had been alive when God breathed the breath of life into him, we should then be able to say that this spirit is other and separate from the breath of life of the animals, since Adam would then be already alive. But Adam did not move until the spirit of life was breathed into him. Therefore the spirit of life, which was breathed into Adam, was the animal spirit, and this very animal spirit was the rational soul, and all is one and the same, in the sense that at the moment when the animal soul entered into man, there was given unto him also reason and reflection, what one calls the rational soul." It is to Deut. 12:23 and to Lev. 17:14 that Descartes also refers for

his doctrine regarding souls of animals. See Henri Gouhier, *La pensée réligieuse de Descartes*, Paris, 1924, p. 225.

28. Servetus, p. 179: "Ex semine manifeste eliciuntur animantium aliorum animae ac etiam humanae, accedenti ipsi homini divinae mentis halitu . . ." On p. 260: "Si constat brutorum animas elici ex semine, et nobis esse cum eis plurima communia, constabit quoque nostras ex semine quodammodo elici." In da Costa, p. 65: "It is clear as daylight, that man begets the soul of another man by natural procreation, in the same way as an animal begets another animal of its own kind . . ." On p. 66 ". . . the divine order and institution which, by the force of God's word by means of semen is laid within each creature: each begets its own kind, and thus the kinds continue and increase."

29. Servetus, pp. 234 f.: "Qui ante mortem Christi mortui sunt, ad infernum ducti sunt, quasi a Deo oblitioni traditi, exceptis paucis, quos futuri Christi fides fovebat. Hinc sepulchrum vulgo dicebatur terra perditionis et oblivionis, ps. 88. Idem sacris literis erat sepulcri et inferni nomen, ut simul ad sepulcrum, et infernum iretur . . . Ut corpus peccato animam traxit, ditionique subiecit: ita cum corporis sepulcro subicitur anima tenebris, morti et inferno." Da Costa, pp. 68 f., quotes Psalm 88:11–13, and comments: "Here it is denied that the dead praise God and rise again, for where they dwell there is no life, nor is there any spirit in the grave, the land of decay, the land of gloom and oblivion, and only the living can praise God. . . ."

30. As the basis of this conception, encountered in the teachings of Marcion, the radical-minded Tertullian recognizes an inconsistent form of Epicureanism: "Si aliquem de Epicuri schola deum affectavit Christi nomine titulare, ut quod beatum et incorruptibile sit neque sibi neque alii molestias praestet (hanc enim sententiam ruminans Marcion removit ab illo severitates et judiciaris vires), aut in totum immobilem et stupentem deum concepisse debuerat (et quid illi cum Christo, molesto et Judaeis per doctrinam et sibi per sensum?), aut et de ceteris motibus eum agnovisse (et quid illi cum Epicuro, nec sibi nec Christianis necessario?)" *Adv. Marcion* I, 25.

31. *Gesammelte Schriften*, ed. G. B. Mendelssohn, IV, 2, pp. 70 ff. In the text immediately preceding the passage quoted, Mendelssohn says: ". . . Epikur, *so leidlich er auch in der Moral philosophiert*, dennoch in der Metaphysik der seichteste und suffisanteste unter allen Dogmatikern genannt werden kann; . . . Selbst die Gründe, die hier wider die Unsterblichkeit der Seele angeführt werden, scheinen mir so unerheblich, dass sie zwar zu den Zeiten des Lucrez, nach dem damaligen Zustande der Religion und der Weltweisheit, von einem Philosophen konnten vorgebracht werden; zu unsern Zeiten aber in der Philosophie eine so schlechte Figur machen, dass sie kaum beantwortet zu werden verdienen."

32. To whom Mendelssohn of course does not belong; cf. his commentary on Ecclesiastes.

33. On p. 99, da Costa puts forward his views on the ancient contention that religion is an indispensable precondition of human society.

CHAPTER III

ISAAC DE LA PEYRÈRE

34. "Quelques lettres inédites de I. de La Peyrère." *Plaquettes Gontaudaises*, No. 2, Paris Bordeaux, 1878, p. 13. Jean Pierre Niceron, *Mémoires*, Paris, 1730, ch. xii, p. 81. Andreas Räss, *Die Convertiten seit der Reformation*: nach ihrem Leben und aus ihren Schriften dargestellt, Freiburg i. Breisgau, 1868, VII, 114. Heinrich Graetz, *Geschichte der Juden von den ältesten Zeiten bis auf die Gegenwart*, X, Leipzig, 1897, pp. 83 f. Article on La Peyrère by Alfred Bertholet in *Religion in Geschichte und Gegenwart*. Article on La Peyrère by Kerker in *Wetzer und Weltes Kirchenlexikon*.

35. "Conditi orbis epocham non ducendam esse ab illo principio quod vulgo figitur in Adamo; naturalis est suspicio, omnibus insita cogitatione rerum vel mediocriter imbutis. Videtur enim altius et a longissime retroactis seculis petendum illud principium: tum ex antiquissimis Chaldaeorum rationibus: tum ex vetustissimis Aegyptorum, Aethiopum et Scytharum monumentis: tum ex nupere detectis terrenae machinae partibus: tum et ex regionibus illis incognitis, ad quas novissime percrebuit navigando pervenisse Batavos: et quarum homines verisimile est non fuisse ab Adamo propagatos.

"Illa eadem et mihi olim inciderat suspicio; cum puer adhuc vel audirem, vel legerem historiam Geneseos . . . Sed quamvis haec animo meo insideret dubitatio; nihil tamen de illa audebam proferre, quod non saperet receptam opinionem de Adamo primo omnium hominum creato: donec incidi in versus duodecimum, decimum tertium, et decimum quartum, c. 5 Epist. D. Pauli ad Romanos . . ."

Richard Simon writes in similar vein to La Peyrère: "Pour moi plus je lis votre ouvrage, plus je suis convaincu, que vous avez d'abord imaginé ce plan des Adamites et des Préadamites, et que vous avez ensuite cherché dans l'Ecriture des passages pour l'établir." (*Lettres choisies de M. Simon*, Amsterdam, 1730, Tome II, Lettre 1.)

36. Gustav Frank, *Geschichte der protestantischen Theologie*, Leipzig, 1865, II, 75.

37. A. de Quatrefages, *L'espèce humaine*, Paris, 1877, pp. 21 f.

38. "The broadened geographic outlook and no longer blindly obedient intelligence made of Isaac Peyrère . . . one of the most paradoxical writers of his time, one who boldly asserted: *rationalis sum, et rationi conveniens nihil a me alienum puto*, and refused to be placed among the *abnormes miraculorum assertores*." Gustav Frank, p. 67.

39. "They [sc. the Socinians] above all sought to prove that the Law is done away with, and hence also the judicial ordinances. For in these we find much which is in conflict with the promise of *eternal life* revealed in the New Covenant, and in conflict also with the highest and purest *love* which is prescribed in the Evangel. Here one already senses that polemic peculiar to deism which was to arise much later. In that polemic, the specifically New Testament conception of mercy and loving-kindness is applied as the decisive standard to the revelation as conveyed in the Old Testament. This in its turn calls into question the identity of the two Testaments." (Diestel, "Die Socinianische Anschauung vom Alten Testament in ihrer geschichtlichen und theologischen Bedeutung," in *Jahrbücher für Deutsche Theologie*, VII, pp. 735 f., Gotha, 1862. Here Diestel has particularly in mind Morgan, p. 776. (On Morgan, cf. G. V. Lechler, *Geschichte des englischen Deismus*, Tübingen, 1841, pp. 370 ff.) Morgan's view of the Old Testament conception of God and also his view of Mosaic law are in striking harmony with the corresponding teachings of the Gnostics and of Marcion. There is need for investigation of the relation between the gnostic and the Epicurean tradition. It would seem to me that such investigation must take its bearings from the point of view adopted by Tertullian in his critical disquisition on Marcion's conception of God (see Note 30).

40. ". . . cum religio res naturalis nequaquam sit (alioqui non invenirentur nationes omni prorsus religione carentes; quales nostra aetate quibusdam in locis inventae sunt, ac nominatim in regione Bresilia . . .) . . . sed, si vera est, patefactio sit quadam divina . . ." *Fausti Socini Senensis Opera* (Bibliotheca Fratrum Polonorum) Amsterdam, 1646, I, 273.

41. ". . . quid vere in hominibus naturaliter sit positum, quod attinet ad religionem. In omnibus enim hominibus naturaliter est aliquod justi atque injusti discrimen, aut certe in omnibus hoc situm est, ut cognoscant et fateantur, justum injusto anteponi debere, honestum turpi. Hoc autem nihil aliud est, quam Dei verbum quoddam interius, cui qui obedit, ipsi Deo obedit, etiamsi alioqui ipsum Deum ne esse quidem, aut sciat aut cogitet" (*ibid.*, p. 539). The theory of the primacy of moral truths (as the

word of God within us), as opposed to knowledge of God, and in addition the theory of the revealed nature of the truth inherent in religion, is also for Spinoza the heart and core of his conception of religion. The influence of the Socinians is apparent also in Spinoza's distinction between those parts of the Scriptures which are necessary for salvation and therefore clear and unambiguous, and those parts of the Scriptures which are not necessary to salvation, but are merely historical, as also in his hermeneutics'' (cf. Diestel, pp. 740 f.). Spinoza's own library contained a copy of the Socinian Ludovicus Wolzogen's *De scripturarum interprete* (the work itself was not available to me).

42. "Qui igitur animo voluntateque admodum alienus est a probitate et sanctitate, ab hisque moribus, non potest adduci, ut credat, id esse verum, ex quo sequeretur, illi curandum esse, ut et his et illis sese exornaret." Socinus, *Opera* I, 276.

43. *Ibid.*, pp. 273, 277.

44. ". . . Perfectiora etiam quam Moses, et constantiora honesti praecepta tradidere Philosophi, tum Stoici, tum Peripatetici . . . At omnis illorum spes morte terminabatur; vel si quam animarum post mortem felicitatem suspicarentur, et nescio quos campos Elysios somniarent, tamen nec sibi nec aliis certam eius rei spem facere poterant. At immortalitate patefacta, et aditu ad eam toti humano generi aperto, omnia officii genera patuerunt, omnium firma constitit ratio, ibi summa Dei et hominum con-junctio, ibi hominum inter ipsos necessitudo enituit, vel potius tum demum vere constituta est; ibi proposito tanto pietatis praemio, nihil tam durum tamque arduum esse in virtute potuit, quod praestari ab homine aut non possit, aut non debeat. Hanc natura ad virtutis complementum desiderabat, hanc ad ejus amorem omnium homi-num animis inserendum, ad omnes ejus difficultates superandas deesse quodammodo conquerebatur, cum quaedam (ut diximus) praeciperet virtutem officia, quae sine vitae melioris spe suscipere, hominis videretur sibi irati et imprudentis." Johannes Crellius, *Ethica Christiana* (Bibliotheca Fratrum Polonorum), p. 444.

45. Socinus, *Opera* I, 273; Crellius loc. cit.; Ludovicus Wolzogen, *Commentarius in Evangelium Matthaei, Prolegomena in Novum Testamentum*, cap. ii.

46. Socinus, *ibid.*, pp. 274 f.

47. ". . . considerandum est (disputet contra quivis) si recipiatur Novo Testamento, non posse ad ipsam religionis summam quidquam fere momenti habere, quamcunque Veteris Testamenti depravationem, cum nihil non levis momenti potuerit esse in Vetere Testamento, quod Novo non contineatur; nec quidquam illius recipiendum sit quod non conveniat cum iis, quae in hoc sunt scripta. Adeo ut utiles quidem plures ob causas sit lectio Veteris Testamenti iis, qui Novum recipiunt, id est, hominibus Christianae religionis, sed tamen non necessaria. Hocque ideo dictum volumus, ut eodem tempore respondeamus iis (si tales fuerint) qui, ut auctoritatem Veteris Testa-menti minuant, atque ostendant, scripta illa fuisse depravata, dicturi sint, multa in eo legi, quae nihil prorsus cum quibusdam conveniunt, quae in Novo Testamento leguntur. Quandoquidem ita suo tempore et vera fuerunt et sancta. Sed postea qualit-atem mutarunt, cum mutatum est Testamentum . . ." Socinus, p. 271.

48. *Socinus*: ". . . cum jam homo natura mortalis esset, ob delictum illud suae naturali mortalitati a Deo relictus est, quodque *naturale* erat, id in delinquentis *poenam*, prorsus necessarium est factum. Quare qui ex ipso nascuntur, eadem conditione omnes nasci oportuit: nihil enim illi ademptum fuit, quod naturaliter haberet, vel habiturus esset" (I, 541). "Per peccatum inquit Paulus Rom. 5:12, mors in mundo intravit: id est, moriendi necessitas, sive mors aeterna, non autem mortalis conditio, sive ipsa mors naturalis . . ." (II, 261).

La Peyrère: "Mors naturalis hominum, creatur ex natura ipsa mortali hominum: nec causatur ex condemnatione mortis decretae in Adamum, quae mors legalis est" (*Systema theologicum, ex Prae-Adamitarum hypothesi.* Pars prima, 1655, I, 3).

"Neque vero condemnatio mortis vibrata in Adamum, et in omnes homines in

Adamo: quicquam addidit morti naturali, qua Adamus et homines omnes, lege creationis et formationis suae, mori debuerunt; praeter condemnationem ipsam, quae mysterio et spiritu constitit" (*ibid.*, V, 3).

49. *Socinus:* "Nam si peccatum . . . immortalitatem naturalem homini abstulisset, Jesus Christus qui peccatum abstulit, eiusque propriam vim omnem ac poenas illi proprie constitutas delevit, mortalitatem quoque naturalem abstulisset ac delevisset: quod tamen non fecit" (I, 537).

La Peyrère: "Peccatum certe Adami nihil addidit naturae hominum peccatrici, praeter merum reatum, qui mystice intellegi debuit"(*Systema theol.* V,3)."Restituit ergo Christus homines in quem locum acceperat illos Adamus. In locum scilicet peccati non imputati ex lege. Et evaserunt homines, post legem extinctam in Christo, illud ipsum quod erant ante legem latum in Adamo . . . ille homo naturalis . . . qui non in morte Christo extinctus est: Sed qui virtute resurrectionis ejus extinguetur olim. . . . Quo tempore et novissima inimica destruetur mors (*Systema theol.* V, 6).

50. *Socinus:* "Homo quia est ex terra factus, natura sua mortalis et corruptioni subjectus; et, *ex accidente*, quia divinum praeceptum violavit, morti aeternae obnoxius est: ita ut, quod ad immortalitatem attinet, nihil illi cum Deo commune sit, et *insuper*, ob peccata sua, hostis illius evasit. Necesse est igitur, quo cum Deo in gratiam redeat, et in spem vitae immortalis venire possit, ut Deus omnia ei peccata remittere, et *immutata ejus natura*, e mortis servitute eum vindicare velit. Jam vero Deus, pro pura bonitate et misericordia sua, *utrumque* praestare decrevit, dummodo hominem, antea patratorum peccatorum poeniteat, et is in posterum, non ad terrenam et carnalem, sed ad caelestem et spiritualem normam, vitam suam conformet" (I, 281). "Est quidem in hominibus, nullo prorsus excepto, ad peccandum (ut sic loquar) possibilitas, quia nimirum Deus voluntatem liberam et ad bonum et ad malum dedit" (I, 541).

La Peyrère: ". . . non desunt qui asseverent, homines numquam morituros, si Adamus numquam peccavisset. Quasi vero immortalitas, quae vita aeterna est, et quam sola perficere potuit recreatio; quae secunda creatio est; utpote penes quam solam immortalitatis potestas degat: comparari potuerit hominibus, vi et virtute creationis primae, quae natura sua corruptioni et morti oboxia est. . . . Debuit Adamus mori naturaliter, et causa pure naturali, ex quo materia corruptibili et mortali compactus est . . . Mors naturalis Adami, peccatum naturale Adami, et vitium ipsum corruptionis, ex materia ejus corruptibili innatum, consequuta est" (*Systema theol.* I, 3).

51. "Peccatum ante legem non imputatum, vocare liceat Naturale: Quatenus a nulla prohibitione legis pependit, sed a puris et pravis naturae humanae appetitibus ortum habuit. Peccatum post legem imputatum, vocare detur Legale: quatenus a mera legis transgressione originem duxit. Mortem rursus concedatur dicere illam Naturalem, quae ex mea hypothesi peccatum naturale consequuta est. Mortem vero illam Legalem, quae peccatum legale ulta est" (*ibid.*, I, 1).

52. "Crucifixus est cum Christo vetus Adam, et vetus homo legalis noster: sed vivit adhuc in nobis ille homo naturalis, vere noster, qui non in morte Christi extinctus est: Sed qui virtute resurrectionis ejus extinguetur olim, cum nos plena sanctificatione Deus induerit: quae resurrectio, et recreatio nostra perfecta et plena futura est" (*ibid.*, V, 6).

53. "Divina lex [sc. Adamo data] naturam hominum mutare constituit" (*ibid.*, I, 1). "Creditur vulgo: imputatum fuisse Christum mortuum hominibus, quia eisdem imputatus fuerat Adamus peccator. Frustra sunt qui illud putant. Imo contra; imputatus fuit Adamus peccator hominibus, ut eisdem imputaretur Christus mortuus. Non enim referri debuit Christus ad Adamum; sed vice versa, referri debuit Adamus ad Christum. Tendunt scilicet omnia ad finem suum propter quem sunt omnia. Mysteriorum vero omnium finis fuit Christus . . . Neque alia de causa peccatum Adami imputatum fuit hominibus, quam ut mors Christi quae hominum peccata procuraret,

et recreationem eorundem faceret, imputata illis foret" (V, 2). "Naturam produxit creator Deus. Legem tulit recreator, vel secundus creator Deus idem" (V, 5). "Paradiso autem ejecti sunt, et vita aeterna interdicti, mortales et mortui ex peccato Adami homines; mystice et parabolice: ut beneficio mortis et resurrectionis Christi, pateret eisdem aditus ad Paradisum eundem; et vita aeterna fruerentur, non mystice et parabolice, sed vere et reapse, quibus datum foret electis"(V, 7).

54. "Imputatio ergo peccati Adamici quae nos duxit ad finem illum; salutem hominum, non perditionem fecit. *Benignitatis* igitur et *misericordiae* plena fuit, *non feritatis et crudelitatis*, ratio illa divinae legis, qua hominibus vel insciis, imo neque dum natis, noxa Adami imputata est. Imputatum etenim fuit Adami peccatum hominibus insciis, ut illis etiam insciis acquireretur justitia Christi: quae salus est Domini" (V, 6).

55. Wilhelm Dilthey, *Gesammelte Schriften* II, 141.

56. Socinus, *Opera* I, 273, 538. In this Socinus' followers deviate, by making concessions to the ecclesiastical point of view. Cf. Diestel, pp. 772 f.

57. "Ponamus certe Mundum cum Adamo conditum: at non ido sequeretur, scientias, artes, et disciplinas omnes, cum Adamo itidem conditas. Erant quidem in principio, et ante rerum principium, summae scientiarum omnium rationes et causae in Deo: sed illarum semina tantum jacta fuere in Adamo, quo tempore formatus est: quae non nisi cogitatione et ratiocinio, cultura et tempore, et Adami potentia educi potuerunt . . . Adamus, quatenus homo . . . non potuit nisi paulatim, et successione temporis, scientias, artes, et disciplinas apisci . . ." (*Systema theol.* IV, 1).

58. This holds in particular for the deterministic theory of modern naturalism.

59. Dilthey, p. 132.

60. "Non ergo is sum qui putem imputationem peccati Adamici labefactavisse naturam hominum: neque rursus illis assentior qui nihil concedunt imputationibus. Suum sibi locum relinquo naturalibus, et mysticis. Naturalia naturaliter accipienda existimo: mystica mystice intelligenda censeo" (*Systema theol.* I, 2).

61. "Imputatio ex alieno delicto, mera est juris fictio extra Theologos: apud Theologos mera est ratio mysterii. Constet ergo, neque fictiones juris, neque rationes mysterii, vel hilum naturae officere potuisse . . ." (I, 2). "Facilius autem vim mysterii illius concipiet, quicumque intellexerit rationes fictionum juris, quae juris fuere mysteria . . ." (V, 1).

62. "Erratur, quoties generalius accipitur quod specialius debuit intelligi" (IV, 3).

63. *Ibid.*, IV, 3 ff.

64. "Nam et verbum Dei verum est: et ratio Matheseos vera est" (IV, 5).

65. "Solent omnes qui libris Mosaicis scrupulose addicti sunt, inventiones scientiarum, artium, disciplinarum, et rerum omnium, vel ad Adamum, vel ad Adami referre posteros. Ratione illa tantum, quia nullus homo prior Adamo legitur apud Mosem. Hoc illi autumant, argumento eodem quo putant, antiquissima omnia, tum naturalis, tum humanae historiae, monumenta, libris sacris, praecipue vero Mosaicis, contineri" (IV, 1). (This passage forms the introduction to the critical investigation of the Bible.) ". . . erat instituti nostri ostendere: utrum Chaldaei et Aegyptii, disciplinas et artes illas omnes potuerint consequi intra illud tempus quod numeratur, ab Adamo, usque vel ad Abrahamum Chaldaeum, vel ad Mosem Aegyptium. Certe, si res haec bona mente, et bona fide peragitur, nemo erit qui non censeat tempus illud angustissimum, vel ad minimarum et trivialium artium deprehendenda experimenta; ne dicam scientiarum altissimarum, qualia fuere Astronomiae, Astrologiae, et Magiae, curiosa observata, expendenda et demonstranda" (III, 11).

66. "Eliminabimus ergo hinc legem Mosaicam, cui nullus erat locus in negotio peccati originalis, et Adamici . . . Et certe Mosaica lex Judaeis tantum lata et promulgata fuerat, neque vero caeteris hominibus" (I, 1).

67. "Lex sane Mosaica jus suum, illudque praecipuum, habuit apud Judaeos; sed suum successive tempus, distinctum ab aliis et primis legibus Judaicis. Qualis mos est apud omnes populos, quorum posteriores leges priores antiquant. Imo proprie, constitit lex Mosaica in caeremoniis peculiaribus; in peculiari ratione sacrificiorum; et in peculiari jure Sacerdotii. Quae non erant in usu ante Mosem; et a Christo abrogata sunt" (*Exerc.* ii).

68. "Opinione, ut saepe fit, et vulgato magis consensu, quam exquisita veritate credi videtur, Adamum fuisse primum omnium hominum qui in luminis oras prodierunt. Illud enim neque dicunt usquam, neque intelligunt sacrae et canonicae paginae. Imo e contra, colligitur ex iisdem, quod probare in promptu erit; alios homines Adamum antecessisse. Adde, quod ex positione hac, quae statuit primos homines ante Adamum creatos, clarior multo apparet historia Geneseos. Conciliatur eadem cum se ipsa. Conciliatur item miris modis cum monumentis omnibus profanis, sive antiquis sive recentioribus; Chaldaeis puta, Aegyptiis, Scythis et Sinensibus. Conciliatur vetustissima rerum creatio, quae exponitur capite primo Geneseos, cum hominibus Mexicanis quos non ita diu Columbus penetravit. Conciliatur eadem cum hominibus illis Australibus et Septentrionalibus, qui nondum cogniti sunt. Quos omnes . . . probabile est creatos fuisse cum terra ipsa in terris omnibus, neque ab Adamo propagatos" (*Exerc.* viii).

69. "Etsi difficultates quadam in ea [sc. Scriptura] occurrant: Est tamen Scriptura Sacra, *praesertim novi foederis*, facilis et perspicua, in iis, quae ad salutem prorsus sunt necessaria" (*Racovian Catechism*, Qu. 36).

70. *Systema theol.* IV, 1.

71. ". . . inusitatae illae et insolentes coelestium species, quas divinis scriptoribus oblata legimus; inusitatis et insolentibus loquendi formulis descriptae et expressae. Ludos dicas fere omnes schematis enthei, quos nobiscum balbutiens Deus, miris modis fecerit hominibus" (*ibid*).

72. *Ibid.*

73. "Sed quis tam acri judicio erit, ut divinum autographum, ab humano apographo, separare queat? . . . Atqui sane non ita difficulter secernere erit apographum ex autographo; ubi auctor apographi se ipsum prodit, et ingenue fatetur, ex quibus libris librum suum composuerit. Difficultas in eo est, nosse in apographo, quae sunt excipientis; et quae autographi, a quo ille hausit qui excepit . . . Quidni ratio nostra, ubi ponderibus et modulis suis utitur; divino praecipue adjuta auxilio; divina ab humanis excernere poterit? Tum si pater Isaac coecus distinxit vocem Jacob, a manibus Esau: quidni mens nostra coelesti lumine irradiata, distinguere poterit vocem Dei, a manibus hominum?" (*ibid.*, IV, 2).

74. *Ibid.*, IV, 1, 2.

75. "Quae obscura sunt in sacris, quas manibus versamus, paginis, elucidare; confusa in illis et turbata digerere; omissa revocare; manca et mutila restituere; pugnantia conciliare; perspecuitati meae (si qua mihi est) non conceditur: tum neque plenam, ex illarum lectione, de origine Mundi notitiam habere; neque historiae sacrae seriem totam callere; neque Prophetias clare intelligere; neque vim mysteriorum efficacem perfecte cognoscere" (*ibid.*, IV, 2).

76. "Patet ex praedictis, Apostolum posuisse hoc loci due tempora. Unum, quo peccatum et mors primitus intraverunt in mundum, et pervaserunt in omnes homines: quo peccatum primitus imputari, mors regnare coepit. Alterum, quo quidem peccatum et mors erant in mundo, sed non imputabantur, non regnabant; nullo jure

pervaserant in omnes homines; non vivebant. Peccatum tunc temporis erat mortuum; mors erat mortua, et nullus erat sepulchri aculeus" (*Exerc.* xii).

77. The phrase "state of nature," as here used, intends the condition of human reason unaided, perhaps having already attained complete development. The polemical intention of the speech may well explain the apparent contradiction to the theory, for which La Peyrère otherwise plainly and expressly stands, of the original imperfection of man.

78. " 'O vos!' dicet ille [sc. Prae-adamita, "qui viderit utriusque status homines; et sub statu naturae creatos, et sub statu legis positos"], 'sub statu legis constituti: vos ego alloquor. Attendite et videte; quae differentia fuerit inter me creatum ante legem, et vos a lege sive post legem progenitos. Vivebam ego quondam sub statu illo naturae, qui a vestris praesentitus, sed neque dum cognitus fuit . . . Haec ita mecum gerebantur sub statu naturae, ante legem et Adamum. Vobis autem sub statu legis constitutis; et ab Adamo, vel post Adamum genitis, res aliter longe se habuit. Peccatum enim illud quod mihi erat simpliciter et naturaliter peccatum, sub natura, ante legem et Adamum: peccatum idem illud a lege et Adamo, vobis coepit esse imputatum et duplex. Peccatum quod mihi erat mortuum, quod non originem acceperat, quod non vivebat: quod cum patrabem, vivebam: sive quod perinde est, propter quod non moriebar morte, sub natura, ante legem et Adamum: peccatum idem illud, a lege et Adamo, originem accepit, intravit in mundum, et vixit in vobis. Mors quae mihi naturaliter tantum contingebat, sub natura, ante legem, ante transgressionem legis, vel ante peccatum Adami: mors eadem illa, a lege et peccato Adami, coepit regnare in vos, et imputationis causa vobis infligi. Mors mihi erat simplex ante legem et Adamum: mors vobis fuit duplex, ex quo coepit esse regnans, a lege et Adamo, propter peccatum Adami' " (*Exerc.* xviii).

79. "At inquies. Quomodo censeri et cogitari potest, homines illos qui Adamum praecessisse intelligendi sunt, peccavisse ad similitudinem transgressionis Adami; et mortem ex transgressione illa retro regnavisse in illos? Satisfaciam huic quomodo, per alias quaestiones factas in quomodo. Et solverit illam qui unam harum solve. Quaero e contra. Quomodo per transgressionem illam Adami, per peccatum illud originale, censetur et cogitatur natura omnis corrupta, et labefactata omnis creatio? Quomodo censentur et cogitantur peccavisse, non dicam Infantes, sed neque dum etiam nati homines in peccato Adami? . . . Quaero itidem. Quomodo censetur et cogitatur peccatum Adami imputatum Gentilibus illis hominibus, qui nati sunt ab Adamo, sive post Adamum? . . ." (*Exerc.* xxi).

80. Carl Siegfried, *Spinoza als Kritiker und als Ausleger des Alten Testaments*, Naumburg, 1867, p. 7.

81. Cf. *Plaquettes Gontaudaises*, No. 2, pp. 8 f.

82. *Systema theol.* I, 9, 10.

83. *Du Rappel des Juifs*, pp. 166–212, 304 ff.

84. *Ibid.*, II.

85. "Deprecatio Isaaci Peyrerii ad Sanctissimum Patrem nostrum Pontificem optimum maximum Papam Alexandrum VII. super libro edito, cui titulus est: Prae-Adamitae etc.," 1658.

86. La Peyrère was in the service of Prince Condé.

87. Richard Simon, *Lettres choisies*, Vol. II, Lettre 2.

88. *Ibid.*, Lettre 4. (In the light of this, Graetz' comment on p. 84 of his *Geschichte der Juden*, vol. X, should be amended.)

89. *Plaquettes Gontaudaises*, No. 2, p. 34.

90. *Du Rappel des Juifs* appeared in 1643, the *Systema theologicum* in 1655, and the "Deprecatio" in 1658. His last years (he died in 1676) were spent with the Congrégation de l'Oratoire in Paris. It was at this time that Richard Simon knew him personally. Simon reports: '*Toute son application* dans sa rétraite étoit de lire le Texte seul de l'Ecriture, pour fortifier de certaines visions qu'il avoit sur la venuë d'un nouveau Messie qui devoit rétablir la nation Juive dans Jerusalem."

91. "Creaverat nempe Deus gentiles primo, et primae creationis homines. Formavit deinceps Judaeos, et promissionis et secundae creationis filios" (*Systema theol.* II, 10). This is immediately followed in the same chapter by the interpretation, already quoted in our text, of the two accounts of the creation of man. This interpretation will be found again in the work of the English deist Blount, who also treats critically —as did La Peyrère in his *Systema* IV, 4–6—the miracles of the sun standing still, the recession of the shadow on the sundial, the shoes and garments in use during the forty years of wandering in the desert; cf. Lechler, *Geschichte des Englischen Deismus*, p. 123. La Peyrère is thus representative of the evolution from Socinianism to English deism.

CHAPTER IV

THOMAS HOBBES

92. *De Homine*, Ep. ded.: "Contigit autem sectioni huic, ut duae partes ex quibus constat sint inter se dissimillimae. Est enim altera difficillima, altera facillima; altera demonstrationibus, altera experientia constans; altera a paucis, altera ab omnibus intelligi potest. Itaque conjunguntur quasi ad Praecipitium. Sed necessarium erat, ita scilicet postulante totius operis methodo. Homo enim non modo *Corpus naturale* est, sed etiam civitatis, id est (ut ita loquar) *Corporis Politici* pars. Quamobrem considerandus erat tum ut homo, tum ut civis; id est, ultima Physicae cum principiis Politicae conjungenda erant, difficillima cum facillimis."

93. *Leviathan*, Introduction: "Nature (the Art whereby God hath made and governes the World) is by the *Art* of man, as in many other things, so in this also imitated, that it can make an Artificial Animal. . . . by Art is created that great LEVIATHAN called a COMMON-WELTH, or STATE (in latine CIVITAS) which is but an Artificiall Man; . . ."

94. *De Corp.* VI, 7: "Philosophia civilis, morali ita adhaeret ut tamen distrahi ab ea possit; cognoscuntur enim causae motuum animorum non modo ratiocinatione, sed etiam uniuscujusque suos ipsius motus proprios observantis experientia." *De Cive*, praef. ad lect.: "Itaque factum est, ut quae ordine ultima esset [sc. Sectio de Cive], tempore tamen prior prodierit; *praesertim* cum eam, principiis propriis, experientia cognitis, innixam, praecedentibus indigere non viderem."

95. *De Corp.* I, 7: "Harum . . . omnium utilitatem [sc. of technical achievements] causa est philosophia [sc. physics and geometry]. Moralis vero et civilis philosophiae non tam ex commodis quam ab ea cognita quam ex calamitatibus quae ab ejus ignoratione habemus, aestimanda est. Calamitates autem omnes quae humana industria evitari possunt a bello oriuntur, praecipue vero a bello civili; hinc enim caedes, solitudo, inopiaque rerum omnium derivatur." The recklessness of the exaggeration (*calamitates omnes*—Hobbes speaks as though both disease and the science of medicine were nonexistent) betrays his predominant interest in avoidance of *death by violence.*

96. Ferdinand Tönnies, *Thomas Hobbes, Leben und Lehre*, 3. vermehrte Auflage, Stuttgart, 1925, p. 117. An intermediate stage is represented by the classification of "the several subjects of Knowledge" in Ch. ix of the English version of *Leviathan*. Tönnies sees—as does Dilthey (*Gesammelte Schriften* II, 375 ff.)—in the conception of

one universal science, progressing from the abstract to the concrete, Hobbes' scientific ideal and also that of positivism in general. But if this *ideal* is taken as guide, one will fail to do justice to the essential *motives* of critique of religion in particular.

97. *De Hom.* XI, 15: "De jucundis quorum est satietas, quales sunt voluptas carnis, quia jucunditas eorum fastidio compensatur, et nimis nota sunt, et eorum aliqua faetent, nihil dicam. . . . Bonorum autem maximum est, ad fines semper ulteriores minime impedita progressio. Ipsa cupiti Fruitio tunc cum fruimur appetitus est, nimirum motus animi fruentis per partes rei qua fruitur. Nam vita motus est perpetuus, qui cum recta progredi non potest convertitur in motum circularem." See further: *Elements of Law natural and politic*, Pt. I, VII, 5-7; VIII, 2-5; IX, 15, 21; X, 3.

98. *Lev.* xi : "I put for a generall inclination of all mankind, a perpetuall and restlesse desire of Power after power, that ceaseth onely in Death. And the cause of this, is not always that a man hopes for a more intensive delight, than he has already attained to; or that he cannot be content with a moderate power: but because he cannot assure the power and means to live well, which he hath present, without the acquisition of more."

99. *De Cive* I, 2: "Quicquid autem videtur Bonum, jucundum est, pertinetque ad organa, vel ad animum. Animi autem voluptas omnis, vel *gloria* est (sive bene opinari de se ipso) vel ad gloriam ultimo refertur; caetera *sensualia* sunt, vel ad sensuale conducentia, quae omnia *commodorum* nomine comprehendi possunt." I, 5: "Cumque animi voluptas omnisque alacritas in eo sita sit, quod quis habeat, quibuscum conferens se possit magnifice sentire de se ipso: impossibile est quin odium et contemptum motuum ostendant aliquando vel risu, vel verbis, vel gestu, vel aliquo signo; . . ." Cf. *Lev.* xiii.

100. *De Corp.* I, 6: "Finis autem seu scopus Philosophiae est, ut praevisis effectibus uti possimus ad *commoda* nostra, vel ut effectibus animo conceptis per corporum ad corpora applicationem, effectus similes quatenus humana vis et rerum Materia patietur ad vitae humanae usus, industria hominum producantur." I, 7: "Quanta autem sit philosophiae utilitas imprimis vero Physicae et Geometriae tum optime intelligemus, cum praecipua humani generis, quae nunc sunt commoda, enumeravimus, et institutiones eorum qui eis fruantur cum eorum institutionibus qui eis carent contulerimus."

101. *De Corp.* I, 2: "Philosophia est effectum sive phaenomenon ex conceptis eorum causis seu generationibus, et rursus generationibus, et rursus generationum quae esse possunt, ex cognitis effectibus per rectam ratiocinationem acquisita cognitio."

102. *Lev.* xii: ". . . it is peculiar to the nature of Man, to be inquisitive into the Causes of the events they see, some more, some lesse; but to all men so much, as to be curious in the search of the causes of their own good and evill fortune. . . . whereas there is no other Felicity of Beasts, but the enjoying of their quotidian Food, Ease and Lusts; as having little, or no foresight of the time to come, for want of observation, and memory of the order, consquence, and dependence of the things they see; Man observeth how one event hath been produced by another; and remembereth in them Antecedence and Consequence; and when he cannot assure himselfe of the true causes of things (for the causes of good and evill fortune for the most part are invisible), he supposes causes of them, either such as his own fancy suggesteth; or trusteth to the Authority of other men, such as he thinks to be his friends, and wiser than himselfe."

103. This is to be deduced from collating the definition of philosophy (*De Corp.* I, 2, see Note 101 above) and the passage from *Leviathan* quoted in Note 102, with *De Corp.*, I, 1: "Versari mihi inter homines videtur hodie Philosophia, quem admodum frumentum et vinum fuisse in rerum natura narratur priscis temporibus. Erant enim ab initio rerum vites et spicae sparsim per agros, sed satio nulla. . . . Similiter,

Philosophia, id est, Ratio naturalis, in omni homine innata est; unusquisque enim aliquo usque ratiocinatur, et in rebus aliquibus; verum ubi longa rationum serie opus est, propter reactae methodi, quasi sationis defectum deviant plerique et evagantur."

104. In *Lev.* xii, religion is shown to derive from the search after causes: ". . . the solicitude whereof [sc. good and evil fortune] both enclines to fear, and hinders them from the search of the causes of other things; and thereby gives occasion of feigning of as many Gods, as there be men that feigne them."

105. *Lev.* xii and xi *vers. fin.*

106. *De Corp.* I, 2: ". . . sensionem atque memoriam rerum, quae communes homini sunt cum omnibus animantibus, etsi cognitiones sint, tamen quia datae sunt statim a natura, non ratiocinando acquisitae, non esse Philosophiam."

107. *Elements* I,III; *De Corp.* XXV, 7, 9; *Lev.* ii, xii.

108. As did Descartes; cf. Hobbes, *Objectiones ad Cartesii Meditationes*, Obj. I.

109. "If this superstitious fear of Spirits were taken away, and with it, Prognostiques from Dreams, false Prophecies, and many other things depending thereon, by which crafty ambitious persons abuse the simple people, men would be much more fitted than they are for civil Obedience" (*Lev.* ii).

Hobbes is concerned with elimination of fear of spirits, not for the sake of tranquillity of mind, but only to the end that the common people should not be diverted from civil obedience by predictions made by self-styled prophets ("inspired individuals").

110. *Elements* I,X, 3.

111. See Notes 98, 99.

112. *De Hom.* XI, 6: "Bonorum autem primum est sua cuique conservatio. Natura enim comparatum est ut cupiant omnes sibi bene esse. Cujus ut capaces esse possint, necesse est cupiant vitam, sanitatem, ut utriusque quantum fieri potest securitatem futuri temporis. Contra vero malorum omnium primum mors, praesertim cum cruciatu; nam tantae possunt esse vitae aegritudines, ut nisi earum finis propinquus praevideatur, faciant mortem inter bona numerari."

113. *De Cive* I, 7: "Fertur enim unusquisque ad appetitionem ejus quod sibi bonum, et ad fugam ejus quod sibi malum est, maxime autem maximi malorum naturalium, quae est mors; . . . ." *Ep. ded.*: ". . . qua quisque mortem violentem tanquam summum naturae malum studet evitare." Cf. *Elements* I, XIV, 6.

114. *De Cive* I, 2n.

115. *De Cive* I, 7: "Juris naturalis fundamentum primum est, ut quisque vitam et membra sua quantum potest tueatur." This derives from the fact that death is feared as the greatest of all natural ills.

116. *De Cive* I, 3–4. The trinity: gloria, commoda (lucrum), defensio, occurs again with the same intent in the corresponding portion of *Leviathan* (ch. xiii).

117. *De Cive* I, 2.

118. This is not contradicted when Hobbes (in a less central passage) reverses the order, and derives the striving after honor from the striving after power (*Lev.* ch. viii): "Desire of Power, of Riches, of Knowledge and of Honor. All which may be reduced to the first, that is, Desire of Power. For Riches, Knowledge and Honor are but severall sorts of Power." The natural relation between power and reputation, clearly presented in *Elements* I, VIII, 3–5, remains intact, and is indeed recognized also in *Leviathan*, as the sequence in ch. x shows.

119. *Elements* I, IX, 2.

120. *De Cive* III, 32: "Sunt igitur leges naturales summa Philosophiae moralis:

cujus praecepta hoc loco [sc. in the context of political theory] ea tantum tradidi, quae pertinent ad conservationem nostram, *contra pericula quaea discordia oriuntur.* Sunt autem alia praecepta naturae rationalis, ex quibus aliae nascuntur virtutes [sc. temperantia et fortitudo]." The same distinction between the social virtue of justice and the other cardinal virtues appears in *De Hom.* XIII, 9.

121. The question whether Hobbes was timid and suspicious in personal relations, as Tönnies denies, apparently against an opinion advanced by Dilthey, has little bearing on this. It is probable that Dilthey did not intend his assertion in this sense. The part played in Hobbes' life by concern for his personal safety is moreover brought out by Tönnies himself; and this concern is, according to Hobbes' own explanation, identical with fear and mistrust. (Cf. Tönnies, p. 71, and Dilthey, II, 462.) That the unqualified predominance of the security-motive in the founding of a commonwealth can not be explained by the conditions prevailing in Hobbes' own time, is shown by comparison with Spinoza's political theory, which centers more on freedom than on security.

122. For greater clarity we set out the central sequence of Hobbes' thought in the following table:
    a) Bonorum primum: life; malorum primum: death (death by violence).
    b) Bonorum maximum: unimpeded progress to ever further goals; malorum maximum: death.
    c) Desire; Fear.
    d) Inequality; Equality.
    e) Happiness; Right.
    f) Pride; Humility.
    g) Revelation; Reason.

123. *Elements* II, VI–VIII; *De Cive* XII, 2; *Lev.* xxix, xlii.

124. *Lev.* xii.

125. *Lev.* ii, viii, xii, xxix, xxxii.

126. *De Corp.* I, 7, taken in conjunction with I, 1; *Lev.* xiii. See also Descartes, *Discours de la Méthode* I.

127. Tönnies, p. 68, where several observations of this kind are collated.

128. *De Hom.* XI, 8: "Sapientia, Utile. Nam praesidium in se habet nonnullum. Etiam Appetibile est per se, id est, Jucundum . . . Divitiarum quam Sapientiae cupido major. Vulgo enim non quaeritur haec nisi propter illas. Et illas si habent, etiam hanc habere videri volunt. Non enim qui sapiens est (ut dixere Stoici) dives est; sed contra, qui dives est sapiens dicendus est."
This is surely not polemic against the Stoa, as Dilthey takes it to be (II, 294), but the ironic recognition of the predominant vulgar assessment, which is to be taken seriously only because it predominates.

129. On this there is an important comment by Dilthey, unfortunately only a fragment, published from his posthumous papers (II, 376).

130. *De Corp.* XXVI, 1; *Lev.* xi, xii; *Object. ad Cart. Medit.* V.

131. *Elements* I, XI, 4–5; *De Corp.* V, 4, VII, 2, VIII, 1; *Lev.* xxxiv, App. c. 3; cf. Tönnies pp. 124 f.

132. F. A. Lange, *Geschichte des Materialismus*, I, 376 (Reclam).

133. *De Hom.* XII, 5; *De Cive* XV, 5 ff.; *Lev.* xxxi.

134. See Chapter IX of this study.

135. *De Corp.* Ep. ded.; *De Hom.* XIV, 13; *Lev.* viii, xii.

PART TWO

INTRODUCTION

136. Spinoza quotes as his source the collection of Maimonides' letters which, "as he remembers," he "has read in the past" (*Tr.*, p. 167 n.).

137. ". . . causas, quae me ad scribendum impulerunt, docebo. Miratus saepe fui, quod homines, qui se *Christianam* religionem profiteri iactant, . . ." (*Tr.* praef., pp. 3 f.).

CHAPTER V

THE CRITIQUE OF ORTHODOXY

138. ". . . quid de rebus, limites nostri intellectus excedentibus dicere possumus, praeter id, quod ex ipsis prophetis ore, vel scripto nobis traditur?"(*Tr.*,p. 2) "Ipsa [sc. Scriptura], quae humanis figmentis minime indiget, . . . humana commenta pro divinis documentis haberi . . ." (*Tr.* praef., p. 5). ". . . quod tota eius [sc. Scripturae] rerumque spiritualium cognitio ab ipsa sola, et non ab iis, quae lumine naturali cognoscimus, peti debeat" (*Tr.* praef., p. 6).

139. Spinoza says in his reply to Blyenbergh, already cited (*Ep.* 21): "Video . . . nullam demonstrationem, licet pro demonstrationis legibus solidissimam, apud te valere, nisi conveniat cum ea *explicatione*, quam vel ipse, vel alii theologi, tibi haud ignoti, sacrae Scripturae *tribuunt*."

140. "Verum quidem est Scripturam per Scripturam explicandam esse, quam diu de solo orationum sensu et mente prophetarum laboramus; sed postquam verum sensum eruimus, necessario iudicio et ratione utendum, ut ipsi assensum praebeamus" *Tr.*, pp. 167 f.).

141. This is required also for genuine Bible science, which sets out to establish, without any concern for critique of religion, what the Bible in fact says. This however lies outside the field at present under consideration.

142. "Non ergo mirum, quod *antiquae* religionis nihil manserit praeter eius externum cultum . . ." (*Tr.* praef., p. 4). "Qui autem . . . rationem et philosophiam theologiae ancillam facit, is *antiqui* vulgi praeiudicia tamquam res divinas tenetur admittere et iisdem mentem occupare et obcaecare . . ." (*Tr.*, p. 166).

143. ". . . plerique tanquam fundamentum supponunt . . . ipsam [sc. Scripturam] ubique veracem, et divinam esse; id nempe ipsum, quod ex eiusdem intellectione, et severo examine demum deberet constare: et quod ex ipsa, quae humanis figmentis minime indiget, longe melius endoceremur, in primo limine pro regula ipsius interpretationis statuunt" (*Tr.* praef., p. 5).

144. Spinoza takes his bearings by the doctrine of Rabbi Jehuda Alpakhar. Cf. *Tr.*, ch. xv (first half).

145. "Quid autem Deus sit, et qua ratione res omnes videat iisque provideat, haec et similia Scriptura ex professo et tanquam aeternam doctrinam non docet. Sed contra *prophetas* ipsos *circa haec non convenisse* iam supra ostendimus; *adeoque de similibus nihil tanquam doctrinam spiritus sancti statuendum*, tametsi lumine naturali optime determinari possit" (*Tr.*, pp. 88 f.).

146. *Tr.*, ch. xiii–xiv *passim*; cf. in particular the summing-up at the end of ch. xiv, which closes with the following words: "[lector] sibi persuasum habeat, nos non eo scripsisse animo, ut *nova* introduceremus, *sed ut depravata corrigeremus*, quae tandem aliquando correcta videre speramus."

147. In his "Tractat. theol.-pol. . . . ad veritatis lancem examinatus," Jena, 1674, Johannes Musaeus says, after quoting a series of passages which speak of the Cross: "Unde merito miramur, Auctorem provocare tam audacter ad Scripturam, eique tribuere, quod vel religionem totam, vel illius fundamentum totum constituat in obedientia erga Deum: cum contrarium nullibi non Scriptura doceat. Et fundamentum quidem religionis constituit ex conceptis verbis in Christo Jesu, non in obedientia erga Deum" (par. 51). The passages quoted by Musaeus in this connection, characteristically enough, do not occur in any part of the *Tractate*.

148. Diestel, pp. 716 ff.

149. *Epp.* 73, 75, 78; *Tr.* pp. 7, 56 f., 144 ff.

150. ". . . dico . . . me de Deo, et natura sententiam fovere longe diversam ab ea, quam *Neoterici* Christiani defendere solent. Deum enim rerum omnium causam immanentem, ut ajunt, non vero transeuntem statuo. Omnia, inquam, in Deo esse, et in Deo moveri cum *Paulo* affirmo, et forte etiam cum omnibus *antiquis* philosophis, licet alio modo; et auderem etiam dicere, cum *antiquis* omnibus Hebraeis, quantum ex quibusdam traditionibus, tametsi multis modis adulteratis, conjicere licet" (*Ep.* 73. Cf. *Ep.* 21).

151. "Attamen nec ille [sc. Paulus] etiam aperte loqui vult, sed, ut ipse ait, cap. 3 v. 5 et cap. 6 v. 19 ejusdem epist. [sc. ad Rom.], humano more loquitur, quod expresse dicit, cum Deum justum vocat, et sine dubio etiam propter carnis imbecillitatem Deo misericordiam, gratiam, iram, etc. *affingit*, et ingenio plebis, sive (ut ipse etiam ait cap. 3 v. 1. 2 epist. I ad Corinth.) hominum carnalium sua verba accomodat" (*Tr.*, p. 51). Compare with this the first of the basic teachings of Scripture: "Deum, hoc est, ens supremum, summe iustum et misericordem, sive verae vitae exemplar existere" (*Tr.*, p. 163).

152. Spinoza treats of this divergence in the *Tractate* at the end of ch. xi, and also in *Epistles* 75 and 78.

153. *Tr.*, p. 81. Here we see the concrete meaning that the equality in value of the Old Testament and the New has for Spinoza: Solomon and Paul both teach as philosophers (cf. *Tr.*, pp. 52–54). When he speaks of the higher significance of the New Testament, what he has in mind is that Jesus the Christ stands higher than Moses the law-giver, and the Apostles higher than the prophets.

154. "Deus enim, ut prima et immutabilis veritas est, ita nec opiniones falsas Prophetis inspirare, nec in praeiudiciis et opinionibus falsis eos relinquere, per suam immutabilem veritatem, potuit" (Musaeus, par. 73). Similarly Blyenbergh in *Ep.* 20.

155. "Quod si ratio, quamvis reclamat Scripturae, tamen plane submittenda est, quaeso, an id cum vel sine ratione ut caeci facere debemus? Si hoc, stulte sane et sine iudicio agimus; si illud, ex solo igitur rationis imperio Scripturam amplectimur, quam igitur, si eidem repugnaret, non amplecteremur" (*Tr.*, p. 168). "At interim eos absolute excusare non possumus, quandoquidem rationem in auxilium vocare volunt ad eandem repellendam, et certa ratione eandem incertam reddere conantur" (*Tr.*, p. 173).

156. "Haec nisi certitudo [sc. testimonium Spiritus] adsit quolibet humano iudicio et superior et validior, frustra Scripturae auctoritas . . . argumentis munietur . . . siquidem nisi hoc jacto fundamento, suspensa semper manet. Sicuti contra, ubi semel communi sorte exemptam religiose ac pro dignitate amplexi sumus, quae ad eius certitudinem animis nostris inserendam et infigendam non adeo valebant, tunc aptissima sunt adminicula" (Calvin, *Inst. christ. relig.* I, 8, 1). "Aliae sunt nec paucae nec invalidae rationes, quibus sua Scripturae dignitas ac maiestas non modo asseratur piis pectoribus, sed adversus calumniatorum technas egregie vindicetur: sed quae non satis per se valeant ad firmam illi fidem comparandam, donec eius reverentiam

coelestis Pater, suo illic numine patefacto, omni controversia eximit . . . quae vero ad eam confirmandam humana exstant testimonia, sic inania non erunt, si praecipuum illud et summum, velut secundaria nostrae imbecillitatis adminicula, subsequantur. Sed inepte faciunt qui probari volunt infidelibus, Scripturam esse verbum Dei: quod, nisi fide, cognosci nequit" (*ibid.*, I, 8, 13).

157. "Imo dum student mathematicis demonstrationibus Theologiae veritatem et authoritatem ostendere, et rationi et lumini naturali authoritatem adimere, nihil aliud faciunt quam ipsam Theologiam sub rationis imperium trahere, et plane videntur supponere, Theologiae authoritatem nullum habere splendorem, nisi lumine naturali rationis illustretur. Et, si contra iactant se interno Spiritus Sancti testimonio omnino acquiescere, et nulla alia de causa rationem in auxilium vocare, quam propter infideles ad eosdem scilicet convincendos, nil tamen fidei eorum dictis habendum, . . . Ex praecedente enim capite [sc.xiv] evidentissime sequitur, Spiritum Sanctum non nisi de bonis operibus testimonium dare; . . . De veritate autem et certitudine rerum, quae solius sunt speculationis, nullus Spiritus testimonium dat, praeter rationem . . ." (*Tr.*, pp. 173 f.).

158. ". . . quod (ut omnes, ni fallor, fatentur) hoc lumen supranaturale donum sit divinum fidelibus tantum concessum. At prophetae et apostoli non fidelibus tantum, sed maxime infidelibus et impiis praedicare solebant, quique adeo apti erant ad mentem prophetarum et apostolorum intelligendam" (*Tr.*, p. 98).

159. *Tr.*, pp. 16–18, 76 f., 172. On p. 18 of the *Tractate* we read, "signa non nisi ad prophetae persuadendum dabantur." But on p. 172 we read, "verum prophetam a falso dignosci ex doctrina et miraculo simul." The contradiction is evident. In our context interest centers only on the view represented by Spinoza in the later passage: the sign as "objective" criterion of revelation ("hac tantum de causa Scripturae, hoc est ipsis prophetis, credere tenemur, nimirum propter doctrinam *signis confirmatam*" (*Tr.*, p. 172).

160. ". . . si quis doctrinam aliquam integram nationem, ne dicam, universum genus humanum docere, et ab omnibus in omnibus intelligi vult, is rem suam *sola experientia* confirmare tenetur, rationesque suas, et rerum docendarum definitiones ad captum plebis, quae maximam humani generis partem componit, maxime accomodare, non autem eas concatenare, neque definitiones, prout ad rationes melius concatenandam inserviunt, tradere; . . . Cum itaque tota Scriptura in usum integrae nationis prius, et tandem universi humani generis revelata fuerit, necessario ea, quae in ipsa continentur, ad captum plebis maxime accomodari debuerunt, et *sola experientia* comprobari" (*Tr.*, p. 63).

161. "Quae Scriptura docere vult, quae solam speculationem spectant, haec potissimum sunt; nempe dari Deus sive ens, quod omnia fecit et summa sapientia dirigit et sustentat et quod hominum summam habet curam, nempe eorum, qui pie et honeste vivant, reliquos autem multis suppliciis punit et a bonis segregat. Atque haec Scriptura sola experientia comprobat, nempe iis, quas narrat, historiis . . ." (*Tr.*, p. 63).

162. Batalerius, *Vindiciae miraculorum*, Amstelodami, 1674, par. 28: ". . . fateor item, nescire me, quibus in oris illud vulgus inveniatur, quod supra dixit existimare, ex nulla re clarius existentiam Dei probari posse quam ex miraculis, . . ." Cf. Regner a Mansvelt, *Adversus anonymum theologico-politicum*, Amstelodami, 1674, cap. xi.

163. "Quamvis enim in rebus ad Religionem spectantibus, lusciosa et corrupta ratio sibi relicta, nihil boni vel praestet, vel possit, . . . quod Ethnicorum exemplo satis patet; . . . tamen cum lumen lumini non sit contrarium, nec verum vero, sintque fidei Mysteria super rationem, non contra veram rationem, non debet simpliciter recta ratio a Theologicis exulare, aut cum illa ψευδονύμῳ Philosophia confundi, de qua Col. 2, 8" (Maresius, *Collegium Theologicum*, Groningae, 1645, loc. I, par. 15). ". . . fides et philosophia non in hoc differunt, quod haec veritatem, illa obedientiam et pietatem,

pro fine habeat, ut rursum ineptit Auctor [sc. Spinoza], sed in hoc conveniunt, quod utraque sit virtus intellectualis, verum enuncians affirmando et negando; differunt autem in eo, quod fides enunciat verum, a prima veritate revelante super-naturaliter patefactum . . ." (Musaeus, par. 67).

164. ". . . plerique tanquam fundamentum *supponunt* . . . ipsam [sc. Scripturam] ubique veracem et divinam esse; id nempe ipsum, quod eiusdem intellectione et *severo examine demum* deberet constare, . . . *in primo limine* pro regula ipsius interpretationis statuunt . . . sedulo statui Scripturam de novo integro et *libero animo examinare*, et nihil de eadem affirmare nihilque tanquam eius doctrinam admittere, quod ab eadem clarissime non edocerer" (*Tr. praef.*, p. 5).

165. Batalerius, par. 20, 28; Regner a Mansvelt; Musaeus, par. 78–79; Quenstedt, *Theologia didactico-polemica sive Systema theol.*, Wittebergae, 1685, p. 535; Buddeus, *Theses Theologicae de Atheismo et Superstitione*, Jenae, 1717, cap. iii, par. 5, cap vii, par. 5, Buddeus, *Institut. theol. dogm.*, Lips. 1724, lib. II, cap. I, par. 28, 30; cf. Hunzinger, *Das Wunder*, Leipzig, 1912, pp. 10–14. Among Jewish theologians this conception of miracles is defended by Saadia Gaon among others, in *Emunoth vedeoth* III (Slucki, p. 62): "Human power is too slight to subjugate the elements and to transform the natures of things; when such events take place through a human being, they prove that that man is a messenger of God."

166. Proper understanding and just assessment of Spinoza's critique (and that of the Enlightenment, generally speaking) is made impossible both by rejection "as a matter of course" of the traditional conception of miracles by those trammeled in seventeenth century prejudices, and by the modern re-interpretation of the concept of miracle, through which—intentionally or unintentionally—the fact is glossed over or suppressed that the genuine significance of miracles is direct action by God on corporeal things. Pascal clearly brings this out when he says "Les miracles prouvent le pouvoir que Dieu a sur les coeurs, par celui qu'il exerce sur les corps" (*Pensées*, ed. Giraud, Paris, 1924; no. 851; cf. nos. 805, 806, 808).

167. Oldenburg to Spinoza: ". . . multis tollere videris miraculorum auctoritatem et valorem, quibus *solis* divinae revelationis certitudinem adstrui posse, *omnibus fere* Christianis est persuasum" (*Ep.* 71). Batalerius (par. 3): ". . . *vulgo* dicimus, multa miracula facta esse ad Christianae religionis confirmationem; quae et Apostoli et Evangelistae omnes, aliique infiniti, nobis commendarunt pro evidentibus, ac solidis, et *solis, fere dicam*, ejus documentis."

168. Cf. further von Tessen-Wesierski, *Die Grundlagen des Wunder-Begriffes nach Thomas von Aquin*, Paderborn, 1899, p. 132: "Da nun Gott durch seinen direkten Eingriff in die geschöpfliche Natur sein Wesen in aussergewöhnlicher Weise offenbart, als durch die gewöhnliche, natur-gesetzliche Unterstützung, Leitung und Erhaltung der geschöpflichen Dinge und ihrer Kräfte, so kann er auch aus diesem aussergewöhnlichen Wirken von den *vernünftigen* Geschöpfen besser erkannt werden. Diese *bessere, reinere und klarere* Erkenntnis Gottes ist daher auch der *eigentliche Zweck* seiner supranaturalen Thätigkeit." (Not italicized in the original text.) Even Calvin, who however concedes no more than human and secondary value to proof by miracles— a proof which he considers to be essentially ineffective in itself—finds that God manifested Himself as Creator of the sun, the most splendid of all created things, in that he created plants and caused them to thrive prior to the creation of the sun. In the same context Calvin refers also to the miracles accorded to Joshua and to Hezekiah (*Inst.* I, 16, 2). Buddeus, *Theses theologicae*, cap. iii, par. 5: "Cum enim non modo christianae religionis veritas, sed et numinis existentia *valide* ex iis [sc. miraculis] demonstrari queat. . . ."

169. *E.g.* Hettinger-Weber, *Fundamentaltheologie*, Freiburg (Breisgau), 1913, p. 212.

170. Spinoza to Oldenburg (*Ep.* 75): "Humanum imbecillitatem tecum agnosco.

Sed te contra rogare mihi liceat, an nos homunciones tantam naturae cognitionem habeamus, ut determinare possimus, quousque eius vis et potentia se extendit et quid eius vim superat? Quod quia nemo sine arrogantia praesumere potest, licet ergo absque iactantia miracula per causas naturales, quantum fieri potest, explicare, et quae explicare non possumus, nec etiam demonstrare, quod absurda sint, satis erit iudicium de iis suspendere . . ." Spinoza to Burgh (*Ep.* 76): ". . . nec turpiter confunde illa, quae *nobis incognita, vel nondum reperta sunt,* cum iis, quae absurda esse demonstrantur, . . ."

171. The conclusion that he drew from this (on the basis of a denial in principle of the possibility of miracles), that these events did not occur in reality, but only in imagination—can here be left out of account. Cf. pp. 186 ff. and 212 f.

172. ". . . quoniam miracula ad captum vulgi facta fuerunt, quod quidem principia rerum naturalium plane ignorabat, certum est, *antiquos* id pro miraculo habuisse, quod explicare non poterant eo modo, quo vulgus res naturales explicare solet, recurrendo scilicet ad memoriam, ut alterius rei similis, quam sine admiratione imaginari solet, recordetur; tum enim vulgus rem aliquam se satis intelligere existimat, quum ipsam non admiratur. Antiqui itaque et omnes fere in hoc usque tempus nullam praeter hanc normam miraculi habuerunt" (*Tr.*, p. 70). "*Tempore Josuae* Hebraei . . . cum vulgo credebant, solem motu, ut vocant, diurno moveri, terram autem quiescere, et huic praeconceptae opinioni miraculum, quod iis contigit, quum contra quinque illos reges pugnarent, adaptaverunt; non enim simpliciter narraverunt, diem illum solito longiorem fuisse, sed solem et lunam stetisse, sive a suo motu cessavisse, quod ipsis etiam *tum temporis* non parum inservire poterat ad ethnicos, qui solem adorabant, convincendum et ipsa experientia comprobandum, solem sub alterius numinis imperio esse, ex cuius nutu ordinem suum naturalem mutare teneatur" (*Tr.*, p. 78). Cf. the summary given at the beginning of ch. xiii of the *Tractate*, of results derived from applying scientific method to the text of Scripture, and which give proof of the unscientific, vulgar character of the Bible.

173. The complete context of positive criticism is not made fully explicit until Hume's Enquiry X, in which he concretizes the claim of necessity in science as understood by Spinoza, into the claim of probability.

174. "Nec tantum hujusmodi res [sc. matters belonging to natural science and mathematics], sed etiam alias majoris momenti Prophetae . . . ignoraverunt; nihil enim singulare de divinis attributis docuerunt, sed admodum vulgares de Deo habuerunt opiniones . . ." (*Tr.*, p. 23).

175. "Attamen quandoquidem nec de hac traditione, nec de pontificis auctoritate possumus esse certi, nihil etiam certi super his fundare possumus; hanc *enim* antiquissimi Christianorum, illam autem antiquissimae Judaeorum sectae negaverunt" (*Tr.*, p. 91).

176. Burgh: "Dices, mea Philosophia rationi rectae congrua est, caeterae eidem repugnant: sed omnes reliqui philosophi praeter tuos discipulos a te dissentiunt, ac eodem jure idem, quod tu de tua, ipsi de se, suaque Philosophia praedicant, teque, sicut tu illos, falsitatis errorisque arguunt."

Spinoza: "Dices, te in interno Spiritus Dei testimonio acquiescere, reliquos autem a scelestorum Spirituum Principe circumduci, ac decipi; sed omnes qui extra Ecclesiam Romanam sunt eodem jure id, quod tu de tua, ipsa de sua praedicant." Calvin (*Inst.* I, 5, 12): "Rude et indoctum vulgus omitto. Sed inter Philosophos, qui ratione et doctrina penetrare in coelum conati sunt, quam pudenda est varietas?"

177. In Stolle's report as handed down (see Freudenthal, *Lebensgeschichte,* p. 222) we read that Spinoza was "excommunicated because he was accused of rejecting the Pentateuch, as a human book which Moses never composed."

178. Spinoza "made so bold as to suspect that these people [sc. the Pharisees] went so far as to modify somewhat the predictions of their prophets in the light of later events, for the sake of thus maintaining the appearance of firm predictions." According to a contemporary report, Spinoza said this in the course of conversation. Carl Gebhardt discovered this report. See his *Inedita Spinozana* (*Sitzungsber. der Heidelberger Akademie der Wiss.*, Phil.-Hist. Klasse, Jahrgang 1916, 13 Abhdl.) p. 11.

179. Spinoza said this in the course of conversation. See Gebhardt, note 178.

180. ". . . Biblia, ut ut sunt, tanquam epistolam Dei, e caelo hominibus missam considerant . . ." (*Tr.*, p. 144). "At plerique . . . statuunt Deum singulari quadam providentia omnia Biblia incorrupta servasse" (*Tr.*, p. 121).

181. "Scio, me olim in libro quodam legisse, virum, cui nomen erat Orlandus furiosus, monstrum quoddam alatum in aëre agitare solere et quascunque volebat regiones supervolare, eum ingentem numerum hominum et gigantum solum trucidare, et alia huiusmodi phantasmata, quae ratione intellectus plane imperceptibilia sunt. Huic autem consimilem historiam in Ovidio de Perseo legeram, et aliam denique in libris Judicum et Regum de Samsone, qui solus et inermis millia hominum trucidavit, et de Elia, qui per aëra volitabat et tandem igneis equis et curru coelum petiit. Hae, inquam, consimiles plane historiae sunt; attamen longe dissimile iudicium de unaquaque facimus; nempe primum non nisi nugas scribere voluisse, secundum autem res politicas, tertium denique sacras; hocque nulla alia de causa nobis persuademus, quam propter opiniones, quas de earum scriptoribus habemus" (*Tr.*, p. 96).

CHAPTER VI

THE CRITIQUE OF MAIMONIDES

182. *Hilkot Melakim* VIII, 11. The tenor of the passage used as evidence by Spinoza is somewhat softened, but not essentially modified, if we use the reading given in the *editio princeps*. Joel calls attention to the difference between the readings in his *Spinoza's theologisch-politischer Traktat auf seine Quellen geprüft*, Breslau, 1870, pp. 55 f. Joel also refers to the *Keseph Mishneh*, which characterizes the passage quoted by Spinoza as Maimonides' own opinion, in other words, as not traditional; he omits to note that this commentator continues: "it [sc. Maimonides' own opinion] is correct."

183. *Moreh Nebukhĩm* I, Introd.(pp. 6–8, 15); 71 (pp. 332–35); II, 25 (pp. 195 f.); 27 (pp. 205–206); 32 (260); III, 51 (p. 435). The figures in parentheses indicate the pages in Salomon Munk's translation, *Le Guide des Égarés*.

184. *Moreh* I, 71, 73; II, 16. The question whether Maimonides' interpretation of the Kalãm is adequate can not and need not be answered here.

185. *Moreh* I, 73.

186. Lucretius I, 140 ff.

187. *Moreh* II, 25 (pp. 197 f. in Munk tr.).

188. Joel, pp. 47 f.

189. *Moreh* I, 51 (pp. 183 f.); 53 (pp. 213 f.); 58 (pp. 241 f.).

190. *Ibid.*, II, 14 (p. 119); 18 (pp. 141 f.); III, 20 (p. 153).

191. *Tr.*, pp. 48 f.; *Moreh* III, 20 (pp. 150–54).

192. *Moreh* III, 41 (pp. 330–32); I, 36 (pp. 137 f.); *Tract. pol.*, II, 6.

193. *Moreh* II, 32 (pp. 262 f.); *Tr.*, p. 1. Maimonides makes the further reservation that the prophecy of Moses is different in nature from the prophecies of the other prophets; cf. *Moreh* II, 35, 39, and also *Yesode hatorah* VII, 6.

194. *Moreh*, Introd. (pp. 10 ff.).

195. Maimonides, *Hilkot teshubah* III, 8.

196. Maimonides rejects in principle the proof through miracles; *see Yesode* VIII.

197. *Moreh* II, 22 (p. 179); 24 (p. 194).

198. *Ibid.*, 23 (p. 182).

199. *Ibid.*, III, 26 (pp. 207–10); 49 (p. 411).

200. *Ibid.*, II, 25 (pp. 195–97).

201. *Ibid.*, 16 (p. 129); 17 (p. 137); 22 (pp. 179 f.); 23 (pp. 185 f.).

202. *Ibid.*, III, 45 (pp. 351 f.).

203. *Ibid.*, II, 25 (pp. 197–98).

204. *Ibid.*, I, introd. (pp. 7 f.); 71 (pp. 332–35); II, 25 (p. 198); III, 54 (p. 459). Cf. the essay by Franz Rosenzweig, "Apologetisches Denken," reprinted in *Kleinere Schriften*, Berlin, 1937, pp. 31–42.

205. *Moreh* II, 40 (p. 310); III, 27; 28; 31 (p. 248); 51 (pp. 437 ff.); 54 (pp. 460 f.).

206. Joel (pp. 44 ff.) has already indicated this concordance. Joel's indications have been used in the present study, and, where necessary, have been completed or amended.

207. *Tr.*, pp. 32 ff.; pp. 45 ff.; cf. *Eth.*, IV, 28; V, 25, 38, 40.

208. The divergence of their views on the *origin* of divine law (according to Maimonides it is essentially revealed, according to Spinoza essentially not revealed) is not taken into consideration in the present context.

209. "In superiore Capite ostendimus, legem divinam, quae homines vere beatos reddit, et veram vitam docet, omnibus esse hominibus *universalem*; imo eam ex humana natura ita deduximus, ut ipsa humanae menti innata, et quasi inscripta existimanda sit. Cum autem caeremoniae, eae saltem, quae habentur in vetere Testamento, *Hebrais tantum* institutae, et eorum imperio ita accomodatae fuerint, ut maxima ex parte ab universa *societate*, non autem ab *unoquoque* exerceri potuerint, certum est, eas ad legem divinam non pertinere, adeoque nec etiam ad beatitudinem et virtutem aliquid facere" (*Tr.*, p. 55). Cf. *Tr.*, p. 47.

210. *Moreh* III, 41 (p. 333).

211. *Moreh* III, 27 (pp. 211 f.).

212. *Tr.*, p. 46 is irreconcilable with this: "Media igitur, quae hic finis omnium humanarum actionum . . . exigit, jussa Dei vocari possunt . . . atque adeo ratio vivendi, quae hunc finem spectat, lex Divina optime vocatur. Quaenam autem haec Media sint, et quaenam ratio vivendi, quam hic finis exigit, et quomodo hunc optimae *reipublicae* fundamenta sequantur, et ratio vivendi inter homines, ad universalem Ethicam pertinet."

213. Cf. *inter alia Moreh* III, 44. For all that, the distinction made (*Moreh* III, 52) between the actions prescribed by the Law, and which have as their aim the *fear of God*, and the views taught by the Law, which have as their aim the *love* of God, comes very close to Spinoza's interpretation of ceremonial Law.

214. Thomas Aquinas, *Summa theol.* II, I, qu. 91, art. 4 and 5; qu. 95, art. i; qu. 99; qu. 107; Calvin, *Inst.* IV, 20; I, 5; II, 11; cf. *Tr.*, pp. 34, 45, 51, 56.

215. Gebhardt, in the Introduction to his German translation of the *Tractate* (Leipzig, 1922) xvii: Spinoza "seeks to prove that the inevitable result of an independent priesthood and even of the institution of prophecy was the greatest harm to the state. In this matter Spinoza's debate with Judaism is entirely at one with the innermost aim of the *Tractate*."

216. Cf. the report in Lucas (see Freudenthal, *Lebensgeschichte*, p. 7).

217. Cf. *Tr.*, pp. 145, 151 f., 157.

218. *Moreh* III, 28.

219. "Quod si quis dicat, non esse quidem opus Dei attributa intelligere, at omnino simpliciter, absque demonstratione credere, is sane nugabitur: Nam res invisibiles, et quae solius mentis sunt objecta, nullis aliis oculis videri possunt, quam per demonstrationes; qui itaque eas non habent, nihil harum rerum plane vident; atque adeo quicquid de similibus auditum referunt, non magis eorum mentem tangit, sive indicat, quam verba Psittaci, vel automati, quae sine mente, et sensu loquuntur" (*Tr.*, p. 156).

220. This is shown by collating *Moreh* I, 35 (pp. 131 f.): "There is no need to inform the multitude of the fact that God has no positive attributes" with I, 60 (pp. 263–66): ". . . whosoever ascribes positive attributes to God has not merely imperfect knowledge of God, but no knowledge of Him whatsoever."

221. *Moreh* I, 50 (p. 180); 33 (p. 117); 35 (pp. 132 f.).

222. *Tr.*, pp. 163 f.; p. 151.

223. *Moreh* I, 35 (pp. 131 f.), 36; III, 28 (p. 214).

224. The basic reason is that in proper speech there is nothing to be said about God, except to state that he is beyond our comprehension. The second reason: if the literal meaning were the true meaning of Scripture, many statements made in Scripture would be contrary to truth, and this would be in conflict with the revealed nature of Scripture. The third reason is that the Divine law fulfils its two functions at one and the same time, by regulating man's communal life by its outer meaning, and by communicating fundamental truths by its inner meaning. *Moreh* I, Introd. (pp. 7–19).

225. *Moreh* II, 32 (pp. 261 f.).

226. *Moreh* II, 36 (pp. 281–84).

227. ". . . adeoque de verso sensu Scripturae, quantumvis claro, non poterit (sc. Maimonides) esse certus, quamdiu de rei veritate dubitare poterit, aut quamdiu de eadem ipsi non constet. Nam quamdiu de rei veritate non constat, tamdiu nescimus, an res cum ratione conveniat, an vero eidem repugnet; et consequenter etiam tamdiu nescimus, an literalis sensus verus sit an falsus" (*Tr.*, p. 100).

228. *Moreh* II, 19; 22 (p. 179); 24 (pp. 193 f.).

229. The will to mediacy of hearing, not merely the actual mediacy of hearing, is the element of revealed religion. In his polemic against the attempts made to understand Scripture from the "religious experience" of the prophets, Friedrich Gogarten on his side misses the point when he completely denies that (in the Scriptural sense) God is heard by men without mediation. He states in his *Theologische Tradition und theologische Arbeit*, Leipzig, 1927, p. 12, note 2: "Man wird vielleicht auf die alttestamentlichen Propheten . . . verweisen, um zu zeigen, dass es auch ein Wort gibt, das Gott dem Menschen unmittelbar sagt. Aber das scheint mir ein Missverständnis zu sein. Denn bei den Propheten ist es ganz klar, dass sie Gottes Wort nur hören in ihrer strengen Gebundenheit an das Volk, und das heisst bei ihnen ja wirklich nicht an eine nationale Idee, sondern an den Nächsten. Es heisst doch, alles vergessen, was die Propheten sagen, sie in dem, was sie sagen, nicht ernst nehmen, wenn man nicht sieht, dass diese Männer kein individuelles, oder wie wir dafür auch gerne sagen, rein religiöses Verhältnis zu Gott gehabt haben, und dass sie gerade als Propheten in der engsten Gebundenheit an ihr Volk und die strengste Verantwortlichkeit ihm gegenüber das Gotteswort hören und sprechen."

Here only this is justified, and it is indeed justified without any reservation whatsoever, that the prophets were not *concerned* with their "direct experience," but with their demands and their announcements; that proper understanding of the prophets is possible to begin with only if we start from what they demand and announce: that therefore the question of what they "experience" is possible only on the basis of radical misunderstanding—or radical critique. Gogarten however himself controverts his important insight by his entirely "metaphysical" assertion that even the prophets do not hear God without mediation. Once Gogarten has taken his stand on a plane which is essentially indifferent, the objection must be put to him on that same level, that the prophets—even if they heard God's word only "by virtue of their close union with their nation"—nevertheless did not receive their message from their nation, but directly from God. The attempt to even out the distinction between prophet and non-prophet, to deny the fact of this difference—a distinction existentially irrelevant, but no less factual for that—is symptomatic of a position from which miracles in the strict sense can no longer be asserted, not even accidentally.

230. *Emunah ramah, in fine.*

231. "Primo itaque, non desumpsi meum argumentum ex eo quod viderem in sensibilibus esse ordinem sive successionem quandam causarum efficientium; tum quia Deum existere multo evidentius esse putavi, quam ullas res sensibiles; tum etiam quia per istam causarum successionem non videbar alio posse devenire, quam ad imperfectionem intellectus mei agnoscendam, quod nempe non possim comprehendere quomodo infinitae tales causae sibi mutuo ab aeterno ita successerint, ut nulla fuerit prima. Nam certe, ex eo quod istud non possim comprehendere, non sequitur aliquam primam esse debere, ut neque ex eo quod non possim etiam comprehendere infinitas divisiones in quantitate finita, sequitur aliquam dari ultimam, ita ut ulterius dividi non possit; sed tantum sequitur intellectum meum, qui est finitus, non capere infinitum. Itaque malui uti pro fundamento meae rationis existentia mei ipsius, quae a nulla causarum serie dependet, mihique tam nota est ut nihil notius esse possit; et de me non tam quaesivi a qua causa *olim* essem productus, quam a qua tempore *praesenti* conserver, *ut ita me ab omni causarum successione liberarem.*" Descartes, *Meditationes, Primae Responsiones* (ed. princeps, pp. 139 f.). Cf. Spinoza, *Tr.*, p. 16: "Et proh dolor! res eo iam pervenit, ut, qui aperte fatentur, se Dei ideam non habere et Deum non nisi per res creatas (quarum causae ignorant) cognoscere, non erubescant philosophos atheismi accusare."

232. Cf. *Tr.*, adnot. vi, in which Spinoza refers to his own presentation of Descartes' theory.

233. *Moreh* I, 26 (pp. 88 ff.); 49 (pp. 176 f.); 51 (p. 182). Cf. *Millot hahigayon* VIII.

234. *Medit.*, ed. princ., pp. 22 f.

235. *Ibid.*, pp. 86 f.

236. *Tr.*, pp. 3–6, in particular p. 6, the "clear corroboration" by Num. 12:6–7. On p. 4: ". . . in somnis, tempore scilicet, quo imaginatio maxime naturaliter apta est, ad res, quae non sunt, imaginandum." Maimonides' doctrine of prophecy (and that of the "philosophers" of his age) is based on the traditional doctrine of the truthful dream; cf. for instance, Averroës' Paraphrase to Aristotle's *De somniis* (Venice, 1560, VII, 169): "Dicamus igitur quod istarum comprehensionum quaedam dicuntur somnia, et quaedam divinationes, et quaedam prophetiae. Et quidam homines negant ista, et dicunt ea contingere casu. Sed negare ea est negare sensata. Et maxime negare vera somnia. Nullus enim homo est, qui non viderit somnium, quod non enunciaverit ei aliquod futurum . . . sermo de istis omnibus idem est, et sermo de quiditate somnii sufficiet: quia esse eorum non differunt nisi secundum magis et minus, sed tantum differunt secundum nomina propter hoc quod vulgus dicit. Dicunt enim quod somnia sunt ab Angelis; et divinationes a Daemonibus; et prophetiae a Deo, aut cum medio, aut sine medio. Et Aristoteles non fuit locutus nisi tantum de somniis." Scientific insights cannot possibly occur in dreams (p. 171).—There is a striking similarity between Spinoza's *Ep.* 17 and Aristotle's *De divin.*, 464 a 27 ff.

237. Thomas Aquinas, *Summa theol.*, III qu. 172, art. I; Calvin, *In harmoniam ex Matthaeo, Marco et Luca compositam Commentarii* (ed. Tholuck), I, 51, and also the

Commentary on Daniel, 2: 2; 2: 4; 4: 4 f.; Maresius, *Videntes sive Dissertatio theologica de prophetia et prophetis*, Groningae, 1659, *passim* (explicitly polemic against Maimonides' theory of prophecy: II, 13).

238. Spinoza's relation to Maimonides on the one hand, and to Descartes on the other, is treated by Joel, *Zur Genesis der Lehre Spinozas* (Breslau, 1871) and by Roth, *Spinoza, Descartes and Maimonides* (Oxford, 1924); Roth over-estimates the importance in intellectual history of Spinoza's relationship to Maimonides, which is doubtless important in Spinoza's philosophical development. Roth does not sufficiently take into account that the theories regarding which Spinoza stands with Maimonides against Descartes (and against the Kalâm) are for the most part not peculiar to Maimonides, but are the common property of the "philosophers." Spinoza's agreement with Averroës is certainly of greater objective importance than his agreement with Maimonides. Our interpretation is to be understood within this limitation, and this is justified, since we are considering Spinoza's relationship to Maimonides not in regard to Maimonides' importance in general in the history of philosophy, but as an element in Spinoza's critique of religion. Cf. further the detailed review of Roth's book by Tj. de Boer, "Maimonides en Spinoza" (*Mededeelingen der Koninglijke Akademie van Wetenschappen*, Afdeeling Letterkunde, Deel 63, Serie A, No. 2), Amsterdam, 1927.

239. This is not contradicted by the fact that Maimonides asserts the inadequacy of scientific knowledge of God, for in so doing he does not assert the independence of faith in relation to science, except for "the multitude." Furthermore, we must bear in mind that Maimonides' theology has its roots in the context of Jewish life and faith, and that for him the scientific foundation is entirely secondary. But at this particular moment we are concerned solely with the position which Maimonides exposes to Spinoza's critique and in so far as he exposes it to that critique. See *supra*, p. 164.

240. Jacob Kramer gives a complete presentation in his dissertation, "Das Problem des Wunders im Zusammenhang mit dem der Providenz bei den jüdischen Religionsphilosophen von Saadia bis Maimuni," Strassburg, 1903. Kramer also offers, as does Joel, textual evidence of the harmony existing between Maimonides and Spinoza in their interpretation of the Biblical accounts of miracles.

241. *Moreh* II, 19 (pp. 148–61); 27; 28 (pp. 209 f.); 29 (pp. 224 ff.).

242. It is rewarding to compare the interpretation of Ps. 148, v. 6, given in the same context by Maimonides and by Spinoza, from this point of view. "He hath also established them for ever and ever: He hath made a decree which shall not pass away." Spinoza relates the passage to the eternity and unchangeability of nature, Maimonides uses words which seem to be to the same effect. What they intend is shown in the commentaries by Ibn Ezra and David Kimchi on the passage, which are written in terms of the same cosmological assumptions as Maimonides' own. Ibn Ezra: "They never change, for they are not composed of the four elements." Kimchi: "They are not like those creatures in which the individuals perish, and the species persists, but their individuals persist as does the species." Thus these exegetes consider as exempt from change—and in this they follow the Psalmist—not nature but the heavens. According to Spinoza, Eccles. 3:14 teaches the impossibility of miracles because it teaches the immutable character of the order of nature; according to Maimonides, the eternal duration of the world, after it was created. Maimonides, as though forestalling Spinoza's interpretation, adds the end of the verse, which, as he asserts, contains an allusion to the miracles (*Moreh* II, 28 and *Tr.*, p. 81). On the passage from Eccles. 1 : 9, which Spinoza uses for the same purpose, cf. Ibn Ezra who also limits unchangeability here to the heavens and to genera and species. Of further relevance in this connection is Maimonides' attempt to explain away the miracle accorded to Joshua, by reason of the presupposed unchangeability of celestial events (*Moreh* II, 35; and also Gersonides on Josh. 10:12).

243. Thomas Aquinas, in his doctrine of miracles (otherwise more radical than Maimonides) does this also, when he considers the miracle accorded to Hezekiah (the recession of the sun) to be a greater miracle than the parting of the Red Sea or the wakening of the dead to life (*Summa c. Gentiles* III, 101). To the best of my knowledge, later Catholic teaching has discarded this view.

244. *Jesode hatorah* VIII, I; *Moreh* II, 35.

245. *Moreh* III, 17 (p. 125).

246. *Ibid.*, 17 (pp. 130, 135); 18.

247. *Ibid.*, 22; 23; 51; 54.

248. This line of argument is indicated in Spinoza's work (*Tr.*, p. 69), and developed by Voltaire in the *Dictionnaire philosophique portatif*, in this article on Miracles.

249. *Moreh* II, 28 (p. 209).

250. Which the above-mentioned argument, characteristic of the Enlightenment, assumes; cf. Spinoza: ". . . alias enim [sc., with the assertion of miracles], quid aliud statuitur, quam quod Deus naturam adeo impotentem creaverit, ejusque leges et regulas adeo steriles statuerit, ut saepe de novo ei subvenire cogatur, si eam conservatam vult . . ." (*Tr.*, p. 69).

251. According to Maimonides, miracles are intended by the words in Eccles. 3:14: "and God did thus, so that He might be feared."

252. A Spanish translation of Calvin's *Institutio Christianae Religionis* was among the books in Spinoza's library (see Freudenthal's *Lebensgeschichte*, p. 160).

CHAPTER VII

THE CRITIQUE OF CALVIN

253. "Si enim in ipsa [sc. Scriptura] inveniremus aliquid, quod lumini naturali esset contrarium, eadem *libertate*, qua Alcoranum et Thalmud refellimus, illam refellere possemus" (*Cog. met.* II, cap. 8, par. 5).

254. "Sed quia eos retinet aliquis pudor ne suas blasphemias audeant in caelum evomere, quo liberius insaniant, se *nobiscum litigare fingunt*" (*Inst.* I, 17, 2).

255. "Mortua est igitur litera, et suos lectores necat lex Domini, ubi et a Christi gratia divellitur, et intacto corde, auribus tantum insonat" (*ibid.*, I, 9).

256. *Ibid.*, I, 16, 7; among the corroborative passages quoted from the Bible by Calvin we find Psalm 104, v. 4, just as in Spinoza's *Tractate* (p. 75) and in the same context.

257. *Ibid.*, I, 16, 3; 17, 6.

258. When Calvin (*Inst.* I, 17, 6) concedes to the Christian heart the possibility (apart from relating all things to providence) of contemplating the subsidiary causes on their own plane, what is intended is of course not relative recognition of physics, but—as is brought out in I, 17, 9—the admonition to give *gratitude* not only to God, but also to men.

259. *Ibid.*, I, 8; 16, 2.

260. Lucretius also mentions the changing seasons as proof of his central assertion: he of course refers only to the obvious regularity of the seasons and of what they bring forth (I, 168 ff.). Cf. *supra*, pp. 43 ff., pp. 127 ff. and p. 150.

261. On the similarity of the positions adopted in the Kalâm and by Calvin, cf. Guttmann, pp. 10 f., 16.

262. *Moreh* II, 19 (p. 147; pp. 161 ff.).

263. "Exclamat David infantes adhuc pendentes a matrum uberibus satis facundos esse ad celebrandam Dei Gloriam: quia scilicet statim ab utero egressi, coelesti cura paratam sibi alimoniam inveniunt. Et quidem hoc verum in genere, modo ne oculos et sensus nostros fugiat quod palam experientia demonstrat, aliis matribus plenas esse mammas et uberes, aliis fere aridas, prout liberalius hunc Deus alere vult, parcius vero alium" (*Inst.* I, 16, 3).

264. *Ep.* 73, 76; *Tr.*, pp. 1 ff., 6 f., 144, 172.

265. *Eth.* III aff. def. 25, 26, 28, 29.

266. *Cog. met.* II, 8, sect. 3; *Tr.*, p. 51; *Tr.* adnot. 34; *Tr. pol.* II, 22; *Ep.* 75.

267. *Eth.* III, 11–15; 53–55; aff. def. 26, 29.

268. *Tr. br.* II, 5; *Tr. de intell. emend.*, in princ.; *Eth.* V, 19.

269. "Religioni, humanum tantum utile intendenti . . ." (*Tr.*, p. 185).

270. ". . . et quamvis *experientia* in dies reclamaret et infinitis exemplis ostenderet, commoda atque incommoda piis aeque ac impiis promiscue evenire, non ideo ab inveterato praeiudicio destiterunt. Facilius enim iis fuit, hoc inter alia incognita, quorum usum ignorabant, ponere et sic praesentem suum et innatum statum ignorantiae retinere, quam totam illam fabricam destruere et novam excogitare. Unde pro certo statuerunt, deorum iudicia humanum captum longissime superare: quae sane unica fuisset causa, ut veritas humanum genus in aeternum lateret, nisi *mathesis* . . . aliam veritatis normam hominibus ostendisset" (*Eth.* I app.). Cf. further Leibniz, *Discours de la conformité de la foy avec la raison*, par. 3: ". . . Que si l'objection n'est point démonstrative, elle ne peut former qu'un argument vraisemblable, qui n'a point de force contre la Foy, puisqu'on convient que les Mystères de la Religion sont contraires aux apparences."

271. Cf. among Jewish theologians Bahya, *Hobot* III, 3; Abr. ibn Daud, *Emunah ramah* (*ed.* Weil), p. 100; Maimonides, *Moreh* I, 5 (pp. 47 f.), III, 24 (pp. 192 ff.), III, 52; *Yesode hatorah* II, 2; Albo, *Ikk.* III, 32.

272. *Jüdische Schriften* III, 361.

273 *Ibid.*, p. 368.

274. Calvin cites the stipulations in Deuteronomy for the execution of Servetus, for which he took the responsibility: "Hic nobis non obtruditur hominum authoritas, sed Deum audimus loquentem, et quid Ecclesiae suae in perpetuum mandet, non obscure intelligimus. Non frustra humanos omnes affectus excutit, quibus molliri corda solent: paternum amorem, quicquid est inter fratres, propinquos, et amicos benevolentiae facessere iubet: maritos revocat a thori blanditiis: denique homines propemodum natura sua exuit, nequid obstaculi sanctum eorum zelum moretur. Cur tam implacabilis exigitur severitas, nisi ut sciamus non haberi suum Deo honorem, nisi quae illi debetur pietas, humanis omnibus officiis praefertur: et quoties asserenda est eius gloria, propemodum ex memoria nostra deletur mutua inter nos humanitas?" (In corroboration Calvin cites Deut. 12:13 ff.) Calvin, *Defensio orthodoxae fidei de sacra trinitate, contra prodigiosos errores Michaelis Serveti Hispani: Ubi ostenditur haereticos iure gladii coercendos esse . . .*, 1554, p. 29.

275. Max Scheler, "Mensch und Geschichte," *Neue Rundschau*, 1926, p. 473. The italics are Scheler's own.

276. Atheism prior to Nietzsche and Nietzsche's own atheism differ in that Nietzsche knew that the "death of God" means the setting of a sun, and not, as Scheler takes it to be, in that Nietzsche's atheism is the first to be a rebellion against God, a moral protest against God. Within traditional atheism one difference is of over-riding importance: whereas the Epicureanism of antiquity turns against religion as against a fearsome illusion, in the modern evolution of atheism what predominates is the struggle

against illusionary happiness for the sake of real happiness. Feuerbach in particular is here representative. He seeks only "dass sie [die Menschen] über den himmlischen Tauben nicht die irdischen aus den Augen und Händen verlieren, und eine mässige, aber *wirkliche* Glückseligkeit einer masslosen, aber *eingebildeten* Seligkeit vorziehen" ("Über meine Gedanken über Tod und Unsterblichkeit"). Heine and the socialists think along these same lines. To Feuerbach the development within atheism presents itself as follows: ". . . während sonst der Atheismus nur eine Sache der Höfe, des Luxus und des Witzes, der Eitelkeit, Üppigkeit, Oberflächlichkeit und Frivolität war, ist jetzt der Atheismus die Sache der Arbeiter, der geistigen sowohl als der leiblichen, und eben damit eine Sache des Ernstes, der Gründlichkeit, der Notwendigkeit, der schlichten Wahrhaftigkeit und Menschlichkeit geworden . . ." (*ibid*). Important as is this difference, whether interpreted as by Feuerbach or otherwise, what is common to the main drift of traditional critique of religion is the conviction that by doing away with religion, human happiness increases, and prior to that the will to happiness.

277. Cicero, *De finibus bonorum et malorum* I, 18, 62. Here the Epicurean Torquatus says: "Igitur neque stultorum quisquam beatus neque sapientiam non beatus, multoque hoc melius nos veriusque quam Stoici" (namely, by reason of the better basis).

278. Dilthey, II, 362, 422, 434.

279. On this, cf. V. Brochard, "La théorie du plaisir d'après Épicure," *Journal des Savants*, 1904, pp. 205 ff.

280. ". . . constitui tandem inquirere, an aliquid daretur, quod verum bonum, et sui communicabile esset, et a quo solo, rejectis caeteris omnibus, animus afficeretur; imo an aliquid daretur, quo invento, et acquisito, continua, ac summa in aeternum fruerer laetitia" (*Tract. de intell. emend.* in *Opera posthum.*, p. 357).

281. *Der junge Despinoza*, p. 249.

282. Regner a Mansvelt: "[nomen miraculi] *praecipue* respicit rerum naturas et iis conformem a Deo constitutum ordinem, praeter quem Deus agit in miraculis, *secundario* vero hominis opinionem formatam vel formandam ex et secundum illum ordinem natura cognitum." Musaeus, par. 78: ". . . Miracula . . . quae Scriptura commemorat talia sunt, ut illa *revera, non ex opinione hominum*, contra vel supra naturam sint, . . ."

CHAPTER VIII

THE ANALYSIS OF REVEALED RELIGION

283. *Eth.* II, 29 and schol.; 40, schol. 2; 41. *Tr. de intell. emend.*, Opp. II, 10–12; 22; 32.

284. Besides, Spinoza, even at this point, goes into the matter of why prejudices arise only with the intention of eliminating prejudices: ". . . verum haec ab humanae mentis natura deducere, non est huius loci. Satis *hic* erit, si pro fundamento id capiam, quod apud omnes debet esse in confesso."

285. *Ep.* 54, vers. fin.; *Eth.* III, def. 3; post. I; affect. gener. def.; IV, 8.

286. *Tract.* praef. I; *ibid.*, pp. 32 f. The term "consilium" indicates reflection on means to the previously established end: one takes counsel with oneself only in regard to matters whose outcome is uncertain. (Cf. Arist., *Eth. Nic.* III, 5; Thomas Aquinas, *Summa theol.* II, I, qu. 14). Thus even the first sentence of the *Tractate* unambiguously defines in which domain of human life religion has its home.

287. What follows is based on the first page of the Preface to the *Tractate*. The passages from the *Tractate* and from Spinoza's other writings, here used to complement the text, are quoted in the text itself.

288. *Tr.*, pp. 1, 9 f., 13 f., 19, 30, 67; *Eth.* III, 12–13; 53–55, corr. I, schol.; IV, 57 schol.; *Ep.* 52, 54. "Omne humanum genus est avidum nimis auricularum"—thus also in Lucretius in a similar context (IV, ll. 576 ff.).

289. ". . . [superstitio] non ex ratione, sed ex solo affectu, *eoque efficacissimo* oritur" (*Tr.* praef., p. 2).

290. The concord between Spinoza and Epicureanism in the analysis of religion, and also the limit of this concord, stand out plainly if one compares what has been said in the text with the following lines from Lucretius (V, ll. 1236–40):

> denique sub pedibus tellus cum tota vacillat,
> concussaeque cadunt urbes dubiaeque minantur,
> quid mirum, si *se temnunt* mortalia saecla
> atque potestatis magnas mirasque relinquunt
> in rebus viris divum, quae cuncta gubernent?

CHAPTER IX

THE STATE AND THE SOCIAL FUNCTION OF RELIGION

291. "Verum enimvero si regiminis Monarchici summum sit arcanum, ejusque omnino intersit, homines deceptos habere, et metum, quo retineri debent, specioso Religionis nomine adumbrare, ut pro servitio, tamquam pro salute pugnent, . . .; nihil contra in libera republica excogitari, nec infoelicius tentari potest. . . ." (*Tr.*, praef., p. 3).

292. *Eth.: Plerique*, qui de affectibus et hominum vivendi ratione scripserunt, . . . non communi naturae potentiae, sed nescio cui naturae humanae vitio tribuunt, quam propterea flent, rident, contemnunt, vel, *quod plerumque fit, detestantur*; et qui humanae mentis impotentiam eloquentius vel argutius carpere novit, veluti divinus habetur.

Tr. pol.: Affectus, quibus conflictamur, concipiunt *philosophi* veluti vitia, in quae homines sua culpa labuntur, quos propterea ridere, flere, carpere vel (*qui sanctiores videri volunt) detestari solent.* Sic ergo se rem divinam facere et sapientiae culmen attingere credunt, quando humanam naturam, quae *nullibi* est, multis modis laudare et eam, quae *revera* est, dictis lacessere norunt. Homines namque *non ut sunt, sed ut eosdem esse vellent,* concipiunt.

293. The connection between Utopias and religion is brought out in *Tr. pol.* I, 5.

294. *Ibid.*, V, 7.

295. "Lex [sc. naturalis] ergo eo ipso, quod praecipit media ad pacem, praecipit bonos mores, sive virtutes. Vocatur ergo moralis" (*De Cive* III, 31). Cf. Tönnies, *Hobbes*, pp. 197 f.

296. *Elements* Pt. I, xiv, 11, 13. *De Cive* I, 4, 12. One does not reach the core of Hobbes' theory if one—admittedly in accord with many of his utterances—defines the state of nature as dominated by the passions, and the civil state as dominated by reason.

297. "And from this diffidence of one another, there is no way for any man to secure himself so reasonable, as Anticipation; that is, by force, or wiles, to master the persons of all men he can, so long, till he see no other power great enough to endanger him: And this is no more than his own conservation requireth, and is generally allowed" (*Lev.* xiii).

298. ". . . nec hic ullam agnoscimus differentiam inter homines et reliqua naturae individua" (*Tr.*, pp. 175 f.)

299. Thus even fools and madmen act *summo naturali iure* (*Tr.*, p. 175). Even though Hobbes speaks of the natural right of God, and also of animals (*Elements* Pt. II, iii, 9; *De Cive* viii, 10, xv, 5), in so doing he *subsequently* and metaphorically extends a claim derived from the human situation, whereas for Spinoza human natural right is a special form of the natural right derived from God, and *primarily* granted to all beings.

300. For this reason Spinoza turns against Hobbes: "ratio pacem *omnino* suadet" (*Tr.*, adnot. 33); for Hobbes justifies war as rational in respect to the concrete situation of man in the state of nature.

301. *De Cive* I, 4. Cf. *Lev.* xxi, in which Hobbes distinguishes between iniquity (in relation to natural right) and injury (in relation to civil right); Spinoza consistently applies both terms as synonymous (*Tr.*, p. 182).

302. If Spinoza's pathos is to be rightly understood, we must compare the passage "Pisces a natura determinati sunt ad natandum, magni ad minores comedendum, adeoque pisces summo naturali jure aqua potiuntur et magni minores comedunt" (*Tr.*, p. 175), with his actual behavior. Colerus reports (and there is no reason to doubt the truth of his report):

"When Spinoza was at home, he was no burden to anyone, but spent most of his time sitting quietly in his room. When he was weary from his investigations, he came down and conversed with the other inmates of the house on everything that was going on, even of trifles. He also took pleasure in smoking an occasional pipeful of tobacco; when he sought some other diversion, he would catch a few spiders and have them fight one another; or he caught a few flies, tossed them onto the spider's web, and greatly enjoyed watching this combat, even laughed at it. He also used to take his magnifying-glass, and observe the smallest midges and flies through it, and engaged in his investigations." If one speaks in this context of "cruelty" (as does Schopenhauer), it is meaningless; but even to speak of "scientific interest" (as does Freudenthal) is to misjudge the level of the pleasure experienced by Spinoza: not the mere *lex naturae*, but the *summum naturale ius*, which belongs to all events, and therefore also to the victory of the stronger, is the correlate of the pleasure felt by Spinoza as *spectator*: the actors are the large fish and the small fish, the rulers and their subjects, whose power and struggle are modes of the eternal power and necessity of God.

303. The formal distinction between natural right as subjective title, and natural law as objective obligation (*Lev.*, ch. xvi), does not sufficiently bring out the internal connection.

304. The striking contradiction in Hobbes' *Leviathan*, ch. xv (Molesworth, p. 133) is to be reduced to this relationship of mutual independence.

305. In the sense of perfection independent of duration (*Eth.* IV, praef.).

306. Spinoza's political theory stands or falls by the proposition that contracts are not binding. The state is founded not on contract, but on the power of all its citizens. On the other hand, "A free man never acts by fraud, but always by good faith." Proof: What should a man's conduct be in a case where he could by breaking faith free himself from the danger of present death? Would not his plan of self-preservation completely persuade him to deceive? This may be answered by pointing out that, if reason persuaded him to act thus, it would persuade all men to act in a similar manner, in which case reason would persuade men not to agree in good faith to unite their forces, or have any general laws, which is absurd. (*Eth.*, Pt. IV, prop. 72 et schol., as given in Elwes' translation [London, 1884], p. 235.)

307. "Le seul idéal d'avenir conçu par ce peuple fut une sorte d'économie en politique; sa force révolutionnaire vint du désir domestique d'avoir ses coudées franches à table et son aise complète sous l'auvent de ses *steedes*." Balzac, *La recherche*

de l'absolu, p. 477, *La Comédie humaine*, ed. Marcel Bouteron, IX (Paris, Bibliothèque de Pléiade, Paris, 1937).

308. The historical condition underlying this judgment is the Revolt of the Netherlands.

309. There is a close connection between this and Spinoza's derivation of aristocracy and monarchy from democracy. The emergence of an aristocracy from democracy is justified by rights of privilege against aliens, and finally by property-rights. Spinoza does not question these rights (*Tr. pol.* VIII, 12).

310. "Libera enim multitudo maiori spe, quam metu, subacta autem maiori metu, quam spe ducitur: quippe *illa vitam colere, haec autem mortem tantummodo vitare studet*; illa, inquam, sibi vivere studet, haec victoris esse cogitur, unde hanc servire, illam liberam esse dicimus" (*Tr. pol.* V, 6).

311. "Spinoza's speculative interpretation of religion, by reason of its aristocratic exclusiveness, requires as complement a form of religion which is accessible also to the common people. It is the same problem which we have already met with in the thought of the Arab Aristotelians. Even the solution, taken in the most general sense, is the same" (Guttmann, p. 56).

312. ". . . verbum Dei . . . proprie significat legem illam divinam (de qua in 4. cap. egimus), hoc est, religionem toti humano generi universalem sive catholicam; qua de re vide Esaiae cap. I, vers. 10 etc., ubi verum vivendi modum docet, qui scilicet non in ceremoniis, sed in caritate et vero animo consistit, eumque legem et verbum Dei promiscue vocat" (*Tr.*, p. 148). The *lex divina*, which is treated in ch. iv of the *Tractate*, is the standard by which the philosopher lives. On the demand made by revelation Spinoza says: ". . . obedientia erga Deum in solo amore proximi consistit" (*Tr.*, p. 154). Cf. further *Tr.*, p. 142: ". . . quamvis religio, prout ab apostolis praedicabatur, nempe simplicem Christi historiam narrando, sub rationem non cadat, eius tamen summam, quae potissimum documentis moralibus constat, ut tota Christi doctrina, potest unusquisque lumine naturali facile assequi."

313. "Omnes absolute obedire possunt" (*Tr.*, p. 174).

314. "Amor enim Dei non obedientia, sed virtus est, quae homini, qui Deum recte novit, necessario inest. At obedientia voluntatem imperantis, non rei necessitatem et veritatem respicit" (*Tr.*, adnot. 34).

315. ". . . ex mediis, quae sibi ipsi parare solent, concludere debuerunt, dari *aliquem vel aliquos* naturae rectores . . ." (*Eth.* I, app.).

316. This seems to be contradicted by a passage in the Preface to the *Tractate* (p. 2): ". . . ex hac itaque superstitionis causa [sc. timore] clare sequitur, omnes homines natura superstitioni esse obnoxios (quicquid dicant alii, qui putant, hoc inde oriri, quod omnes mortales confusam quandam numinis ideam habent)." Naturally the primary idea of God, common to all men, is not the reason, the characteristic reason, for superstition, and yet essentially it precedes superstition.

CHAPTER X

SPINOZA'S READING OF THE BIBLE, BIBLE SCIENCE AND CRITIQUE OF THE BIBLE

317. Should one feel inclined to call Spinoza's conception of Scripture "unhistorical," one must not disregard the fact that the "unhistorical approach" common in the Age of Enlightenment was already understood historically by the Enlightenment itself, and not only by its critics and historians. Spinoza characterizes the "prejudices" to be found in Scripture as "*antiqui vulgi praeiudicia.*" The attribute

"ancient" is here to be understood in the sense of "antiquated, raw, barbaric." Such characterization presupposes the historical point of view. The "unhistoricity" of the Age of Enlightenment is primarily to be defined as the mode of treating the present, understood *as* present, as an absolute. This form of historical consciousness is the presupposition for despising the dark past, for the failure to understand the past in its peculiar character, for the lack of interest in that peculiarity, just as on the other hand the critical attitude towards the present, the self-criticism of the age, is the presupposition for what we call, in the narrower sense applied by the Romantics, the historical view-point. Cf. also pp. 115, 133 f., 178 ff.

318. Cf. the analysis of prejudices in *Eth.* I, App. on the basis of the assumption: "omnes homines rerum causarum ignari *nascuntur.*"

319. ". . . unusquisque tam in religione, quam in reliquis sui nominis gloriam *incepit* quaerere . . . ut religio in exitiabilem superstitionem *declinaret* . . ." (*Tr.*, p. 208).

320. ". . . novi . . . aeque impossibile esse vulgo superstitionem adimere ac metum . . ." (*Tr.* praef., p. 8).

321. ". . . atque hoc praecipuum est, quod in hoc tractatu demonstrare constitui; ad quod apprime necesse fuit, praecipua circa religionem praeiudicia, hoc est, antiquae servitutis vestigia indicare, tum etiam praeiudicia circa summarum potestatum ius, quod multi procacissima quadam licentia magna ex parte arripere, et specie religionis multitudinis animum, gentilium superstitioni adhuc obnoxium, ab iisdem avertere student, quo omnia iterum in servitium ruant" (*Tr.* praef., p. 3).

322. ". . . jam autem felix profecto nostra esset aetas, si ipsam etiam ab omni superstitione liberam videremus" (*Tr.*, p. 144).

" . . . nos non eo scripsisse animo, ut nova introduceremus, sed ut depravata corrigeremus, quae tandem aliquando correcta videre speramus" (*ibid.*, p. 166).

323. "Primis Judaeis religio tanquam lex scripto tradita est, nimirum quia tum temporis veluti infantes habebantur. Verum imposterum Moses (Deut., cap. 30, vers. 6) et Jeremias (cap. 31, vers. 33) tempus futurum ipsis praedicant, quo Deus suam legem eorum cordibus inscribet" (*Tr.*, pp. 144 f.). Cf. Gal. 4:1–3 and Col. 2:14.

324. In the chapter on *lex divina* (ch. iv), all the Scriptural texts adduced in corroboration of *lex divina* are taken from Proverbs or from Paul's Epistles to the Romans and to the Corinthians.

325. The account given here is based on ch. vii of the *Tractate.*

326. "His enim omnibus [sc. casibus librorum Scripturae] ignoratis, minime scire possumus, quid auctor intenderit aut intendere potuerit; quum contra his probe cognitis nostras cogitationes ita determinamus, ut nullo praeiudicio praeoccupemur, ne scilicet auctori, vel ei, in cuius gratiam auctor scripsit, plus minusve iusto tribuamus, et ne de ullis aliis rebus cogitemus, quam de iis, quas auctor in mente habere potuerit, vel quas tempus et occasio exegerit" (*Tr.*, pp. 95 f.).

327. Gebhardt, *Inedita Spinozana*, pp. 7–13.

APPENDIX

ON THE SOURCES OF DA COSTA

The limits of the agreement between da Costa and Servetus appear from the following juxtaposition:

Da Costa: ... accidit ... ut ... accederem sententiae illorum, qui legis veteris praemium et poenam definiunt temporalem, et de altera vita et immortalitate animorum minime cogitant, eo praeter alia nixus fundamento, quod praedicta Lex Mosis omnino taceat super his, et nihil aliud proponat observantibus et transgressoribus, quam praemium, aut poenam temporalem. . . . Christiani . . ., qui ex speciali fide in lege Evangelii fundata, ubi expresse mentio fit de aeterno bono et supplicio, animae immortalitatem et credunt, et agnoscunt. (Gebhardt, p. 108.)

Servetus: Populi Judaeorum mundana iustitia tunc erat, ut ad tempus in terra illa bene viveret favore divino. Nostra vero, ut aeternam vitam iam vivamus . . . Praemia, quae lex promittebat, erant eis omnia carnalia: nec ipsi solent, nisi carnalia a Deo petere . . . Poenae et maledictiones legis, omnes erant carnales et mundanae Levit. 26 et Deut. 28 . . . De poena damnationis aeternae non erat ibi apertus sermo . . . At Christus, qui solus aeternam vitam intulit, solus aeternas damnatis fore poenas, operte mundo declaravit, magnus undique magister. Nemo igitur intelligat, illos olim ideo dici carnales, quia futuram gloriam non sperarent, ut de solis Saducaeis dicitur. Judaei eam hodie sperant ac etiam Mahometani, et nihilominus sunt maxime carnales. Carnales vocamus homines, qui spiritum regenerationis non assequuti carnales habent iustificationis ritus. (*Christianismi Restitutio*, 1553, pp. 321–23)

As a source for da Costa one has to consider, besides Servetus, especially Socinus. Socinus adduces seven arguments in favor of man's original mortality (in the first chapter of his *Praelectiones Theologicae*, which is entitled: Primus homo etiam ante lapsum natura mortalis fuit.—*Op*. I, 537). The second, third and fourth arguments appear again in da Costa.

Da Costa: The weakness, from his origin, that he required

Socin: Secundo. Quia jam escis utebatur et cibo, Gen. 1:29.

food and drink, does not speak in support of it [that Adam was created immortal] . . . (Gebhardt 79, 12–15)[1]

Ubi autem immortalitas est, ibi escis ciboque non est locus.

. . . it does not follow [from Gen. ii:7] that the spirit which gave life to Adam's body would have been an immortal spirit without Adam's soul; rather, this passage proves that animals have the same life-spirit as man . . . (79, 23–26)

Tertio. Primus homo etiam ante peccatum corpus animale habuit, igitur et mortale . . . Adamus . . . non modo antequam peccaret, sed in ipsa creatione factus est in animam viventem, Gen. 2:7.

Secondly, [that the human soul is mortal] is proved from this, that God said to man, "On the day on which you eat, will you suffer death." It follows that man was created mortal and subject to death. Else, if by his nature he were immortal, he would not need to die. Further, in saying to him "Dust thou art and to dust thou shalt return," God revealed to man his end (67, 29–68, 4)

Quarto. Primus homo, antequam peccaret, jam erat terrenus; nempe, quia e terra formatus fuerat . . . Peccatum igitur non mortalitatis naturalis, sed necessariae mortis causa fuit. Nec aliter intelligi debet comminatio illa, In quacumque die comederis ex ea, moriendo morieris etc. Gen. 2:17. . . .

For the 4th argument cf. also from Socinus' *Summa Religionis Christianae* (Op. I, 281):

Homo quia est ex terra factus, natura sua Gen. 2:7, 1 Cor. 15:47, mortalis Gen. 3:19, 1 Cor. 15:48 et corruptioni subiectus; et, ex accidente, quia divinum praeceptum violavit, morti aeternae obnoxius est. Gen. 2:17, 3:19. . . .

The following argument also belongs to the same context:

---

[1] We use the emendation made by Porges (*Monatsschrift für Gesch. und Wiss. des Judent.*, 1923, p. 215); otherwise, we follow Gebhardt's German translation as far as the Portuguese text is concerned.

To the argument that man would not have been made in God's image if he were not immortal, we counter that it would be foolishness to require that man be God's image in every aspect and function; if God is almighty, man, his image, is not therefore almighty. . . . Man is thus image and in a certain sense a copy of God; but he is a shadow of His wisdom itself. He rules over creatures and is almost like God, but he does not rule like God (75, 29–76, 12)

Dei imago et similitudo, ad quam conditus est homo, ne in ipsa quidem mente ac ratione, unde omnis iustitia in illum derivari poterat, praecipue consistit, sed in dominatu rerum omnium, praesertim inferiorum, sex illis diebus a Deo creatarum, ut satis patet ex loco ipso, ubi primus homo ad Dei imaginem et similitudinem factus fuisse narratur, Gen. 1:26 (*Op.* I, 539)'

Demus in omnibus rebus creatis aliquam esse similitudinem creatoris: Quid tum? Num propterea res creatas creatori prorsus similes esse oportet? Certe longe aliud est, aliquam similitudinem habere, et in omnibus esse similem . . . Possunt ergo res creatae aliquam creatoris similitudinem retinere, nec tamen immortales esse. Homo autem cur potissimum ad Dei imaginem factus dicatur, ex eo loco, ubi id primum dictum fuit, liquido apparet, hoc est, quia dominium datum est illi in universa opera Dei. (*Op.* II, 258)

I have nowhere found in Servetus the anti-trinitarian argument: "It is a contradiction to be God and to be able to have been made, created or generated," which does not indeed occur in da Costa as an anti-trinitarian argument (cf. Gebhardt 76, 7–8). The following argument of Socinus reminds one of that argument:

Censeo, istud (sc. the doctrine that Christ is generated from God's substance) merum esse humanum commentum, . . . ipsi sanae rationi penitus repugnans, quae nullo modo patitur, ut

Deus animalium corruptibilium more ex sua ipsius substantia generet, utve unica illa numero Dei essentia vel dividatur, vel multiplicetur, vel unica numero et integra manens, pluribus fiat communis (*Op.* I, 655).

How current the scriptural proof used by da Costa against immortality was in the sixteenth century appears from a comparison of da Costa's arguments with the arguments attacked by Calvin in his writings "Psychopannychia, qua refellitur quorundam imperitorum error, qui animas post mortem usque ad ultimum iudicium dormire putant" (in *Calvini Opuscula,* 1563). Calvin says of his opponents: locum Salomonis (sc. Eccl. 3:18–21) in nos, quasi fortissimum arietem, impellunt (p. 66); compare with this the frequent use of this passage by da Costa (65, 21–23; 66, 22–25; 73, 13–19; 73, 26–31; 76, 32 ff.). According to Calvin the opponents of the doctrine of immortality use in addition especially the following Scriptural passages which recur in da Costa in the same context:

> Ps. 78:39 (da Costa 69, 20 ff.—Calvin 92)
> Ps. 88:11 f. (da Costa 68, 27 ff.—Calvin 97)
> Ps. 115: 17 f. (da Costa 69, 4–6—Calvin 97)
> Ps. 146:2–4 (da Costa 77, 22 ff.—Calvin 91, 107)
> Job 7:7–9 (da Costa 69, 25 ff.—Calvin 112)
> Job 34:14 f. (da Costa 78, 2 ff.—Calvin 114)

Cf. furthermore this reasoning of da Costa (79, 12 ff.) with the parallel recorded by Calvin: "And even assuming that Adam had been created immortal . . . under the condition that he kept the Law which had been imposed on him, in that hour in which he transgressed it, he lost immortality."[2] Calvin: Obiiciunt . . . animam, tametsi immortalitate donata esset, in peccatum tamen prolapsam: qua ruina, immortalitatem suam obruerit ac perdiderit. Haec constituta erat poena peccato, . . . (p. 55).

---

[2] According to Porges.

ON THE SOURCES OF THE *TRACTATUS THEOLOGICO-POLITICUS* AND THE *TRACTATUS POLITICUS*[3]

I. CLASSICAL AUTHORS

1. *Thucydides*

In the Fifth Book of his History (para. 103) he makes the Athenian ambassadors say to the Melians: . . . μὴ βούλεσθε . . .
. . . ὁμοιωθῆναι τοῖς πολλοῖς, οἷς παρὸν ἀνθρωπείως ἔτι σώζεσθαι, ἐπειδὰν πιεζομένους αὐτοὺς ἐπιλίπωσιν αἱ φανεραὶ ἐλπίδες, ἐπὶ τὰς ἀφανεῖς καθίστανται, μαντικήν τε καὶ χρησμοὺς καὶ ὅσα τοιαῦτα μετ’ ἐλπίδων λυμαίνεται.

The passage must be considered as a source, not immediately for the *Tract. theol.-pol.* (praef.), but for Hobbes, who, in contrast to Spinoza, attaches central importance to the notion of "invisible powers" in his analysis of religion, and who, as the translator of Thucydides, knew this author very well.

2. *Cicero*

Tr. 32 f. (Bruder III, 12–14) Omnia, quae honeste cupimus, ad haec tria potissimum referuntur, nempe res per primas suas causas intelligere; passiones domare sive virtutis habitum acquirere, et denique secure et sano corpore vivere . . . media, quae ad secure vivendum et corpus conservandum inserviunt, in rebus externis praecipue sita sunt; atque ideo dona fortunae vocantur, . . . Attamen ad secure vivendum et iniurias aliorum hominum, . . ., evitandum humana direc-	*De off.* II, 5, 18–6, 20. Etenim virtus omnis tribus in rebus fere vertitur, quarum una est in perspiciendo quid in quaque re verum sincerumque sit, quid consentaneum cuique, quid consequens, ex quo quaeque gignantur, quae cujusque rei causa sit, alterum cohibere motus animi turbatos, quos Graeci πάθη nominant, appetitionesque, quas illi ὁρμάς, oboedientes efficere rationi, tertium iis, quibuscum congremur, uti moderate et scienter, quorum studiis ea, quae natura

---

[3] These notes could not be used in the preceding study; perhaps they will be useful for further work; they supplement the observations made especially by Joel and Leopold. It goes without saying that the parts of this compilation are of very unequal worth, and that the compilation is in need of being supplemented in every respect.

tio et vigilantia multum iuvare potest. Ad quod nullum certius medium ratio et experientia docuit, quam societatem certis legibus formare . . . et omnium vires ad unum quasi corpus, nempe societatis, redigere.

desiderat, expleta cumulataque habeamus, per eosdemque, si quid importetur urbis incommodi, propulsemus ulciscamurque eos, qui nocere nobis conati sunt, . . . Magnam vim esse in fortuna in utramque partem, vel secundas ad res vel adversas quis ignorat? . . . Haec igitur ipsa fortuna caeteros casus rariores habet, . . . ab inanimis procellas, . . . At vero interitus exercituum, . . . civium expulsiones, calamitates, fugae, rursusque secundae res, honores, imperia, victoriae, quamquam fortuita sunt, tamen sine hominum opibus et studiis in neutram partem effici possunt.

Maimonides uses the same tripartition in his discussion of the difference between divine and human law (see *Guide of the Perplexed* II, 40, III, 27–28, 31, 51, 54).

3. *Curtius Rufus*

Tr. 188 (Bruder XVII 9) . . . quamvis non perinde animis ac linguis imperari possit, . . .

Histor. Alex. VIII 5 (17) Jovis filium non dici tantum se, sed etiam credi volebat (ṣc. Alexander), tamquam perinde animis imperare posset ac linguis, . . .

4. *Tacitus*

Tr. 191 (Bruder XVII, 25) ad hunc modum Monarchae ad sui imperii securitatem alia excogitaverunt, quae omnia missa facio, . . . ea tantum uti dixi notabo et perpendam, quae

Histor. V, 4 Moyses quo sibi in posterum gentem firmaret, novos ritus contrariosque ceteris mortalibus indidit. profana illic omnia quae apud nos sacra, rursum

in hunc finem olim divina
revelatio Mosen docuit.

concessa apud illos quae nobis
incesta.

Tr. 201 (Bruder XVII, 80)
Amor ergo Hebraeorum erga
patriam non simplex amor, sed
pietas erat, quae simul et odium
in reliquas nationes ita quoti-
diano cultu fovebantur et ale-
bantur, ut in naturam verti
debuerint: quotidianus enim
cultus non tantum diversus
omnino erat (quo fiebat, ut
omnino singulares, et a reliquis
prorsus essent separati), sed
etiam absolute contrarius.

Histor. V, 12
providerant conditores (sc.
templi Hierosolymitani) ex diversitate morum crebra bella.

Tr. 42 (Bruder III, 53)
se ab omnibus nationibus ita
separaverunt, ut omnium odium in se converterint, idque
non tantum ritibus externis,
ritibus caeterarum nationum
contrariis, sed etiam signo cir-
cumcisionis, quod religiosissime
servant.

Histor. V, 5
circumcidere genitalia institue-
runt, ut diversitate noscantur.

Tr. 202 (Bruder XVII, 87)
ad eosdem non tantum in patrio
solo retinendum, sed ad bella
etiam civilia vitandum . . . haec
apprime conducebant; nempe
quod . . . et quod charitas et
amor erga concivem summa
aestimabatur pietas, qui non
parum fovebatur communi
odio, quo reliquas nationes, et
hae eos contra, habebant.

Histor. V, 5
auctae Judaeorum res, et quia
apud ipsos fides obstinata, misericordia in promptu, sed adversus omnes alios hostile odium.

Cf. also *Tr.* III, 14–15 and V, 27 with *Histor.* V, 3: adsensere
atque omnium ignari fortuitum iter incipiunt. Spinoza relies

then on Tacitus in his judgment of the Jewish ceremonial law,
although he knows and rejects Tacitus' point of view:

Tr. praef. 1 (Bruder § 3)
Si quid porro insolitum magna
cum admiratione vident, id pro-
digium esse credunt, quod Deorum aut summi Numinis iram
indicat, quodque adeo hostiis,
et votis non piare, nefas habent
homines superstitioni obnoxii,
et religioni adversi. . . .

Histor. V. 13 (Description of the
siege of Jerusalem)
Evenerant prodigia, quae neque hostiis neque votis piare
fas habet gens (sc. Judaeorum)
superstitioni obnoxia, religion-
ibus adversa.

For the preface of the *Tr.* and generally for Spinoza's critique
of religion, cf. also *Histor.* I, 86: Prodigia insuper terrebant . . .,
insolitos animalium partus, et plura alia rudibus saeculis etiam in
pace observata, quae nunc tantum in metu audiuntur.

For *Tr. pol.* VI, 7 (Reges filios etiam plus timent, quam amant,
. . .) cf. *Histor.* I, 21: suspectum semper invisumque dominantibus
qui proximus destinaretur . . . and also in the Annals the reports
about the conduct of Tiberius toward Drusus and Germanicus.

II. JEWISH AUTHORS

1. *Bahya*

For Spinoza's interpretation of the ceremonial law cf. *Hobot
halbabot* III, 3 (ed. Stern, p. 139):

התורה כללה ענינים לא יוכל השכל לבאר אופני חיובם והם המצות השמעיות...
וכללים משרשי השכליות וזה היה בעבור שהיה העם שנתנה להם התורה בעת
ההיא בענין גובר התאוות הבהמיית עליהן ונחלשו מדעתם והכרתם מהבין הרבה
מן השכליות ונתנה בהם התורה בזה מנהג אחד, ושבו השכליות והשמעיות
אצלם שוים בהערה עליהם ומי ששכלו והכרתו חזקים יתעורר אליהם ויקבלם על
עצמו לשני הפנים.

2. *Maimonides*

Tr. 6 (Bruder I, 21)
(Interpretation of Num. 12:
6–8.)
Si aliquis vestri propheta Dei
erit, in visione ei revelabor (id
est per figuras et hieroglyphica;

Yesode hatorah VII, 6

ומה הפרש יש בין נבואת משה לשאר
כל הנביאים. שכל הנביאים בחלום או
במראה, ומשה רבינו מתנבא והוא ע ר
ו ע ו מ ד ... כל הנביאים על ידי מלאך,
לפיכך רואים מה שהם רואים ב מ ש ל

nam de prophetia Mosis ait,
esse visionem sine hierogly-
phicis); in somnis loquor ipsi
(id est non verbis realibus et
vera voce). Verum Mosi non
sic (revelor); ore ad os loquor
ipsi et visione, sed non aenig-
matibus, et imaginem Dei ad-
spicit, hoc est me adspiciens,
ut socius, non vero perterritus
mecum loquitur; ut habetur in
Exodo cap. 33. v. 11. Quare
non dubitandum est, reliquos
prophetas vocem veram non
audivisse, quod magis adhuc
confirmatur ex Deuter. cap.
34. v. 10, ubi dicitur: פנים...
... אל פנים

וחידה. משה רבינו לא על ידי
מלאך 4) שנאמר פה אל פה אדבר
בו. ונאמר ודבר ה' אל משה פנים אל
פנים, ונאמר ותמונת ה' יביט, כלומר
שאין שם משל, אלא רואה הדבר על
בוריו ... כל הנביאים יראים ונבהלים
ומתמוגגין, ומשה רבינו אינו כן, הוא
שהכתוב אומר כאשר ידבר איש אל
רעהו, 5) כלומר כמו שאין אדם
נבהל לשמוע דברי חבירו, כך
היה כח בדעתו של משה רבינו להבין
דברי הנבואה, והוא עומד על עומדו
שלם. כל הנביאים אין מתנבאים בכל
עת שירצו, משה רבינו אינו כן, אלא
כל זמן שיחפוץ רוח הקדש
לובשתו ונבואה שורה עליו ...

Tr. 3 (Bruder I, 10)
(Ex. 25:22) ostendit, Deum
usum fuisse voce aliqua vera,
quandoquidem Moses, quan-
docunque volebat, Deum ad
loquendum sibi paratum in-
veniebat. Et haec sola, qua
scilicet lex prolata fuit, vera
fuit vox, . . .

Tr. 15 (Bruder I, 47)[6]
. . . quoniam imaginatio vaga
est et inconstans, ideo prophetia
prophetis non diu haerebat,

Moreh II, 36
וכבר ידעת כי כל כח גופני יחלש
וילאה ויפסיד עת ויבריא עת אחרת
וזה הכח המדמה כח גופני בלא ספק

---

[4] Regarding this point Spinoza, following the Christian contention (Gal. 3:19 and
Acts 7:38), deviates from Maimonides.

[5] Ex. 33: 11.

[6] Joel (30) quotes *Moreh* II, 37 as the source. Against this Gebhardt (in a note to his
German translation of *Tr.* 15) observes: "Joël führt mit Unrecht More Nebuchim II
37 als Quelle dieser Stelle an. Die Erklärung der Prophetie bloß aus dem Vorstellungs-
vermögen ist spinozistisch." There is an obvious printing error in Joel's reference:
"37" should read "36". The agreement between Spinoza and Maimonides is possible
because Maimonides does not speak here of prophecy as such but only of the failure
of prophecy, which failure is entirely due to the imagination.

nec etiam frequens, sed admodum rara erat, . . .

ולזה תמצא הנביאים התבטל נבואתם
בעת האבל או בעת הכעס וכיוצא
בהם... וכן עוד תמצא קצת הנביאים
נבאו מדת זמן אחת ואחר כן נפסקה
הנבואה מהם ולא התמידה להם ...

Tr. 58 f. (Bruder V, 16). Cf. with this *Moreh* III, 32, where
Maimonides teaches that God has preserved the sacrifices in the
Mosaic legislation only because men always incline toward the
things to which they are accustomed, and yet in doing so He
demanded that from now on the sacrifices be brought no longer
to creatures but to Himself.

Tr. 155 (Bruder XIII, 11)
notandum, in Scriptura nullum
nomen praeter Jehova reperiri,
quod Dei absolutam essentiam
sine relatione ad res creatas
indicet. Atque ideo Hebraei
hoc solum nomen Dei esse
proprium contendunt, reliqua
autem appellativa esse.

Moreh I, 61

כל שמותיו יתעלה הנמצאים בספרים
כולם נגזרים מן הפעולות וזה מה שאין
העלם בו אלא שם אחד והוא יו"ד ה"א
וא"ו ה"א שהוא שם מיוחד לו יתעלה
ולזה נקרא שם המפורש ענינו שהוא
יורה על עצמו יתעלה הוראה מבוארת
אין השתתפות בה ... והשמירה
מלקרוא אותו להיותו מורה על עצמו
יתעלה מאשר לא ישתתף אחד מן
הברואים בהוראה ההיא...

Cf. furthermore the interpretation of Exod. 33:12–34, 7 given in
Moreh I, 54 with *Tr.* 154, 157 (XIII 9, 22): Deus Mosi cupienti
ipsum videre et noscere, nulla alia attributa revelat, quam quae
divinam justitiam et caritatem explicant.

Tr., adnot. 1. (Bruder I, 1 n)
nomen נבואה (prophetia) . . .
omne prophetandi genus comprehendere.

Moreh II, 32

כל מגיד בנעלם [בעולם] מצד הקסם
ומצד המשער או מצד מחשבה צודקת
הוא גם כן יקרא נביא.

3. *Alpakhar*

The statement which Spinoza records in *Tr.* 167 (Bruder XV,
4 ff.) reads literally as follows (Igrot le Rambam, Amsterdam
1712, p. 24a):

ובידוע שאינו דומה ענין הקדמות לגשמות כלל כי בענין הגשמות יבואו כמה
כתובים מכחישים זה את זה כתוב אחד אומר ויראו את אלהי ישראל וכתוב אחד

אומר כי לא יראני האדם וכתוב אחד אומר ועשו לי מקדש ושכנתי וכתוב אחד
אומר הנה השמים ושמי השמים לא יכלכלוך וכיוצא בזה אמרו רז"ל דברה תורה
כלשון בני אדם... אבל לענין מעשה בראשית כל הכתובים זה לוה מעידים ...
ואינו כדאי מופת חכמת יונית לעקור את הכל שנאמר ובא האות והמופת וגי'.

The comparison shows that Spinoza has inserted into his report
on Alpakhar's opinion the consequence or presupposition of this
opinion, without stating this.

4. *Albo*

Tr. 55 (Bruder V, 2)

Quum autem ceremoniae, eae
saltem, quae habentur in vetere
testamento . . . (Hebraeorum)
imperio ita accomodatae fuerint, ut maxima ex parte ab
universa societate, non autem
ab unoquoque exerceri potuerint, certum est, eas . . . solam
corporis temporaneam felicitatem et imperii tranquillitatem
respicere, proptereaque non nisi
stante eorum imperio ullius
usus esse potuisse.

Ikk. IV, 40

כאשר עיינו ביעודים הגשמיים שנזכרו
בתורה אחד לאחד נמצא שאי אפשר
שיבואו במקום ההוא יעודים רוחניים, כי
היעודים שנזכרו בתורה נמצאו כולם
כוללים לכלל האומה... והוא מבואר
כי היעודים הכוללים לכלל האומה לא
יתכן שיהיו נפשיית שאף אם תהיה
האומה בכללה צדקת וראויה לחיי
העוה"ב אי אפשר שנאמר שהרשע אשר
בה יזכה לחיי העוה"ב למען חמשים
הצדיקים אשר בקרבה... וע"כ הוא
מבואר שהיעודים הכוללים לאומה
בכללה ראוי שיהיו גשמיים בהכרח
וזהו כאשר המדינה או האומה רובה
צדיקים תמלט המדינה או האומה ההיא
מן הגלות או מן הרעב...

Albo asserts just as Spinoza does that there is a connection
between the "this-worldliness" of the Mosaic law and its "sociality," but his intention is entirely different from Spinoza's.

5. *Menasseh ben Israel*

For the understanding of *Tr.* 65 (Bruder V, 47)[7] consider the
following passage from Menasseh's Dissertatio de fragilitate
humana ex lapsu Adami deque divino in bono opere auxilio.
Ex Sacris Scripturis et veterum Hebraeorum libris (Amstelodami
1642): . . . non constituit tantum supernaturalia (sc. Deus in
lege sua): sed et ea quae natura sponte dictat, ut sunt non fura-
beris . . . et similia. Eoque Deus augmentavit leges, ut praemium

---

[7] See note 182 of main text.

acciperet, non qui propter naturam, sed propter Dei voluntatem
istas observasset (p. 85). Menasseh refers to Laniado's Cheli
hemda.

6. Commentaries on the Bible

Tr. 8 (Bruder I, 26) explains רוח in Ezek. 2:2: spiritus seu vis;
Kimchi: רוח שחזקה אותי.

Tr. 8 (Bruder I, 27) explains רוח in Judg. 8:3: spiritus sive impetus; Kimchi: רוח הכעם.

Tr. 9 (Bruder I, 29): . . . res aliqua ad Deum refertur, et Dei
dicitur esse . . . ad rem in superlativo gradu exprimendum, ut
הררי אל montes Dei, hoc est, montes altissimi; 'תרדמת ה
(הררי אל) somnus Dei, id est, profundissimus. On Ps. 36:7
Rashi observes: אל לשון תוקף; Kimchi: ההרים הגבוהים וכן מנהג
הלשון|כשרוצה להגדיל הדבר סומך אותו אל האל.
On 1 Sam. 26:12 ('תרדמת ה) Kimchi: הסמיכות הוא לאחד משני פנים
או פירושו תרדמה גדולה כי הדבר שרוצה להגדילו סומך אותו לאל יתברך
כמו מאפליה שלהבת יה כהררי אל עיר גדולה לאלהים ותהי לחרדת אלהים.
או פירושו להודיע כי התרדמה היתה סבה מאת האל. . .
On Ps. 80:11 (ארזי אל) cedri Dei, ad exprimendam earum
insolitam magnitudinem) Kimchi: הארזים הגבוהים מאד לפיכך קראם
ארזי אל כי כל דבר שרוצה להגדילו סומך אותו לאל.

Tr. 10 (Bruder I, 33) interprets "spirit of the Lord" in the
accounts of Gideon and Samson as: animus audacissimus et
ad quaevis paratus; Raschi on Judg. 6:34: רוח גבורה; Kimchi
on Judg. 13:25: הגבורה והכח.

For the interpretation of 'רוח ה Isa. 11:2 cf. Kimchi *ad loc.*:

hoc est, ut ipse propheta אמר בתחילה רוח ה' ואחר כן
. . . particulatim postea id ex- פירש רוח חכמה ובינה רוח עצה
plicando declarat, virtus sap- וגבורה . . .
ientiae, consilii, fortitudinis etc.

Tr. 10 f. (Bruder I, 33): רוח־אלהים רעה Dei spiritus malus, id est
melancholia profundissima; . . . Dei melancholiam naturalem
melancholiam . . .

Abrabanel on 1 Sam. 16:14: ואמנם מה היה הרוח הזה, הנה המפרשים
לא אמרו בו דבר. . . וחכמי הנוצרים חלקו בזה. . . מהם אמרו שהיה חולי
טבעי שחוריי. . . והיותר מתישב אצלי הוא ששאול אחרי שסרה ממנו
רוח ה'. . . סבבוהו בלהות ומחשבות רעות. . . ומתוך זה נשרף דמו ונתהוה

בו חולי המילא"נקולייא... ויהיה אם כן אמרו מאת השם, פירושו
מסבת היות האל ית' נפרד ממנו, לא שיהיה האל ית' הוא הפועל לחולי
ההוא בעצם.

Tr. 13 (Bruder I, 39) interprets Isa. 48:16: a principio (hoc est,
quum primum ad vos veni; . . . (ut ipse cap. 7. testatus est);
Kimchi: ואדוני אבי ז"ל פירש לא מראש כאשר נבאתי נבואת סנחריב
בגלוי דברתי ...

Tr. 15 (Bruder II, 1): homines rustici, et extra omnem disciplin-
am . . . dono prophetico fuerunt praeditae. In agreement with
this assertion directed against Maimonides, Abrabanel makes
the following note on Amos 1:1, in explicit criticism of Maimonides (*Moreh* II, 32):

אין תנאי הכרחי בהם (בנביאים .sc) למוד החכמות המחקריות
והתפלספותם... ולכן היה שעמוס בהיותו בנוקדים אשר בעיר תקוע עם
היותו בלתי מלומד בחכמה חלה בו הנבואה.

Tr. 16 (Bruder II, 4 f.): . . . ille quidem (*sc.* Abraham) Deo
credebat, nec signum petiit, non ut Deo fidem haberet, sed·ut
sciret id a Deo ei promitti. Id etiam clarius ex Gideone constat; . . . Vide Judicum cap. 6. v. 17.—Abrabanel on Judg. 6
vers. fin.: וגדעון היה שואל האות לראות אם רצון האל יתברך להושיע את
ישראל בידו, לא לנסות יכלתו כי אם לדעת רצונו ...

Tr. 17 (Bruder II, 7)—for the explanation of Ezek. 14:9 Kimchi
too uses 1 Kings 22:20 ff.

Tr. 22 (Bruder II, 29): Licet nobis affirmare, eum (sc. Salomon-
em) rationem inter peripheriam et circuli diametrum ignora-
visse, et cum vulgo operariorum putavisse eam esse, ut 3 ad 1.—
Gersonides and Abrabanel (following a Talmudic utterance)
note on I Kings 7:23 that the numerical relation given in the
passage is to be understood על דרך קירוב .

Tr. 57 (Bruder V, 10). On Isa. 58:8 (Videmus itaque prophetam
. . . etiam post mortem promittere) Kimchi says: תהיה...
הצלחתך זה יהיה בעולם הזה ובעולם הבא.
In a note Spinoza says on יאספך : Hebraismus, quo tempus
mortis significatur. Aggregari ad populos suos mori significat.
Cf. Kimchi *ad loc.*:   כבוד ה' יאספך: אל מקום הכבוד אשר נפשות
הצדיקים צרורות שם בצרור החיים.

Tr. 76 (Bruder VI, 46): Dei iussu mare viam Judaeis aperuit (vide Exod. 14:21), nempe Euro, qui fortissime integra nocte flavit.—Rashbam on Exod. 14:21: כדרך ארץ עשה הקב"ה שהרוח מיבש ומקריח את הנהרות.

Tr. 76 (Bruder VI, 47): ut Elisa puerum, qui mortuus credebatur, excitaret, aliquoties puero incumbere debuit, donec prius incaluerit et tandem oculos aperuerit.—Kimchi on II Kings 4:34: וישם פיו על פיו... ואפשר ג"כ להנשים על הנער לחממו בחום הטבעי היוצא מפיו ומעיניו כי רוב הנסים נעשים עם מעט תחבולה מדרך העולם.

Tr. 78 f. (Bruder VI, 57): In Scriptura enim multa ut realia nar-rantur et quae etiam realia esse credebantur, quae tamen non nisi repraesentationes resque imaginariae fuerunt; ut . . . quod Elias ad coelum igneo curru et igneis equis ascenderit.—Kimchi on II Kings 2:11: ראה דמין רכב אש וסוסי אש.

Tr. 80 (Bruder VI, 62): quum ex consensu Cyri Hierosolymam petierunt, nulla similia miracula iis contigisse constat.—Kimchi on Isa. 48:21: אם נבואה זו על השבי מגלות בבל כמו שהוא בנראה הוא תימה איך לא נכתב בספר עזרא כשספר בצאתם מהגלות שנעשו עמהם נסים אלו שבקע צור בעבורם במדבר.

Tr. 110 f. (Bruder VIII, 34 ff.). The question here treated con-cerning the authors of the books of Joshua, Samuel, etc. is raised by Abrabanel in the Introduction to his commentary on the Prior Prophets. According to Abrabanel the Talmudic assertion that Joshua is the author of the book of Joshua is contradicted by the fact that in that book Joshua's death is narrated and, above all, by the expression which occurs frequently in it, "up to the present day": וכה מאמר עד היום הזה יורה בהכרח שנכתב זמן רב אחרי שקרו הדברים. Cf. VIII, 36: modus etiam loquendi in hunc usque diem ostendit, scriptorem rem antiquam narrare.

In order to prove that Samuel is not the author of the book named after him, Abrabanel, like Spinoza (VIII, 40), refers to I Sam. 9:9; he says on this verse: וזה הפסוק מורה בהכרח שלא כתבו שמואל כי שאול בימיו היה, ואיך יאמר עליו לפנים בישראל כי לנביא היום יקרא הרואה? אבל יורה זה בחיוב מבואר שנכתב זמן רב אחרי מות שמואל ששנו המנהגים.

The limits of the agreement between Spinoza and Abrabanel appear from the final result at which Abrabanel's critique arrives: ומפני זה כלו חשבתי אני שיהושע לא כתב ספרו, אבל שמואל הנביא כתבו וכתב ג"כ ספר שופטים, ולזה לא תמצא שנאמר ביהושע שכתבו, כמו שהעידה התורה על משה רבינו עליו השלום באומר' ויכתוב משה את התורה הזאת ואמר ויהי ככלות משה לכתוב את דברי התורה הזאת על ספר עד תומם ...

Tr. 121 ff. (Bruder IX, 32 ff.). Kimchi on I Kings 17:14 דעתינו בכתיב וקרי כי בגלות נשתבשו הנסחאות והיו מוצאין בנסחא אחת כן ובנסחא אחרת כן ולא עמדו על בירורם וכתבו האחת מבפנים והאחרת מבחוץ.

III. Modern Writers

1. *Machiavelli*

Tr. 178, 182 f. (Bruder XVI, 16 ff., 44 ff.), as well as *Tr. pol.* III, 14 —— *Discorsi* III, 40, 42; *Principe* XVIII (utilitate sublata pactum simul tollitur).

Tr. 180 (Bruder XVI, 34), as well as *Tr. pol.* V, 6 —— *Discorsi* II, 2 (opposition of republics and monarchies).

Tr. 187, 189 (Bruder XVII, 3, 17) —— *Discorsi* III, 6 in princ. (the citizens are more dangerous to the ruler than are foreign enemies).

Tr. 190 f. (Bruder XVII, 20 ff.) —— *Discorsi* I, 11 ff. (the political function of "revelation").

Tr. 212 (Bruder XVIII, 29) —— *Discorsi* I, 26 (a new prince must innovate in everything).

Tr. 212 (Bruder XVIII, 30) populus regiae authoritati assuetus . . . si unum e medio tollat, necesse ipsi erit. . . . alium loco prioris eligere, qui non sponte, sed necessario tyrannus erit.

Discorsi I, 16
Un popolo uso a vivere sotto un principe, se per qualche accidente diventa libero, con difficultà mantiene la libertà. . . . uno populo, il quale sendo uso vivere sotto i governi d'altri, . . . ritorna presto sotto un giogo, il quale il più delle volte è più grave che quello che per poco innanzi si aveva levato d'in su'l collo. . . .

Tr. 213 (Bruder XVIII, 35) (At forsan aliquis exemplo populi Romani objiciet . . .) is directed against Discourses I, 4, 6, where Machiavelli teaches that the seditions of the Roman people in Rome's early period led to the freedom and power of the republic. Spinoza says here of the Roman people that it is *ex seditiosis et flagitiosis hominibus conflatus.* The passage is important because it shows the fact that, and the reason why, the Romans lost for some time the glory, asserted by Machiavelli, of being the classic political nation: the will to security becomes predominant. An earlier and more important testimony to this change in the judgment on Rome is supplied by Hobbes' *De Cive,* Ep. ded. (in princ.).—Cf. *Tr. pol.* V, 2 (rejection of sedition and war), but also VI, 4 (it is no objection to democracy that it gives more occasion for seditions than do the other regimes).

Tr. pol. I, 5 —— *Discorsi* I, 3 in princ. (the premise of politics is that all men are bad).

Tr. pol. III, 9 and VI, 4 —— *Discorsi* I, 45 as well as *Principe* XVII and XIX (in order to rule securely, the rulers must avoid acts of violence).

Tr. pol. V, 4 —— *Discorsi* I, 16 (an unfree people lives like a beast).

Tr. pol. VI, 35 —— *Discorsi* II, 24 (conquered cities must either be made allies or be destroyed, but must not under any circumstances be kept under military occupation).

Tr. pol. VII, 20 —— *Principe* XXI (the king is compelled in the interest of his security and tranquillity to wage wars, namely, in order to occupy the nobility which otherwise would be dangerous to him. Cf. Meinecke, *Staatsräson* 241 f.).

Tr. pol. VII, 27, *Tr. theol.-pol.* 180 —— *Discorsi* I, 58. ("The multitude is wiser and more constant than a prince.") Both Machiavelli and Spinoza quote Livy XXIV, 25 (plebs aut humiliter servit aut superbe dominatur) as authority for the opinion which they reject; the reasoning of Spinoza agrees entirely with that of Machiavelli: the defects for which the authors blame the multitude are to be found in all men; and: it is much harder to persuade a people to a bad or senseless

action than a prince; both Machiavelli and Spinoza begin their
statements with captatio benevolentiae: Machiavelli: Jo non
so se io mi prenderò una provincia dura, e piena di tanta
difficultà, che mi convenga o abbandonarla con vergogna, o
seguirla con carico . . . Spinoza: haec, quae scripsimus, risu
forsan excipientur. . . .

Tr. pol. VIII, 9 —— *Discorsi* I, 35 and III, 24. (Necessity to
limit the duration of the supreme command. *Discorsi* III, 24:
La prolungazione degl'imperii fece serva Roma. Spinoza:
Cuius rei funestissima exempla Roma dedit.)

Tr. pol. VIII, 12 —— *Discorsi* I, 6 (how aristocracy arises out of
democracy: through the immigration of foreigners).

Tr. pol. IX, 13 —— *Discorsi* II, 23 (towns conquered according
to the law of war must either be obliged by benefits or settled
by colonists—in the latter case the indigenous population must
be settled elsewhere—or be completely destroyed).

Tr. pol. X, 1 —— *Discorsi* I, 34, 35, 40 (virtues and defects of
dictatorship).

Tr. pol. X, 3 —— *Discorsi* I, 48 (how the Roman Senate paralyzed
the effectiveness of the tribunes of the people).

2. *Clapmarius*[8]

Tr. praef. 3 (Bruder praef. 9 f.) (Turkish despotism and religion);
Tr. pol. VI, 4 and VII, 23 —— *De arc.* VI, 20: Turcae etiam
habent occulta sua consilii imperii ac dominationis, ut sunt
violenta gubernatio, magno metu maximisque superstitionibus
induere plebem, consilia agitare non tam pacis, quam belli,
nunquam a bello cessare . . . Caeterum totae et singulae fere
leges Alcorani nihil continent, quam arcana consilia dominationis conservandae augendaeve.

Tr. 60 (Bruder V, 22 ff.) —— *De arc.* II, 2: plebs mavult decipi
quam cogi. II,9: Religione infatuare plebem.

Tr. pol. I, 2, 5 —— *De arc.* I, 1: Nam ut eos qui libertatis amantes
sunt, vel imperii avidi, in officio contineas aperta ac regia via

---

[8] Cf. Carl Gebhardt, Spinoza gegen Clapmarius (Chronicon Spinozanum III,
344–47). Clapmarius' De arcanis rerum publicarum, from which the passages quoted in
the text are taken, was in Spinoza's library.

frustra es. Quippe apud quos nullus locus est rationis, nullus aut legum, aut philosophicorum praeceptorum usus.

Tr. pol. VI, 6 —— *De arc.* II, 23: Quemadmodum etiam nimiae divitiae principibus merito suspectae sint, ut de Aruntio notat prudens scriptor, quem Tiberius "ut divitem suspectabat," et Annal. 11 "caveri vim atque opes principibus offensas" . . . *De arc.* III, 12: ne quis summam rei gestae ad se trahat: militiae auspicia et gloriam propriam esse summi principis.

Tr. pol. VIII, 9 (hoc apprime necesse est, ut nullus in Patriciorum numerum recipiatur, nisi qui artem militarem recte noverit. Subditos autem extra militiam esse, ut quidam volunt, inscitia sane est).

De arc. II, 6: In republica igitur optimatum, arma habere oportet (sc. optimates), et nisi habeant, puniri: plebs vero impune armis carebit.

De arc. II, 7: In aristocratia certe eos, qui primas tenent in Republica sedes armis exerceri oportet, indicta gravi poena, ne id faciant: plebeis vero impune ab armis abstinere licet.

Tr. pol. VIII, 9 (Caeterum . . . dux . . . ex solis Patriciis eligendus, qui annum ad summum imperium habeat, nec continuari in imperio, nec postea eligi possit; . . .). —— *De arc.* II, 11: in qua (sc. Aristocratia) nemini diu summum Imperium, ac praesertim bellicum, destinandum est . . . Quo magis cavendum est, ne quis eundem magistratum bis gerat.

Tr. pol. VIII, 16 —— *De arc.* II, 3: poena dicenda est patriciis ac divitibus, nisi ad comitia veniant: plebi vero et pauperibus poena remittenda est. Qua speciosa fallacia fascinata plebs, operis domestici sui suorum sustentandorum causa occupata, facile emanebit.

Tr. pol. VIII, 39 (ne duo sanguine propinqui simul in subselliis locum occupent) —— *De arc.* II, 12: arcanum illud . . . ne duo ex una familia, vivo utroque, non solum magistratus essent, sed ne quidem uno tempore in Senatu, . . .

3. *Petrus Cunaeus*

Petrus Cunaeus states the purpose of his De Republica Hebraeorum libri tres (ed. noviss. Lugd. Batav. 1632) in the Ep. Ded.

as follows: Inspiciendam . . . offero rempublicam, qua nulla unquam in terris sanctior, nec bonis exemplis ditior fuit . . . ipsum Deum immortalem, autorem fundatoremque habet, . . .

On *Tr.* 202 (Bruder XVII, 85) cf. Cunaeus I, 2: . . . Mosis jussa secutus summus dux Josua est. Universam enim regionem in duodecim partes divisit, atque habitandam totidem tribubus dedit. Mox singularium tribuum familias numeravit, et pro capitum multitudine certum cuique modum agri, atque proprios fines dedit. Ita provisum est, uti eadem aequalitate omnes continerentur. Quae esse prima cura bonis reipublicae moderatoribus solet . . . praeclaram legem quandam Moses tulit, qua effectum est, ne paucorum opulentia quandoque caeteros opprimeret, neu mutatis studiis cives ad novas artes peregrinasque ab innoxio labore se converterent. Ea fuit lex agraria, quae vetuit ne quis venditione aut ullo contractu plenum dominium fundi sui transferret in alium. Nam et iis, qui egestate compulsi agrum vendidissent, redimendi jus quovis tempore concessit, et ni redemtus esset, restitui eum gratis in Jubilaei celebritate jussit.

The connection between Spinoza's critique of religion and the economic tendency of his age becomes visible when one compares *Tr.* 207 (Bruder XVIII, 2): talis (sc. Hebraeorum) imperii forma iis forsan tantum utilis esse posset, qui sibi solis absque externo commercio vivere, seseque intra suos limites claudere et a reliquo orbe segregare velint; at minime iis, quibus necesse est cum aliis commercium habere [9]—with the following utterance of Cunaeus (I, 4): "Nos neque terram habitamus, quae mari vicina est, neque negotiationibus gaudemus, neque earum causa nobis consuetudo cum aliis gentibus est. sed sunt urbes quidem nostrae procul a mari sitae: ipsi autem nos regionem bonam incolentes, hanc cum labore exercemus." (Joseph. contra Apion.) Enimvero, cum diversas gentes ita negotiatio sociaverit, ut quod genitum est usquam, id apud omnes natum esse videatur; soli Judaei intra terrae suae fines, iis contenti opibus, quas illic natura producebat, vitam procul commerciis agitavere. Non enim maria transibant, neque exteros visebant, et ab his non visebantur . . . Ac mihi quidem sane Flavius etiam gloriari de Judaeorum obscuritate videtur,

---

[9] Cf. also *Tr.* 62 (Bruder V, 33 f.) and *Tr.* 186 (XVI, 67).

cum in mediterraneis locis eos agere, et nullum aditum esse ad
eos mercatoribus peregrinantibusque ait. Ita enim diutissime
incorruptos mores servavere, nihilque rerum ad copiam et
luxum pertinentium illatum est, quibus perire potentissimi
populi solent.

4. *Hobbes*

Tr. 3–6 (Bruder I, 9 ff.) —— Leviathan xxxvi: Explanation of
"Prophecy" (among the passages used Exod. 7:1); Scriptural
proof that prophecy takes place through vision or through
dreams; privileged position of Moses' prophecy (Num. 12:6–8;
Exod. 33:11; Acts 7:35) brought into connection with the
political position of Moses—cf. *Tr.* 193 (XVII, 37) and *Tr.* 1
(I, 1) (vicem Dei agere).

Tr. 7 ff. (Bruder I, 26 ff.) —— Lev. xxxiv: Explanation of "Spirit"
(among the passages used Gen. 1:2; Exod. 31:3; Judg. 6:34;
13:25; 14:6, 19; 1 Sam. 11:6; Isa. 11:2; Ezek. 2:2; Job 27:3);
primary meaning: fine invisible body; metaphorical meaning:
disposition or inclination of the mind, outstanding faculty,
extraordinary disease of the mind.

Tr. 148 (Bruder XII, 18–22) —— Lev. xxxvi: Explanation of
"Word of God"; primary meaning: what God has said to the
prophets; metaphorical meaning: God's wisdom, power,
decree, fatum; furthermore: words of equity and reason even
if not proffered by a prophet, the dictate of *recta ratio*, which is
inscribed in the hearts of men.

Tr. 193 (Bruder XVII, 36 ff.) —— Lev. xl: Political constitution
of the Hebrews; the authority of Moses based on a covenant;
the priests subordinate to Moses; Moses the sovereign. (On the
post-mosaic times the judgments of Hobbes and Spinoza differ
entirely.)

Tr. 228 (Bruder XX, 20 ff.) —— Lev. xxix, as well as *De Cive*
XII: seditiosae opiniones. Cf. *Tr.* 220 (Bruder XIX, 35): . . .
seditiosam opinionem (veniam verbo duriori precor) . . .

Tr. pol. V, 2 (Homines enim civiles non nascuntur, sed fiunt.)
—— *De Cive* I, 2: Polemics against the concept of man as
ζῷον πολιτικόν; man is made capable of living in society not by
nature, but by education.

5. *La Peyrère*

Jacob Thomasius in his Programma of the year 1671 indicates an agreement between Spinoza and La Peyrère regarding the treatment of Biblical accounts of miracles; he has in mind the fundamental agreement in the explanation of the Joshua and Hezekiah miracles, as well as of the Flood.

Tr. 22 (Bruder II, 27) —— *Syst. theol.* IV, 5: Accipiendum ergo ita est miraculum hoc: ut cum Sol ipse revera occumberet; neque cessaret interea celestis et naturalis rerum ordo: fulgor Solis, sine Sole ipso, et miraculo maximo, superesset in Atmosphaera, vel regione vaporum illa, quae civitati Gabaonicae, coeli et aëris medio, incubabat . . .

Tr. 23 (Bruder II, 31) —— *Syst. theol.* IV, 7: Diluvium Noaicum non fuisse effusum super universum terrarum orbem, sed super terram Judaeorum.

For *Tr.* 81 (Bruder VI, 67): eam (sc. naturam) fixum atque immutabilem ordinem servare, . . . Philosophus praeterea in suo Eccl. cap. I. vers. 10. clarissime docet, nihil novi in natura contingere; . . . cf. *Syst. theol.* III, 5: Aeternitatem quinetiam Mundi conjecere . . . per aeternum tenorem illum, et perseverantem constantiam, qua Mundus permanet, et qua semper sui similis est. Quocirca et immutabilem dixere illum: quia talis semper fuerit, et talis semper futurus sit, qualis nunc est. Quo refer Ecclesiastae illud capite 1. . . . (sc. v. 10).

COMMENTS ON
DER BEGRIFF DES POLITISCHEN
BY CARL SCHMITT

COMMENTS[1] ON
DER BEGRIFF DES POLITISCHEN[2]
BY CARL SCHMITT

I

SCHMITT'S TREATISE is intended to serve inquiry into the "order of human things," in other words, into the State. In view of the fact that to-day the State has become problematic to a degree which has not been the case for centuries, understanding of the State requires radical foundation, "a simple and elementary presentation" of the basis of the State, in other words, of the political; for "the concept of the State presupposes the concept of the political."

This thesis, with which the investigation into the concept of the political begins, must be understood according to Schmitt's own general principles of understanding. According to these principles, the proposition that "the political is prior to the state" cannot be meant to express an eternal truth, but only a present truth. For "all mind is only present mind"; "all concepts in the mental sphere, including the concept 'mind,' are in themselves pluralistic, and are to be understood only from concrete political existence"; "all political concepts, representations and words [have] a polemical meaning; they envisage a concrete antithesis, and are bound up with a concrete situation. . . ." If these principles hold, we must ask: To what extent does the present situation force one to recognize the State as founded in the political? In the face of which counter-claim does the political stand out as the foundation of the State?

The present situation is characterized by the fact that a process which has lasted for three centuries has "drawn to its close." The age of which the end is present before our eyes is "the age of neutralizations and de-politicalizing." The de-politicalizing is not the chance result, or even the necessary result, of the modern development, but its original and essential goal. The movement in

---

[1] From *Archiv für Sozialwissenschaft und Sozialpolitik*, 67:6.

[2] *Der Begriff des Politischen*. Mit einer Rede über das Zeitalter der Neutralisierungen und Entpolitisierungen neu herausgegeben von Carl Schmitt, München und Leipzig, 1932.

which the modern mind has attained to its maximum effectiveness, liberalism, is in fact characterized by the *negation* of the
political. If liberalism has now lost its evidence, if "another
system" must therefore be opposed to it, then the first word
against liberalism surely is affirmation of the political. And if it is
the case that liberalism, by its negation of the political, believed
that it could found the State or, more precisely, rational society,
the thought inevitably emerges that the State is understandable
only from affirmation of the political, now that liberalism has
foundered. Thus Schmitt's fundamental thesis is altogether
determined by his fight against liberalism; that thesis can be
understood only as a polemical thesis, only "from the concrete
political existence."

Schmitt's task is determined by the fact that liberalism has
failed. The failure took place in the following manner: Liberalism
negated the political; by so doing, liberalism did not banish the
political from the world, but only concealed it. Liberalism brought
about that politics is carried on by means of anti-political speech.
Liberalism has not killed the political, but merely killed understanding of the political, and sincerity regarding the political.
To clear the obfuscation of reality which liberalism has caused, the
political must be brought out and shown to be completely undeniable. Liberalism is responsible for having covered over the
political, and the political must once again be brought to light,
if the question of the State is to be put in full seriousness.

It does not suffice that the failure of liberalism is recognized as a
fact; that liberalism is shown refuting itself, in every political
action it takes; nor does it suffice to point out "that all clear-eyed
observers . . . despaired of finding here [*i.e.*, in liberalism] any
political principle or any consistency in thinking." It is not even
sufficient to have reached the insight that the manifest inconsistency of all liberal policies is the necessary consequence of denying
the political in principle. What is required is to replace the
"astoundingly consistent systematics of liberal *thought*," which
reveals itself in the inconsistency of all liberal *policies*, by "a
different system," by a system that does not negate the political,
but brings the political into full recognition.

Schmitt is aware that the "astoundingly consistent system of
liberal thought," "in spite of all defeats, is even today in Europe
not replaced by any other system," and this suffices in itself to

characterize the significance of his attempt: for by this awareness he stands alone among the opponents of liberalism, who usually carry in their pocket a fully worked-out illiberal theory. By making the statement just quoted Schmitt indicates the fundamental difficulty with which his own enterprise has to contend. For if it is true that "the system of liberal thought" "is still not replaced by any other system in Europe," it is to be expected that even he, when presenting his own views, is forced to make use of liberal elements. This explains the provisional character of Schmitt's assertions. Schmitt himself expressly admits the fact. His intention is to do no more than provide "a theoretical framework for an immense problem"; the theses of his study are "to be thought of as a *starting point* for objective discussion." Because of this, the critic is in duty bound to consider more wherein Schmitt differs from the prevailing view than wherein he follows it.

II

Schmitt expressly refrains from offering "an exhaustive definition" of the political. The "essence of the political" is from the outset identified with the specific character of the political. He takes this attitude because of his deep-seated mistrust of the liberal answer to the question "what is the genus within which the specific difference of the political must be defined?" In seeking a path to an original answer, he rejects the obvious and widely accepted liberal concept: that the genus to which the political and hence the State belongs is "culture," i.e. the totality of "human thought and action" which divides itself into "different, relatively independent regions," into "provinces of culture" (Natorp). Schmitt would remain within the horizon of this answer if he were to say, as at first glance he seems to say: just as "in the field of morals, the ultimate distinctions are good and evil, in aesthetics, beautiful and ugly, in economics, useful and harmful," so, "the specifically *political* distinction . . . is the distinction of friend and foe." This coordination of the political with other "provinces of culture" is, however, explicitly rejected: the distinction of friend and foe is "not equivalent and analogous to those other distinctions"; the political does not constitute "a peculiar and new province." This means: the understanding of the political requires a fundamental critique of at least the prevailing concept of culture.

This critique is not maintained by Schmitt throughout. He

too—following the mode of speech prevailing within a whole literature—occasionally speaks of the "various, relatively independent
fields of human thinking and of human action" or of the various
"spheres of human life and thought." In one passage he expresses
himself in such a way that to a superficial reader he may seem to
intend to bring the political to recognition in a way similar to the
way liberalism has brought to recognition the autonomy of the
aesthetic, of morality, of science, of economics. His intention, it
would appear, was to counter liberalism, but in the pattern of the
liberal striving after autonomy. How little this is Schmitt's
intention is shown even by the quotation-marks with which he
encloses the word "autonomy" in the phrase " 'autonomy' of the
various fields of human life." It becomes still more manifest in his
emphasis on the "*matter-of-courseness*" with which liberalism "not
merely recognizes the 'autonomy' of the various fields of human
life, but overfavors their specialization and even their complete
isolation." Schmitt's remoteness from the prevailing conception of
culture becomes perfectly clear in the following indirect characterization of the aesthetic: "The way from the metaphysical and the
moral to the economic is via the aesthetic, and the way via even
the most sublime aesthetic consumption and enjoyment is the
surest and most facile way to a universal 'economization' of
mental and spiritual life . . ." For the predominant conception of
culture in any case includes recognition of the autonomous value
of the aesthetic; we leave it open whether that conception is not
altogether constituted by such recognition in the first place. From
this arises at least Schmitt's demand that the prevailing conception
of culture should be replaced by another conception of culture.
That substitution would have to be based on the insight into the
specific character of the political.

As has already been pointed out, Schmitt expressly refrains
from any "exhaustive definition" of the political. Starting from the
fact that "the various, relatively independent fields of human
thought and action" (the moral, the aesthetic, the economic, and
so on) have "their own criteria," by which they are constituted
as relatively independent, he inquires into "the criterion of the
political." The criteria in question have the character of "final
distinctions," or, more precisely expressed, of ultimate "contraries," good-evil, beautiful-ugly, etc. Schmitt defines "the specifically political distinction as the distinction friend-foe." Here

"foe"—and thus also "friend"—is always only the public foe (friend), "a totality of men which is at least potentially a fighting group opposing another totality of the same kind." Of the two moments of this point of view (friend-foe), the moment "foe" clearly is dominant, as appears from the fact that in his more detailed explanation of this point of view, Schmitt actually speaks only of what "foe" means. One may say: every "totality of men" first looks out for friends, indeed has friends, only for the reason that that totality already has enemies; "in the reference to a concrete opposition the essence of political relations is contained." "Foe" takes precedence over "friend" because "the concept of foe"—as distinguished from the concept of friend—implies "the real possibility of a struggle," and because, from the possibility of war, from the "*Ernstfall*," from "the most extreme possibility," "human life takes on its specifically political tension." The possibility of war however does not merely constitute the political as such. War is not merely "the most extreme political means," it is the "*Ernstfall*" not merely in one "autonomous" domain, but for man simply, since it bears "on the real possibility of *physical killing*, and continues to have this bearing." This character of the political shows that the political is fundamental and not just a "relatively independent universe of discourse" among others. The political is the "authoritative." In this sense it is to be understood that the political is "not equivalent and analogous" to the moral, the aesthetic, the economic and so on.

This characterization of the political has the closest possible connection with the critique, adumbrated by Schmitt, of the prevailing conception of culture. This critique questions the "autonomy" of the various "fields of human thought and action." In accord with the prevailing conception of culture, the various provinces of culture are "autonomous" not merely in relation to one another, but prior to that, "culture" as a whole is taken as "autonomous," the sovereign creation, the "pure product" of the human mind. This conception makes us forget that "culture" always presupposes something which is cultivated: culture is always *cultivation of nature*. Originally that means: culture develops the natural disposition; it is careful cultivation of nature—whether of the soil or of the human mind; in this it *obeys* the indications that nature itself gives. However, it may also mean: overcoming nature by obedience to nature (*parendo vincere*, in Bacon's phrase). In that case, culture is not so much faithful cultivation of nature as a harsh and cunning fight *against* nature. Which understanding of culture is accepted depends on how nature is understood: whether as an order seen as a model or whether as disorder which is to be removed. In either view culture is cultivation of nature. "Culture" is to such an extent cultivation of nature that it can be understood as a sovereign creation of the mind only if the nature being cultivated is taken to be the *opposite* of mind, and has been *forgotten*. Since we understand by "culture" above all the culture of *human* nature, the presupposition of culture is, above all, human nature, and since man is by nature an *animal sociale*, the human nature underlying culture is the natural living together of men, i.e. the mode in which man—prior to culture—behaves towards other men. The term for the natural living together thus understood is *status naturalis*. One may therefore say: the foundation of culture is the *status naturalis*.

In accord with the specifically modern conception of nature—here we disregard the question whether it is possible to speak of any conception of culture except the modern one—Hobbes understood the *status civilis*, which is the presupposition of culture in the narrow sense (i.e. of the cultivation of the arts and sciences), and which itself already rests on a particular culture, namely, on a disciplining of human will, as the *opposite* of the *status naturalis*. In this context we disregard the fact that Hobbes conceives the relation between the *status naturalis* and culture (in the widest sense) as an opposition; here we merely stress the fact that Hobbes characterizes the *status naturalis* as the *status belli* simply, and that "the nature of war consisteth *not in actual fighting*, but in the known *disposition* thereto" (*Leviathan*, ch. xiii). That means, in Schmitt's terminology: the *status naturalis* is the genuinely political status: for "the *political* lies *not in the conflict itself*, . . . but in behavior determined by this real possibility." Hence it follows that the political, which Schmitt brings out as fundamental, is the "state of nature" prior to all culture; Schmitt restores Hobbes' conception of the state of nature to a place of honor. This gives us the answer to the question within which genus the specific difference of the political is to be placed: the political is a status of man, indeed, *the* human status in the sense of the "natural," the fundamental and extreme status of man.

Schmitt defines the state of nature in principle differently

from Hobbes. For Hobbes it is the state of war of individuals—
for Schmitt it is the state of war of groups, and especially of
nations. For Hobbes the state of nature is the condition in which
each man is the enemy of every other man—for Schmitt, all
political conduct is directed on *friend* and foe. This divergence
springs from the fact that Hobbes' definition of the state of nature
is polemically intended: the fact that the state of nature is the
state of enmity of all against all is adduced so as to yield a motive
for relinquishment of the state of nature. Against this negation of
the state either of nature or of the political, Schmitt sets the
affirmation of the political.

Even in the case of Hobbes, one is not justified in asserting that
his negation of the political is all-embracing. At the very least,
according to his doctrine, the state of nature persists in the
relationship between nations. The "political" in Schmitt's sense of
the word (i.e. the "natural" character of the relations between
groupings of men) is not brought into question by Hobbes' polemic against the state of nature as the state of war between individuals, which Schmitt implicitly adopts in his remark explicitly based on Hobbes regarding the relation between protection
and obedience. However, in Schmitt's view, it is essential to the
political grouping that that grouping may "demand . . . from those
belonging to a nation *readiness to die*," and the legitimacy of this
demand is at least qualified by Hobbes: the man in the battle-
ranks who deserts by reason of fear for his life acts "only" dis-
honorably, but not unjustly (*Leviathan*, xxi). The rights of the
State do not go beyond the right to demand *conditional* obedience,
in other words, obedience which is not incompatible with saving
or preserving one's life: for protection of life is the ultimate reason
of the State. Therefore man is otherwise in duty bound to unconditional obedience, but not to risking his life. For death
is the greatest evil. Hobbes does not recoil from the consequences,
and expressly denies the character of virtue to courage (*De
hom.*, xiii, 9). The same attitude comes out in Hobbes' definition of
the *salus populi*: it consists

1) in defense against the enemy from without;
2) in maintaining peace within the state;
3) in the just and modest acquisition of wealth by the individuals, which is more easily attained by industry and thrift

than by victorious wars, and which is promoted in particular by
the cultivation of the sciences of mechanics and physics; and

4) in the enjoyment of innocuous freedom (*De Cive*, XIII, 6
and 14).

As soon as "humanity" becomes the subject or object of
planning, these principles cannot but lead to the ideal of civilization, i.e. to the demand for the rational and universal society as a
single "union of consumers and producers." Hobbes is to a much
higher degree than, say, Bacon the originator of the ideal of
civilization. By this very fact he is the founder of liberalism. The
right to the securing of bare life, i.e. the only natural right that
Hobbes recognizes, has the character of an inalienable right of
man, i.e. of a claim of the individual which precedes the State and
determines the purpose and the limits of the State. The manner in
which Hobbes lays the foundation for the natural right to the
securing of bare life suggests the whole system of the rights of man
in the liberal sense, even assuming that it does not make these
indispensable. Hobbes differs from full grown liberalism only by
what he regards as the obstacle against which the liberal ideal of
civilization is to be established in a determined fight: the obstacle
is not corrupt institutions or the ill will of a ruling stratum, but
man's natural malice. Hobbes establishes liberalism in an illiberal
world against the (*sit venia verbo*) illiberal nature of man, whereas
his successors, ignoring their presuppositions and goals, trust in
the original goodness of human nature, guaranteed by God's
creation and providence, or, basing themselves on scientific
neutrality, hope for an improvement of human nature to which
man's experience of himself does not entitle him. Hobbes attempts
to overcome the state of nature to the extent to which it can be
overcome, while he faces the state of nature, whereas his successors,
dreaming of a state of nature or allegedly possessing a deeper
insight into man's history and therewith into his essence, forget the
state of nature. But—this justice must be accorded to his successors
—that dream and that oblivion are in the last instance only the
consequence of the negation of the state of nature, or of the
affirmation of civilization, that was begun by Hobbes.

If it is true that the final self-consciousness of liberalism is the
philosophy of culture, then we may sum up as follows: liberalism,
sheltered by a world of culture and unable to see beyond it,

forgets the foundation of culture, the state of nature, i.e. human nature as dangerous and endangered. Schmitt goes back against liberalism to its originator, Hobbes, in order to strike the root of liberalism in Hobbes' explicit negation of the state of nature.[3] Whereas Hobbes, living in an illiberal world, lays the foundation of liberalism, Schmitt, living in a liberal world, undertakes the critique of liberalism.

III

To the liberal negation of the political, Schmitt opposes the affirmation of the political, i.e. the recognition of the reality of the political. For the affirmation of the political, in Schmitt's explicit view, it is a matter of indifference whether the political is held to be desirable or abhorrent. It "is neither for war nor for militarism, neither imperialist nor pacifist" in intention. Schmitt sets out to do no more than to ascertain what *is*. That does not mean that he considers his exposition as "free of value-judgments," or that he—whether from concern for the scientific character of his investigation, or for freedom of personal decision—is anxious to leave open all the possibilities of taking an evaluating position toward the political. His concern is rather to close all possibilities of this kind: the political *cannot* be evaluated, cannot be measured by the yardstick of an ideal; applied to the political, *all* ideals are nothing more than "abstractions," or, *all* "normativities" are nothing more than "fictions." For the political is constituted by reference to "the real possibility of physical killing" of men by other men, and "there is no rational aim, no norm however correct, no programme however impressive, no social ideal however beautiful, no legitimacy or legality, which could justify that men kill each other for its sake."

The affirmation of the political has as result the *unpolemical* description of the political. As such it is opposed to Hobbes' polemical description of the state of nature. Hobbes had presented the state of nature as impossible in itself: the state of nature is the state of war of every man against every other man; in the state of nature every man is the enemy of every other. According to

---

[3] In the first version of his treatise Schmitt had described Hobbes as "by far the greatest and perhaps the only truly systematic political thinker" (*Archiv für Sozialwissenschaft und Sozialpolitik*, Vol. 58, p. 25). Now he speaks of him as only "a great and truly systematic political thinker." In fact he is *the* anti-political thinker, if we understand "political" in Schmitt's sense.

Schmitt, the subjects of the state of nature are not individuals, but communities; and furthermore not every community is the enemy of every other community, there existing not only the possibility of hostility but also the possibility of alliance and neutrality. The state of nature thus understood is in itself *possible*. But that it is also *actual* is shown by the whole history of mankind up to our own time. Perhaps there will one day be a completely de-politicized condition of humanity; "whether or when this condition of the world and of humanity will occur, I know not," but in any case "as yet that condition has not come to pass" and therefore it would be "a dishonest fiction, to assume it as existing . . ."

Now one cannot leave matters—Schmitt least of all—at asserting that the depoliticized condition is "*as yet* not come to pass" or that "war as a real possibility is *still* present *today*." In the face of the fact that there exists in our time a powerful movement which strives to achieve the complete elimination of the real possibility of war, in other words, the elimination of the political; in the face of the fact that this movement exercises a great influence not only on the mode of thought of the age, but also decisively determines actual conditions (this movement having led to the point that "*today* war is probably neither something pious, nor something morally good, nor something lucrative," whereas in earlier centuries war could be all of these things), in the face of these facts, we cannot but ask, looking beyond today: granting "that war is still present today as a real possibility," will it still be such to-morrow? or the day after to-morrow? In other words, even though the elimination of the political has not *up to our time* been successfully achieved in any way, is this elimination not still possible in the future? is this not a possibility at all?

To this question Schmitt gives the following answer: the political is a basic characteristic of human life. In this sense, politics is destiny; therefore man cannot escape from the political. The inescapable nature of politics is shown by the contradiction from which man cannot extricate himself, whenever he makes the attempt to eliminate the political. This effort is hopeful only when it itself becomes political, in other words, when it is itself "strong enough to group all men into friends and foes," when it might be able to drive "the pacifists into *war* against the non-pacifists, into a 'war against war.' " The war against war will then be undertaken as "the definitively final war of humanity." Such a war is however "of necessity, particularly intensive and in-human," because in that war the enemy is fought "as an in-human monster . . . which must not merely be repelled, but totally annihilated." It is not to be expected that when mankind has behind it a war of particularly inhumane character it will be particularly humane and therefore unpolitical. Thus the effort to do away with the political for the sake of humanity will have as its necessary consequence nothing other than an increase and heightening of inhumanity. Therefore if it is stated that the political element is a basic characteristic of human life, in other words, that man would cease to be man by ceasing to be political, what is also being stated is precisely that: man ceases to be human and humane when he ceases to be political. If man's effort to eliminate the political necessarily involves man in contradictions, this attempt is in the end not honestly possible. "To curse war as murder, and then to require of men that they wage war, that they kill and let themselves be killed, for the sake of a 'war to end war,' is manifest deceit."

The political is thus not merely possible, but also actual; and not only actual, but also necessary. It is necessary, because it is given in human nature. Hence the opposition between the negation and the affirmation of the political leads us back to a controversy on human nature. In the final instance, what is in question is whether man is by nature good or evil. In this context, "good" and "evil" are however "not to be taken in any special moral or ethical sense." But "good" is to be understood as "harm-less," and "evil" as "dangerous." This then is the ultimate question: "whether man is a dangerous or a harmless being, a risk or not a risk." "All genuine political theories" presuppose the dangerous character of man. The assertion that man is dangerous is then the ultimate presupposition of the affirmation of the political.

The train of thought that we have just summarized is hardly Schmitt's last word; it is surely not his deepest word. It conceals a reflection that leads to an entirely different result, one that cannot be reconciled with it.

Schmitt describes the thesis of man's dangerous character as the ultimate presupposition of the affirmation of the political: the necessity of the political is as certain as the dangerous character of man. But is man's dangerous character absolutely certain? Schmitt himself characterizes the thesis of man's dangerous character as a "presumption," as a "profession of faith regarding man." Yet if man's dangerous character is only presumed or believed, not genuinely known, it is possible also to assert its contrary and to attempt to eliminate this character which *hitherto* has indeed always been a fact.

Schmitt concedes that the political is in principle threatened, by stating "whether and when this [*sc.* completely a-political] state of the world and of humanity will come to pass, *I do not know.*" Now the political could not be menaced, if, as Schmitt repeatedly and at various points asserts, it were utterly inescapable. One must therefore qualify his assertion that the political is inescapable as follows: the political is inescapable so long, but only so long, as at least one antithesis exists which is—if only potentially—political. In fact, this limitation is made by Schmitt himself in the argument against pacifism that has been previously adduced; for his argument presupposes that the antithesis between pacifists and non-pacifists does not disappear. Hence the political is only conditionally inescapable; in the last analysis the political remains endangered.

If so, the position with regard to the political must be more than recognition of its reality; there must be a defense of the threatened political, a genuine affirmation of it. It is therefore necessary to raise this question: Why does Schmitt affirm the political?

The political is threatened if the dangerous character of man is threatened. Hence the affirmation of the political is the affirmation of the dangerous character of man. How is this affirmation to be understood? If it is intended as *political*, it cannot—since it is political—have "any normative, but only an existential, meaning." The next question which must be put is: does a "totality of men, engaged in a war," *affirm* the dangerous character of their enemy? does it *wish* for dangerous foes? And one cannot but answer this in the negative, with the same meaning that underlies the utterance of C. Fabricius when he heard that a Greek philosopher stated pleasure to be the greatest good: If only Pyrrhus and the Samnites were of this opinion as long as we are engaged in war against them! In the same way a nation engaged in war wishes to be dangerous, not for the sake of the dangerous quality

itself, but for the sake of its salvation from the danger. The affirmation of dangerousness as such, then, does not have a political
meaning but only a "normative," moral meaning. Reduced to its
adequate expression, it is the affirmation of force as the force which
builds the State, of virtù in Machiavelli's sense. Here again we
find ourselves recalling Hobbes, who conceives the characteristic
of inspiring fear (which he rejects, as he rejects the state of nature)
as the virtue of the state of nature, but understands this characteristic as glory or courage. Thus a warlike morality seems to be the
ultimate legitimation for Schmitt's affirmation of the political,
and the antithesis between negating and positing the political
seems to coincide with the antithesis of pacifist internationalism
and bellicose nationalism.

Is this really the case? It becomes doubtful, if one reflects on
the determined manner in which Schmitt refuses to oppose the
pacifists from the point of view of bellicism. And it must be
contested, as soon as one has made a closer study of how Schmitt
arrives at the dangerous character of man as the ultimate presupposition of the affirmation of the political. After he has twice
rejected the pacifist ideal, by adducing that this ideal is of no
import in the present situation, either for behavior in that situation or for understanding it, he finally recognizes the possibility in
principle of a "world-state," as a completely a-political "co-
operative of consumers and producers" embracing the united
human race, and on this basis he raises the question, "to which
men will fall the awful power lying in a worldwide economic and
technological centralization?" In other words, which men will
rule in the "world-state"? "This question is not in any way to be
done away with by hoping . . . that the government of men by
men will have become superfluous because in that time men will
be completely free: for that precisely is the question: *for* what will
they be free? This question may be answered by optimistic or by
pessimistic suppositions," i.e. by the optimistic supposition that
man will then have ceased to be a dangerous being, or with the
pessimistic supposition that he will still be a dangerous being. The
question "Is man dangerous or not?" emerges then in the face of
the question "Is the government of men by men necessary or
superfluous; will it always be so?". Hence dangerousness means
"being in need of being governed." And the ultimate struggle takes
place not between bellicism and pacifism (or nationalism and

internationalism) but between the "authoritarian and anarchistic theories."

The controversy between the authoritarian and the anarchistic theories turns on the question whether man is by nature evil or good. "Evil" and "good," are here *not* to be taken in any specifically *moral* or ethical sense." The words are to be understood in the sense of "dangerous" or "not dangerous." What this means becomes clear in the light of the twofold significance of "evil" to which Schmitt refers. " 'Evil' may appear as corruption, weakness, cowardice, stupidity, but also as 'rudeness,' instinctiveness, vitality, irrationality, and so on . . ." In other words, "evil" may be understood either as *human inferiority* or as *animal force*, as *humana impotentia* or as *naturae potentia* (Spinoza, *Eth.* III, praef.). If "evil" is not intended in the moral sense, then only the second connotation counts. It is in the latter sense that "the political philosophers of the seventeenth century (Hobbes, Spinoza, Pufendorff)" have described man in the state of nature as "evil," i.e. "like the *beasts* moved by their drives (hunger, cupidity, fear, jealousy)." But it is necessary to wonder why these philosophers, Hobbes in particular, took man to be "evil as are the beasts." He could not but understand evil as *guiltless* "evil," since he denied the existence of sin. And he could not but deny sin, because he did not recognize any primary human obligation preceding all claims or "rights" (i.e. justified claims), because he understood man as being by nature free, in other words, under no binding obligation. For Hobbes, the basic political fact was natural right as the justified claim of every individual, while duty or obligation was a *subsequent* restriction of that right. Setting out from this, it is impossible to raise objections of principle against the proclamation of the rights of man as claims of the individual on the State and against the State, against the distinction between Society and the State, and against liberalism, assuming liberalism is not indeed the inevitable consequence of Hobbes' starting point. And once one understands man's being evil as the innocent "evil" of beasts, but of a beast which can become prudent through damage suffered and hence can be educated, one's expectations from education indeed eventually rest on mere "presumption": the "presumption" will determine whether one expects little, as did Hobbes himself who became therefore an adherent of absolute monarchy; whether one expects more as did liberalism; or whether one expects almost anything, as does anarchism. The antithesis between good and evil loses its sharpness, it even loses its significance, as soon as "evil" is understood as innocent "evil," and therewith goodness itself becomes an ingredient of evil. In order to launch the radical critique of liberalism that he has in mind, Schmitt must first eliminate the conception of human evil as animal evil, and therefore as "innocent evil," and find his way back to the conception of human evil as moral depravity. Only by so doing can Schmitt remain in agreement with himself, if indeed "the core of the political idea is the *morally* exacting decision" (*Politische Theologie*, p. 56). For this requirement, the modification undertaken by Schmitt of Hobbes' thought, and of the thought of Hobbes' successors, is insufficient, and not merely insufficient, but actually contradicts that requirement. Whereas in the final instance Hobbes brings out the natural and therefore innocent evil, so that that evil may be combated, Schmitt speaks with unmistakable sympathy of an "evil" which is no longer to be taken in the moral sense. This sympathy is nothing other than admiration for animal power, and the same must be said of this admiration as what Schmitt says of the aesthetic in an already quoted passage. In addition, the inadequacy reveals itself immediately in the fact that what he admires is by no means an excellence, but rather a deficiency, a need—the need of being ruled. The dangerous character of man, which was brought to light as his need for being governed, can be fittingly regarded only as a moral inferiority. As such it must be recognized as existing, but it cannot be affirmed as good. What then does the affirmation of the political mean?

The reason why Schmitt affirms the political, and does not limit himself to merely recognizing it as actual or necessary, appears most clearly in his polemic against the ideal which corresponds to the negation of the political. In the end Schmitt does not regard this ideal as utopian—he concedes, be it said, that he does not know whether its realization is possible or not—but he abominates it. That Schmitt does not make a moralizing display of his conviction, but tries to hide it, makes his polemic all the more effective. Here are his own words: "if . . . the distinction between friend and foe were to disappear, even as the merest possibility, there would be nothing but a world-view devoid of politics. There would be culture, civilization, economic life,

morality, law, art, *entertainment* and so on, but there would be
neither politics nor the State." We have emphasized the word
"entertainment," because Schmitt does his utmost to make entertainment fade almost to a vanishing-point within a series of serious
human activities; in particular, the "and so on" following on
"entertainment" hides the fact that "entertainment" is in actual
fact the final member of the series, its *finis ultimus*. Schmitt thus
conveys the following thought: the opponents of the political
may say what they will, they may justify their plans by appeal to
the highest concerns of man; their good faith is not called in
question; granted that world-view, culture and so on need not *of
necessity* be entertainment; but they *may become* entertainment.
On the other hand, it is impossible to name politics and the State
in the same breath with "entertainment"; the only guarantee
against the world becoming a world of entertainment is politics
and the State; hence what the opponents of the political have in
mind is to bring into being a world of entertainment, a world of
fun, a world devoid of *seriousness*. "A completely pacified globe,"
says Schmitt in an earlier passage, "would be a world freed from
politics. It is thinkable that such a world might contain many *very
interesting* oppositions and contrasts, competitions and intrigues of
every kind, but there could not meaningfully be any opposition
by reason of which the sacrifice of life could be required of
men . . ." (italics supplied). Here, too, what Schmitt concedes to
the ideal condition that pacifists have in mind, what *strikes*
him in this condition, is its capacity for entertainment, for being
"exciting." Here, too, he is at pains to cover the critique contained
in describing this state of affairs: "*perhaps* very interesting." It is
to be taken as a matter of course that he has no intention of
casting doubt on the fact that the world, devoid of politics, is
interesting. There is nothing of which he is more convinced
than that that world is highly interesting ("competition and
intrigues of every kind"); the "perhaps" does no more than call
into question whether interest of this character is of a nature to
claim the interest of any human being worthy of the name.
The term both hides and reveals the *nausea* felt for this particular
quality of interest, which becomes possible only once man has
forgotten what are the things that count. Thus it becomes clear why
Schmitt rejects the ideal of pacifism (more precisely, the ideal of
civilization) or why he affirms the political: he affirms the political

because he realizes that when the political is threatened, the serious-ness of life is threatened. The affirmation of the political is in the last analysis nothing other than the affirmation of the moral.

The result reached is not different, if one takes a closer view of Schmitt's characterization of the modern age as the age of depoliticization. This characterization surely does not mean that in the nineteenth and twentieth centuries politics do less to determine men's fate than in the sixteenth and seventeenth centuries. Mankind today, no less than in earlier times, is divided into "totalities potentially engaged in fighting." What has changed fundamentally is not the *fact* of struggling, but the object of the struggle. What is the object of the struggle depends on what is regarded as important, as authoritative. Different centuries regard different things as authoritative: in the sixteenth century, it was theology, in the seventeenth metaphysics, in the eighteenth morals, in the nineteenth economics, and in the twentieth century technology. In each century a different sub-stantive concern is the central concern. Politics, since it does not have a substantive field of its own, is thus never the "central field." Whereas the "central fields" vary, politics remains constantly determinative of men's fate. But in this function, politics is always dependent on what is at any given time man's ultimate concern. "Even the State [draws] its reality and strength from whatever is at the time the central concern, because the decisive themes of contention between the groupings of friend and foe are determined by the substantive concern which is authoritative at the time." The precise significance of the de-politicizing that is characteristic of the modern age is therefore to be discerned only by under-standing which law prevails in the "sequence and gradation of the varying central fields." This law is the "tendency towards neutralization," in other words, the effort to reach a base, which "makes security, evidence, agreement and peace possible." Agree-ment and peace are meant in the sense of agreement and peace at any price. Yet agreement can always be reached in principle about the means to an already established end, whereas the ends are always controversial: we disagree with one another and with ourselves always only about the just and the good (Plato, *Euthy-phro* 7 b-d and *Phaedrus* 263 a). If therefore one wishes agreement at any price, there is no other way than to abandon altogether the question of what is right and to limit one's concern exclusively to the means. Thus it becomes intelligible that modern Europe after it had decided to seek for a neutral plane as such in order to escape from the struggle about the right faith, arrived eventually at the faith in technology. "The plausibility of today's widely held belief in technology depends upon another belief, i.e. that technology is the absolutely and finally neutral ground . . . As compared with theological, metaphysical, moral and even economic questions, over which controversy may well be never-ending, the purely technical problems have a quality refreshingly objective: they are capable of completely convincing solutions . . ." But this neutrality of technology is only apparent. "Technology is always instrument and weapon only, and for the reason that technology serves everyone, it is not neutral." In this characteristic of apparent neutrality we plainly see the absurdity of the attempt to discover a "ground absolutely and finally neutral," or to reach agreement at any price. Agreement at any price is possible only as agreement at the price of the meaning of human life, for such agreement is possible only when man abandons the task of raising the question regarding what is right, and when man abandons this question, he abandons his humanity. But when he asks the question of what is right in earnest, there arises (given "the inextricably problematic character" of what this question is about) conflict, life-and-death conflict: by the seriousness of the question of what is right, the political—the division of the human race into foes and friends— is justified.

The affirmation of the political is the affirmation of the state of nature. Schmitt opposes the affirmation of the state of nature to the Hobbesian negation of the state of nature. The state of nature is the *status belli* simply. Thus, it seems, the affirmation of the state of nature can have no other meaning than to support bellicism. This appearance dissolves as soon as one grasps what return to the state of nature signifies for Schmitt. Affirmation of the state of nature does not mean affirmation of war, but "relinquishment of the security of the *status quo*." Security is relinquished, not because war is something "ideal," but because one must return from "dazzling representation," from the "comforts and convenience of the existing *status quo*," to the "cultural or social void," to the "mysterious, unimpressive origin," to "undefiled, uncorrupted nature," so that "by virtue of pure, unpolluted knowledge . . . the order of human things" may arise afresh.

If then according to Schmitt's ultimate view the affirmation of the political rests on the affirmation of morality—how can one reconcile with this the polemic, pervading his whole essay, against the (alleged) primacy of morality over the political? The simplest explanation is that in this polemic he understands by "morality" a specific morality, i.e. a morality that essentially contradicts the political. "Morality" is for Schmitt always— at least in the context here under discussion—"humanitarian morality." This means however that Schmitt accepts his opponents' view of what constitutes morality instead of questioning the claim of humanitarian-pacifist morality to be the true morality; he remains under the spell of the opinion he combats.

The polemic against morals—against the "ideals" and "normativities"—does not indeed prevent Schmitt from passing a *moral* judgment on humanitarian morals, on the pacifist ideal. Admittedly, he is at pains, as we have already shown, to conceal this judgment. Through this concealment a fundamental difficulty finds expression: the fact that the political is endangered makes an evaluation of the political inevitable, and at the same time insight into the essence of the political creates doubt as to the legitimacy of an evaluation of the political. For adopting a posture of evaluation would be a "free, untestable decision, which concerns no one except the deciding individual himself"; it would be essentially "a private affair." But the political lies outside the domain of all private preference: its character is that of *obligation* transcending the private. If it is presupposed that all ideals are private, and therefore not binding, then obligation can be comprehended not as such, not as duty, but only as inescapable necessity. This then is the presupposition that disposes Schmitt to assert the inescapability of the political, and, as soon as he finds himself unable, on account of the nature of the matter, to maintain that assertion, it disposes him to conceal his moral judgment. This presupposition, however, is, as he himself stresses, the one characteristic of the "individualistic-liberal society."

Let us now make clear what, in principle, affirmation of the political in abstraction from the moral, what the primacy of the political over the moral would signify. To be political means to be directed toward the "*Ernstfall*," toward war. Hence the affirmation of the political as such is affirmation of fighting as such, regardless of the object of the fighting. This means: he who affirms the political as such, is neutral towards all friend-foe groupings. However much this neutrality may differ in kind from the neutrality of the man who denies the political as such, who ever *adopts* the attitude of affirmation of the political as such, and therewith is neutral to all friend-foe groupings, is not minded "to place himself outside the political totality . . . and to live solely as a private individual"; he does not have the *will* to "neutralization," to avoidance of decision at any cost, but on the contrary is determined towards decision. As directed towards *decision of whatsoever character*, such determination makes use of a sphere beyond all decisions, of a possibility originally opened for the sake of neutrality. Whoever affirms the political as such, respects all who are willing to fight; he is quite as tolerant as the liberals, but with the opposite intention. Whereas the liberal respects and tolerates all "honestly held" convictions, so long as these respect the legal order or acknowledge the sanctity of *peace*, whoever affirms the political as such, respects and tolerates all "serious" convictions, in other words, all decisions leading up to the real possibility of *war*. Thus the affirmation of the political as such proves to be liberalism preceded by a minus-sign. And with this Schmitt corroborates the truth of his statement that "the astoundingly consistent . . . systematics of liberal thought is today in Europe not yet replaced by any other system."

The affirmation of the political as such can therefore not be other than merely the first word from Schmitt against liberalism. It can do no more than prepare the way for a radical critique of liberalism. In an earlier writing Schmitt said of Donoso Cortes: he "despises the liberals, whereas he respects atheistic and anarchistic socialism as his mortal enemy . . ." (*Politische Theologie*, 55). The struggle is fought out alone between mortal enemies: the "neutral," who seeks to act as intermediary between them, who seeks some middle way, is pushed aside by both of them with unqualified contempt—with rude insults or under maintenance of the rules of courtesy, according to the character of the individuals in question. The "contempt," the disregard, is to be taken literally: they do not "regard" him; each seeks only a view of the enemy; the "neutral" obscures this view and obstructs the line of fire; he is gestured aside: the enemies never look at him. The polemic against liberalism can therefore have no meaning other than that of a subsidiary or preparatory action. It is undertaken only to clear the field for the decisive battle between the "spirit of technology," the "mass faith of an anti-religious, this-worldly activism" and . . . the opposite spirit and faith, which, it seems, does not yet have a name. In the end, two completely opposed answers to the question of what is right permit no mediation and no neutrality (cf. the remark on "two-membered antitheses" and "three-membered schemata" or "constructs"). Schmitt's ultimate concern is then not the fight against liberalism. For this very reason the affirmation of the political as such is not his last word. His last word is "the order of human things."

This is not to deny that the polemic against liberalism too often seems to be Schmitt's last word, that too often he becomes entangled in the polemic against liberalism and thus is drawn away from his primary purpose and is detained on the plane created by liberalism. This involvement is no accidental failure but is the necessary consequence of the principle that "all concepts of the spiritual-intellectual sphere . . . can only be understood from the concrete political existence" and that "all political concepts, ideas and words have a polemical meaning." This principle, which itself is altogether based on liberal presuppositions, is counter-acted by Schmitt *in concreto* when he opposes to Hobbes' polemical concept of the state of nature his own unpolemical concept of the state of nature; and he rejects that principle explicitly when he expects to gain the order of human things by virtue of "a pure, unpolluted" knowledge. For pure, unpolluted knowledge is never, except accidentally, polemical; and pure, unpolluted knowledge cannot be gained from "the concrete political exist-ence," from the situation of the age, but only through a return to the origin, to "undefiled, not corrupt nature."

We have said above that Schmitt is undertaking the critique of liberalism in a liberal world. We meant by this that his critique of liberalism takes place within the horizon of liberalism; his illiberal tendencies are arrested by the as yet undefeated "systematics of liberal thinking." The critique of liberalism that Schmitt has initiated can therefore be completed only when we succeed in gaining a horizon beyond liberalism. Within such a horizon Hobbes achieved the foundation of liberalism. A radical critique of liberalism is therefore possible only on the basis of an adequate understanding of Hobbes. To show what is to be learned from Schmitt for the execution of this urgent task was therefore the main concern of our comments.